"Frank Kelly is a confidant of mine and I greatly appreciate his friendship, expertise and enthusiastic support of World Lacrosse. Frank, the entire Kelly family and FCA are an integral part of the fabric of the sport and growth of the Creator's game around the globe. Frank has earned great respect and I am excited for the lacrosse world and others to experience this uplifting book of real-life stories."

JIM SCHERR
CHIEF EXECUTIVE OFFICER – WORLD LACROSSE

"Frank Kelly is a multi-dimensional and impactful leader whose love for the Lord, lacrosse and FCA are contagious. In this book, Frank takes us on a deep dive into his incredible journey and many dynamic paradigm-shaping stories of family, faith, FCA and lacrosse."

SHANE WILLIAMSON
PRESIDENT – FELLOWSHIP OF CHRISTIAN ATHLETES

"In many ways, Frank Kelly has been the heart and soul of FCA Lacrosse, and this book is a compelling tribute to the history of the game we love, and to many of the incredible people who have influenced it throughout the years. It is filled with personal anecdotes and stories that truly bring the past to life."

HANK JANCZYK
LEGENDARY LACROSSE COACH (2ND ALL-TIME NCAA WINS) – GETTYSBURG COLLEGE

"When I speak at various sports and faith-based events, I often say that I thank God for Jesus Christ, my husband, and Frank Kelly. Frank and his family have been key to the growth and influence of FCA in Baltimore City and beyond. I am grateful he has taken the time to capture his story and so many other incredible God stories of light being shined in places of darkness. Sit back, relax, and let the light of this book refresh and encourage you."

SIRENA ALFORD
BALTIMORE CITY FELLOWSHIP OF CHRISTIAN ATHLETES METRO AREA DIRECTOR

"Frank Kelly and FCA Lacrosse represent the best of the Creator's game—a community of people who believe in the value of team sports and benefit from the fellowship that such unity provides. This book captures many stories that will hopefully inspire more fellowship around the game while practicing the golden rule: 'Do unto others as you would have them do unto you.'"

STEVE STENERSEN
FORMER PRESIDENT & CEO – USA LACROSSE

"I was fortunate to coach two of Frank Kelly's sons and three of his nephews, and Frank's brother, Bryan, walked closely with me during one of the most difficult times in my life. Frank has helped me become a better Christian, husband and father, and I believe Influence and The Creator's Game will encourage and help you in your relationships as well."

JOE BRESCHI
NCAA NATIONAL CHAMPION LACROSSE COACH – UNIVERSITY OF NORTH CAROLINA

"Frank and the entire Kelly family have huge hearts for God, and they have influenced countless lives throughout Baltimore, the state of Maryland and across the world. This book shares some of those amazing stories in a fun and refreshing way."

MATT STOVER
NFL SUPER BOWL CHAMPION AND ALL-PRO KICKER

"Frank Kelly is a highly respected business leader, and as CEO of Kelly Benefits, has leveraged his platform to share God's love and truth in practical and compelling ways with many business leaders and others in his sphere of influence. As the head of a faith-based business leaders' organization, I often say that CBMC is to the marketplace what FCA is to the sports world. I am thrilled that Frank has chosen to share his story and other stories of influence, hope and true transformation."

DAVID MEYERS
PRESIDENT – CHRISTIAN BUSINESS MEN'S CONNECTION USA (CBMC)

"I played lacrosse at Baltimore City College High School and the University of Maryland, so I always appreciated Frankie Kelly's toughness and tenacity on and off the field, and that he is a role model who walks the talk. In Influence and The Creator's Game, readers will learn about perseverance, teamwork and serving those in need at home and around the world."

C.A. DUTCH RUPPERSBERGER
UNITED STATES CONGRESSMAN – MARYLAND 2ND DISTRICT

INFLUENCE

and

THE CREATOR'S GAME

My Story and Stories of Family, Faith and Lacrosse

FRANK KELLY III

with Bill Tamulonis

FOREWORD BY JON GORDON
Wall Street Journal Best-Selling Author of The Energy Bus and The Hard Hat

SCHMITZ PRESS

ISBN: 979-8-218-31600-6
Library of Congress Control Number: 2023936848

www.MyStoryGift.com – Bill Tamulonis
Book design and layout by Jennifer Kozak, KLUTCH, Inc.
Cover design by Jennifer Kozak and Heather Kness

Printed by Schmitz Press, in the United States of America.

Francis X. Kelly III
c/o Kelly Benefits
1 Kelly Way
Sparks, MD 21152

www.FrankKellyIII.com

DEDICATION

It has been said that "A coach will influence more people in a year than most people will in a lifetime."[1]

I dedicate this book to all the coaches I had along the way and for their influence in my life, especially Augie Miceli, Mike Thomas, Tom Keigler, Haswell Franklin Jr., Richie Moran and Arlie Marshall.

Every coach I had challenged, encouraged and influenced me in unique and different ways. To each one I am grateful, especially those coaches who sparked and grew my love for lacrosse—the Creator's game.

CONTENTS

FOREWORD

Frank Kelly and I share a lot of common bonds. We are both former college lacrosse players. We were both faceoff men. Frank no doubt had a higher winning percentage than me. We both played at Cornell University. We both played for legendary coach Richie Moran, who deeply impacted each of our lives. We are both men of faith who gave our lives to God during a time of anguish, suffering and pain. We both knew that God was what our soul longed for and needed when we needed Him most. We both love the Fellowship of Christian Athletes (FCA) and have experienced the incredible impact it has had on our lives, our families and many others.

That's why I'm excited that Frank has written this book where he shares the incredible journey of his life and love for the Creator and the Creator's game and the many stories, events and miracles that he experienced while giving his life to God, the game and others. I can say without a shadow of a doubt that FCA Lacrosse is what it is today because of Frank Kelly and thousands of athletes, coaches, parents and families are the beneficiary of his time, passion, love and commitment to making people and the world better.

I can't wait for you to read about the Miracle in the Mountains and how it all got started. It's one of my favorite stories of all time and gives you an introduction and foreshadowing of the amazing future God had planned for FCA Lacrosse and the blessings and favor He would provide to everyone involved. As you read this book, Frank takes you on a special journey where you'll meet many unique characters, laugh at humorous stories, feel the special bonds and relationships that developed, see the blessings, and witness a modern movement of God through His creation (us) and His game (lacrosse).

Some people think God already did all the miracles He's going to do, but the Creator is not done creating, and I love how Frank shares countless stories and examples that demonstrate how God is still transforming hearts, minds, and souls and doing miracles today.

I'm smiling right now at the fact that you and others are reading these words and knowing that as you read this book, you will be encouraged and inspired. Most of all, I believe you will feel a greater sense of hope in understanding what God did, what He can do and what He wants to do in your life too.

Influence and The Creator's Game is not just about Frank's story and the stories of others, it's about your story as well. The Native Americans called lacrosse "the Creator's game" and played it to honor the Creator. You too honor the Creator in the way you live your life and the faith you have on your journey.

I hope this book strengthens your faith. Knowing Frank Kelly, watching his impact and hearing these stories over the years has certainly strengthened mine.

God bless you!

Jon Gordon
Wall Street Journal Best-Selling Author of The Energy Bus and The Hard Hat

INTRODUCTION

"In the beginning God created the heavens and the earth."

Genesis 1:1

The Haudenosaunee, also known as the Iroquois, played the game we know as lacrosse for much more than a trophy.

They played to settle inter-tribal disputes between their six nations—the Onondaga, Mohawk, Oneida, Cayuga, Seneca and Tuscarora—which inhabited much of northeastern North America, including most of what is now Upstate New York.

They played lacrosse as a medicine game to promote the healing of individuals, communities and nations. Although their young warriors were already tough, they played to prepare for combat and for recreation at their festivals. Most importantly, they played "for the pleasure of the Creator."

Folklore alleges that when French Jesuit missionaries first observed the game in the 1630s, they noticed how the sticks made of hickory or ash used to scoop, throw and catch the wooden ball in its rawhide webbing resembled "la crosier" staffs their bishops carried, so they called the game *lacrosse* ("the cross"). Others trace the origin of the name to the expression "jouer à la cross" ("play cross country") used to describe various games played with curved sticks in France.

Alfred Jacques, the well-known Onondaga lacrosse stick-maker, reminds us that "the Creator wants us to play lacrosse, the Creator watches lacrosse games and the real name for lacrosse is 'Dey-Hon-Tshi-Gwa'-Ehs.'"[1] Dao Joa Dre of the Cayuga Nation notes, "Sometimes other people have said, 'It sounds like you guys invented lacrosse' and I say, 'No, we never invented it, our Creator established it here on Earth.'"[2] And the Mohawk Nation calls lacrosse "Tewaaraton," meaning "an instrument of peace."

Whatever the origin of the game's Native American name, most Haudenosaunee or Iroquois, and the more than 60 countries around the world that now officially play lacrosse, collectively acknowledge it as and call it, "the Creator's game."

By the 1740s, French colonists took up the game and in 1856, a Montreal dentist, Dr. William George Beers, founded the Montreal Lacrosse Club. Beers wrote a rule book, redesigned the stick, switched to a rubber ball and shortened the field to a half-mile (880 yards!).

Iroquois teams traveled all the way to England to play exhibition games before the Queen and, in 1868, after a friendly game against a baseball team in Troy, New York, a group in Troy established the first lacrosse club in the U.S.: The Mohawk Lacrosse Club.

Lacrosse was played officially in the 1904 and 1908 Summer Olympics and as an exhibition sport in the 1928 and 1932 games. The sport continued to grow in popularity through the 1900s as more high schools and colleges formed leagues. In 1971, Cornell defeated the University of Maryland to win the inaugural NCAA Division I Men's Lacrosse Championship. The Eagle Pro Box Lacrosse League, a men's professional indoor lacrosse league, launched in 1987 and Major League Lacrosse, a professional outdoor field lacrosse league, was formed in 2001, followed by the Premier Lacrosse League that was established in 2019. Today, lacrosse is one of the fastest-growing sports in the world.

My brother John was the first in our family to play the Creator's game. As my Irish twin, born a year and week after me, he always wanted to blaze a different trail. John was a risk taker, and a bit of a rebel at heart, so naturally he was the one who wanted to play this weird sport called lacrosse. Moving from Brooklyn, New York to Philadelphia and then later to Baltimore when John and I were young, our parents had never even heard of lacrosse.

My younger brothers David and Bryan soon followed John's path and dropped baseball to start playing this crazy game. As four brothers, we played "two vs. two" everything, so I played a little backyard lacrosse with them, but I insisted lacrosse was for wimps.

I played football and baseball from the age of seven. Football was my passion, and I was good enough to get recruited by legendary coach Augie Miceli during eighth grade and was offered a small scholarship to attend Calvert Hall College High School, which had one of the top football programs in the state of Maryland.

I was also a decent Little League baseball player. My dad grew up as a strong baseball player himself, and his father, my grandfather, actually played semi-pro baseball in the Wall Street League. As the oldest of the Kelly brothers, my dad usually coached my baseball teams and helped me develop as a solid third baseman and pitcher. So, although my passion was football, I still planned to play baseball in high school as well.

It was in eighth grade when one of my youth football coaches really came after me to play lacrosse, which is a spring sport. I had little interest and told him I played travel baseball in the spring, and besides, I could barely catch or throw. He encouraged me that lacrosse was a great fit for football players with my skill set, and that I could come to practices and games whenever they didn't conflict with baseball. In hindsight, I am really surprised he made that offer since it was a high-level Junior A team, but I decided to quietly take him up on it and ended up making four or five practices and played in a few games. My stick skills were terrible, but the team was so strong that he put me into every game I attended, and I could run, hit and get ground balls. Coach loved my toughness, speed and intensity, but I was a football and baseball player, period!

Little did I know God had other plans for me that would include a spiritual awakening on a lacrosse field in college, where the Creator's game would be used to draw me into a personal, life-changing relationship with Him, the Creator of heaven and earth, and alter the trajectory of my life forever.

After college, I would be introduced to something else that would have a major impact on my life, my family and many others—an organization called the Fellowship of Christian Athletes, or FCA.

I learned that FCA had been founded in 1954 by a young basketball coach in Oklahoma named Don McClanen, who had been cutting press clippings of professional and college athletes and coaches who publicly praised God for their successes on and off the field. With the support of Branch Rickey, one of the most influential men in sports who broke Major League Baseball's color barrier by signing Jackie Robinson with the Brooklyn Dodgers, and a large donation from a Pittsburgh businessman, McClanen launched his vision to use the platform and influence of athletes and coaches to share God's love and truth through sports. To this day, many would say the one-word definition of FCA is "Influence."

Influence and The Creator's Game: My Story and Stories of Family, Faith and Lacrosse chronicles how the Creator's game and FCA have helped shape my life, as well as the lives of my family and countless others around the world, to more fully connect with the Creator of not only lacrosse, but all of life.

Everyone likes a good story, so I hope this book of stories, which I have done my best to recall and retell as accurately as possible, helps connect you to the Creator in personal, real and life-changing ways. Above all, I hope it pleases the Creator.

Sports

ward Christian Athletes in '92

Squad' upsets Turtles

O. Williams
tor

upposed to be a case of
ans being thrown to the

the be whs raced
Vail Lacrosse Stub
Greene Turtles jump
2-0 lead over the
on Friday afternoon, vith
the expectation of winning
ighter was posked
four fourth. qon quarter and
verume, th Xhocs a
nade up could: the ACA
s 9-8, ever, the soul brught
ated to al out picks bracket for
uration.
CA, the VLC, making its first
blout appes ance, sed, used a
wn as the kd bod us defense
nbination of us defense

and sheer hustle to shut down the
No. 1 seeded Turtles' potent offense, anchored by Towson State
middie Rob Shek and former
Syracuse All-American Gary Gait,
one of the all-time leading scorers
in the Major Indoor Lacrosse
League.

Gait, who had seven goals in a
22-7 Greene Turtles' shellacking of
the Vail Lacrosse Club in
Thursday's opening round, was un-
able to get into the swing of things
Friday, scoring no goals on six
shots.

"I just wasn't on today at all,"
Gait said. "(Thursday) everything
was going in, (Friday) nothing was.
I'd say it was the difference. but
think it was the lack of activity.

Though David Kelly had the
game-winning goal at 3:14 of the
second overtime, it was the

Please see *Lacrosse* pa

PART I

Miracle in the Mountains

CHAPTER 1

Ask, Seek, Knock

"Ask and it will be given to you; seek and you will find;
knock and the door will be opened to you."

Matthew 7:7

I t was the summer of 1991, one night during the fourth year of our Fellowship of Christian Athletes (FCA) Lacrosse Camp at Gettysburg College. After a long day of lacrosse, fellowship and huddles, approximately 80 young campers settled into their dorms for the night. Around 10 p.m., my friend Dan Britton, my brother Bryan, and a couple others and I went to the campus pizza shop for a little break and some good food and drink.

What could we do to more effectively share God's, or our Creator's, love and truth with the top players in the lacrosse world? How could we make a greater impact?

"Wouldn't it be cool," Dan asked, "if we put together a team to go out to that huge tournament in Colorado?"

The Vail Shootout in Colorado was the Daytona 500 of lacrosse, a highly competitive international tournament, the second biggest in the world behind the World Games.

"That would be cool," we agreed, "but it would be almost impossible to pull together a competitive team of players who would want to be a part of a faith-based team like that."

Really, how many guys did we even know who would consider being a part of a team of players who loved lacrosse, yet were open and even desirous to grow in their relationship with God while wanting to be a light to others?

As FCA did not sponsor teams, the whole idea sounded like a crazy long shot. I suggested that maybe we could talk to Athletes in Action (AIA) since I had been involved with AIA at Cornell. They had a division that specialized in team outreaches in sports like basketball and wrestling; maybe it would be possible to form our lacrosse team under their ministry umbrella.

Despite our doubts, Dan said he would check into it.

We prayed: *Lord, if this is of You, you're going to have to open doors.*

In September, a couple of months after camp was over, Dan called a guy named Skip at the Vail Shootout office and asked to enter a team for the following summer. Skip laughed and told Dan that people can't just call and enter the tournament; it sells out years ahead of time.

"Can you put us on the waiting list?" Dan asked.

"There's no waiting list."

"What if a team drops out?"

"Teams don't drop out of this tournament."

"Can you just write down my name and number and call me if there's an opening?"

Skip grunted, "Okay. Whatever."

When Dan told me about his conversation with Skip, I was actually relieved because I didn't really think we could fill out a competitive team, even if they accepted us.

We heard nothing for months and the door seemed closed. I hadn't given Vail much thought until Dan called me the second week in May. "You're not going to believe this," he said, "but the Vail Lacrosse people just called me at my office. They had a team drop out. If we call them back and commit by tomorrow at 10 a.m., we're in."

"Are you kidding me?" My mind started racing, my heart was beating fast, and doubts flooded my mind. "Let me call my wife," I said.

I called Gayle and told her what happened. "What do you think?"

Gayle loves travel and adventure. "Go for it! Let's do it!" she said.

"But I don't know if we will even be able to put together a team, especially this late, with only five or six weeks before the tournament," I said.

"It will come together," she said. "I think we should do it."

Twenty Flights

Dan told me we had to send in an $880 registration fee. I was still early in my career in our family's business and Gayle didn't make much money as a teacher and coach at a private school, so it wasn't like we had extra money, but we wrote the check. On faith, Gayle booked 20 non-refundable flights—you could do that in 1992—at $300 a pop and charged them on our credit card. We prayed we would find enough players to pay us back and take us off the hook for the $6,000.

Dan had originally called AIA to see if they could help with our team, but the discussion didn't go very far, and it didn't matter since we were on the waiting list and unlikely to get into the tournament anyway. After the call from Skip and our decision to "go for it," Dan called AIA again, but there was no real interest on their part, and it seemed like God was steering us in a different direction. We ended up calling Dal Shealy, the president of FCA, and told him about our idea of taking a faith-based lacrosse team to the Vail tournament.

"Do you mind if we go as a team under the banner of FCA and wear an FCA jersey that we will design?" we asked.

"We have not had teams like this before, but let me think about it," he said. After further discussion and reflection, Dal agreed. Dan, who was then on staff with FCA, and I assured him we would do our best to represent FCA with excellence.

I began the recruiting with my brothers, John, David and Bryan, who all agreed to come, which was huge because they all played lacrosse at a high level in college. Bryan recruited Steve Mason, who had been an All-American goalie at Roanoke College, and several of his University of North Carolina teammates, including Steve Muir, who was a big, strong, fast midfielder. I called my teammate and best friend from Cornell, Steve Paletta, an outstanding defenseman. "I'm in," he said. "That's a tournament I've never won."

"Don't expect to win it with us," I said, "but we're going to have fun."

To fill out a roster, we even invited several guys who just graduated from high school and who were involved with our Calvert Hall FCA Huddle, including Andy Hilgartner and Brian Hubbard, both of whom later played at Michigan State. Our recruiting pitch was simple: "We are going on a retreat to the mountains of Colorado where we are going to play in the top lacrosse tournament in the world. If you love lacrosse and are open to growing in your relationship with God, please join us."

Guys called their friends and the friends of their friends, and we found players like George Glyphis, who played at Virginia, and Tim Spears, who had played at Towson University. The night before we left for Vail, nineteen guys showed up for practice at St. Paul's School in Baltimore and a cookout afterward at my parents' house. Somebody brought their friend, Glen, who had played "club lacrosse" at Liberty University, which was not exactly a lacrosse power at the time.

"Glen, we could use one more player. Do you want to go with us?" we asked.

"Sure, I've got nothing else to do."

After dinner, Steve Paletta, our only player who had ever played in the Shootout, stood up to address the team. It sounded more like a warning than a pep talk.

"Listen, guys, I've gone to Vail on teams loaded with talent and gotten crushed. I don't want to scare you, but we have to have the proper perspective about what we're in for. This is going to be a battle. We have to prepare ourselves for that."

Dan Britton said that he laid awake all that night thinking, *This might be the dumbest thing we've ever done in our lives. Are we going to embarrass ourselves and the Lord? Couldn't we come up with a better way to impact the lacrosse world?*

MORE TO THE STORY...

We Can Do This – Gayle Kelly

"A lot has to be done to pull a team together," Frank sighed when he told me about the opportunity to play in Vail.

I started doing the mental math. *There's Frank. He has three brothers. They all know tons of lacrosse players.*

"We can do this," I said.

I booked 20 flights because that's the number where the group discount kicked in. The airline needed names, so I made them up—listing my college roommates and other random friends and family names. Neither Frank nor I had ever been to Vail, so it wasn't easy to arrange all the accommodations and transportation—there was no Expedia or Yelp in 1992.

All this while I was nursing a nine-month-old. But it was so cool to see God confirm our decision to go every step along the way.

CHAPTER 2

God Squad Upsets Turtles

"Now to him who is able to do immeasurably more than all we ask or imagine,
according to his power that is at work within us, to him be glory...
throughout all generations, for ever and ever! ..."

Ephesians 3:20-21

On the two-and-a-half-hour drive from the Denver airport to Vail, we were all blown away by the majesty of the Rocky Mountains. When we arrived in Vail, we had a light practice to acclimate to the thin air. We were all exhausted, gasping for breath, and drinking a lot of water.

The next day we played our first game against an all-star team from North Carolina. We had no idea what to expect. We had a handful of talented and experienced players, but our last five guys had just finished high school or their freshman year at college and we were playing in the Open Division, where most players were in their mid to late twenties. There was no professional outdoor lacrosse in existence so many players at the Shootout were considered the best in the world at that time.

The whistle blew and we got off to a slow start. We fell behind early and looked like a team that had never played together before. I began to doubt if we would ever score.

My dad—"Big Frank" we call him—joined us on the trip. He wanted to see his four sons all play together—this was the first and only time that had ever happened—and, by God's grace, we broke the ice and scored. And before you knew it, all four of us scored in that game, including Bryan, a defenseman. We won the game, 12-6. After the game, we knelt in a huddle to thank God for bringing us to such a beautiful place, and for allowing us to come away with at least one victory on the field.

Our reward was a matchup the next day against the two-time defending champions, the Greene Turtle team. The local newspapers called them "the greatest team ever assembled in the 20-year history of the tournament." They

The first and only time all four Kelly brothers played together on the same team. (L to R) John, me, David, Bryan

had no idea what to call us since it was our first year there. All we knew was that the Greene Turtle was going to destroy us.

Dave Pietramala, a future Hall of Fame defenseman on the Greene Turtle and future head coach at Johns Hopkins University, summed up his team's reaction to playing us in a documentary that was later produced about the game: "Who is this team? What are they? Why are they here?"

My brothers, David and Bryan, and I flashed back three weeks. We had played together for Maryland Lacrosse Club (MLC) that year and faced Mt. Washington Lacrosse Club—with Dave Pietramala and Gary Gait, who was known as "the Michael Jordan of lacrosse"—in the United States Club Lacrosse Association (USCLA) South Division Championship game. We fell way behind but staged a fourth-quarter comeback and closed to within a goal. With seconds left, David scored to tie the game. We beat Mt. Washington in overtime and went on to win the USCLA Championship a week later on Long Island against Brine Lacrosse Club out of New England.

But this game against the Greene Turtle team was very different. Our FCA team had neither the talent nor depth of our MLC team, and the Greene Turtle had all-stars from Mt. Washington Lacrosse Club and other clubs.

Against the Greene Turtle, "The only thing we had going for us," my brother Bryan said, "was that maybe the Greene Turtle guys would not take us seriously and get caught up in the evening activities the night before the game, and maybe we could keep it close."

Here we are playing Greene Turtle in primetime on July 4th weekend on Ford Field, the main stadium field (named after former President Gerald Ford), packed with thousands of fans.

As we gather on the field, before the opening whistle, I tell the team, "Here's the deal, let's not worry about the score. The only question we're going to ask ourselves at the end of the game is, did we play as hard as we could with the gifts God gave us? This game is going to be all about effort.

"The Lord tells us in His Game Plan (the Bible), that 'whatever you do, work at it with all your heart, as if for the Lord, not man.'[1] Guys, today we play for the Creator, our Lord, not for our wives, girlfriends, parents, the fans, or anyone else. Look up at the mountains. Imagine the Creator, who we believe is Jesus, sitting on the top of that mountain enjoying us. Let's play as hard as we can for Him!"

Forty-five seconds into the game, we are already behind 2-0, and we know we're in trouble. I call a timeout, bring us together, and remind the guys, "We can't play for the scoreboard. We have to keep our eyes on the Lord and we have to stay together and cover for each other. We know we're underdogs. We need to play with all our hearts as if for the Lord and we can't quit or give up no matter what happens."

After my rousing pep talk, we fall behind 3-0, then 4-0. We finally score to make it 4-1, then 4-2, then 5-2, then 5-3, and the butterflies and nerves begin to settle a bit and we even hear some of the fans starting to cheer for us, the underdog; like cheering for the Washington Generals against the Harlem Globetrotters; or for David to take down Goliath. The score at halftime is 5-5. I violate my own rule—the spirit is willing, but the flesh is weak—and ask Gayle to take a picture of the scoreboard. (I think that is the only time someone has ever taken a picture of a scoreboard at halftime.)

To start the second half, Greene Turtle scores early and we fall behind 7-5 but come back to tie it 7-7 at the end of the third quarter.

Greene Turtle retakes the lead 8-7, but with about three minutes left, we score to send the game into overtime. I ask Gayle to take another picture of the scoreboard, showing 8-8 at the end of four quarters.

The game is still tied toward the end of overtime when Greene Turtle's Gary Gait—the legend out of Syracuse whom many regard as the greatest to ever play the game—has the ball. Gait, a 6'2", 210-pound stud, barrels toward the goal, covered by a guy on our team named Tucker Bailey, who had just graduated from high school.

I'm watching from the sideline. I turn to a teammate next to me and say, "This game's over."

I don't know how it happened, but the next thing I see is Gait's stick helicopter checked and knocked loose from his hands, spinning in the air, and the ball rolling on the ground. Tucker somehow de-twigged Gary Gait, and we're heading to double overtime.

I win the ensuing faceoff and pass the ball to Mike O'Keefe, a Penn State graduate who had a short stick covering him. My defender leaves me to double-team the ball, and I get the ball back, ten yards from the goal, dead center, wide open. I fire a bullet toward the upper right corner of the net.

Greene Turtle's goalie, Jim "Beardy" Beardmore, who had been the NCAA Goalie of the Year at the University of Maryland, with his quick reflexes blocks my shot with his left elbow, but the ball deflects off Beardy to one of our top players on the crease, Tim Spears, who catches it and shoots toward an empty goal.

Greene Turtle's Dave Pietramala, whom ESPN's Leif Elsmo called "the world's best defenseman," dives into the cage. The ball deflects off his helmet, right to Dan Britton who scoops it up behind the goal. Dan spots my brother, David, on the backside of the crease and feeds him the ball. David's middle name is Eugene, and his teammates at the University of North Carolina called him "Eugene the Scoring Machine." David shoots. He scores, and FCA beats the Greene Turtle team in double overtime.

It was like a shot heard around the lacrosse world. Half of the fans erupted in pandemonium; the other half sat in stunned silence. Big Frank ran out onto the field to join in the celebration. After mobbing David and then shaking hands with the shocked and angry Greene Turtle players, who would now be relegated to the losers' bracket (which had never happened before or since), we quietly dropped to our knees in a huddle to give thanks and praise to God, who showed us how a little faith could become a "Miracle in the Mountains."

The local newspaper, the *Vail Daily*, now had a new name for us. "God Squad Upsets Turtles," read their headline.

This picture of our team after the Greene Turtle game has been labeled "The Power of Prayer" and is a symbol of FCA Lacrosse to this day.

MORE TO THE STORY...

The Power of Prayer – Big Frank (My Dad)

What could be better than joining my four sons on a retreat in the Rocky Mountains and watching them play lacrosse together on the same team? Only watching them win the game known as "The Miracle in the Mountains."

I had been to many games before watching my sons play at Calvert Hall, then Frank at Cornell, John at Washington College, and then David and Bryan at the University of North Carolina (UNC), but I had never seen all four of them play together on the same team. And I had never seen a game like that, even though I had seen both David and Bryan win national championships at UNC.

I rushed out on the field with the rest of the team to smother David after he scored the winning goal. After shaking hands with the Turtle players and coaches, we walked to a corner of the field, got in a huddle, then dropped to our knees to give thanks and praise to God. It is something I will never forget, and I thank God for that special experience.

Tape It Up – David Kelly

"I'm not sure, Frank. I'm married and have a child—I'm retired from lacrosse."

That was my answer when Frank asked me to play in the Vail Shootout. But Frank is Frank, and he is very persistent and he wouldn't let me say no.

"Why don't you come out with us? It'll be fun. You've never been to Vail. You'll love it and we really need you on the field and off," Frank insisted, and I relented.

In the first quarter of the Greene Turtle game, I chased a ground ball and Ronnie Klausner, a Greene Turtle defenseman who is in the Towson University Hall of Fame, takes a full swing at my kneecap and splits it open. I howl in pain and hobble off the field as my knee starts bleeding.

You're done for the day," the trainer tells me. "You need to go to the medical center and get stitches."

"Can't you tape it up and I'll get stitches later?" I ask.

"You're not going to be able to walk later."

"Yeah," I said, "as soon as I stop playing, I won't be able to walk, so I want to finish the game."

The trainer tapes me up and I go back on the field, but I can't run full speed. Have you ever been smashed in the knee with a brick? That's what it feels like.

Fortunately, I don't need full speed when, in the second overtime, Danny Britton scoops up the ball behind the goal and moves to his right. I cut backside and he hits me with a perfect pass that I catch and quick-stick into the empty cage. I know it's going in the second I let it go.

I raise my arms in victory and within seconds, the whole team charges me. I'm in the middle of the pile, which is why you can't find me in the picture of the team kneeling and praying.

The fans were shocked. Walking around town afterward I would overhear people asking each other, "Did you know FCA beat Greene Turtle? Can you believe it?" To me it was just another game, but it turned out to be much bigger than that.

I'm All in Now – Stephen Paletta

In February of 1991, the company I worked for had an underground pipe project in Baltimore City. I called Frankie and asked if I could stay at his house for a few days and maybe up to a week while we completed the job. But the project developed major complications and I ended up living in the Kelly's basement for over a month.

It was during that extended, unplanned stay that Frankie and Gayle helped me come to understand what it meant to have a personal relationship with the Creator, God, through his son Jesus Christ. A few months later, Frankie called me about playing with FCA in Vail, so I was still young in my faith. I had some questions about the Bible—it has all those miracles; how come I had never seen one?

After we arrived in Vail and had our first FCA practice, I wanted to slip away to meet some old friends but Frankie announced, "Come on, everybody in. It's time for fellowship."

"Fellowship? Really Frankie?" I said.

"Yep, that's one of the main reasons we are here. Let's keep our hearts and minds open to what God might say to us through His Word and through each other's stories."

I didn't anticipate how powerfully God was going to show up in those fellowship times. God broke me down. He moved me out of my egoism and individualism. He molded us and connected us as a team through the life stories and faith stories we shared.

But I still thought Greene Turtle would destroy us. I thought of us as a ragtag team, and we were going up against Division I All-Americans at every position. When we fell behind so early, I thought, *This is going to be the longest lacrosse game ever.* The fans snickered at us—"the Christians were being fed to the turtles" was how one sportswriter put it. As we mounted our comeback, I could hear a change in the crowd. Most started cheering for us.

After the victory, kids came up to us asking for our autographs. Parents asked us to explain what FCA was and why we played for them.

It was that game, it was on that field, at that moment, that I said to God, "Hey, that's it. You showed me a miracle. Without your divine intervention, there's no way we could have stayed within ten goals of that team. I'm all in now."

I still have questions for God, but from that point forward, I've had a committed faith and personal relationship with Jesus Christ.

I believe the FCA victory over Greene Turtle was a pivotal moment in the lacrosse world. In many ways, the Vail Shootout was always a big party where lacrosse happened to be played. The tournament directors considered closing it down because the social life atmosphere often got out of control. Teams changed their behavior from that moment forward. I don't mean the parties and drinking stopped completely, but the tournament became more about the quality of the lacrosse than the parties.

I give all the credit to God and FCA.

Catching a Vision – Gayle Kelly

Frank never mentions it because the altitude wreaked havoc on all the players, but his asthma flared up the day of the Greene Turtle game. At the end of the first half, when he came over to me gasping for air, I thought he was going to ask me to find some kind of medical help. But what he said was, "Gayle...can you...quick...take a picture of the scoreboard?"

That victory was so, so fun, but there were greater victories on the trip, especially at mealtimes. Most nights, my sister-in-law Tee and I cooked dinner for the 20 guys and other family and friends. While most other teams hit the bars at night, our guys sat around and talked about their struggles in life and asked questions about faith and what it meant to have a personal relationship with God. The experience built my own faith. Too often I had compartmentalized my life. In Vail I saw, in action, the benefits of merging something that you love—it could be lacrosse or anything else—with faith in Jesus. I caught a vision of an integrated life more clearly than I had ever seen before.

CHAPTER 3

Bumps, Bruises and Blisters

"Even youths grow tired and weary, and young men stumble and fall; but those who hope in the Lord will renew their strength. They will soar on wings like eagles; they will run and not grow weary, they will walk and not be faint."

Isaiah 40:30-31

Although the spiritual impact of the victory over the Greene Turtle team was immediate, the next day we played Team Colorado, another perennial powerhouse, in the semifinal game. They were thrilled that we had knocked off Greene Turtle and cleared an easier path to the championship game.

The manager of Team Colorado was Brett Davy, whose son, Brett Jr., had played with David and Bryan at UNC. He told Big Frank that he noticed our team praying before and after each game and told him, "We've got one up on you today. We hired a minister to come and pray with our team before we play you."

Team Colorado's head coach and top player, Peter Schaffer, was a sports agent for Barry Sanders, the star running back of the Detroit Lions. He knew that the Lions team chaplain lived in Colorado and had asked him to come and pray with the team. Big Frank had watched Team Colorado interact with the chaplain, but things did not go as planned. When they called the guys in for prayer, Big Frank saw a lot of rolling eyes and heard a lot of grumbling curse words. It ended up being a very rough game with some hard hits and trash-talking, but our FCA team did our best to keep our cool and we were fortunate to score a goal in the last minute to win.

"I give the coach credit for trying," Big Frank said, "and thank God that our guys handled the pressure in a God-honoring way."

Who could believe that at noon the next day, FCA would be playing Mt. Washington Tavern for the championship of the Vail Shootout?

The tournament officials contacted us with a request. "The championship game tomorrow will be on cable TV and broadcast to millions of people across the country. Can you please wear real jerseys?"

We had been wearing cheap, red and white pinnie tank tops—practice jerseys really—over a T-shirt. We had slapped a number on the back and the FCA cross logo on the front, which technically violated the rules because uniforms were supposed to have numbers on both the front and back. Some of the numbers and logos were peeling off.

We laughed. "It's not like we have a stash of nice jerseys we've been waiting to pull out. This is all we got." The top teams like Greene Turtle, Colorado and Mt. Washington all had amazing uniforms.

Going into the championship game against Mt. Washington Tavern, we were running on fumes. My brother John's ankle hurt so bad he "iced" it in the Colorado River every night—alongside my brother David who was icing his knee. A number of

My former Cornell teammate, Steve Paletta, was not the only one wrapping and icing up after four games in four days.

our guys were pretty banged up, and a bunch of us had really bad fever blisters on our lips from the bright sunshine and dry Colorado air.

We didn't exactly feel our best, but we were believing God to help us rise up, renew our strength and help us finish strong.

MORE TO THE STORY...

You've Got to Play with Us – John Kelly

"John, you've got to play with us in Vail," Frank pleaded. "This could be the first and maybe only time the four Kelly brothers play together on the same team. I realize you haven't played for a while, but you're in better shape than any of us. You can run all day!"

I agreed to go and started fiddling around with my stick which I hadn't touched in five years. I had traded it for a bike and was as fit as I ever was from racing on mission trips to Costa Rica, Mexico, Venezuela, and across the U.S. with Athletes in Action.

Team Colorado, whom we faced in the semifinal game, was strong, but I knew many of them, including my old college roommate from Washington College, Steve Beville. We played together in three Division III Championship games, unfortunately losing to Hobart each time.

I knew Team Colorado wanted to win this game badly, and had a lot of confidence against us, but they must have been a little worried as well and brought in some extra help.

"Hey, JK, we've got a pastor coming in," Steve told me while we were warming up before the game. "We're not going to let God be only on your side." We were fortunate to win that game in a nail-biter.

Sharing that experience with my wife, Tee, was great too. While I played, met with the guys in our daily huddle and fellowship times, and nursed my bumps and bruises, Tee worked with Gayle to serve our team meals. She was also on the sidelines, cheering us on and sharing with other spectators who asked about the true meaning and purpose of our FCA team. Gayle and Tee were a big part of our success on and off the field and would have plenty of fans to interact with during the championship game the next day.

CHAPTER 4

Did That Really Happen?

"But thanks be to God, who gives us the victory through our Lord Jesus Christ."

1 Corinthians 15:57 (ESV)

In the championship game, we did something we had never done before—scored first. *Here we go!* But we quickly fell behind and trailed 9-2 going into the fourth quarter. We rallied to close the gap to 9-7 late in the game.

During the comeback, David scored what had to be the most bizarre goal of the tournament. We were in a drop back, or sloughed ride, so all three of our attackmen were in a zone between the restraining line and midfield line. Mt. Washington's goalie,

Me winning a fast-break faceoff in the championship game against Mt. Washington

Quint Kessenich, who was twice recognized as the nation's best goalie during his playing days at Johns Hopkins University and is currently a top sportscaster for ABC and ESPN, made a pass to one of his stud defensemen, Steve Kisslinger, who was super dangerous with the ball in his stick. Somehow, David jumped the pass and intercepted it with one hand outstretched and took off for the goal.

Even with a bad knee all taped up, he still somehow got by Kessenich and was in a footrace with three Mt. Washington defenders towards the goal. Kisslinger, a former Towson University All-American who was named one of the top 30 professional indoor players of all time, got to the goal just as David shot and decided to grab the side of the goal and literally flip the goal over. David's shot goes through everything – through the front of the crease, through Kisslinger's legs and right out the back of the goal.

"What the heck was that?" asked Leif Elsmo, ESPN legend and television broadcaster for the game. "You don't see that very often!" You can actually still watch the highlights of the game and that crazy sequence today on YouTube by searching *Vail Lacrosse Shootout Mt. Washington Tavern vs. FCA 1992*.

My brother David's shot (and Mt. Washington defenseman Steve Kisslinger flipping the goal) in the championship game

Unfortunately, we lost that game 10-7, but God gave us other victories in ways we never imagined.

Dan Britton, me and my son Frankie (nine months old) with the consolation trophy

We barely had time to stay for the awards ceremony. When Gayle booked our flights, she figured we would not be playing in the finals on Sunday afternoon and would be done by late morning. She also knew some of us had to be at FCA Camp at Gettysburg College on Monday morning and booked a 5 p.m. flight back to Baltimore. We shook hands with the Mt. Washington team and hoisted the consolation trophy.

Our goalie Steve Mason, my brother Bryan, and I were each selected to the All-Tournament team, so they did that presentation after the championship game as well, which further delayed our trip to the airport which was more than two hours away. We had pre-packed our three vans and took off to the airport—still in our uniforms—and sat in a Fourth of July weekend traffic jam. We smelled the brakes burning out on one of the vans. *Will we make it?*

In full panic mode, we pulled up to the departing flights curb and scrambled to unpack the vans. Gayle called the airline and begged them to hold the plane, and they delayed takeoff for 40 minutes. Gayle then called the car rental office and told them we were in danger of missing our flight and would leave the vans at the departing flights drop off curb with the keys on the seats. (Imagine doing that today—we would have been arrested!)

We rushed to the gate and caught the flight, some of us still wearing our uniforms and cleats, most of us nursing bumps, bruises and sun blisters on our lips, and all of us excited that God had done something bigger than any of us could have asked or imagined.

We landed at Baltimore/Washington International Airport around 11 p.m., and it was midnight before we picked up all of our luggage and equipment. Dan Britton drove directly to Gettysburg College for our FCA Lacrosse Camp. I caught a few hours of sleep at home before driving to camp in the morning.

Dan and I smiled and shook our heads when we saw each other the next day. *Did that really happen?*

Scan to check out the FCA Lacrosse Miracle in the Mountains documentary.

The 1992 FCA Lacrosse Team

MORE TO THE STORY...

They Had IT – Dal Shealy

When Dan Britton asked me if the lacrosse team that he and Frank Kelly were taking to Vail could wear the FCA logo, I didn't think very long about it.

I coached football for over 40 years before I was named president of FCA, and built some of my teams from scratch, so I knew what it took to pull that off. I was confident that Dan and Frank, who are like two peas in a pod, also had what it took to bring together a team that would honor God and FCA.

Sure enough, they built a team with *IT*. There are athletes, there are good athletes, and there are athletes that have *IT*—the intangibles to know what it takes to step up, to overcome, and do what's necessary to win.

FCA President Dal Shealy, pictured above with FCA's famous "Influence" print, graciously allowed us to play under the banner of FCA.

That team had *esprit de corps*, which comes from the heart and soul of the athlete and spreads like a virus and turns the team into a force to be reckoned with.

Success breeds success and little did they know that the Miracle in the Mountains team would spark the strategic development of other FCA sports-specific ministries and new ways to share the influence and message of FCA that would keep going and going and going.

God Works in Broken Plays – Dan Britton

I love how God works in broken plays—things you don't expect and at times when you least expect them. Like when a group of FCA camp leaders share dreams around a pizza. Or a team drops out of a tournament for the first time in the tournament's history. Or a shot deflects off a defender's helmet and leads to a game-winning goal.

I believe God met us in the mountains and did supernatural work in everyone. He moved something in us or revealed something to us in every game and each night in our fellowship and sharing times.

On the second night, one of the guys broke down weeping because he wanted to surrender his life to the Lord. In the middle of a conversation over ice cream in downtown Vail, one of our players told me he wanted to turn his life over to Christ. We met together back home for Bible study over the next six months.

God's work extended beyond our team. Families would come up to us after the games and tell us they were vacationing in Vail, saw the lacrosse games while driving down the freeway, stopped to watch, and found our FCA team. "Seeing you here is such an encouragement to us," they would say.

Some of us knew players on other teams. There we were playing against them but also desiring to honor God. That opened doors for sharing the Good News. We discovered there were more believers in the lacrosse world than we realized, but they were isolated. Many found new boldness when they realized they were not alone

Kelly Hepting, who came with the Greene Turtle to watch the coaches' and owners' kids during the games, told us that as she observed the FCA team, she thought to herself, *They have something that I want; that I don't have.* Watching our FCA team, on and off the field, drew her into a personal, life-changing relationship with the Lord and, years later, her sons played for FCA.

The media took note. They called us "The God Squad," and joked that we always played with a man up because God was on our side. They had fun with us, but they didn't make fun of us. I thought it was awesome that they respected our team and, in their own way, helped spread our message.

After our loss to Mt. Washington, ESPN broadcaster Leif Elsmo said on the broadcast, "The biggest story of this tournament was the Fellowship of Christian Athletes, the fact that they got to this final. The goals from this team are goals that make you believe in the value system of this country again."

Playing in the Vail Shootout wasn't about winning the games. It was about being obedient to what God put in our hearts, taking that step of faith, and allowing God to orchestrate whatever he wanted to come from it.

I learned that there is power in a specific passion. You can put your love for Jesus alongside your passion for lacrosse or anything else, get a group of like-minded believers together, and start dreaming. Anything is possible with God, right?

I'm Not Scared – Bryan Kelly

I had graduated from the University of North Carolina in 1991 and we won the National Championship that year, so I recruited my good friends and teammates, Gregg Langhoff, a great attackman, and Steve Muir, a big, strong middie, to join us in Vail. Without Steve, we never would have had the success we had on the field.

More than 20 years after the 1992 Miracle in the Mountains, in 2015, Steve was struck with an aggressive form of cancer. I visited him in the hospital and as we talked, he told me that he knew he wasn't going to make it. "Bryan, obviously I don't want to die," he said. "I want to be with my wife and my kids. I love them. But I'm not scared, because I know where I'm going. Back when we played in Vail, I accepted Christ there on the mountain. I'm at peace."

Steve died and transitioned from life on earth to eternity in the presence of God, on September 4, 2015, and we have provided opportunities for his sons to play on some of our FCA lacrosse teams over the years. I still miss Steve and his fun personality, but I am so thankful he had that FCA Lacrosse experience in 1992 and made the decision that he did—a true miracle in those mountains.

Steve Muir (Left) and Gregg Langhoff

Sports

ward Christian Athletes in '92

Squad' upsets Turtles

D. Williams
tor

upposed to be a case of
ans have thrown to the

the irving thrown
Vail Lacrosse Shoot
Greene Fields Jump
co less
from the
the three
eights
our return to
vercome points lasted
ade about
9-8
eve
ated to
ration
A, the
tout appe
n as the
bination of

and sheer hustle to shut down the
No. 1 seeded Turtles' potent offense, anchored by Towson State
middie Rob Shek and former
Syracuse All-American Gary Gait,
one of the all-time leading scorers
in the Major Indoor Lacrosse
League.

Gait, who had seven goals in a
22-7 Greene Turtles' shellacking of
the Vail Lacrosse Club in
Thursday's opening round, was un-
ble to get into the swing of things
day scoring two goals or six
shots.

"I just wasn't on today," all
Gait said. "(Thursday) everything
was going in, (Friday) nothing was
I'd say it was the altitude, but
think it was the evening activities

Though David Kelly had the
game-winning goal at 3:14
second overtime, it wa

A
ted
club
was

Please see Lacrosse pa

PART II

It's Great to Be Here

Family Foundations

"Why do you call me, 'Lord, Lord,' and do not do what I say?
As for everyone who comes to me and hears my words and puts them into
practice, I will show you what they are like. They are like a man
building a house, who dug down deep and laid the foundation on rock..."

Luke 6:46-48

Many people in FCA point to the Miracle in the Mountains game in Colorado as the birth of FCA Lacrosse, a new area of ministry focus under the umbrella of FCA. While it helped put FCA Lacrosse on the map, I trace its genesis back eight years earlier to Schoellkopf Field during my sophomore year at Cornell University in 1984.

But before I explain that I would like to share a little about my family, how I got connected to the Creator's game and how God used the Creator's game to ultimately connect me to Him.

My dad was born in Brooklyn, New York and moved with his family to Philadelphia when he was young, as his dad, Francis X. Kelly, had accepted a sales position with a food packaging company. His mother, Margaret McPartlin Kelly, graduated from Adelphi University, which was a big deal for a woman in the 1930s. This would be her first time leaving Brooklyn as well.

My father ended up meeting my mother, Marguerite Janet DeMaine, during his junior year at Villanova University. My mom was born and raised in the Springfield, Pennsylvania area just outside of Philadelphia and was the first in her family to attend college, a two-year school called Gwynedd Mercy. Her dad, John R. DeMaine, worked for the Philadelphia Gas & Electric Company and her mom, Marguerite Delvecchio DeMaine, was a second-generation Italian, who worked hard at home and ran a tight ship.

After my dad graduated from college, he took a sales job with Armour Foods, and a year later married my mom. Three years later in 1964, I was born in Bryn Mawr Hospital outside of Philadelphia and my parents tell me they drove me home a few days later in the middle of a blizzard. Around that time, my dad took a new sales job selling engineering equipment for Eugene Dietzgen Co.

In 1965, my brother John was born and a couple of years later, my dad's company decided they wanted to open an office in Baltimore. When the opportunity presented itself, he accepted the challenge to move his young family to Baltimore, just like his father had done a couple of decades prior leaving Brooklyn for Philadelphia.

Shortly after arriving in Baltimore, my brother David was born. And a little over a year after that, Bryan was welcomed into the family. My mom had her hands full with four sons under the age of five.

AA *and Prayer Meetings*

It was 1971 when my dad came to the realization that he had a problem with alcohol. Just like his father before him who got sober two years before his death at age 46, and his grandfather, who died because of his alcoholism, my dad had what some refer to as the "Irish Virus." He was functional and never lost his job or his family, but deep in his heart he knew he had a problem. He courageously chose to get involved with Alcoholics Anonymous, and, by working the twelve steps of AA, got sober.

It was during that time that he decided he wanted to have more control of his work destiny as well, so he chose to pursue a career in insurance. He started with Aetna but didn't love individual life insurance sales, so after six months he joined an agency called Tidewater. He had met one of the owners of Tidewater through AA, and was excited to sell different kinds of insurance, including health insurance directly to small businesses.

During this time, my parents chose to open our home to our foster sister, Sharon. Sharon was six years old when she started spending weekends with our family. She lived at St. Vincent's Orphanage because both her parents, although alive, were incapacitated and not able to care for her. Sharon never took our family name but lived with us on and off until she was eighteen years old. She still calls my mom weekly and is blessed to be the mother of three sons and a number of grandchildren.

After being sober for several years, my dad still felt like something was missing in

1970s fashion at its finest! Family picture with me standing to the right of my mom

his life. He was sober but wasn't free of the fear and anxiety that drove some of his drinking habits.

Both my parents were "religious," coming from strong Irish Catholic and Italian Catholic backgrounds, but neither were free, nor had the peace that the Bible talks about. For several years, my dad was a daily communicant, which means he went to mass or church every day, but the feelings of guilt and anxiety persisted.

As a family, we went to church every Sunday, but my brothers and I didn't pay much attention, as our goals were survival, being "good enough" to get some donuts after church, and not being bad enough to get "the belt." The last thing on our minds was growing in a relationship with God.

Some friends invited my parents to a "Prayer Meeting." At first, it sounded kind of weird to them, but they both felt drawn to give it a shot. The group met in the basement of the church's main school building. When they arrived, they didn't know what to expect.

It was there that they heard the Gospel presented in a way they had never heard before. That night, they opened their hearts and lives to receive Jesus and the Holy Spirit in a personal and real way. As the Lord came in, much of the anxiety and fear my dad battled went away. That night was the beginning of a new peace, joy and freedom in both of their lives.

That night was also the first time my parents left my brothers and me home alone. Sharon was not there, so I was the oldest, and thus, "in charge." I don't remember exactly how it all happened, but when our parents came home all hell had broken loose—we accidentally left the oven on, unfinished pizza on the kitchen table and in the oven, burning. The upstairs toilet had overflowed and we didn't clean it up, so brown water was leaking into the family room below. We had also somehow torn the towel rack in the bathroom off the wall and broke my parents' bed, where we had been having two-on-two wrestling matches. We then went to bed, so when my parents came home with a new joy of the Lord upon them, it didn't take long to realize there was going to be some opposition to this new life in the Spirit.

Business and Politics

It would be two years later in 1976 that my parents started a small insurance business in the basement of our home. With five children under the age of fourteen, they made the decision to double mortgage their house (because they couldn't get a line of credit from a bank) and move forward with the idea of pooling small businesses together into a larger group of at least 100 employees, so these small groups could get access to better quality health insurance benefits at a much lower rate than they could get on their own.

Blue Cross Blue Shield of Maryland (BCBS) agreed to put together a pooled association health insurance plan for the Baltimore County Licensed Beverage Association. My dad got the association's "endorsement," but would have to go out, solicit and bring in the small business liquor stores, bars, and restaurants (ironically, five years after he stopped drinking alcohol). My mom would handle all the enrollments, answer all service calls, and then bill and collect the premium from each of the small groups. The first bills my mom sent out were handwritten on carbon paper.

Our parents started Francis X. Kelly Associates, Inc. in May 1976 in the basement of our family home.

My parents added an administrative fee that was built into the rates, so after they collected the premium from each small group, they kept their administrative fee and then passed the remaining premium for each of the groups through to BCBS, who looked at it as one big group.

When they started the business, they got on their knees at the end of their bed, asked for God's blessing and expressed their desire to provide for their family and to benefit the community. They had no huge goals, but the business slowly began to grow.

Two years later in 1978, my dad got involved in fighting a large state property tax increase. After attending a community meeting with hundreds of people in attendance, he was recruited to help lead a protest in Annapolis, the capital of Maryland. After that march, a number of people asked him to run for State Senate. He had no political aspirations, had only lived in Maryland for around ten years, had just started a business in the basement of our home a couple of years earlier, and had a wife and five kids he needed to provide for.

He didn't think it was a great idea, but decided to pray about it with my mom and a friend and spiritual mentor he met through the Prayer Group he attended, named Stelman Smith. Together, they discerned he should run, so with my mom's blessing, he did.

And sure enough, he won. He would go on to serve three four-year terms and rise to be vice chair of the powerful Budget and Taxation Committee.

Each legislative session began around January 15th and ended around April 15th, so with Big Frank spending most of his time in Annapolis for three months of the year, my mom was more than busy with the business and her five children.

CHAPTER 6

No Ordinary Ham and Egger

"Therefore encourage one another and build each other up..."

1 Thessalonians 5:11

My brothers, sister and I all attended the local public elementary school at the end of our street. We walked to and from school and had a ton of fun playing with our friends in the neighborhood and local pool. And we were fortunate to play sports through the Cockeysville-Springlake Recreation Council (CSRC).

I will never forget my first football team—the Orange Crush. My brother John and I were on the same team. He was seven years old, and I was eight. We got to the championship game and beat the mighty White Mustangs. I can't remember to pick up milk on the way home from work, but I can

Our 1972 Orange Crush team, with me (top row, far right with glasses) and my brother John (middle row with glasses)

still remember almost every detail of that game, including Coach Long and the trophy we all received at the awards banquet at Martin's West after the season. There was something about that experience that burned deep in my heart and soul, even as a little boy.

The spring before, I played on my first baseball team, the Green Tigers, coached by my dad. We started the season with T-ball, then finished with coach pitch. We were decent but didn't win anything special that I recall.

I often say that "I peaked in sixth grade," which was my last year at Pot Spring

Elementary School. I emerged as a leader in the classroom, was elected president of the school and, more importantly to me, was a leader on the playground.

In football, I was maybe average to slightly above average until about seventh grade. It was then that a switch flipped, and I went from being decent to being pretty good—and very tough.

I was farsighted and wore glasses that had thick lenses and magnified my eyes. My brother John wore glasses too and between us, our glasses were always broken on at least one corner, sometimes both corners, and sometimes in the middle as well. When we couldn't find tape to tape them back together, we would use Band-Aids, so we were easy targets for teasing. I also chipped my front tooth in seventh grade so between the taped-up, extra-thick glasses, and my busted-up smile, I definitely did not win "best looking" in my class and ended up developing a pretty big chip on my shoulder.

On the field, I wanted to prove my toughness and became a mean, borderline "cheap" football player. I played "until the whistle blew," to the end of each play, just like the coach told us. I would hit anyone, anywhere, as hard as I could until the whistle blew. No one was going to laugh at me and my brother.

I also ran the football that way. On the Orange Crush, I was an offensive lineman. By eighth grade I was one of the top running backs in the area. I loved running the ball and running people over. I loved delivering the blow to any would-be tackler and loved breaking tackles and scoring touchdowns.

Despite my attitude on the football field, my mom reminded me and my brothers daily to keep an eye out for anyone on our teams or in our classes who was struggling or being left out. Our mom had a special needs sister, and she modeled and prioritized empathy as a character trait in each of her children. Because of my mom, my heart and mind often go to the outcast, the underdog, or the one furthest out. I didn't realize it then, but she was shaping my heart and mind in how I would desire to relate and connect with people for years to come.

A Weird New Game

When I was in seventh grade and my brother John was in sixth grade, he decided to drop baseball and play a sport my parents and our family knew nothing about—lacrosse. Really, it wasn't that surprising given John was always the one taking risks and trying new things. Of course, he wanted to play this "weird" new game! It was only later that I learned that lacrosse is actually the oldest team sport played in North America.

It wasn't long before my younger brother David and Bryan jumped on board. Despite my protests that lacrosse was for "wimps," I eventually got dragged into their backyard scrimmages so they could play two on two... pretty much the way we played everything growing up. But our backyard battles didn't do too much to change my mind about the game.

As I shared in the Introduction, when I was in eighth grade, I got asked my one of my youth football coaches to play lacrosse on the CSRC Junior A Team—one of the top teams in the state. I wasn't interested, especially given I played travel baseball in the spring, which would conflict with the timing of the lacrosse season. My lack of stick skills (I could barely catch and throw the ball) made it a no-brainer for me to say no. But my coach wouldn't take no for an answer. He said he could work around my baseball schedule and explained how my strengths as a football player made me a great fit for the Creator's game.

Quietly, I decided to give it a try and ended up attending a handful of practices and, even though my skills were rough to say the least, the coach made sure I got playing time in each of the games I attended. Although it was nice to have the encouragement of the coach, who complimented my athleticism and hustle, I had a clear picture of my sports future, and lacrosse was definitely not in it.

The Hall

After my eighth-grade football season, I got calls from the football coaches at Calvert Hall and Loyola Blakefield, two of the top Catholic high schools in the area. I visited Loyola and liked Coach Joe Brune, but after visiting Calvert Hall and meeting Coach Augie Miceli, I knew "The Hall" was for me! They had a blue-collar edge and were one of the top-ranked high school football programs in the state.

I also seriously considered going to our local public high school, Dulaney, which would have been the natural fit coming

Coach Augie Miceli

from Ridgely, our public middle school that I attended. Almost all my good friends were going there, and I liked the idea of a co-ed school.

My parents had only started their business two years earlier. It was still operating out of the basement of our home and they didn't have a lot of extra money to afford the $1,000 Calvert Hall tuition. Coach Miceli and Calvert Hall came up with a $500 scholarship/financial aid package that was enough to help me and my family to say "Yes" to the Cardinals.

When I arrived at "The Hall," I chose to try out for the fresh-soph football team. I made the team and didn't start at first, which was really tough for me. I was also in advanced classes and felt in over my head. I started to doubt my decision and was leaning strongly towards transferring out and joining my friends at Dulaney, when some much-needed encouragement came my way.

In our football game against Archbishop Curley High School, I finally got my first start and somehow ended up having a big game. Brother Gregory Cavalier, my advanced French teacher (which was a class full of sophomores that I was struggling to keep up in), read the bulletin to the class, saying, "Hey, our little freshman here is 'no ordinary ham and egger.' Yesterday he rushed for 250 yards and had four touchdowns in the first half of the game vs. Curley." The timely words of encouragement from Brother Gregory, who joked that his nickname was "The Rock" because he was so tough, and a couple of sophomores in that class, Rick Roesner and Andrew Kimmel, were key to me staying at Calvert Hall.

Yet, Brother Gregory's words about my performance on the football field also reminded me further of what I had come to learn—that if you scored touchdowns, runs or goals, people liked that. I was realizing that if I performed at a high level, I felt good about myself and if I didn't, I felt inadequate and unworthy. It started in seventh and eighth grade and by high school, sports were on their way from being games to gods (or idols) in my life.

Coach Mike Thomas

After my freshman football season, one day walking down the hallway, Mike Thomas, the Calvert Hall varsity lacrosse coach, approached me. He wanted me and several other freshman and sophomore football players to play lacrosse. I told him I didn't play lacrosse and that I was planning to play baseball. He said he heard I played a little lacrosse in eighth grade. He was persistent and even said he thought that I could be a lacrosse All-American someday. *What? No way!*

I can't remember exactly how it happened, but several other football players and I decided to play lacrosse in the spring, and we all made junior varsity. Our stick work was terrible, but we could run, hit and hustle.

Our coach was Tom Keigler, a history teacher who was a USA National Lacrosse Team defenseman and one of the top players from his era. Coach Keigler had a quiet disposition, and he made me believe that I could play this game. He is definitely one of the best and most influential coaches I have had in any sport. He fanned a barely flickering flame into a fire of passion for the Creator's game.

Football and Faceoffs

My sophomore year, I made varsity football and through our weekly challenge drills, was able to climb the depth chart and beat out a junior and senior ahead of me to earn a starting position at cornerback. In my first varsity start, I had two interceptions in the first half, mainly because the Cardinal Gibbons quarterback threw the ball right into my chest two times. Our 1979 team went undefeated, won the Maryland Scholastic Association (MSA) A Conference Championship, and was the number one ranked team in the state of Maryland. It was Calvert Hall's last undefeated football team.

I somehow made varsity lacrosse that spring, and can still remember running up the field with the ball in my stick in the MSA Championship game at Towson University in front of thousands of lacrosse fans, thinking, *What am I doing here?* We lost that game, but my love for the Creator's game was growing by the day.

Football was still my passion, and I was thankful to start at running back my junior and senior year and loved returning kicks and punts. Our senior year, we went 11-1, with our only loss coming to Archbishop Rummel, a game we flew to and played in New Orleans.

I was fortunate to be 3-0 in wins over our archrival Loyola in the annual Thanksgiving morning Turkey Bowl that was played at old Memorial Stadium, where the Baltimore Colts played. The history, tradition and fanfare of that game made it feel like a championship game every year, regardless of the teams' records.

MAKING TRACKS. Calvert Hall halfback Frank Kelly looks for running room against Loyola.

Calvert Hall proves it's best with win over Loyola

I was honored to be a captain my senior year (#24) with Mark Kauffman (#40), Carl Epple (#72) and Anthony Guarino (#63), who each went on to play college football.

In lacrosse, Coach Thomas made me a center middie and faceoff man. When Coach Thomas asked me to faceoff, I had no idea what I was doing. Faceoffs are a critical part of every game, as that is the method of beginning play at the start of each game, each quarter and after each goal that is scored. It is where two opponents face each other in the center of the field, then work to gain control of the ball for their team after the official blows a whistle to start play. It's a critical position, because the team who earns the most possessions usually has more scoring opportunities, and thus, a better chance to win the game, so I wanted to get better at it to help our team.

I was learning that the keys to facing off well were concentration, quickness, technique and strength. I was focused, quick and strong, but my technique was terrible. I had a long way to go if I ever wanted to be good as a center middie and faceoff athlete.

I started at faceoff and first midfield my junior and senior years, but since I had never been to a lacrosse camp or received one-on-one instruction, I wasn't the "prettiest" or "smoothest" player. Somehow as a senior, I emerged as one of the top players in the highly regarded MSA A Conference and my passion to hopefully play lacrosse in college was growing as well.

Pushing the Boundaries

One of the challenges with making a varsity sport as a freshman or sophomore in high school is the exposure to upperclassmen, who tend to push the boundaries with alcohol and partying. I had pretty much decided I was not going to drink alcohol or do drugs because of my family's history with alcoholism and my commitment to football and lacrosse. But once I got sucked into some of the drinking games and the competition part of it, I was on my way. And various opportunities with girls that I was meeting led me down some paths I wasn't planning on taking either.

I remember when I first started partying and all that went with it. I felt guilty and uncomfortable but over time, I got more and more calloused to that sense of conviction. Like lifting weights, when you first start, your hands get blistered and hurt, but over time the callouses build up and you don't feel it at all after a while. I knew I was doing things that were not best for my body or soul, but most other guys on the team were doing it, so I joined in and eventually became a leader in the party scene too.

CHAPTER 7

Go Big Red

"'For I know the plans I have for you,' declares the Lord, 'plans to prosper you and not to harm you, plans to give you hope and a future.'"

Jeremiah 29:11

By my senior year of high school, I had developed a "work hard/play hard" mentality. The drinking age in Maryland at the time was eighteen, so as a senior, it was easy to buy alcohol and get served in most bars. Most of my friends and I were not afraid to push the boundaries.

I still took football and lacrosse seriously and was fortunate to be named a captain of each team. I also studied hard, and although I wasn't one of the smartest guys around, I ended up in the top ten of my class of nearly 300 graduates and was elected senior class president.

My goal was to go to the best college possible where I could play top-level Division I lacrosse and also play football. My most appealing offers were a full scholarship to Washington and Lee University (W&L), a half scholarship to the University of Virginia, acceptance into Harvard University with no financial aid, and a small grant from Cornell University.

I liked coach Jack Emmer at W&L, and I could play football there. Coach Ace Adams at Virginia was very positive, and used his top assistant Bruce Arena, who had played soccer and lacrosse at Cornell, to recruit me. Neither of them was big on the idea of me trying to play football at Virginia. Coach Bob Scalise from Harvard was very gracious as well. But of my four main options, Cornell's lacrosse reputation impressed me the most. They played in four national championship games in the 1970s and won three—including the first-ever NCAA Lacrosse National Championship game in 1971 against the University of Maryland.

I remember when I was in seventh grade, watching their 1977 National Championship game victory over Johns Hopkins with my brother John and our neighbor and John's lacrosse friend, Danny Llewellyn, on the classic Saturday sports anthology show, ABC's *Wide World of Sports*. (Remember "The thrill of victory and the agony of defeat"?) I had horsed around with lacrosse in the backyard with John and Danny but had not yet played on an organized team, when Danny saw something nobody else had yet seen. He said to me, "Frankie, I could see

The News American — Gene Boyars
SAME OBJECTIVE: Gilman's Harry McCambridge and Calvert Hall's Frank Kelly vie for possession during Tuesday's game. Gilman won, 12-8. Prep roundup on 6C.

This picture appeared in our local newspaper with me fighting for a faceoff. Cornell Coach Richie Moran was at that game and decided to recruit me.

you playing lacrosse at Cornell." Little did I know that legendary Cornell Coach Richie Moran would actually recruit me one day.

In March of my senior year, Coach Moran came to see me play in person. The game was at Calvert Hall and we played Gilman, whom I never beat in lacrosse in my high school career (although I never lost to them in football, which was more important to me at the time). Although we lost the game, I somehow had one of my best games of the year, scoring three goals, assisting another and winning a bunch of faceoffs.

In May of my senior year in 1982, I took my second recruiting trip to Cornell on a rare warm, sunny day in Ithaca, New York. Cornell beat Hobart, their local rival, in front of thousands of fans all seated in the famous crescent side of the stadium. After the game, Coach Moran reminded me of all the other lacrosse players who had also played football at Cornell like Eamon McEneaney, Bill Marino, and Bobby Henrickson and encouraged me that I could do the same. He also reminded me of my exact stats from the Calvert Hall vs. Gilman lacrosse game. His memory was incredible.

I wanted to play football and lacrosse in college, and Cornell seemed like the perfect fit, but my parents' insurance business was only six years old and money was still tight. I thought I should pick W&L or Virginia because they were great schools, offered the scholarship money, and would be the cheapest options. Others said, "How can you possibly say no to Harvard—it is a no-brainer, and you've got to go there."

On the ride home from Cornell, my father asked me my thoughts and we shared the pros and cons of each option. I tried to make it sound like Harvard and Cornell were too far away and that the cheapest options would be best, but he could sense my heart leaned toward Cornell. He suggested that we pray about the decision, which he did out loud in the car. After that, he asked, "If money were not an issue, where would you like to go?"

"Cornell," I sheepishly answered, and he agreed. We stopped somewhere on Route 81 on our drive home and found a payphone to call my mom and share the news of my decision.

Somehow, my parents worked out the finances, which would ultimately involve me having a part-time job at Cornell and taking on some relatively small student loans.

It was official, I would be heading to Ithaca!

CHAPTER 8

I Can Do All Three

"Pride goes before destruction, a haughty spirit before a fall."

Proverbs 16:18

I didn't know anyone when I arrived at Cornell for freshman football practice in the summer of 1982. At that time in the Ivy League, freshmen could not play varsity, but I was just happy to be playing football again.

The athletic director met with the team and said, "Gentlemen, welcome, and congratulations on being at Cornell. There are three things you can do here but you can only do two well, and you need to choose wisely. You can be a student and an athlete and fulfill your potential on the field and in the classroom. Or you can be a student and a party boy but you will never fulfill your potential on the athletic field. Or you can be a party boy and an athlete, and you will flunk out of here. Choose wisely!"

I sat there thinking, *Hmm, I think I will try all three.* My first semester I decided to take nineteen credits instead of the normal fifteen credits (to try to get ahead of schedule academically), played football, and joined Chi Psi, a fraternity full of football and lacrosse players.

Every Saturday night, Chi Psi and other fraternities hosted parties with free beer—one set of fraternity parties would go from about 10 p.m. to 1 a.m., then other fraternities hosted after-hour parties that began around 1 a.m. That's where things got wild, crazy and out of control. A number of us thought it was cool to stay up on Saturday nights until the sun came up Sunday morning. I had not factored the need for sleep into my calculation and the partying began to mess with my body.

I was playing running back on the freshman football team, along with about a dozen other guys, when Coach Pendergast made an announcement. "I need some guys who are willing to put the team first and serve the team. We only have four defensive backs. I need three or four of you running backs to volunteer to focus on playing defensive back."

I loved running the ball at Calvert Hall but had also played defensive back there, so I tried to do the right thing and volunteered to make the switch. The only thing I asked was if I could please return punts and kicks so I could at least touch the ball sometimes, and the coaches agreed.

In our final game of the season against Mansfield State—a school I had never even heard of—we were trailing 3-0 in the fourth quarter. I received a punt on about our own 30-yard line and broke free in the open field with two blockers in front of me and only one defender to beat for a touchdown. One blocker took out the defender at about the five-yard line and there was nobody to stop me— except my other blocker, who stumbled into me and knocked me out of bounds at the one-yard line. The Mansfield State defense made a goal-line stand, our kicker missed a field goal attempt, and we lost 3-0. That was the highlight of my Cornell football career and a microcosm of our season.

At Calvert Hall, we were the top-conference MSA champs almost every year. We only lost three football games over three years, and one was my senior year, when we flew to New Orleans, got some southern "home cooking" from the referees, and lost our only game of the year to Archbishop Rummel. My freshman year at Cornell, we lost every game.

I played football for the Big Red my freshman and part of my sophomore year, until an injury ended my season.

At least towards the end of the season, the football coaches invited me and a few other freshman players to practice with the varsity team for the last two weeks, which I took as a good sign and a great opportunity. Unfortunately, on the last play of the last practice before the varsity's last game, I was playing defensive back and came up to make a tackle when a guy stepped on the top of my foot. His metal cleat pierced a nerve and it felt like a lightning bolt had shot through my foot, up my leg, through my arms, and out the top of my head. I limped to the locker room and figured I would rest my foot over the weekend before starting to train for lacrosse season.

I was anxious that I had missed fall lacrosse practice because of football so on Monday morning after football ended, I put on my sweatpants, gray-hooded sweatshirt, and Chuck Taylors (I looked like Rocky Balboa—I love that movie!) and went for a run. By the way, Chuck Taylors are terrible running shoes, but I didn't know better.

What is Phineoctopeine Powder?

As lacrosse season was fast approaching and I continued to train, the nerve in the top of my foot was still hurting and I was still running with a slight limp, but I knew I had to be prepared to get off to a strong start.

I will never forget my first lacrosse practice freshman year. Because I played football and missed "fall ball" lacrosse practices, I was a total rookie when spring practice began on February 1st. I was excited, but anxious, and dressed and ready to go plenty early in the locker room. Fifteen minutes before practice started, Coach Moran came up to me.

"Hey, Kelly."

"Yes, Coach."

"I need you to go down to the training room and get me some Phineoctopeine Powder."

"Some what?" I asked.

"Some Phineoctopeine Powder. Just go down to the training room and tell them Coach Moran needs some Phineoctopeine Powder."

"Yes Coach, I'll go," I said, and bolted to the training room. I didn't want to be even one second late for practice. When I got to the training room, I told our trainer, Tom Lavigne, "Hey. Coach Moran sent me here to pick up some Phine-uhh...Phone-o..."

"Oh, you need some Phineoctopeine Powder?" Tom asked.

"Yeah, that's it. And I'm in a rush. Please give me some and I'll take it right to him."

Tom opened a drawer, then closed it, opened another drawer, then another, and said, "We're all out. You are going to have to go over to Teagle Hall and go to the equipment cage and ask the equipment manager."

"Oh my God," I thought, "I'm going to be late for my first practice." I took off like a rocket in my lacrosse equipment (minus gloves and helmet). When I got to the equipment cage, I shouted, "Hey! Is anyone in there? Coach Moran needs some Phineoctopeine Powder." An older man came out of a closet area and asked me what I needed. "I need some Phineoctopeine Powder for Coach Moran, quickly. Practice starts in five minutes."

He took his time and opened a cabinet, then shut it, then opened another cabinet drawer, and shut it. "Sorry, we're all out. You need to go down to the medical center."

"What?!" That was a quarter mile down the hill. I took off like a rocket, again. The people at the medical center had no idea what I was talking about. They said they had never heard of Phineoctopeine Powder. I ran back up the hill, cleats clacking on the cement, and into our locker room next to Schoellkopf Field. I grabbed my helmet, gloves, and stick and ran out onto the field.

Coach Moran barked at me for being ten minutes late. "But Coach," I pleaded, "they were all out of Phineoctopeine Powder in the training room, they were all out over in the equipment room at Teagle Hall and they sent me to the medical center. They said they never heard of Phineoctopeine Powder."

Coach started laughing and said, "Kelly, get in the line drill, you're late." My teammates, several of whom had been duped the same way during fall ball, bent over laughing and let me in on the prank. There was no such thing as Phineoctopeine Powder.

Coach almost got me again a few days later when he asked me to go down to the training room to get him a "bucket of steam." I was so eager to please him I would have done just about anything he asked, but I didn't fall for that one.

I was old-school: respect authority and work hard to please your elders, especially your coach. I called him "Coach Moran." Most people, even some of the players—especially the guys from Long Island—called him "Richie." (To the day he died on April 24, 2022, at the age of 85, he was "Coach" or "Coach Moran" to me.)

I always marveled at the Long Island guys who would give the business right back to Coach Moran. At one practice, a teammate (he'll remain nameless) took Coach Moran's can of Diet Coke, which he drank every day while getting dressed for practice in the same locker room as us players, and punched a hole in it right under the opening. When Coach lifted the can to his mouth the Diet Coke poured down the front of his white shirt. A lot of the guys laughed out loud but I held it in. Coach got the last laugh—he ran us into the ground that day.

It's Great to Be Here!

Coach Moran always started practice with his signature whistle. No metal whistle, no fingers, just a loud, piercing whistle. To this day, if I heard it, I would know immediately it was him and I would react.

Cornell's weather can be a little cold in February and March but Coach Moran reminded us daily that "It's great to be here!" He loved to joke and laugh and have fun. Sometimes at water breaks during practice, he would pull the team together, turn us toward the famous Cornell Schoellkopf Crescent side of the stadium, and have us sing a song like "God Bless America." But in our practice drills and games, he was all business.

As the season unfolded, it turned out to not be a lot of jokes and laughter for me, and the last thing on my mind was "It's great to be here!"

Coach Moran would eventually write a book titled It's Great to Be Here!, *but I wasn't feeling too great about the start to my Cornell lacrosse career.*

CHAPTER 9

Pain

"Not only so, but we also glory in our sufferings, because we know that suffering produces perseverance; perseverance, character; and character, hope."

Romans 5:3-4

A couple of weeks into practice, my foot pain, limp, and all the running we did on the old-time, pavement-covered AstroTurf field led to deep pain in both of my shins. I had shin splints—bad ones! I took a lot of aspirin, lived with ice bags wrapped around my shins, and never missed a practice, as I had no choice but to play through the pain.

Freshmen were permitted to play varsity lacrosse, so I was competing against other freshmen to make the team and against everyone for playing time. I went up against our senior faceoff specialist, Tarik Ergin. At 6'2" and 210 pounds, he was much bigger than me but, more importantly, technically more skilled than me. When I lined up for faceoffs against Tarik, the whistle would blow and the ball would disappear before my eyes. In high school, I used my athleticism to scrap and scrape and fight for the ball like a wrestler. Tarik used the proper technique to snag the ball before I ever moved.

Two other freshman middies, Jeff Doughty and Greg Ripich, both from the Syracuse area, had learned faceoff mechanics in part from legendary Syracuse faceoff man, Kevin Donahue, and I began to pick their brains. I had never been shown much faceoff technique and at this level, my athleticism alone was not going to get it done.

We would stay after practice for hours to work on faceoffs and our technique and I began to add skill to my quickness and strength. I owe a lot of my success in lacrosse to Jeff and Greg because they shared what they knew with me. We spent a lot of time together and had goofy nicknames for each other. We called Jeff "Chippo" in honor of his adopted brother from Liberia. We called Greg "Guido" because that was actually his middle name, and they called me

"Frankie" or "Down the Line Chippo Beater" after one of the faceoff techniques they taught me which I got really good at. Here we were competing against each other for playing time, yet working with each other to become the best faceoff men we could be. I am grateful for our friendship, even to this day.

I also thought I was holding my own among the midfielders and figured I was somewhere between second and third midfield on the depth chart. The second midfield would always get playing time. The third midfield might see the field late in a game if the score was lopsided.

Put On Your Street Clothes

The game I had circled on the schedule freshman year was against Syracuse in the Carrier Dome—the big-time lacrosse I went to Cornell for. My mom and dad drove up for the game. A couple of my brothers came. The girl I was dating came. All my new fraternity brothers were there. I was out on the field warming up, pumped with adrenaline. Two minutes before the opening faceoff, Coach Moran called for me and another freshman to come over to him.

"Hey guys, there's a new Ivy League rule. We can only dress 25 players for the game, and we have 27 here. I need you two to go in the locker room and put on your street clothes."

"What?!" I was devastated. I had no way of communicating with my family, who were up in the stands in the Carrier Dome, to tell them what happened. I could not even speak. I changed, came out on the sidelines wearing a shirt and tie, made eye contact with my family, and did everything in my power to hold back tears for the next three hours. I didn't even know if we won or lost the game.

That's the way the rest of my freshman season unfolded. My legs hurt so bad the training staff sent me for an X-ray, but they saw nothing, and couldn't really ease the pain of the terrible shin splints. I didn't play enough to earn a letter. I had lost 20 pounds from the grind of the seasons and from the partying, which clearly caught up to me (the athletic director was right).

I would call home to complain to my parents and talk about transferring. My friends at Navy, North Carolina and Virginia were all starting and playing. My dad would listen and empathize and tell me the same thing he told me my senior year of high school: "Frankie, until you make God your priority, you're not going to find peace. You can look for it on the football field, the lacrosse field, the party scene, or someday with your job or money, but you are not going to find true peace until your relationship with God through His son, Jesus Christ, is your priority."

I heard what he said, but it kind of went in one ear and out the other. It just didn't connect or make sense to me. I was a little religious and I would go to church some Sundays at the 5 p.m. Mass at Anabel Taylor Hall. I was usually so hungover though that I just went through the motions. It was kind of like "checking a religious box" but it had little to no impact on the way I lived my life the rest of the week. I would pray, but it sounded something like, "God, I don't think I am doing the right things at night, so please forgive me... but I still can't wait for next Thursday and Saturday night."

I got a bone scan on my legs when I got home for the summer and learned that I had forced myself to play not only with shin splints but, for at least four weeks, with stress fractures in both legs. Despite the pain, football and lacrosse had become such idols in my life that I did not miss a single practice.

Now my idols were beginning to crumble.

CHAPTER 10

She's Perfect for You

"A wife of noble character who can find? She is worth far more than rubies."

Proverbs 31:10

I spent the rest of the summer after freshman year in physical therapy, lifting weights, and training in a pool and on a bike. Although I had been cleared to run, my legs hurt too much to run on a regular basis. I had to be ready for football season. I couldn't lose that.

One hot, humid Saturday morning that June, my mother woke me up at what felt like the crack of dawn—I was not feeling good at all from the previous night's activities. My mother managed our household on a tight budget, so when Cohen's, our well-known neighborhood clothing store, held a sidewalk sale, it was time to go shopping. No matter what.

"No, Mom, I don't want to go. I'm not doing that this morning."

She said, "If you don't go, you won't have any clothes for school in the fall. It's now or never."

I dragged myself out of bed. I was kind of dating a girl who worked at Cohen's, so at least I could see her. When I got there, she was so busy, she could barely say hello.

While I was hanging around the parking lot where a number of tables were set up, all of a sudden, a girl was looking at the same table of sports clothes as me, and we got to talking. I found out that her name was Gayle Schmith, that she graduated from Dulaney High School (where I would have gone if I left Calvert Hall), and that she ran cross country and played some lacrosse and field hockey at Mary Washington College (now University) in Virginia. For the summer she was working as a lifeguard at the Top Field Condominiums pool. I liked her right away.

Top Field, *hmmm*. I remembered that my dad's good friend, Dutch Ruppersberger, belonged to the same pool. Dutch and my father became friends after they ran against each other for a seat in the Maryland State Senate in 1978. My dad won, but later worked on Dutch's successful campaigns for County Council, County Executive, and the U.S. Congress, where Dutch has served since 2003. He also played lacrosse at the University of Maryland.

I called Dutch. "I just met a girl at the Cohen's sidewalk sale. Her name's Gayle Schmith. I think she's a lifeguard at your pool."

"Frankie, I love Gayle. She's perfect for you," Dutch said.

"Can you do a little digging and find out, you know, what her situation is?"

I waited by the phone, which in those days hung on our kitchen wall. About an hour later, Dutch called me from the pool.

"Guess what, she doesn't have a boyfriend. Do you play tennis?"

I said, "I can play tennis if I have to. I'm not very good. I don't really play tennis and I'm nursing shin splints and stress fractures from the season, but if I have to, I'll play tennis with her."

"Great. Let me call you back."

Another hour later, Dutch called again. "How about an Orioles game?"

"That would be perfect!"

Our first date was a double date at an Orioles game with my brother John and his girlfriend. I remember exactly what Gayle wore—a blue and white striped sleeveless blouse and a blue jean skirt. I remember we sat in the upper deck, section 34, where Wild Bill Hagy drank a lot of beer and led his famous "O-R-I-O-L-E-S" chants.

After that night, Gayle apparently went home and checked in with her mom, who was in bed. Her mom asked her how the date went. Gayle told her it went great, but that she was concerned that she had just met the guy she was going to marry and she was only nineteen years old. Her mom said, "Go to bed, honey!"

Ground Balls Win Games!

At the Orioles game, Gayle mentioned how much she liked tennis, so for our second date, we grabbed our rackets and headed to Seminary Park to play. Only one problem—it was evening and the lights on the court weren't working. I panicked for a minute, then decided to pull my car up and shine the headlights onto the court. That made switching sides after every odd-numbered game even more important than usual because the headlights only lit up half the court.

Gayle admired my persistence and determination to figure out how to get something done when it looked like it couldn't be done.

We played tennis again—in the daytime—soon after at the Dulaney High

School courts. As we were walking across the athletic fields to leave, we ran into a friend, Geoff Nordberg, who had played lacrosse at Dulaney and was playing in college at Johns Hopkins.

Geoff and a few other guys were playing catch and had a couple of extra lacrosse sticks laying around. Gayle and I both picked one up and tossed the ball around with them. Somebody dropped a pass and Gayle and I took off after the ball. We're both pretty competitive. I say she bumped into me and ricocheted off me, but she claims I blew through the ball, threw an elbow into her ribs and sent her flying in the air. I was so focused on the ball that I didn't realize what I had done until I saw Gayle eight feet away picking herself up and dusting herself off.

"Oh, I'm sorry, are you okay?"

Geoff has never stopped needling me about it. "You must have really wanted that ground ball to knock your girlfriend almost into the bleachers."

God uses the Creator's game in mysterious ways.

MORE TO THE STORY...

God's Timing is Perfect – Gayle Kelly

The first time I remember seeing Frank was Thanksgiving morning of my senior year of high school.

I woke up a little late and turned on the small black and white portable TV with rabbit ears that sat on top of my dresser. By chance, the annual Calvert Hall vs. Loyola Turkey Bowl game was on. It was being played at the old Memorial Stadium, where the Baltimore Colts and Orioles played at the time.

Soon after I turned on the TV while I was fixing my hair, they did a segment on the National Football Foundation Scholar-Athlete award winner—Calvert Hall senior captain, Frank Kelly. They flashed a picture of Frank and gave all these statistics and accolades about him, but the words of the announcer faded into the background as my mind began to wander.

This was not like me at all, but as I watched that brief feature on Frank, I got this clear impression that "I'm going to marry that guy some day."

I wasn't even that into guys. I had a high school boyfriend, but we were really just friends. If there was a "least likely to get married before age 30" award, that would have been me.

It's pretty amazing that we did not know each other, since our homes were only a few miles apart. I went to Cockeysville Middle School, which fed into Dulaney High School and he went to Ridgely Middle School, which also fed into Dulaney. But since he went to Calvert Hall, we ended up having all these friends in common at Dulaney, but somehow, we never really connected.

I still don't remember officially meeting Frank until that fateful day at Cohen's Sidewalk Sale after our freshman year of college, but apparently, we must have ended up crossing paths at a party during the spring of our junior year, as my dear friend Mary Beth many years later showed me what I wrote in her high school yearbook: "Mary Beth – I hope we have as much fun at the beach as we did the other night at the party at your house when I met Frank Kelly. Oh baby, what a Fox!"

Frank often says if he had gone to Dulaney, he probably would have tried to date me and messed things up. Only God knows, and only God's timing is perfect.

CHAPTER 11

Peace

"And the peace of God, which transcends all understanding,
will guard your hearts and your minds in Christ Jesus."

Philippians 4:7

I stopped by the Top Field Condominiums pool before I began my long drive back to Ithaca for football to say goodbye to Gayle. I gave her a bright red Cornell T-shirt, and although we were not in an exclusive boyfriend/ girlfriend relationship, I did not want her to forget about me as she went back to Mary Washington.

A few weeks into my sophomore football season, I was playing well but the throbbing pain returned in my shins. The trainers sent me for another bone scan, which again showed stress fractures in each shin. I missed the remainder of the football season, and I missed the fall lacrosse season. My world and my gods or idols were crumbling, and I was angry, frustrated and unsettled.

During this time of disappointment, frustration and pain, a guy crossed my path at Cornell named Pete Shaifer, a wrestler. He was genuinely excited about his faith and talked to me about having a relationship with God. He kind of sounded like my dad, but I could better relate to another athlete. I still didn't get it or understand what a personal relationship with God looked like or meant, but he planted seeds that influenced me later.

I worked out hard in the weight room on the stationary bike and in the pool (I was a terrible swimmer), but I kept my legs from any pounding (no tennis!) in preparation for lacrosse season, which started February 1st. Three weeks into the lacrosse season, the pain came back. I could barely walk and if I got stress fractures a third time, my athletic career would clearly be over. So here I was in serious pain and still on the third-string midfield as a sophomore when I thought I would start and play as a freshman. Coach Moran was riding me hard, but that was how he tried to motivate players he thought should be doing better.

Stripped Three Times

After one of my roommates, Kevin Casey, a long pole defenseman, stripped the ball from me in a one-on-one practice drill, Coach Moran screamed, "Kelly, go again!" Kevin stripped me again.

"Get your 'bleeping bleep' out there and go again," Coach screamed.

In front of the entire team, Kevin, just doing his job, took the ball from me a third time.

Using some choice words, Coach led me to believe I would never, ever play at Cornell.

I stumbled to the end of the line drill, and that was it. I was devastated. Tears in my eyes, standing on Schoellkopf Field, a little opposite Teagle Hall, close to the scoreboard, I prayed to the Creator as I understood Him, *Lord, God, Jesus, If I never play football or lacrosse again, I need you. I don't know if I am supposed to receive you, believe you, accept you, but whatever it is, I want you in my life and I want to prioritize my relationship with you, so please forgive me for doing things my way, and I ask you to help me become the person you want me to be.*

In my mind, lacrosse and football were over. I didn't realize it at the time but flashing back to my freshman year and watching that Syracuse game in my street clothes from the bench, was part of God saying "Frank, I have something better for you and more important for you than lacrosse."

I am often reminded of a story I heard of a father who gave his little daughter a set of plastic pearls when she was young. She loved them dearly, but as she grew older, they became chipped and scratched. The father came to his daughter one day and said, "Honey, I want you to give me your pearl necklace." But she held them tightly and would not let go. She thought nothing could be better.

Over time, the father slowly pried her fingers off the plastic pearls, took them away, and as she let go, he later chose to give her a necklace of real pearls. I think that's what God was trying to do for me—to pry my hands off the false god of the plastic pearls of football and lacrosse success that I embraced so tightly. He had something better for me than plastic pearls. But first I had to let them go.

I finally let go of the plastic pearls. I called my dad that night and told him, "Dad, during practice today I cried out to God and told Him if I never played football or lacrosse again, I wanted to prioritize Jesus in my life and that I wanted a relationship with Him." My dad prayed with me over the phone and thanked God for opening my eyes and my heart.

The Power of Praise

He then said, "Frank, the most practical thing I can tell you to do now is to praise and thank God every minute you can. You don't have to go to church to praise God. You can be anywhere at any time and praise Him in your heart and mind." I later learned that when you praise Him and thank Him, you are expressing faith and inviting Him into your situation.

"So, when you're walking across campus, thank God that you can walk," my dad said. "Thank Him that you can see, that you are at Cornell, that you are on the team. Thank Him for everything that you can think of."

Then my father added, "And Frank, this is going to sound crazy, but the tougher and harder the situation, the more you want to praise Him. So, when you go out on that field, if Coach

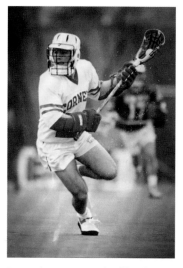

My senior year on Schoellkopf Field, where two years earlier I got "confirmed in my heart" in the middle of lacrosse practice

Moran is being tough on you and your shins are hurting, thank the Lord. Praise Him." I learned it is not so much thanking Him *for* the situation, but praising Him *in* the situation.

The next day, walking from my fraternity house, Chi Psi, up to Schoellkopf Field, through the Arts Quad, past the Ezra Cornell statue, I prayed, *Thank you, God, that I can walk, even if I am in pain. Thank you that I can see. Thank you, God, it's freezing but I can feel the cold. Thank you for the sun and clouds, and for the trees.*

Before practice that day, I stretched out my legs and iced down my shins as had become my ritual, but they were still hurting and I was not at my best. I did something at practice that frustrated Coach Moran. Trying to get through to me, he grabbed my helmet and shook my head and screamed at me. Under my breath, in the heat of the moment, I was thanking God. *Thank you, God, that Coach Moran sees potential in me. Thank you that I am on this field. Thank you for my teammates.*

I was third or fourth string and Coach was all over me, but for the first time, I felt peace. No anger, no fear. Peace!

Confirmed in My Heart

I grew up in a faith tradition where at the age of thirteen or fourteen, it was time for the sacrament of confirmation. It didn't really matter if I was ready yet, or understood what was going on, it was more of a religious box that had to be checked.

Despite getting kicked out of confirmation class more than once for goofing around with spit balls and worse, I got "confirmed" as an eighth grader at St. Joseph's Catholic Church in Cockeysville, Maryland, and we had a party back at our family's house. I got some nice gifts and money inside cards that had pictures of upside-down doves or flames of fire on them, which unbeknownst to me, represented the Holy Spirit, the third person of the Trinity, who was supposed to come into my life at confirmation if I sincerely committed my life to Jesus, the Creator and His church, which I did not do at that time.

I have heard it said that "the distance between religion and relationship is eighteen inches, or the distance from your head to your heart."

As I reflect, I now say that I got "confirmed in my head" as a fourteen-year-old at St. Joseph's, but got "confirmed in my heart" as a 20-year-old sophomore in the middle of lacrosse practice on Cornell's Schoellkopf Field. It was there, at the end of that drill, that I stood on my own two feet apart from my parents, and fully opened my heart and life to Jesus, the Creator, as I understood Him.

I didn't realize it at the time, but that is when I believe the gift I was supposed to receive at the time of my eighth-grade confirmation—the Holy Spirit—actually came upon me and into my life. I later learned that Jesus said, "...unless one is born again he cannot see the kingdom of God."[1] I had been born physically in 1964, and here 20 years later on a lacrosse field, I experienced a spiritual birth and for the first time, began to see things I had not seen before.

I had a lot to learn about this new spiritual life, a personal relationship with God, and the Holy Spirit.

MORE TO THE STORY...

Set Him Free – Big Frank (My Dad)

Frank called me several times a week during his freshman and sophomore lacrosse seasons. He would vent his frustrations with his injuries and playing time, and I would listen and encourage him as best I could. I knew from my recovery from alcoholism that his battle was more against the spirits of fear and anxiety than they were against the physical and emotional pain. During one of our calls, I prayed for Frank to be delivered of this frustration and angst, and I had a sense that God was at work in his difficult situations and that the Lord was going to set him free. When he called me the night after the practice where he decided to prioritize the Lord in his life, we prayed together over the phone. We thanked the Lord for his amazing grace, mercy, freedom and blessing.

CHAPTER 12

God Wink

"I waited patiently for the Lord; he turned to me and heard my cry.
He lifted me out of the slimy pit, out of the mud and mire; he set my feet on a rock
and gave me a firm place to stand. He put a new song in my mouth, a hymn of
praise to our God. Many will see and fear the Lord and put their trust in him."

Psalm 40:1-3

The season opened three weeks later, over St. Patrick's Day weekend, at Adelphi University. Adelphi was in Division I in 1984 and they were ranked preseason in the top ten in the country that year. We were ranked in the top five. Two days before the game, Coach posted the travel roster. I was the last name on the list. A year earlier, I would have been very frustrated. *Why am I the last name on the list? I'm better than that guy above me.* But when I saw my name this time, I prayed, *Thank you, God, that I am on the list. Thank you that I am on the team. Thank you for my teammates and friends in this locker room.*

Peace!

It was a cold, rainy day when we played Adelphi. I stood on the sidelines in my sweatpants trying to stay warm, down where the reserve players stand at the end of the bench, praising God in my mind. "Thank you, Lord, that I am here. Thank you that my grandmother Kelly graduated from Adelphi. Thank you that my shins are feeling a little better," (not that it really mattered because I was probably not going to play in the game).

Adelphi had an All-American center middie faceoff guy named Todd Lawson, a big stud, who was dominating our first- and second-string faceoff men. We were losing 8-3 in the third quarter, and I began to hope that Coach would call my name. For the next faceoff, he called for Kevin Cook, our All-American attackman and probably the best player I ever played with. But he was not a faceoff specialist. If it was a year earlier, I would have been absolutely fuming over the snub, but not that day. I thanked God that I could see and hear, and that I was there on that cold, rainy, muddy field.

"Cookster," as many called him, lost the faceoff and Coach turned to me.

"Kelly, you've got the next draw."

No one plays in a Division I lacrosse game wearing sweatpants, but I was so cold, and I didn't have time to take them off when Adelphi scored again and I had to run out to take the faceoff. Sweats and all and barely able to feel my hands because of the cold, I won the faceoff. When I came off the field, I got some high fives and then pulled off my sweats. I took the next faceoff and won again. And the next one. By the middle of the fourth quarter, I had won a bunch of faceoffs and we tied the score at 11-11. I had an assist, and I scored a goal.

Facing off against Adelphi my sophomore year in March 1984, when God chose to give lacrosse back to me in tangible ways

We lost the game 13-12 but in the locker room after the game, my teammates were saying, "Frankie, you were totally possessed out there, man!" On the bus, Coach Moran came over to me and said, "Hey, Kelly, that was one of the best games I have ever seen anyone play off the bench. Great job!"

At that moment, I literally felt like God "winked" at me. I had no deal with God. No quid pro quo. I didn't tell him three weeks earlier on the turf at Schoellkopf Field that I would give him my life if He would give lacrosse back to me. I thought my lacrosse career was over, and I had peace with that—His peace that surpasses understanding. For whatever reason, God chose to bless me that day. And although I didn't realize it at that time, when my teammates said I played like I was possessed, I now believe that it was God Himself in the form of the Holy Spirit who played through me that day.

Little did I know, what God had planned for me on the lacrosse field in the future.

I started the next game and had more success. A few weeks later against a local rival, Cortland State, I won over 80% of my faceoffs and scored four goals and had three assists, unheard of for a center middie.

God graciously chose to lift me out of the pit and miry clay. I went from *fourth string, my career is over; gone,* to starting the next three years, taking the majority of faceoffs, and even playing on the first midfield and extra-man offense unit.

I had given lacrosse to God, and He had chosen to give it back to me.

MORE TO THE STORY...

A Coach and a Prankster – Coach Richie Moran

I'm known as a coach who can be a pretty good prankster (like asking my young players to go get me "Phineoctopeine Powder" or a "bucket of steam"). I ran a highly structured program, so to motivate my players to buy in, I wanted to help them loosen up and enjoy themselves. I also used pranks to help a player take his mind off something that was bothering him, such as an injury, or a bad game or a personal problem.

Players would sometimes misinterpret my pranks and wonder, "Does Coach even like me?" but I didn't just like my players, I loved them.

Frank Kelly was definitely loved and appreciated by his coach. I had a lot of compassion for him, because I knew how eager he was to play both football and lacrosse, and what a setback his shin splints and stress fractures were for him.

If I had a list of top ten players based on their work ethic and preparing for a season, Frank would be on it. He was energetic, enthusiastic, and always in great condition. A remarkable competitor.

Frank was the leading faceoff man in the history of Cornell until just recently, and that's mostly because they started playing sixteen games in a season and the most Frank ever played was twelve. So there should be an asterisk on the all-time faceoff leaders. But without a doubt, Frank was very, very good at that skill, and he could handle a stick.

Frank was always well-respected by my assistant coaches, his teammates and fraternity brothers. He matured tremendously as a leader over his years at Cornell. The faculty enjoyed having him in their classes—I know because I checked up on him.

Everyone had nothing but positive things to say about Frank Kelly.

Sports

ward Christian Athletes in '92

Squad' upsets Turtles

, Williams
or

pposed to be a case of
ns lying down to the

and sheer hustle to shut down the
No. 1 seeded Turtles' potent offense, anchored by Towson State
middie Rob Shek and former
Syracuse All-American Gary Gait,
one of the all-time leading scorers
in the Major Indoor Lacrosse
League.

Gait, who had seven goals in a
22-7 Greene Turtles' shellacking of
the Vail Lacrosse Club in
Thursday's opening round, was un-
ble to get into the swing of things
goals on six

"I just wasn't on today
Gait said. "(Thursday) everything
was going in, (Friday) nothing was
I'd say it was the altitude, but
think it was the evening activitie

Though David Kelly had
game-winning goal at 3:14
second overtime, it wa

Please see *Lacrosse* pa

PART III

Power from on High

CHAPTER 13

Into the Word

"Your word is a lamp to my feet and a light to my path."

Psalm 119:105 (ESV)

In high school, my first job was at a local gas station. It was during the gas shortage crisis in the late 1970s, so I was on an island pumping gas into four cars at a time for an entire eight-hour shift. In the summers, I also worked on the maintenance crew at our local fairgrounds, and for a couple of summers was a lifeguard at a local pool, which was a lot of fun.

During the summer leading into my junior year at Cornell, I worked in the family business telemarketing liquor stores, bars and restaurants about the association health insurance plans available to them. I was also calling gas stations, since the Service Station and Automotive Repair Association was a new client. I was trying to generate leads for the new salesperson my parents had hired.

Gayle and I continued to date that summer, but I had a hard time trying to explain to her my newfound relationship with God, and my lifestyle was still a little wild. We were not "exclusive" boyfriend and girlfriend yet, but spent a lot of time together.

I decided not to play football my junior year, since my sophomore football season was crushed by the stress fractures in my legs, and God had blessed my efforts on the lacrosse field.

I am very glad I gave college football a shot, so I would have no "what ifs" or regrets in the future. Giving up football also enabled my body to get some much-needed rest and recovery from the prior season.

As I arrived back in Ithaca to start my junior year, I had greater peace with God but I was still unsure of what it all meant and how to live out my faith and articulate it to others. My former football teammate, Jeff Caliguire, invited me to a fraternity/sorority Bible study he and his fraternity brother, Gregg Stutts, were starting at his fraternity house—Sigma Chi.

"When do you meet?" I asked.

"Mondays at 9 p.m."

That's exactly when Monday Night Football came on, which I loved watching with my housemates. I lived with five Chi Psi fraternity brothers who played football or lacrosse, all partiers, and I would be embarrassed to tell them I was missing Monday Night Football for a Bible study. We considered Sigma Chi a rival fraternity so that wouldn't go over well either and, on top of all that, the house was off-campus and hard to get to. But I felt I should go and told Jeff I would be there.

I used laundry as my cover. At 8:30 p.m., I made my way toward the door, hoping no one would see me, carrying a small Bible in the bottom of my mesh laundry bag full of dirty clothes. "Frankie, where are you going?" a couple of my housemates asked.

"Gotta do laundry," I said, which was half true. I planned to drop off my laundry on the way to the Bible study and pick it up on my way back.

The only Bible I owned was a little one my father gave me for Christmas in 1977.

I had not read that Bible that he had given me, but I had read the note he wrote in it: "Dear Frank, The solutions to any problem are in this great book. Try to read a chapter each day of your life and you will be happy. The words in this book come directly from God through the Holy Spirit to you. Seek God first in all areas of your life and you will be guaranteed success. Pray regularly Frank, and always remember how much I love you. - Dad"

As I arrived a little late and very jittery, one of the Sigma Chi brothers welcomed me into the house and pointed up the stairs to where the group was meeting. I walked into the Bible study and among the eight or so people there was a girl whom I had seen over the weekend at about 3 a.m. during one of the Saturday night (into early Sunday

The note my dad put in the small pocket Bible he gave me for Christmas in 1977

morning) after-hour fraternity parties. I later learned her name was Janine. *What is she doing here?* I thought. I'm sure she was thinking, *What is he doing here?* At this time, I had one foot in my new faith-based world, and one foot still firmly planted in the secular world. God was at work in both of our lives at least to the point where we were both there.

"Hey Everyone! Welcome to our fraternity/sorority Bible study. To start tonight, we would like everyone to turn in their Bible to the book of Ephesians," Jeff said.

Ephesians? Oh my God, what is that? After panicking, I quietly turned to the girl next to me. "Can you please tell me where Ephesians is?"

"Oh...It's easy," she said. "Just remember, Go Eat Pop Corn."

"What?"

"Galatians—Ephesians—Philippians—Colossians. Ephesians is right after Galatians."

"Uh, okay, thank you."

I never found one verse that Jeff and Gregg referenced that night. I faked my way through and never said a word. But I noticed that everyone was very excited about their faith. They were not carrying some religious burden. They talked about their relationship with the Lord and their passion and excitement for Him.

I couldn't find any verses the second week either, but after I called home and told my mom I was attending a fraternity/sorority Bible study, she sent me a new Bible with big tabs sticking out the side with the names of all the books so I could flip right to them. That Bible was a lifesaver.

Jeff Caliguire (Left) and Gregg Stutts (Right) led the fraternity/sorority Bible study that would change my life.

MORE TO THE STORY...

Squeeze Play – Jeff Caliguire

When Frank came into our room where we were hosting the fraternity/sorority Bible study, he was so nervous he just bolted to the first place he saw to sit down—the middle of a beat-up orange futon, only as wide as a car, that three girls had already squeezed onto. There was no way a fourth person could fit, and Frank practically knocked two of the girls off the futon, forcing one of them to the floor. That left Frank sitting next to Carol, the girl who tried to help him find the book of Ephesians by telling him it was after Galatians.

Frank was amazed that there existed fraternity and sorority members who were excited about their relationships with God and learning the Bible, and that triggered a hunger in him for God's Word. He was always there for our weekly study and Sunday night dinners.

The two of us also met for lunch at the student union for informal chats about how to grow in our relationship with God. Even though I had become a follower of Jesus only eight months earlier—after four car accidents, a knee surgery, an emergency appendectomy, and a relationship break-up drove me to ask, *What am I doing with my life*, and open the Bible and turn my life over to Christ—Frank saw me as a spiritual mentor and asked a thousand questions.

He would rub his hands together a hundred miles an hour, or run his hands through his hair, and ask something like, "As a follower of Jesus, is it still okay to get drunk?" I suggested he read Ephesians 5:18, which says, "Do not get drunk on wine, which leads to debauchery. Instead, be filled with the Spirit..."

We had so many amazing conversations about life and faith, and fortunately continue to have such amazing conversations even to this day, where Frank is often pointing me to truth in God's Word as well.

CHAPTER 14

Sharing the Good News

"And the things you have heard me say in the presence of many witnesses entrust to reliable people who will also be qualified to teach others."

2 Timothy 2:2

One night during the Sigma Chi Bible study, someone shared a quote with me from a famous 17th-century French philosopher, Blaise Pascal, that really hit home. It said, "There is a God-shaped vacuum in the heart of every man which cannot be filled by any created thing, but only by God, the Creator, made known through Jesus."

I could look back and see how I had been trying to fill that God-shaped vacuum in my heart with all kinds of "created things" like success on the football or lacrosse field, or in the classroom, or even in the party scene, but that fulfillment was always temporary and fleeting. I had learned on the lacrosse field and was continuing to learn how God, the Creator, through Jesus, could fill the void and was sensing that I should share this discovery with others.

After a few weeks of attending the Bible study, I nervously decided to invite one of my good friends on the lacrosse team and my fraternity brother, Kevin Frank. Kevin was the other player that Coach Moran sent into the locker room with me to change into street clothes at the Syracuse game our freshman year. Kevin had an injury-riddled career at Cornell—he blew out an ankle one year and fractured his neck another.

"Kevin," I said, "you're not going to believe this, but I've been going to this fraternity/sorority Bible study thing. It's kind of cool and I've been thinking of inviting you. But I can understand why you wouldn't want to come. If I were you, I probably wouldn't come, but I still thought I should tell you about it and was thinking about inviting you but I'm not sure."

"Are you inviting me or not?" he asked.

"Yeah, I think you would like it so why don't you come?"

Kevin went with me the next Monday. His first Bible study. The first person I ever invited to any faith-based event, and soon after, he tells me, "This is it. This is what I've been looking for," and fully surrenders his life to the Lord, his Creator. All in! I had never seen anything like it.

Pieces of the Puzzle

I'm very grateful for the faith tradition I grew up in and I'm thankful that my parents took me to church and allowed me to attend a great Catholic high school—Calvert Hall. Through that background, I received all the pieces to the faith puzzle, but I had no idea how those pieces fit together. I knew about religion, rites and rituals, but I did not understand the concept of a relationship with God.

After crying out to the Creator and inviting Jesus into my life on the lacrosse field, then reading and discussing the Bible with other college students and athletes, the pieces of the puzzle came together in a way that I could better see and understand the bigger picture of God's work in my life and His desire to have a personal, daily, life-changing relationship with me.

Kevin and I began to bring new people, like his roommate and our teammate Steve Paletta, to the Bible study every week. The group grew from eight to ten to twelve to fourteen then up to twenty. "You guys are like evangelists!" Jeff told us.

"What's that?" we asked.

"You're out sharing the Word."

We were just sharing with our friends from our fraternity and the lacrosse team and even at the bars about how cool a personal relationship with God and this Bible study thing was. It was real, practical and fun. Some people thought we were joking, but those who came were impacted as well.

By December, Kevin and I had an idea to start a Bible study for athletes at our fraternity, Chi Psi. We figured that if we were hurting, other athletes were probably hurting also, even if they didn't show it. If God wanted us to play a part in ministering to them, we were willing.

We asked Jeff and Gregg if they would lead the group if we invited some athletes to attend. "That would be great," they said.

A week before our first meeting, Jeff and Gregg came to Kevin and me and said, "We've been thinking and praying about it, and we think the two of you should lead the Bible study at Chi Psi. You can call it Athletes in Action or AIA—the ministry that's a part of CRU and where we get our materials."

We were stunned. I had been to about ten Bible studies in my whole life,

Kevin even fewer, and they wanted us to start leading one in a week?

"We can't," Kevin and I told them. "We don't know what we're doing."

"You can do it," they insisted. "We'll come to support you, but you guys lead it."

The Lodge

The Chi Psi house, known as "The Lodge," was a beautiful mansion-like house near the famous Johnson Art Museum, and we started our AIA group on a Sunday night with six or seven guys in a small room on the top floor. The next week, eight or ten came. It kept growing and we moved to a larger room. One of our lacrosse goalies, Chris Modesti, and his roommates graciously let us use their room because it was the biggest bedroom in the house. After a few more weeks we moved to the library with 30, 40, sometimes 50 athletes coming.

Sunday night was also the time I usually called home. One week I told my mom I had just come from our Bible study.

"What do you mean, your Bible study?"

"Kevin and I started a Bible study for athletes at Chi Psi."

"You and Kevin Frank started a Bible study at Chi Psi?"

"Yes."

"That's fantastic! What are you using? Are you using a Bible study guide?" she asked inquisitively.

"What is that?" I asked.

"Are you using a concordance?"

"A what?"

"What exactly are you and Kevin doing?"

"Well, a few days before the study, we discuss and pray about a topic, like success and failure, or winning and losing, or pressure and stress. We then open the Bible and look for a few relevant verses we could read and then share some thoughts and facilitate a discussion. That's about all. But more people come every week."

"Oh my gosh!" she rejoiced. She recognized that despite our lack of knowledge and experience, God was working through Kevin and me.

Chi Psi – The Lodge

MORE TO THE STORY...

Is This How God Answers Prayer? – Kevin Frank

I was going through some hard times. I missed my entire sophomore lacrosse season with a hairline fracture in one of my vertebrae. When I came back my junior year, I suffered severe ankle sprains. I was struggling academically. I didn't feel safe and was trying to find where I belonged.

Frank and I and other guys from Chi Psi usually went to the "Hangover Mass" in the late afternoon on Sundays, and one week amid my struggles, I really prayed from my heart. *God, I don't know if you're there. I don't know if I believe in you. But I do know that I've been hurting people and hurting myself and I don't know how to live any differently from the way I'm living and everyone around me is living. So, if you're there, come to me. If you're not there, I'm gonna keep doing what I've been doing, because it's all I know.*

Later that same night, I hear a tap on my door—not a knock, but a tap. I open the door and there's Frank. He looks up and down the hallway to make sure no one sees him or hears him.

"What's up?" I ask.

Frank looks up and down the hallway again, then whispers like he's giving me some kind of top-secret information.

"You won't believe what I did last week."

"Frank, why are you whispering? I'm right here. What did you do?"

In a hush, still making sure nobody else can hear him, he says, "I went to a...I went to a Bible study."

Bible study? All I can picture is Monty Python and the Holy Grail—people in bathrobes smacking a Bible against their foreheads and chanting.

Frank stumbles over his words but manages to eke out, "Something in me is telling me to invite you."

My first thought is, *Absolutely not. Why would I do something like that?* I thought that somehow, I was better than anyone who would go to a Bible study. Didn't people come to watch me play lacrosse?

Then I remember my prayer, *God, if you're there, come to me,* and make the connection. *Oh my God, is this how God is coming to me—through Frank Kelly?* A priest I could understand, but a party animal?

My mind is racing in a thousand different directions. *Could this be how it works? Could this be how God answers prayer? If it is, I'd better say "yes."*

"Okay, I'll go with you," I told Frank.

The Bible study introduced me to a universal God who has a personal and intimate and tender love for His creation, including me. Sharing my heart with God and with a group that cared about all of me, not only the player on the field but also the deeper person below the surface, changed the trajectory of my life.

All In – Jeff Caliguire

Almost instantly, Frank started bringing a posse of lacrosse players and football players to the Bible study. One week he brought a cute girl and told me, "Caliguire, I give you two weeks before you invite this girl I am bringing to the study on a date—her name is Mindy."

Little did Frank know that Mindy had been in a similar place to Kevin Frank spiritually, and had recently cried out to God, even questioning His existence. When Frank invited her, she couldn't believe it, as she just that day had asked God to please confirm if He was real. She had dated Frank some the prior year, and she knew him as a bit of a "wild man," so she wondered if he was being sincere when he first invited her right there in Mann Library.

As more of his friends came, Frank and his fraternity brother and teammate, Kevin Frank, approached Gregg and me with the idea of starting a Bible study "for athletes" at their fraternity. (Apparently, they didn't consider the crew team rowers and polo players in my fraternity to be real "athletes.")

"Awesome," we said, "and you guys should lead it."

"We thought you two would lead it," Frank said.

"Let us think about it, but I think you should lead it. It's your group."

Frank rubbed his hands together a hundred miles an hour, ran his hands through his hair, and agreed to lead the study with Kevin if Gregg and I came to support them.

Leading that Bible study catapulted Frank's maturity and growth in the Lord. He would always share the story of how he hit rock bottom and then connected with God, which was a powerful example that resonated with the many seekers there. He and Kevin didn't preach. They read God's Word, then asked thought-provoking questions and facilitated discussions without judgment, which created an environment where people saw themselves on an exploration.

And Frank was right about Mindy and me. We've been married for over 35 years. Frank was the best man in our wedding, and he has been there for me and Mindy through thick and thin.

CHAPTER 15

Filled with the Spirit

"Do not get drunk on wine, which leads to debauchery.
Instead, be filled with the Spirit..."

Ephesians 5:18

After attending the fraternity/sorority Bible study for a couple of months, it became clear to me that most of the attendees had a joy, excitement, and depth in their relationship with God that I lacked. And although I was inviting others to check out the Sigma Chi Bible study, I knew I wasn't "all in" yet. I wasn't having as much fun in the party scene either. I felt like I was on a fence with one foot in the secular world, wanting to please my fleshly desires, and one foot in the spiritual world, wanting to please and enjoy the Lord. I was not experiencing the best of either. Sitting on a fence is never comfortable, and that was certainly true for me in this season of life.

During one of my Sunday night calls home, when I was sharing the tension in my heart and mind, my mom began to talk with me about the Holy Spirit. Little did I know the Holy Spirit was actually in my life since I committed my life to the Lord back in February on the lacrosse field. I didn't realize it was the Holy Spirit who had played through me in the game against Adelphi my sophomore year when my teammates told me, "Frankie, you were totally possessed out there!" Without question, that wasn't only me playing.

I grew up in a faith tradition that believed in the Trinity—Father, Son and Holy Spirit—but I understood nothing about the Holy Spirit. "Frankie, you need to learn about the Holy Spirit," my mom advised.

In early December, 20 of us from Chi Psi planned to go to the George Thorogood concert on campus. He's the rock star best known for his hits "Bad to the Bone" and "I Drink Alone." At the concert pre-party at Chi Psi, the guy handing out tickets realized he had only nineteen tickets and 20 of us planned to go. There was some real tension about who was going to be left out when I gave him my ticket back. "I don't need to go," I said. "I have something else I can do."

The sold-out concert was on the same night as the Christmas party the fraternity/sorority Bible study and CRU were hosting. I made my way to the Christmas party, which turned out to be a lot of fun.

I ended up having a great conversation with this girl when I asked her if she knew anything about the Holy Spirit. She said, "Believe it or not, I just read a book about the Holy Spirit that was awesome and I will be happy to give you a copy."

A few days later she brought me a copy of *The Holy Spirit: The Key to Supernatural Living* by Bill Bright, the founder of CRU.

Light Bulbs Lit Up

As I read the book, light bulbs lit up left and right in my mind. Before when I had thought of the Holy Spirit, I thought of *Star Wars*—"May the force be with you"—some nebulous cosmic force that moved out in the heavenlies. But I learned that the Holy Spirit is a person, He is God, and if we fully surrender our lives to the Lord, then the Holy Spirit that indwells us after we commit our lives to Jesus can live through us with full power, every day.

From the book, I learned the three keys to being filled with the Spirit, which helped me examine myself.

First is the willingness to surrender every area of our life to the Lord. *Okay, I already gave Him the most important things to me—football and lacrosse. I guess next would be the other areas of my life, like girls, the party scene, my future, etc.*

The second key is confessing every known sin to the Lord and desiring to repent and choose God's best. I learned that once the Holy Spirit is in us, He promises to never leave us, but that unconfessed sin is like a wet blanket on the flame of the Holy Spirit that quenches the power of the Spirit in and through us. That made me a little nervous because *Hey, I am willing to confess my sin but I don't think I can stop some of the things I'm doing.*

The book emphasized that we might not be able to change everything right away, but if we tell the Lord we are willing to change, the Holy Spirit will lead us and give us the power to choose God's best. *Wow, so I don't have to grind it out!* I told the Lord that if He could change me and help me to choose His best, I was open.

The third key was the hardest for me: the willingness to do whatever God wants us to do with our lives. I thought it would be okay to decide what I would do for the Lord and ask Him to bless it. But God says, *Surrender. Give me your life and I will lead you in what I created you to do.* Was I willing to go all in and become anything God wanted me to be or do—A priest? A missionary? Marry a woman I wasn't attracted to? (I had a distorted view of God's love and grace at that time.)

I had surrendered lacrosse, but my whole life? God might mess it up.

But as I continued to read and learn about the Holy Spirit and His power, I reached the point where I knelt down in my room in our ugly house there on Williams Street in College Town, trembling, with tears in my eyes, and prayed, *God, if you want me to be a missionary to Africa or China or to become a priest, as much as that does not appeal to me right now, whatever you want, I want to do Your will. Now, Holy Spirit, please fill me.*

I did not hear thunder or see lightning, but from that point forward I began to see things happening around me and through me that I now realize was the Holy Spirit, including having the courage to help start, lead and invite friends and teammates to our new AIA Bible study for athletes at Chi Psi.

I still went to parties because I love people and having fun, and I still drank, but my 20 beers declined to fifteen, ten, six, down to nursing a couple.

One of the key verses from the book about the Holy Spirit that spoke to me was ironically from the book of Ephesians, the book in the Bible that Jeff asked us to turn to at my first Bible study. In Ephesians 5:18, the Apostle Paul wrote to the church in Ephesus, "Do not get drunk on wine, which leads to debauchery. Instead, be filled with the Spirit..." Once I experienced being filled with the Holy Spirit, God took away my desire to get drunk with wine and I learned I would much rather be filled with the Spirit than anything else.

Spiritual Food

Evidence of the Holy Spirit's power in me started to show up in a number of ways, including a real passion and excitement to share God's love and truth with others, and to be an encouragement in all my relationships.

As I was walking across campus after class one day with a teammate, he said, "Frankie, I need to talk to you about something."

"Yeah, what's up?"

"I feel like you're taking this Bible stuff too seriously, and you're missing out. You're not partying hard like you used to. I think you're going to look back and really regret all that you're missing because you seem to be all into this religion thing."

I said, "You know, I really appreciate you sharing that with me. It shows how much you care. And I thank you for having the courage to confront me and share that.

"But you know how hungry we are after practice on a Friday afternoon and how we love the pizza and wings from the Souvlaki House? We talk about it all week; can't wait for Friday night. It's hard to explain, but that's how I actually now hunger for God's Word. I enjoy it and can't wait to read it and although I can't completely understand it, it's like food for the Holy Spirit, also known as the Comforter or Helper, who is living in me."

I know some of my friends thought I was crazy, but my desire to love, bless and encourage them only grew.

Power to Do the Right Thing

One weekend, a girl came up to me at a party. I knew who she was because I had noticed her before. I thought she was the most beautiful girl on campus and I had admired her for years from a distance, but I never tried to meet her because she seemed to always have a boyfriend who was a big man on campus.

"Hi. You're Frank Kelly," she said.

She knows my name? Wow!

"Yeah," I said, "I'm surprised you know who I am."

"Oh, I know who you are."

We talked for about 20 minutes, then she said, "I have to leave now. Would you mind walking me home?"

"Sure," I said, and we had a pleasant walk to her house.

"Do you want to come in?" she asked.

"Okay."

She took me directly to her bedroom, sat on the bed, and pulled me over to her.

"What?! Are you kidding me? I had a number of different girlfriends in high school and at Cornell, but never before had an opportunity like this presented itself this quickly in such a clear and compelling way.

"I'm sorry but I can't do this," I said, and I got up and left.

In the past, I was looking for those kinds of situations. But it just did not feel right and the Holy Spirit led me, empowered me, and guided me right out the door. I couldn't believe it—but there I was praising God the whole way home for giving me the power to do the right thing.

MORE TO THE STORY...

You Have No Idea What God Has Planned for You – Stephen Paletta

Frankie's commitment or surrender to the Lord on the lacrosse field his sophomore year was a private thing. He didn't say anything to me or any of his friends about it at first, but I noticed in our junior year that he had greater peace and joy and he wasn't going as crazy in the party scene. I didn't find out that he was slipping off to Bible studies until he invited me and a bunch of others from the fraternity.

I laughed when he invited me. "Are there any good-looking girls?" I asked.

"There are," Frankie said.

"Okay, I'll come."

Kevin Frank was there. He was one of my apartment-mates and I had seen the radical change in him since he started attending. He was always a crazy partier and very popular with the girls, but one day in our apartment he walked away from the table where we were sitting around drinking and I never saw him get drunk again. He was still fun but he was now totally focused on pleasing God.

The Bible studies that Frank and Kevin led at Chi Psi opened my eyes to the Scriptures, and I started attending church again on Sundays.

Going into my junior year, I was considered one of the top defensemen in the country, a captain on our team, and headed for first-team All-American honors. Frankie introduced me to the idea of playing for God, which seemed a little bizarre, but I figured if I play for God, I'll probably be a much better player. I dedicated my season to God and after the first day of practice, I grabbed a teammate and said, "Let's stay after practice and do one more drill." As we ran through the drill, I tore my ACL and blew out my knee. My All-American season ended before it started.

I was angry at Frankie, angry at God, angry at the world. Frankie came to see me and I was cursing God, but Frankie remained calm. "I am so sorry. I can't explain it, Steve, but I know God loves you and has a plan for you," he told me.

I laid into a priest at church one Sunday—the first and only time I ever cursed at a priest. "Who in the hell is this God that you profess and is supposed to be looking out for me?"

"You have no idea what God has planned for you," the priest said. "It's much bigger than a lacrosse season."

"No, Father, I think you're full of *bleep*, and I'm never coming back here again," I said, and stormed out.

Two years later, in 1987, I was a redshirt, or fifth-year senior, because I had sat out a season and had a year of eligibility left to play. I wasn't the defenseman I had once been but I still started, played every game and our team went undefeated until we lost by a goal to Johns Hopkins in the national championship game. That season I spent a lot of time in the training room strengthening my knee, and one day my trainer pointed to a freshman gymnast rehabbing her knee—same knee and same injury as mine. "Steve, I think you should go over and say hello to her," he suggested. "She could use some encouragement."

"No, I don't think so. I'm not interested. I just want to work on my knee and get outta here."

"Oh no, you want to talk to that girl," he insisted.

I reluctantly walked over and introduced myself, and we hit it off. Christine and I dated, and years later got married. Today we have three beautiful daughters who would all end up playing lacrosse with FCA and Division I college lacrosse with one at Brown and two at Cornell.

Frankie and the priest were right. God had ideas for me that were bigger than a lacrosse season. Today, I tell people that one of the best things that ever happened to me was blowing out my knee on the first day of practice my junior year. Only God knew that as a fifth-year senior I would be on one of the best teams in Cornell history and meet a freshman gymnast who would become my wife and the mother of our children.

CHAPTER 16

The Spirit Is Willing

"...The spirit is willing, but the flesh is weak."

Matthew 26:41

Our junior year lacrosse season was challenging in many ways. In a pre-season scrimmage vs. Army, I somehow bruised my heel and could barely walk, let alone run. At least with the shin splints, I could still practice in pain. The heel bruise sidelined me for a couple of weeks, which was frustrating, but God gave me peace.

Kevin was battling injuries too, dealing with the recovery from his prior ankle sprains and hairline fracture in his neck vertebrae. And our good friend Steve Paletta, who was a preseason first team All-American, was planning a surgery for his knee since he tore his ACL on our first day of practice. God never said new life in Him was going to be easy.

When I returned from my injury, I still started every game, but our team lost a number of tough one-goal games and we did not qualify for the eight-team NCAA playoff field. Cornell was used to winning national championships, so not making the playoffs was a heavy burden to bear.

Our AIA Bible study at Chi Psi, however, was booming with growth. We moved from a small bedroom to a larger bedroom on the second floor and finally to the library area, which could easily hold 50 or more people.

Kevin Frank (Left) who helped me lead the AIA Bible study pictured with Cornell wrestler Peter Shaifer, who challenged and encouraged me to pursue and prioritize a relationship with God

The CRU staff at Cornell came to Kevin and me that spring and said, "God's working through your Bible study and we think it would be great if you could go to the AIA Ultimate Training Camp this summer in Colorado. It's a two-week camp, all Division I athletes who are trying to live out their faith, and you'll learn how to apply God's Word and truth to your life as an athlete on the field and off."

"That sounds great!" I said. "I'd love to go." When I told my parents about it, my mom said, "Well, Frankie, I wasn't going to tell you yet, but we have a surprise 21st birthday gift for you."

"Really? What is it?"

"I've talked to Gayle. Her brother Steve is getting married in Germany this summer, and we're sending you to the wedding so you can visit Gayle in Paris and then go to the wedding with her. Happy Birthday!"

Gayle was studying abroad in Paris that semester, and I wanted badly to see her. I had never been to Europe and had only flown on an airplane a couple of times, so I was excited, but there was one problem. The wedding overlapped with the AIA camp.

I told the people from AIA about my dilemma, and they said that if I could only come to the second week of the camp, it would still be worth it, so I made my travel plans for Europe and Colorado.

The Flesh is Weak

As my relationship with God was growing and becoming stronger, so was my relationship with Gayle. After being filled with the Holy Spirit, I began writing to her regularly, explaining all that I was learning about God and His Word.

And she was growing as well. That year when I went home for Christmas break, I was able to share the Good News in a way that she could better understand. She would later join a Bible study at Mary Washington that would help her grow in her relationship with God as well.

Although we didn't make it official, we were now both dating each other exclusively. As I was growing in my faith, my desire to honor, bless and encourage her was growing as well.

On my first day in Paris, Gayle and I went for a walk and ended up back at the apartment of the French family she was living with, and where I would be staying for a couple of days in an extra bedroom they had.

I told her how excited I was about my relationship with God and how I was growing in my faith. "I want to honor God and you and keep things pure between us. I don't think we should even hold hands or kiss while I'm here because one thing seems to lead to the next thing for me. Are you okay with that?"

"That's fine with me," she said.

I was so relieved to get that off my chest, I said, "Well, let me just give you one hug."

Here's where I was reminded again that the spirit is willing, but the flesh is weak, and that being filled with the Holy Spirit is a minute-by-minute, day-by-day, ongoing decision.

She was so beautiful. I still remember her outfit—a pink sweater dress, with these white French lace stockings, and she was wearing a light perfume that smelled really good as well. The hug led to a kiss. I started kissing her like crazy, or as Gayle says, I began to maul her. She graciously pushed me away.

"But you just said…"

"I know, I'm sorry. I'm sorry," I said, and that ended our physical contact, for a while, anyway.

In Germany, Gayle and I stayed at her father's house. He was a retired Lieutenant Colonel, and her brother was also in the military as an Army Ranger. Two days before the wedding, I stepped on a rusty nail in the backyard. I got a tetanus shot but somehow had strep throat as well and ended up having an allergic reaction to the shot. I've never been sicker in my life.

"Would you like a cup of tea for your throat?" Gayle asked.

My throat was so sore I could barely swallow, and with the pain in my foot and the rest of my body, I couldn't move.

"Thanks, I'd like that," I said.

Gayle was not a tea drinker. She brought me a cup of tea with all the tea leaves floating around the top. I took a sip, then started spitting out the tea leaves.

"Oh," Gayle said. "I thought they would dissolve like hot chocolate."

"That's okay, thanks anyway." And then the words slipped out, "I love you," I told her, for the first time. That changed everything for Gayle. Her feelings toward me grew much more affectionate.

I was too sick to attend the wedding but felt well enough a few days later to go with Gayle to visit her friends in Florence, Italy before I had to fly home. I was a little nervous boarding the sixteen-hour overnight train ride from Florence to Paris by myself—the guy whose only idea of a vacation was a three-hour drive to Ocean City, Maryland.

Each car had two sets of triple bunk beds. I rode and tried to sleep with strangers from France and Germany in the bunks above and across from me. When the train arrived in Paris, I caught a cab to the airport and was on time for my flight. Not bad for a guy who had never been out of the country before.

I flew the six hours to Baltimore and told my parents all about my trip. They were so excited to hear everything, because they had never been to Europe either. The next day I was on an early morning four-hour flight to the AIA camp in Colorado Springs.

Holy Spirit Connections

Jet-lagged and exhausted, I arrived at the camp just in time for the Ultimate Training Camp Competition, which was a 24-hour, nonstop series of activities and competitions designed to teach us how to compete under stress. I'm naturally competitive, and by then I had plenty of practice operating without sleep and pushed myself to finish.

I didn't know anyone when I arrived at the camp, and everyone was already hanging out in small groups with their new friends. Fortunately, God led me to two people whom He would use to make a significant impact on me and my family for many years to come.

The first was Mike Echstenkamper, a former professional baseball player in the New York Yankees organization, who was new on staff with AIA. He became the AIA campus director at the University of North Carolina and would years later pour into my brothers David and Bryan, and my son Frankie when they played there for UNC.

I also became fast friends with a gymnast from Penn State, who was very excited about her faith, named Kristen Minor. Her friends called her Tee. She was the first girl I met who was passionate about her relationship with God and understood the challenges and pressures of being a college-athlete. We just connected and understood each other on a deeper level. The following school year we visited each other at our campuses, and she was a great encouragement to me in this relatively new faith journey.

It was also at this camp that I learned about what the AIA staff called a "Praise Performance," which meant competing out of a desire to praise and thank God, our Creator, for the opportunity to compete. So much of my life, I competed with a sense that I should be angry and channel that anger and fear of failure to make me great. Although anger and fear are intense motivators, over time they are not healthy, and instead of enhancing performance, they can actually limit an athlete's freedom and ability to perform.

The AIA staff challenged us to put a small cross somewhere visible to remind ourselves of Jesus, and the sacrifice He ultimately made for us. I ended up putting a small cross on my lacrosse gloves and would look at that symbol when I was on the sideline or before a faceoff—not as a good luck charm but as a reminder of what is most important in life.

My junior year when we got to order our Cornell ring, I chose to have a gold cross engraved into the red stone to remind me of God's goodness and grace. I still wear that ring and it acts as a reminder to this day.

We were also encouraged to use our sport, instead of allowing our sport to use us. One way to use our sport, and any success we had on the field, was to give public glory and thanks to God, and use our platform and influence in our sport to share the Good News with those who might listen because of our position.

I was beginning to have an appreciation and understanding of what some call "sports-based ministry." Little did I know the long-term impact these truths would have in my future.

CHAPTER 17

Eternity in My Heart

"He has made everything beautiful in its time.
He has also set eternity in the human heart;
yet no one can fathom what God has done from beginning to end."

Ecclesiastes 3:11

After my Ultimate Training Camp experience with AIA, I entered my senior year at Cornell with a desire to live for what I learned is called the "Great Commandment" (loving God with all my heart, soul, mind and strength, and loving my neighbor as myself) and the "Great Commission" (to go and share God's love and truth with others). This was a drastic change from my sophomore year, when I lived in The Lodge with all my new fraternity brothers.

Our Chi Psi cartoonist and my fraternity brothers captured it in the caricatures he drew of me, with their input about my lifestyle differences between those two years, which I share at the end of this chapter.

I decided to run for an officer position at Chi Psi, which would allow me and a roommate of my choice to move back into The Lodge for our senior year. Although I washed dishes at Chi Psi to cover my fraternity fees, I didn't live there my junior year. Mostly sophomores lived in the house and I had a desire to influence them and use the house as a gathering place for fellowship. I was elected vice president (although I ended up serving as president—that is another story!) and Kevin Frank agreed to move back into the house as my roommate. We made our senior year about trying to be a light for God's glory and sharing the Good News of God's love and truth in a relevant way with our fraternity brothers, lacrosse teammates, and others.

It turned out that there was an AIA staff person at Syracuse University named Walt Day, and after he heard about the volunteer AIA movement at Cornell, he decided to come and meet with Kevin and me about once a month. He shared different ideas with us, and ultimately shared our stories with a local sportswriter he knew who worked for the *Syracuse Herald American.*

This reporter, Scott Conroe, wanted to feature Kevin and me in a series he was calling *Christianity in Sports: The College Experience.*

Kevin and I had the opportunity to tell both our faith and athletic stories, which the reporter cast in a positive light.

The reporter captured our desire to let other people know that as followers of Jesus, we wanted to do our best and use our talents to the fullest, and he included my comments about my decision to try to keep Christ at the center of my life.

Kevin and I also did our best to dispel the myth that Christian athletes don't want to compete hard and win, and the reporter heard us. "Their commitment to living in a Christian manner hasn't lessened their competitiveness," he wrote. "Far from it."

As a senior, I was fortunate and honored to be elected a captain of the lacrosse team and then an officer in the Red Key Scholar-Athlete Honor Society, as I desired to earn the trust and respect of my peers.

Senior Season Challenges

Our senior lacrosse season was again full of unique challenges and disappointing one-goal losses, and despite being a captain trying to help lead the team in a positive direction, we had an odd chemistry and never really "clicked" or fired on all cylinders. The biggest disappointment was our game against the University of Pennsylvania on famous Franklin Field in Philadelphia.

We were winning 7-3 midway through the third quarter, and I was having a very good day at the faceoff X against their All-American center middie. We actually dominated the first two and a half quarters, and we should have been winning 10- or 11-3, when something happened that I have never seen before.

As I remember it, one of our players got called for a high hit and a two-minute unreleasable unsportsmanlike conduct penalty. One of our captains couldn't believe the call. He confronted the referee and accidentally bumped into him, resulting in another two-minute unreleasable penalty. Then Coach Moran went crazy and got another unreleasable unsportsmanlike conduct penalty himself! We would be three men down with unreleasable penalties.

Coach Moran decided to use our "man down" faceoff guy (instead of me), who was coming into the game cold facing off "one against three." We lost the next three faceoffs, and Penn scored three goals during those penalties. We went on to lose the game by a goal. It cost us the Ivy League Championship, and any chance of making the eight-team NCAA playoff field. I have never been more down after a game, and it still bothers me to this day.

Thinking About the Future

Senior year was also about planning for the future. Studying business management and marketing in the Cornell College of Agriculture and Life Sciences, I decided to interview with Procter and Gamble, but I ultimately felt prompted to explore missions instead, which scared and excited me at the same time.

A turning point came after reading *C.T. Studd—Cricketer and Pioneer*, the biography of a missionary that Gary Reubling, a Towson University football player, gave me. Gary played for Coach Phil Albert, the highly respected head coach of the Towson Tigers, who influenced the spiritual development of many of his players. Gary and I had met the summer prior through a

With my dad, wearing his signature green hat (so I could find him in the stands) after my last game on Schoellkopf Field—a win over Brown

college-athletes gathering in the Towson area, which was near my family's home.

C.T. Studd was a member of the "Cambridge Seven," a group of student-athletes at Cambridge University in England in the 1880s who all heeded a call to the mission field. Studd and most of "The Seven" grew up in fairly wealthy families who questioned their need to go to China or India or Africa to share the Gospel when, as well-known athletes, they had a platform at home in England.

Studd's poetic answer really challenged me: "Some would rather live within the sound of chapel bells. I would rather run a rescue shop within a yard of hell." Wow! C.T. Studd was "all in."

A second missionary biography also inspired me. That year, during a CRU/AIA winter conference the week after Christmas in Philadelphia, where nearly a thousand college students gathered for fellowship and biblical teaching, someone challenged me to read a book entitled *Shadow of the Almighty: The Life and Testament of Jim Elliot*, written by Elliot's wife, Elisabeth. In the book, she tells the story of how Jim Elliot, a former college wrestler, and four other missionaries in Ecuador were brutally martyred by the Auca Indian tribe they were trying to reach with the Good News in 1956.

After her husband's tragic death, she and one of the other martyred missionary's wives later returned to the Ecuador jungles and spent two years as missionaries to the same tribe members who killed their husbands. Ultimately, the Aucan Indians who had killed their husbands came to experience and receive God's love and grace and became followers of Jesus.

Jim Elliot's well-known quote, "He is no fool who gives what he cannot keep to gain what he cannot lose," and C.T. Studd's well-known verse, "Only one life, 'twill soon be past, Only what's done for Christ will last," impressed on me the truth I had been learning from God's Word that on the timeline of eternity with no beginning or end, our lives, even if we lived to be 100 years old, were like a small pinpoint and that there are only three things that last forever: God, His Word, and the souls of men and women.

As I pondered graduation and job possibilities, I knew I wanted to invest my life in those three things. I wanted to invest my life in eternity.

See the difference between my sophomore (Left) and senior year Chi Psi fraternity caricatures.

CHAPTER 18

The Calling

"But you will receive power when the Holy Spirit comes on you;
and you will be my witnesses in Jerusalem,
and in all Judea and Samaria, and to the ends of the earth."

Acts 1:8

As I approached graduation from Cornell, my father came to me with an offer. "Frankie, I feel God has blessed us with this insurance agency, so before you go off to save the world, I'd love it if you spent at least one year in the business."

At the time, the business consisted of him, his partner Gary Chick (who he had brought into the business six months after my parents had started it), Gary's wife Betty, my mom, a couple of salesmen, and some of my friends' moms from the neighborhood working 9 a.m. to 3 p.m.

I love my mom, but working with her and my friends' moms from the neighborhood was not the kind of job I envisioned after graduating from Cornell. And besides, I wanted to live for something I thought would be more eternally significant and had signed up for a summer missions trip to Japan with CRU and AIA. I had not yet made any long-term plans.

"Ehhh. Thanks Dad! Let me think about it," I said. "Can I give you an answer when I get back from Japan?"

I also needed to factor Gayle into this equation. She decided to turn down job offers in San Francisco and Washington, D.C. in order to come back to Baltimore so we could spend time together and see if our relationship was meant to be long term.

When I decided to do the summer mission to Japan, she was not thrilled, but she understood that I needed to explore this as a vocational option. She ended up graciously supporting me and knew she needed to hold our relationship loosely and with open hands, as did I.

Give and It Will Be Given to You

After a week of orientation with hundreds of other U.S. college students in Tokyo, they sent me and a group of about 50 others to Okinawa to build relationships and look for opportunities to share the Gospel with university students. We met students by tutoring them in English and playing basketball with them during free time.

I did not know at the time, but lacrosse had recently been introduced in Japan and was just beginning to grow as a sport there. I would much rather have been playing lacrosse with them, as my basketball skills were not pretty, but at the end of the day, it was all about having some fun, breaking down walls, and building relationships.

One of the guys in our group was a rising junior at Virginia Tech named Scott. One day, I noticed his shirt and

Meals were a great time for conversations with my new Japanese friends.

commented how much I liked it. We were about the same size, and the next day, he handed the shirt to me, cleaned and folded, and said, "I want you to have this." A few days later, I saw him do the same thing with his sunglasses after someone commented how cool they looked—he took them right off his head and gave them to the guy.

I couldn't help but ask him why he was giving all his nice stuff away when he told me he had decided to make a verse in the Gospel of Luke his theme for the summer, and he challenged me and the others in our group to memorize it. I had not memorized too many Bible verses before, but his example inspired me to do it. After all, I could remember football plays, lacrosse scouting reports and things I needed to know to pass exams.

The verse captured the words of Jesus in Luke 6:38, when he said, "Give, and it will be given to you. A good measure, pressed down, shaken together and running over, it will be poured into your lap. For with the measure that you [give], it will be measured to you [in return]."

By the end of the summer, I had memorized that verse and little did I know how much it would shape my thinking about giving my time, talent, treasure and testimony for decades to come.

I had no idea another verse would come my way soon afterwards that would change the trajectory of my life forever.

Five Words

We each lived in the homes of Japanese families who followed Jesus, which was a very small percentage of the population, and on Sundays we attended church with them. I was not fluent in Japanese, so it was difficult to follow what was going on in the service, but I did recognize the melodies of the music—they sang some of the same songs we sang back home, but in Japanese.

I had a comfortable bed on the floor in my Japanese host family's home.

While I was in Japan, I interviewed for a possible staff position with AIA, as I wanted to be open to God's leading and direction in my life. It was more of an exploratory conversation and something I wanted to better understand.

After church one Sunday, a group of us went to a local beach for some sun, fun and a little rest. I brought my Bible with me in my backpack and later in the day, decided to get some quiet time and reflection. By chance (or "God-incidence"), I turned to the Book of Acts, which is the first book in the Bible after the four Gospels, and read the first chapter. In verse 8 were the last words Jesus spoke to His followers 40 days after his resurrection and right before he ascended into heaven, when he said: "But you will receive power when the Holy Spirit comes upon you; and you will be my witnesses in Jerusalem, and in all Judea and Samaria, and to the ends of the earth."

For some reason, the words of this one verse literally jumped off the page. I had learned about and experienced the power of the Holy Spirit during my junior year and God had given me a great passion to be a witness to His love, grace and truth, but for some reason, the word that hit me hardest that day was *Jerusalem*. There I was in Japan, less than two percent Christian, which for a kid from Baltimore is the "remotest part of the earth," yet God gave me a strong sense that He wanted me to go back home and start in my Jerusalem, which was Baltimore.

Still sitting on the beach, another word came to me. It wasn't audible but it was clear. *Business. Hmm. What does that mean?* I got the strong impression that I was supposed to honor my dad's request and spend at least one year in my parents' business. I figured I could waste one year of my life working in something as eternally insignificant as an insurance and benefits company. (Although, I would soon learn that there is no eternally insignificant work if it is done in an effort to honor and serve God, the Creator and others.)

Then a few minutes later another word came to me: *School*. That made no sense. And I don't know why, but when the word "school" came, I sensed it was Calvert Hall. It would end up being much more than that.

I was still sitting there on the beach and received another word: *Lacrosse*. Again, inaudible but crystal clear. That made no sense to me either because I had just finished my career at Cornell with a bizarre and challenging season, losing multiple games by a goal, and not being selected into the eight-team NCAA Division I playoff field. And besides, there were no pro lacrosse leagues, so my lacrosse career was over as far as I knew. I felt the Lord had put a lid on lacrosse for me.

Another word came to me: *Friends*. I thought about all my Calvert Hall friends, elementary and middle school friends, and my college friends who thought I had gone off the religious deep end. *What do you mean you're going to Japan to "share the Gospel?"* It might have made a little sense to them if I was going to serve orphans or widows or the homeless, but going just to share God's love and the truth about how people can be rightly connected to their Creator, through a relationship with Jesus Christ? That's weird. I wanted to share with them what

I had learned about God's greatest priority (or Great Commandment) and what it meant to love God completely, love others compassionately, and love ourselves correctly.

I was also prompted to think about my parents and their friends. I knew their faith had become personal, real, and life-changing through the charismatic renewal movement in the

It was on this beach in Okinawa where I sensed God's calling one Sunday afternoon.

Catholic Church, but I didn't think they had been trained in sharing with others how they could more fully experience a personal relationship with God. The Lord gave me a passion to help others learn how to share God's love and truth more effectively.

Re-Entry

My flight home from Japan stopped over in Los Angeles. Gayle had timed a visit to her college friends in California so she could pick me up at the airport. She was glad to see me, but after ten minutes in the car, I unloaded on her.

I was a little excited about my experience in Japan and wanted to be faithful to God's call on my life. "You have to know something if we are going to keep dating," I said. "If you're not willing to be a missionary's wife, or a pastor's wife, a poor man's wife, not willing to live in a tent anywhere in the world, we have no future together. I can't guarantee you anything about where God is going to take me and us."

It was great to see Gayle when I landed in Los Angeles.

Understandably, my ultimatum didn't go over well.

Her wide eyes said, "Okay?!"

Gayle recalls, "I hadn't seen Frank for over two months and I was really excited to meet him at the airport when he flew in from Japan. But right away he was very passionate and clear about following God's call in the future, no matter where it led and let me know that if I wasn't on board, then, well, *See ya*."

"We had planned a few days for sightseeing in California. We'd be standing in line at Universal Studios and other tourist attractions and Frank would talk with anyone who would listen about the Good News. He was wise and tactful, but fearless. It wasn't that I didn't want him to

I was a little intense when I landed, but still loved to have fun —even with Gayle and me feeding the dolphins at Sea World.

be a missionary or follow Jesus; I was just thinking, *I haven't seen you in months. Let's have a conversation. How about asking me how I feel about the future?*"

Gayle was gracious with me and God was patient with both of us. Over time Gayle saw my heart behind it, and it became both of our desires to pursue God's best.

Family Business

When I returned to Baltimore, I thanked my father for supporting me on the trip and told him I felt called by God to honor his request and work a year in the business. He was thrilled to have his son working as a salesperson.

"Frank, this is great," he said. "As I told you before, our business is all about relationships, and through relationships, you can impact lives. You will have a tough job to do but you won't have to punch a clock, so you can have great flexibility with your time. Flexibility gives you quality of life, and quality of life is more important than money. You can be in business and still be an ambassador for the Lord's love and truth and have the flexibility to do things outside the business as well."

I asked my parents if they would be willing to let me come to their church small group and discuss with them some ideas on how to more effectively share their faith.

My dad would often paraphrase the words of St. Francis of Assisi and say, "Share the Gospel at all times and only use words if necessary." In other words, live the Gospel and leave the results to God. I reminded them that God's Word says, "...faith comes by hearing, and hearing by the Word of God"[1] and that the best way to share God's love and truth is with both word and deed. And as the Scriptures remind us, we should "...be prepared in season and out of season..."[2] or at all times, to give the reason for the hope that is in us. They graciously agreed to let me come and share what I had learned.

When I ended up meeting with my parents and the three other couples in their group, I decided to use a small booklet from AIA called *The Four Spiritual Laws,* which started with the simple statement that "God loves you and has a wonderful plan for your life." The booklet covered the key elements of the Gospel that I like to reference as (1) God's Position—He is perfect, holy, loving, kind, and gracious; (2) Our Condition—we are sinners who are broken and separated from God; (3) God's Provision—His Son, Jesus Christ, who lived and died and rose again so that our sins can be forgiven; and (4) Our Decision—to accept, reject or neglect God's incredible gift of Jesus Christ and His love, grace and cleansing.

We even worked on writing out our personal faith stories around those four key elements of the Gospel message, and what our lives were like before and after coming into a personal relationship with God, so that we would each be better prepared to share the greatest news of all time, in season or out.

My parents and the other couples, who were great family friends, were gracious and humble to meet with me, a 22-year-old college graduate who they had known since I was a young boy. They had to be kind of chuckling and shaking their heads a little in disbelief that "Frankie Kelly" was trying to help them more effectively share their faith.

God does have a sense of humor!

PART IV

Small Beginnings

Saturday, July 4, 1992

Sports

...vard Christian Athletics in '92

...Squad' upsets Turtles

..., Williams

...r

...pposed to be a case of
...ns ly... thrown to the
... with heavily favored
... Vail Lacrosse Sho... at
... Gree... was jump...
...0 lea...
... Fri... while
... v... pocke...
... athlet...
... nter... b...
...oun reputation... arters and
... ertime pe... iods l... CA
...de... wo... p... the... nted
... iou... lo... of... club
...9-8, a... v... of... f... was
... ever... se... volle... ... et for
...ed to... ... ... bu... ation.
...A, the ... ... ts first
...out appo... ... become
... as the ... ... d," used a
...ination of ... ... defense

and sheer hustle to shut down the
No. 1 seeded Turtles' potent offense, anchored by Towson State
middie Rob Shek and former
Syracuse All-American Gary Gait,
one of the all-time leading scorers
in the Major Indoor Lacrosse
League.

Gait, who had seven goals in a
22-7 Greene Turtles' shellacking of
the Vail Lacrosse Club in
Thursday's opening round, was un-
able to get into the swing of things
Friday. Gait scored no goals on ...
sho...

"I just wasn't on toda, at all,"
Gait said. "(Thursday) everything
was going in, (Friday) nothing was.
I'd say it was the altitude, but I
think it was the evening activitie...

Though David Kelly had the
game-winning goal at 3:1... the
second overtime, it wa...

Please see *Lacrosse* pa...

CHAPTER 19

Huddle at The Hall

*"Pray also for me, that whenever I speak, words may be given me so that
I will fearlessly make known the mystery of the gospel, for which I am
an ambassador... Pray that I may declare it fearlessly, as I should."*

Ephesians 6:19-20

W ith my calling to business clarified for the time being, I turned my attention to the next word that I sensed God leading me to, which was *school or schools*, which in my mind, was Calvert Hall.

I invited Calvert Hall's principal, Brother René Sterner, and Calvert Hall's chaplain, Father Jeff, out to lunch. I shared my personal faith story of connecting to the Creator and opening my heart to Jesus in the middle of lacrosse practice my sophomore year at Cornell. Then I shared what I had learned about the Holy Spirit, and my desire to share God's love and truth with others. I told them about my awesome fellowship and Bible study experience with athletes and asked if I could start the same kind of group at The Hall.

"You know, Frank, we already have religion here," Brother René said.

"I know that Brother, but this would be more like a spiritual vitamin supplement, not something that would replace the teachings of the church."

As I mentioned earlier, I had learned that the distance between "religion" and "relationship" is about eighteen inches—from your head to your heart—and told Brother René that this fellowship would help God's Word and truth go from the guys' heads to their hearts. It would help them better understand how to live out their faith on a daily basis in an integrated way on the athletic field, in the classroom, and even in their social life.

"But Frank, when would you do it? After school, all these kids play sports and go to clubs and other activities."

"I thought I could do it one day a week, an hour before school, at 7 or 7:30 a.m."

"But Frank, kids drive an hour from every direction to come to Calvert Hall. Nobody is going to come to school an hour early for a Bible study."

"Well, Brother, if no one comes, I will commit to pray by myself for you and the school during that time." Not that I was some great prayer warrior, but I sensed I was called to do this.

I could tell Brother René and Father Jeff both wanted to say no, but I didn't leave them with any reason. I was volunteering my time and with my prior success as a student-athlete at Calvert Hall and Cornell, I had a little "street cred." And my three younger brothers were Calvert Hall men and had done well on the athletic fields and in the classroom as well. I was willing to sit alone in the room and pray for the school if no one came.

I asked if they would please let me give a two-minute testimony (I had been trained to share my story in two minutes) and an invitation to the 1,200 high school students at the annual Christmas assembly. We would start in January after Christmas break. Brother René hesitantly gave me the green light.

I decided we would call our fellowship Athletes in Action (AIA). We had no official affiliation with that organization, but they were the only organization I knew of from my experience at Cornell.

I Was Mortified

"I was mortified."

That's how my youngest brother Bryan felt when I shared my faith story and plans to start a fellowship for athletes during the Christmas assembly. I thought it went well, but Bryan remembers it a little differently:

"I had watched how Frank and my other two older brothers lived the wild and crazy life of a high school senior, and now I had my turn. I always had a heart for God, but in my insecurity, I cared more about what my classmates thought of me, about being the All-Metro stud lacrosse player, and a cool dude.

"Then Frank stands up in front of the whole assembly—the only thing between 1,200 hyped-up high school boys and Christmas break—and in his passionate style, shares the story of how God worked in his life at Cornell.

"My friends gave me the business afterward. They called Frank a 'Jesus Freak' and told me I was going to turn into a Jesus Freak like him.

"All I could do was shrug and stammer, 'Oh, well, you know, that's my brother.'"

We started our group on Thursday mornings in January 1987, and only a few students showed up. At first, my brother Bryan was angry at me for "wrecking" his senior year by starting this fellowship and Bible study, but then he felt bad for me when hardly any students came and he started to come himself.

Still, we never had to worry about running out of chairs in Room 108, at least not for a while.

CHAPTER 20

Coaching the Cardinals

*"Do you not know that in a race all the runners run,
but only one gets the prize? Run in such a way as to get the prize."*

1 Corinthians 9:24

I was walking down the hallway at Calvert Hall after AIA one Thursday morning, when Mike Thomas, the head varsity lacrosse coach, called out to me. "Hey, Frank, can I talk to you for a minute?" It made me flash back to my freshman year at The Hall when he stopped me and a couple of other freshmen and sophomore football players in the hall and encouraged us to come out for lacrosse.

"Hey, Coach, sure."

He told me that his long-time assistant coach, Dave Creighton, had a conflict and couldn't coach with him that year. "I really need an assistant coach," he said. "Could you be my main assistant? We practice every day from 3:30 to 5:30 p.m. and I would need you here in time for all our games."

"Hmm, I'm not sure. Let me check into it." I talked it over with my dad at the office. He was all for quality of life and flexibility. "If you want to coach, you can coach. Just make sure you get your job done," he told me.

Now I was leading the AIA fellowship and coaching lacrosse for the Calvert Hall Cardinals. As soon as lacrosse tryouts started in mid-February, more guys showed up on Thursday mornings. They had some level of interest in growing in a relationship with God, but their motives weren't always pure and their plans didn't always work out.

Andy Droney, a freshman, came because he thought it would help him get more playing time since he was a faceoff man and I was the new faceoff and midfield coach. Brian Hubbard thought he might get more middie runs out of me by coming, but attendance didn't matter to Coach Thomas.

Andy Hilgartner (who would one day become the head high school boys' lacrosse coach at McDonogh School in Baltimore) was trying to make the varsity team as a sophomore and thought coming to the AIA fellowship would help his chances. But less than an hour into the first practice on the snow-covered tennis courts, he dropped a pass and Coach Thomas yelled to him, "Hey, Hilgartner, report to JV." No counseling session, no one-on-one or family meeting, and no discussion, just cut from varsity.

Andy said, "Yes Coach," and played JV. "I go to Coach Frank's Bible study and I get cut after one practice," Andy complained.

Faceoffs in the Dark

I worked the Calvert Hall faceoff guys hard. "Coach, it's dark," they would say.

"Yeah, I can see that," I would tell them, then pull my car up to the field and turn on the headlights, just like I had done on one of my first dates with Gayle when the lights on the tennis courts didn't come on the night we were playing.

"Let's keep going. We got to get better." *This guy's crazy*, they would think, but for ten straight years, our center middie faceoff guys were the best in our league and earned Division I scholarships.

Coaching allowed me to build relationships with the guys at a much deeper level. I spent two or three hours a day with them so I had time to ask them about their life and family and faith.

Coaching Calvert Hall and Brian "Hubbs" Hubbard about wing play on faceoffs

Also, with sports competition comes vulnerability. The intensity and stress of performance expectations that athletes feel, which for high school kids mostly comes from within themselves, makes them open and responsive to the influence of their coaches.

I saw that influence taking effect on and off the field. I could relate to the pain of getting cut from a team or not playing many minutes, so I could encourage Andy Hilgartner, which helped open the door for the relationship with Christ that he eventually embraced. I got to know Andy Droney well enough to gain his trust and talk to him about becoming a three-dimensional athlete— mental, physical and spiritual. And Brian Hubbard opened up to me about his great-grandmother's battle with cancer and the questions that were raised in his mind about God's goodness.

For any relationship to grow, it takes presence, and with presence comes the opportunity to have greater influence.

MORE TO THE STORY...

The Power of Influence – Brian Hubbard

I was a mere freshman at Calvert Hall when Frank invited me to the new fellowship and Bible study for athletes. "We'll have some breakfast food, learn from God's Game Plan (the Bible), and different coaches and athletes will talk about their life and faith," was how he described it.

I figured, *Well, I respect Coach Frank, I like the other kids and coaches involved in AIA, and I like donuts. This sounds like it could only make me smarter and wiser as an athlete. Yeah, I'd be interested in that!*

We also joked as players that "if I go to the Bible study maybe Coach Frank will put in a good word for me with the head coach." But that was not the case for me—I was cut from JV as a freshman.

At the same time, I started going to the Bible study, my great-grandmother was dying of cancer and living with my family. I was confused because Coach Frank taught us that God is good and God is loving, so why would He allow such a terrible thing to happen to an 85-year-old woman who had been a great person and went to church every week?

During her illness, my great-grandmother slept in my bedroom and I slept on the couch downstairs; Every night when I would go upstairs to grab a shirt, tie, and sport coat out of my room for school the next day, I heard her talking. I thought she was on the phone and would wait until I didn't hear her anymore before going into the room. But one evening I barged in to grab my clothes and saw the phone on the desk and her lying in bed.

"Grandma," I said, "every night I come up here and you're always talking to somebody. Who are you talking to?"

"You always catch me praying," she said.

"Who are you praying to?"

"I'm praying and talking to God."

"Why would you pray to Him?" I asked.

"Because I'm thankful. Thankful for the life I've had. I'm thankful for you, thankful for my family."

It hit me that what I was learning from Coach Frank and what my great-grand-mother was living was real.

It would be a year later when I went to a retreat for athletes that I went back to my room after hearing the speaker reaffirm what Frank was teaching through our huddle and what my great-grandmother was living and I told God, "I want what Coach Frank has. I want what my great-grandmother has. I want to learn more and have a relationship with You and Your Son, Jesus."

I ended up playing three years of varsity lacrosse at Calvert Hall and because I was fast, Coach Frank turned me into a "wing middie" on faceoffs. That turned out to be a great position and role for me and ultimately opened doors for me to play at Michigan State with my Calvert Hall teammate, Andy Hilgartner.

During my senior season at Calvert Hall, we were playing St. Paul's. It was a tough game and we were having some issues with facing off—partly my fault because I played on a wing and wasn't getting to the ground balls fast enough.

We called timeout and Coach Frank pulled me two feet away from the team huddle and got in my ear. He made it clear I needed to pick up my game, and just as he was showing me what I needed to do better, my father, who came to all my games, snapped a picture.

That picture on the previous page is the definition of *Influence*. That is Frank chirping in my ear, pouring into my life, making me better. Sometimes he'd have to kick me a little hard and sometimes he just put his arm around me and loved me.

Just like Frank put his arm around me, today as an adult I want to put my arm around coaches and athletes. If I can influence them through my encouragement or my challenging words, I'm going to do it.

Influence always leads to more influence!

CHAPTER 21

Iron Sharpens Iron

"As iron sharpens iron, so one person sharpens another."

Proverbs 27:17

I enjoyed coaching, and helping build up and encourage the guys along the way. I forgot how tough and at times, negative, Coach Thomas could be. In some ways, he reminded me of how tough Coach Moran was on me my first couple of years at Cornell. I could relate to what the guys might be feeling, and since I was so young, I could quickly remember how I would have liked to be coached.

I was working hard to help the guys fulfill their potential on and off the field, when one week I got a call from two of the top post-collegiate club lacrosse programs in Maryland. The last thing on my mind was playing lacrosse since I basically thought my competitive playing days were behind me after graduating from Cornell.

Because I didn't start playing lacrosse until high school, I didn't really know much about the overall lacrosse scene, and particularly, knew very little about the storied histories of these two elite clubs, called Mt. Washington Lacrosse Club and Maryland Lacrosse Club (MLC). I was flattered to receive calls from Mt. Washington Head Coach Skip Lichtfuss, and MLC's Head Coach, Arlie Marshall.

Although Mt. Washington had been around since 1904 and had an amazing history, I felt led to play for MLC as a midfielder and faceoff specialist. Since MLC practices were going to start in just a couple of weeks, I knew I had to get back in "faceoff shape," and quickly.

Every day, after 45 minutes of instructing and drilling the Calvert Hall faceoff players, I joined in for the last 30 minutes and had them push and train me. We applied what I told the guys was the one verse in the Bible, or God's Game

Plan, about lacrosse and faceoffs which says, "As iron sharpens iron, so one person sharpens another."

We needed to be "iron" for each other, as we practiced and refined our technique. It is almost impossible to practice and improve at facing off alone. And since this door opened for me to play again at a very competitive level, I needed to stay sharp.

MLC's first practice game was coming up against Johns Hopkins University, the perennial powerhouse that Cornell only played once in my career during my freshman year. I did not even dress for that game. I was a little nervous about facing Hopkins on the famous Homewood Field, and had the Calvert Hall faceoff group work me really hard for the week leading up to that practice game.

That MLC team was loaded with former All-Americans and U.S. National Team players, and we crushed Hopkins by a lopsided score in this early pre-season contest. I won close to 80% of my faceoffs, several of which led to fast-break goals, and had a great time surrounded by such talented players.

Hopkins was a very talented team, and later that year went on to win the NCAA National Championship over Cornell. My alma mater was undefeated until that championship game when they struggled to win faceoffs.

It was both exciting and painful to watch my former Cornell teammates play in the Final Four and National Championship games, which were held at Rutgers University in 1987, the year after I graduated. A lot of the guys told me after Cornell's one-goal loss that I would have helped them win it all if I was still on the team. Maybe, but it wasn't God's plan.

Fortunately, I was having fun, and my competitive juices were flowing again working with the Calvert Hall faceoff guys and playing with MLC. With so many amazing players on the MLC team and Coach Arlie Marshall being competitive but laid back in his coaching style, it was the most enjoyment I ever had playing the Creator's game.

Professional Lacrosse

Surprisingly, another lacrosse opportunity opened up for me when a newly established professional indoor league, called the Eagle Pro Box Lacrosse League, started their inaugural season with four teams, including the Baltimore Thunder. The Thunder needed a faceoff guy, and because I was playing so well for MLC, they called me. Suddenly I was a professional lacrosse player, making a whopping $125 per game.

It didn't take long for me to realize that the league seemed more interested in pumping up the fans with rowdy entertainment and fights than quality lacrosse play. I played my first game at the Spectrum in Philadelphia in front of 16,000 people who were mainly Philadelphia Flyers hockey fans. The game felt like a cross between a WWF wrestling match and an out-of-control hockey game. Gayle came to the game and couldn't believe her eyes. We weren't in Ithaca anymore.

Our coaches and my teammates reminded me of the one "unofficial" fundamental rule of this game, which was: "there are no rules!" In all the lacrosse I had ever played, cross-checking—holding the stick with both hands spread apart and using it as a battering rod on the opposing player—was not allowed. In this game, the more crosschecking, the better.

By the second half, it was "kill or be killed." A dozen fights broke out in each game and the referees let them go on because the fans loved them.

Me (#9) getting cross-checked from behind and on the side into the wall, which was all part of the pro box/indoor game

All four teams were owned by the same two guys, so they didn't care who won or lost. They just wanted entertainment and paying fans in the stands, so they loved the fights too. It made no sense to me because most of the players I fought were guys I knew from previous lacrosse teams whom I considered friends!

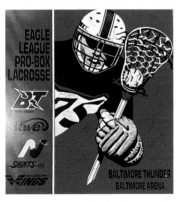

It was exciting to win the inaugural Pro-Box Lacrosse Championship with the Baltimore Thunder in 1987.

Our Thunder team won the championship that inaugural year, beating the Washington Wave, the team coached by Maryland lacrosse legend Buddy Beardmore, and featured star players like Frank Urso (former Maryland legend) and Brad Kotz (former Syracuse All-American). At least there was a reward for enduring the craziness.

In my third year after the league had been rebranded the Major Indoor Lacrosse League (MILL), Vinnie Sombrotto, who played for the New York Saints and worked as a local Teamster Union Leader, tried to organize all the MILL players under the Teamsters Union. I loved Vinnie, but I didn't feel great about becoming a member of the Teamsters. After all, the owners were now paying us $150 per game.

The game atmosphere grew rougher by that third year, especially in Philly. One of our players, Lou Delligatti, who used to play for the Philadelphia Wings but was traded to Baltimore, scored a goal and then jumped up onto the sidewall to taunt his former fans with some trash-talking and hand gestures. The fans retaliated by pelting our bench with beer, soda and hot dogs. I had ketchup and mustard in my hair, in my ears, and all over my uniform.

After that season, I really questioned whether this pro box lacrosse league was for me. And I had to wonder what the Creator was thinking about this crazy version of His game.

CHAPTER 22

The Movement

"He who is faithful in a very little thing is faithful also in much..."

Luke 16:10 (NASB)

By the end of the 1987 school year, fifteen to 20 guys were coming to Room 108 and our fellowship for athletes at Calvert Hall. It had taken less than one year back home in Baltimore—my "Jerusalem"—for the words that made no sense to me on the beach in Okinawa—business, school, lacrosse and friends—to take on meaning.

In the summer of 1987, a friend who knew I was leading the AIA group at Calvert Hall thought it would be helpful for me to meet a guy named Mark Gassman, who lived near Gettysburg, Pennsylvania. Mark was on staff with an organization I had never heard of—the Fellowship of Christian Athletes, or FCA. We met for lunch at a McDonald's in Westminster, Maryland, a roughly equidistant drive for both of us.

I learned that Mark had been a businessperson, like me, and had worked for New York Life Insurance Company when he was recruited to come on staff with FCA to see if he could get the ministry going in the Mid-Atlantic and Northeast areas. There were very few staff in these areas, so Mark was really going to have his work cut out for him. Fortunately, his wife was open to him stepping into this ministry role, but she did not want to live in a big city. Mark let her pick where they would live in the region, and she picked Gettysburg.

Mark explained that FCA was committed to helping coaches and athletes fulfill their God-given potential on and off the field with a special focus on high school and college coaches and athletes. One of their main ministries was sharing "God's Game Plan," or the Bible, through school-based fellowship groups called "huddles." Their approach was to identify coaches and volunteers in the community—like me—and equip them with tools to support a huddle. Over the summer, they ran multi-day sports camps all over the country, but especially in the Bible Belt down south.

"We only have one FCA camp in the Mid-Atlantic and Northeast and it is at Gettysburg College in June," he said. "Why don't you come up for a day? We'll be hosting several different sports. I would love for you to come and check it out."

I took Mark up on his offer. About 200 kids from more than five different states in the region came to the camp to play football, basketball and soccer. They held large-group fellowship times in the morning and evening with gifted speakers, and small-group huddles throughout the day with about ten kids in each group. All the huddle leaders were college athletes who volunteered as coaches at the camp. Pretty cool, I thought.

Former professional and college athletes spoke at the evening program, which also included live music and personal stories from coaches and campers. *This is incredible!*

Before I left, I had to ask Mark one question. "Do you have lacrosse at FCA camps?"

"No, we don't have lacrosse," Mark said, "but if you want to start it next year, you can. We would love to offer lacrosse here."

"Okay, let me think about it," I said.

Initials Don't Matter

When our fellowship at Calvert Hall restarted in September of 1987, I told the guys, "Listen, I went to an FCA camp over the summer and I'm going to change our name to FCA."

"Coach, no. We can't," some said. "We're Athletes in Action. We love AIA."

I said, "Okay. Well, we'll make the transition. For this year, we'll be called AIA/FCA. Next year we'll switch to FCA." I cared more about the mission than the initials, but AIA was more focused on pro and college athletes and teams, and I really liked FCA's tools and resources for middle school and high school coaches, athletes and volunteers so we were an FCA Huddle as far as I was concerned.

Our Calvert Hall Huddle was for all athletes, not just lacrosse players, and it was my understanding that we were the only FCA high school huddle of its kind in the state of Maryland at the time. Soon thereafter, I heard about a college huddle that had recently started less than an hour away at the U.S. Naval Academy in Annapolis, Maryland.

Student-athletes led the Navy FCA Huddle, and Barry Spofford, a captain in the Navy, was the faculty advisor. I don't know how Barry got my phone number,

INFLUENCE

I learned that the Fellowship of Christian Athletes was founded in 1954 by Don McClanen, a basketball coach in Oklahoma who had been cutting press clippings of professional and college athletes and coaches who publicly praised God for their successes on and off the field.

With the support of Branch Rickey, one of the most influential men in sports who broke Major League Baseball's color barrier by signing Jackie Robinson with the Brooklyn Dodgers, and a $10,000 donation from a Pittsburgh businessman named Paul Benedum, McClanen incorporated FCA and launched his vision to use the platform and influence of athletes and coaches to share God's love and truth through sports.

To this day many would say the one-word definition of FCA is "Influence."

FCA founder Don McClanen (Above) and key supporter Branch Rickey (Right) with Jackie Robinson

Scan for a brief history of FCA.

but he reached out to me and asked, as a professional lacrosse player, to come and speak to their huddle, and I asked if Mark Pimpo, the star middle linebacker on the Navy football team and one of their FCA leaders, would speak at Calvert Hall. We continued the "iron sharpens iron" synergy over the years and both huddles continued to flourish.

On my second speaking visit, Barry invited me to come early and eat in the mess hall with all the midshipmen. "And feel free to bring a guest with you," he said.

I decided to bring Gayle with me and we both dressed up. I wore a blazer and button-down shirt and Gayle wore a nice, hot pink dress. It looked even brighter in contrast to all 4,000 Mids dressed in their all-black uniforms seated in the dining hall. As Gayle—who I think is beautiful—and I walked the full length and down the center of the entire dining hall to our seats, I could see some of the guys looking out of the corner of their eyes at the woman in pink. We still laugh about that dinner and Gayle's dress choice.

The Springboard

As our Calvert Hall FCA Huddle grew, I sensed God's prompting to share what we were doing with the students' parents. In the spring of our second year, 1988, we held a banquet in the Calvert Hall cafeteria. I invited Pat Kelly (no relation, although we talked about being brothers all the time after we met at a city ministry outreach), the former Baltimore Oriole baseball player, as our guest speaker. Pat was passionate about his faith and had a gift for sharing the "Good News" in a powerful and inspiring way.

Pat was very expressive and outward in his excitement about his relationship with God. He told a funny story about how one day in the Orioles' locker room, he was praising the Lord and said to Earl Weaver, the crusty Orioles manager, "Hey, Earl, it's great to walk with God. It's great to walk with Jesus!"

Earl sneered, "I would much rather you walk with the bases loaded."

About 100 people attended the dinner—a mix of kids from the huddle, their parents, and siblings. All we tried to do was serve a nice family dinner and share what we were doing on Thursday mornings and why. I had no idea we were bouncing on a springboard of growth.

The parents talked about the banquet with other parents in their neighborhoods and workplaces. The siblings talked about the banquet with their friends in other schools. My phone started to ring. Dulaney High School wanted to start a huddle. Towson High School wanted to start a huddle. Loyola Blakefield wanted to start a huddle, and McDonogh, and Loch Raven. I logged a lot of hours trying to find and encourage coaches, teachers, and students who were excited about their faith and had a desire to start huddles at their schools, and then providing them with Bible study materials, video resources, and connections to guest speakers.

I was so thankful for my flexible work schedule and so grateful for Gayle's support and encouragement every step of the way. God was opening doors into various high schools and there were many more to come.

CHAPTER 23

A Cord of Three Strands

"Two are better than one, because they have a good return for their labor:
If either of them falls down, one can help the other up. But pity anyone who falls
and has no one to help them up. Also, if two lie down together, they will keep
warm. But how can one keep warm alone? Though one may be overpowered,
two can defend themselves. A cord of three strands is not quickly broken."

Ecclesiastes 4:9-12

At the end of my one-year commitment to my dad and the family business, in August of 1987, I spent time reflecting on all that had happened in the year since my graduation from Cornell and my summer mission to Japan. I was trying to discern whether God wanted me to continue in the business and with the other areas of focus, including schools, lacrosse and friends.

In unique and powerful ways, God was at work in all four areas of the calling He impressed upon me just a year earlier.

I was proving to be fairly successful in sales and had vision to grow our sales team and overall business. I had also been connected to a group called Christian Business Men's Connection (CBMC), which was helping me learn how to understand, apply and share God's Word in the marketplace, which was a lot of fun.

Our AIA/FCA Huddle at Calvert Hall was growing and other schools were expressing interest in starting huddles.

I was coaching varsity lacrosse at Calvert Hall and playing club and pro indoor lacrosse at a high level and I saw the possibility of starting lacrosse at a future FCA camp.

God was opening many doors with my friends from college, high school, and even elementary school for me to encourage them in their spiritual journey as well.

The most important "friend" decision I made that year was to ask Gayle Barbara Schmith to marry me. It was February 14, 1987 when I took Gayle to Sabatino's in Little Italy in Baltimore, Maryland. I prayed a lot about the decision, knowing how important and significant it was.

We both came from somewhat religious backgrounds, but when we first met after our freshman year in college, neither of us were rightly connected to God, and neither of us understood what it meant to have a personal, real, daily, life-changing relationship with Him. As we each began to grow closer to God, we grew closer to each other.

And even as I came on strong and passionate about my relationship with God after my transformation at Cornell and mission in Japan, Gayle was gracious and continued to grow in a slow and steady manner. We complemented each other's gifts, passions and dispositions.

A Big Hurdle

As attracted as I was to Gayle physically, mentally, emotionally and spiritually, there was a big hurdle we had to overcome. About six months before our engagement, as our feelings for each other were intensifying, Gayle courageously shared something very significant with me. She told me about some medical complications that could possibly impact her ability to get pregnant and bear children. She asked me to go with her to her doctor so I could understand all the issues and challenges we might encounter if we ever got married and wanted to have children together.

I loved Gayle, yet I knew I wanted to have children and a big family someday. I remember sharing the situation with my mom and dad, and as usual, my mom shared great wisdom and grace as this decision could affect them as potential grandparents.

My mom asked, "Frankie, do you love Gayle?"

"Yes mom, I do!" I replied.

"Do you trust God?" she asked.

Through tears I said, "Yes mom, I think so."

My mom, realizing her oldest son may knowingly marry a woman who had a high chance of not being able to get pregnant, brought wisdom, faith and love to the table.

I literally remember the night I was driving to pick Gayle up to take her to dinner, and then ask her to marry me. I had her parents' blessing. Yet in the back of my mind, I was still questioning until we got to dinner.

I was so nervous at dinner that I barely ate any of the famous Sabatino's salad and chicken parmigiana that we ordered. And although I could remember exactly what Gayle wore on our first date and when I visited her in France, I can't remember anything from that night until after dinner.

After dinner, I told Gayle I wanted to walk around the beautiful Inner Harbor, which she was not too excited about with the sub-freezing temperatures and chilling winds. But my plan was clear as we walked to one of my favorite piers and I got on my knee and asked her to marry me.

My nerves disappeared after I popped the question, and I have not had a single doubt since that night. Gayle was the one for me. She loved God, she loved me, and together we surrendered our future with or without children to God.

She said yes!

Two Are Better Than One

Gayle and I got married on August 22, 1987 at St. Joseph's Catholic Church in Cockeysville, Maryland. We asked Father Victor Galeone, who understood our new love for Jesus and God's Word, to marry us.

Gayle planned just about every part of our wedding so it was really great. My only real job was to get a videographer.

We ended up with about 200 people at our wedding, which unfortunately, did not include everyone we wanted to invite. We had a tight budget, so we had to make some tough decisions.

In an effort to include two of my Cornell lacrosse teammates in the wedding party, I asked them if they could use my camcorder and tripod and do the video for us. That turned out to be a disaster, as they chose to zoom in on various body parts of Gayle's beautiful bridesmaids, even while Father Victor shared God's Word, and even while Gayle and I were praying together on the altar. When we returned from our honeymoon in St. Maarten in late August of 1987, Gayle could not wait to watch our wedding video. I had no clue what they had done, but after about fifteen minutes of watching, she got up, left the room, and has never watched it since.

On a more serious note, we did invite my friend Tee Minor, whom I had met after my junior year at Cornell at the AIA Ultimate Training Camp in Colorado Springs. I asked my parents if she could stay at their house and, of course, they obliged.

One morning, Tee and my father were up early having coffee and chatting in the kitchen. Later that day, my father told my brother John, "You've got to talk to this girl Tee. She is marriage material!"

John wasn't thinking about marriage material at the time but later came to the same conclusion about Tee, and now they are married with six children.

God used John to introduce me to lacrosse, then he used me, and our wedding, to connect him to his beautiful wife.

God had other unique challenges, opportunities and blessings ahead for Gayle and me. Over the years, we have seen and experienced

Our wedding day! August 22, 1987

again and again the reality of one of the scriptures read at our wedding from Ecclesiastes that "two are better than one," and that "a cord of three strands (Gayle, me and God) is not quickly broken."

CHAPTER 24

My Grace Is Sufficient for You

"But he said to me, 'My grace is sufficient for you,
for my power is made perfect in weakness.' Therefore I will boast all the more
gladly about my weaknesses, so that Christ's power may rest on me."

2 Corinthians 12:9

After we returned from our honeymoon in St. Maarten, Gayle and I moved into our first home together.

We decided to rent a small tenant house on the back of a farm in Monkton, Maryland, which was pretty close to where Gayle was teaching high school history and French, as well as helping coach field hockey and lacrosse at an all-girls boarding school called Oldfields.

The farm owner, Mrs. Crosby, only charged us $200 a month for rent, but I was responsible for cutting about seven acres of grass each week, using her Gravely lawn mower, which wasn't fun with the hay fever allergies I had. Gayle actually mowed the grass a few times when the allergies crushed me so bad I could barely see.

We also made a decision to begin attending a nondenominational church that was meeting in the gymnasium of another all-girls school in

Playing a little lacrosse in front of our first home

the city. The church was called Grace Fellowship. The teachings and music were amazing and relevant. They talked a lot about the importance of being in a small group and reminded us that "you learn a lot more in 'circles' than in 'rows,'" so we had been thinking about joining one.

Some of our Catholic friends were concerned that we were not attending a Catholic church, but our priority was being in a church where we were learning God's Word, growing in our relationship with Him and comfortable inviting guests even if they were not Catholic.

It turned out that more than half of the attendees at Grace Fellowship had a Catholic background and were looking for a place where the teaching was practical and relevant to their everyday lives. Plus, I was still very involved with coaching lacrosse and leading the FCA Huddle at Calvert Hall, so I was still connected to my Catholic roots.

In my mind, we weren't "leaving" the Catholic church, but we were open to non-Catholic experiences as long as they were aligned with the truth in the Bible, and our focus became more about Christianity and following Jesus than any one denomination.

After a year on the farm, we decided to buy our first house—a townhouse in a community called Loveton Farms, which was a lot closer to my business office, and still close to Oldfields as well. Once we settled in, we felt led to try and start a small group in our new neighborhood.

One day after church, we decided to take a walk around our neighborhood, and prayed "Lord, we would like to start a small group in our home, so if this is of You, please connect us to others who would be open to joining us."

We were not expecting an immediate response to our prayer, but during that walk, we randomly ran into three other couples along the way who said they would be very open to checking out a small group Bible study if we started one.

Another couple we met later at a neighborhood cookout was Chuck and Ellen Knudsen, who were recently married as well. We somehow built up the courage to invite them, and they had the courage to try something new and potentially uncomfortable for them as well.

My brother David and his new wife, Melissa, also moved into Loveton Farms and joined our small group. That small group was a lot of fun and full of laughter with David's stories and jokes, and we were all learning from each other and from God's Word.

Friendly's

One of the gifts God has given me is the ability to connect with different people in a variety of random ways, that might lead to an invitation. Going back to my Cornell days, I was an "inviter" and loved connecting others to God's love and truth.

One night, I ran into a couple in a very odd way. The last thing I was thinking about that night was inviting anyone to our small group. I'd had a rough weekend, and besides, we were in a Friendly's restaurant on a Sunday night and

I had never met this couple before.

The day before, on Saturday afternoon, I went to see my brother Bryan and his North Carolina Tar Heels lacrosse team play the Loyola Greyhounds on the Loyola University campus. Bryan had been a multi-time All-American defenseman in high school, and I was there to cheer him on with the rest of my family and many of his friends.

Bryan was a junior and had started every game prior that year, but for some reason, the coach benched him and he did not play one minute with all his family and friends there watching. The Tar Heels lost that game. I could relate to the pain he must have been feeling from my experience at our Cornell game at Syracuse my freshman year. It "triggered" something inside of me and I was furious.

I began yelling some things across the field towards the UNC coaches. My frustration and language certainly did not honor God. My flesh got the best of me and I knew that this was not the witness I wanted to reflect, especially as the leader of our FCA Huddle at Calvert Hall.

I knew what I did was wrong and asked God for forgiveness. I was reminded again that with FCA we are not the Fellowship of "Perfect" Athletes and Coaches, but rather the Fellowship of "Broken and Forgiven" Athletes and Coaches. I was thankful for God's grace and forgiveness.

Unfortunately, the next day I blew it again. This time, I was playing in a big game for MLC. It was a close game, and things were not going our way when the referee made a bad call around one of my faceoffs. I can't remember what I said, but he called an unsportsmanlike penalty on me and immediately I was convicted in my spirit. Here I am, a spiritual leader, and two days in a row I fell short.

When I got home, I processed my mistakes with Gayle. The Scriptures say, "...confess your sins to each other and pray for each other so that you may be healed...."[1] I did feel better after sharing my failures and feelings with her, but in a couple hours, seven or eight Calvert Hall athletes would be coming to our townhouse for our FCA "Leaders" Bible study. We were meeting every Sunday night outside of our Thursday morning FCA Huddle to go even deeper into God's Game Plan, and to really share life together. I felt totally unworthy to lead the group, and considered canceling.

When the guys arrived, I shared a little about my struggles and told them we were going to call an "audible" and instead of going down into our basement as usual, we were going to Friendly's for ice cream and that instead of me leading, I would have each of them share their favorite scripture or one thing that they had been learning lately. I was feeling really down, but the plan seemed to work well. I told the group the ice cream was on me, so they all ordered these huge

"Jim Dandy" sundaes, and openly shared from their Bibles.

As we were walking out of the restaurant, a young woman who was sitting at a table with her boyfriend grabbed my arm and asked if I was a minister. I said "no" and wanted to tell her what a sinner I was. She asked what we were doing with the Bibles and what kind of group we were.

When I told her we were a part of an FCA Huddle, her eyes lit up, and she told me she had been involved with FCA when she was a cheerleader in college. The whole time, her boyfriend was rolling his eyes and shaking his head. She then asked if I knew of any fellowship like FCA, but for adults. I mentioned we had just started a small group in our home and gave her my business card.

I never expected to hear from her again, but a couple days later she called me. "Hey Frank, this is Kim Kirkwood, the lady you met at Friendly's Sunday night. Are you still open to me and possibly my boyfriend, Tom Bonvissuto, checking out your small group?"

"Sure," I said.

Then she told me how Tom was basically an atheist, and had been in a band called "Lucifer," so he would most likely not be joining her.

Sure enough, the next week Kim showed up to small group, and somehow convinced Tom to come as well. They were both quiet at first, but over time they really opened up. And Tom was great—he was honest about what he didn't believe and why, and asked really tough questions that other people think, but usually don't have the courage to ask.

Over time, it was amazing to see our neighbors Chuck and Ellen, then our new friends Tom and Kim, come to fully surrender their lives to the Creator and fully embrace Jesus as their Lord and Savior.

Today, they are each leaders who love God, and share His love and truth in a variety of unique and powerful ways. I love being teammates in the Gospel with friends like that.

CHAPTER 25

Lacrosse at FCA Camp

"Many are the plans in a person's heart,
but it is the Lord's purpose that prevails."

Proverbs 19:21

After a year back home in Baltimore and seeing God at work in the different areas He had called me to, I decided to take Mark Gassman up on his offer to start lacrosse as a new option at the FCA sports camp at Gettysburg College. When I called, he was thrilled to give this game he knew nothing about a shot, hoping it would bring more kids to camp to hear the "Good News."

In college, I began the practice of journaling some of my prayers and praises, and keeping notes on things I was learning that I might want to access again in the future. In my 1988 prayer journal, I wrote "God, please raise up 50 kids for this first-ever FCA Lacrosse camp."

I was not sure where the lacrosse campers would come from that first year, but just sensed God wanted me to do it.

God, in His sovereignty, had led two of the relatively few committed and passionate followers of Jesus that I knew of in the lacrosse world at the time to Gettysburg College. Hank Janczyk was the head lacrosse coach there, and Fred Opie, a dynamic long-stick defender who had played at Syracuse University, was a graduate assistant and Coach Janczyk's defensive coordinator.

Coach Janczyk was holding his own lacrosse camp at Gettysburg College the same week as the FCA camp, and Fred was helping him, so I called them. "I'm trying to start lacrosse at the FCA camp the same week as your camp. Can you help me a little?"

Fred Opie (#34) played defense for the Syracuse Orangemen.

"Sure, we can help," they said. The three of us agreed to pray for God to bless this effort.

Frederick Douglass Opie

I met Fred, who was named after the famous abolitionist Frederick Douglass, when we played on the same team at a summer tournament in Connecticut, in 1985. It didn't take long before we discovered we were both believers and followers of Jesus, which was not very common in the lacrosse world at that time. It was easy to feel spiritually alone and isolated as a lacrosse player trying to live out your faith.

I bumped into Fred, literally, a couple years later, after he had graduated from Syracuse and I had graduated from Cornell. Our Maryland Lacrosse Club Team was scrimmaging his Long Island Lacrosse Club Team in an early March exhibition in Baltimore. I had won a fast-break faceoff and was flying down the field when Fred laid me out. It was a clean hit, and he put me on my back. When I looked up, I saw Fred's big smile as he helped me up off the ground. I thought, "Hey, I remember that guy!"

After the scrimmage, we got to talking and had a few laughs about his big hit, and even more importantly, about life, family and faith. We really connected, realizing we were more than just competitors who loved the Creator's game; we were brothers in Christ.

It was providential when three months later, our club teams met for the United States Club Lacrosse Association (USCLA) National Championship on Homewood Field at Johns Hopkins University. Fred's Long Island Lacrosse Club beat our Maryland Lacrosse Club team in a close game, but the crazy thing was

Playing in the 1987 USCLA Championship on Homewood Field at Johns Hopkins University

Being presented the 1987 USCLA Championship Offensive MVP Award—a dyed USA stick

that Fred got named the defensive MVP of the game, and I was named the offensive MVP of the game. Even though the greatest players in the world, including many U.S. National Team players, were on those two teams, there we were, in the middle of the field after the game, holding our awards.

It was the following spring when I reached out to Fred about possibly helping coach the first-ever FCA Lacrosse Camp I was trying to coordinate that summer. I knew Fred was a graduate assistant at Gettysburg College, getting his master's degree in African American history, but I wasn't sure he would be around in the summer during our FCA camp dates. It turned out that Fred was going to be on campus helping Coach Janczyk with his Gettysburg Lacrosse Camp, and he would be able to help between sessions.

Do Not Despise Small Beginnings

Although I prayed and planned for 50 kids, with only two weeks left before the start of camp, Mark Gassman called to tell me that only six had pre-registered for lacrosse. Should we cancel? Hank and Fred were going to be there anyway, so we decided to go forward.

A couple of the FCA football coaches brought their families and they sent a

Fred Opie coaching at FCA Lacrosse Camp

few of their eight- to ten-year-old children over to play lacrosse, so we ended up with a total of nine kids at the first FCA Lacrosse Camp.

Though we only offered boys lacrosse at the time, one of our nine campers was a young girl whose dad was coaching football. She was probably our toughest player, hidden under the boy's helmet, shoulder pads and gloves.

With a 3-to-1 player-to-coach ratio, and the young ages of these lacrosse campers, at times we felt more like the camp daycare option but, at the end of the day, those kids received highly personalized instruction—both in lacrosse and in God's Word. Coach Moran, who was volunteering at Coach Janczyk's camp, also stopped over to support me and talk to the FCA kids, which was great.

Besides lacrosse, the kids had plenty of fun when the FCA campers from all the sports gathered together for meals, swimming, games, music, and the evening fellowship times.

This FCA Lacrosse Camp idea might have legs!

MORE TO THE STORY...

I'll Be There –Fred Opie

Meeting Frank in 1985 was the highlight of that Connecticut tournament for me and, even then, he mentioned that he wanted to do some kind of lacrosse ministry. When he asked me a couple of years later about helping with the lacrosse camp at Gettysburg College, where I had just started graduate school and coaching with Hank Janczyk, I told him, "I'll be there!"

That first camp felt a lot like babysitting, but it was a lot of fun. I was grateful to use the platform and bright light that God shined on me after I scored my long-pole-behind-the-back-goal on national television and in front of a sold-out stadium crowd in the 1985 NCAA Division I Championship game to give glory to God and to help FCA Lacrosse get started.

A Mustard Seed – Hank Janczyk

No matter how many players showed up, I was committed to supporting lacrosse at the FCA camp at Gettysburg College and introducing God into kids' lives through the Creator's game. I believed that Frank had a vision from the Lord and like anything worthwhile, you have to try new ideas and stick to them.

I saw God's hand at work all during those first camps. Frank, Fred, and I each had opportunities to share our faith in the huddles. We had a tone we wanted to set and life lessons we wanted to teach to help the kids grow as people and open up with their friends. The camaraderie and honest sharing we witnessed during the week convinced us there was something right about what we were doing and that lacrosse at FCA is going to happen! We talked about what it could become in the future.

I was amazed at what grew out of the little mustard seed at Gettysburg College in 1988 and honored to be a part of its beginning.

CHAPTER 26

Coaches Are Key

"Do not despise these small beginnings,
for the Lord rejoices to see the work begin..."

Zechariah 4:10 (NLT)

W hen I was at FCA camp coaching lacrosse, I got to interact with Mark Gassman and the other sports' coaches and volunteer leaders. During our mealtimes in the dining hall, I learned a lot, including that someone from FCA usually attended the national coaches conventions for the major sports, such as the American Football Coaches Association convention and the college basketball Final Four luncheon.

The goal of attending was to connect coaches to God and His Word, which FCA often refers to as "God's Game Plan." It was also an opportunity to expose them to the FCA ministry so they might support huddles at their schools and volunteer at FCA summer camps.

Hmmm, maybe I should go to the 1988 US Lacrosse Coaches Convention in December. Hank Janczyk, Fred Opie and Coach Moran would be there. I was coaching at Calvert Hall. *I'll do it!*

At the convention in Connecticut, I suggested to Hank and Fred, "Why don't we try to coordinate an FCA Coaches Breakfast or something? We can try to plant seeds and share about how FCA can support them and their teams."

Our first "breakfast" consisted of about eight people huddled around two round tables with coffee and a couple of boxes of donuts set up in the lobby of the hotel. Hank shared a brief devotion, others shared their personal faith stories, and together we closed with prayer. The group was small, but our hearts were sincere.

Hank gave us some credibility because he was a head coach at a top school, Gettysburg College, and although his first year was 1987, little did we know at the time that over the next 34 years, he would go on to become one of the most successful coaches in NCAA history, accumulating more than 400 wins.

Another coach who came to our early FCA Coaches Breakfasts and gave us credibility was my former Cornell coach, Richie Moran. Although he wasn't at the first breakfast in the lobby, he came to almost every other breakfast or lunch that we hosted over the years. He saw my life change at Cornell and although he wasn't used to the FCA style of outreach, he was always there for me and FCA— in sickness and in health, like he was for so many of his other players as well.

We learned an important lesson our second year at the convention. Instead of just hanging around in the lobby, we wanted to look like a more official group and set up a booth in the exhibition hall among all the equipment suppliers and other vendors displaying their wares. I didn't know what an FCA booth should look like so I asked FCA headquarters in Kansas City to send someone to set up and work the booth.

The guy meant well and worked hard, but all I can say is that as a lacrosse representative, he was a heck of a college football player! He had never heard of lacrosse. Since then, we've set up our booth and worked the convention floor ourselves.

We Can Always Ask Hank

Hank recalls, "Frank, Fred, and I did most of the speaking at the first few breakfasts that FCA held at the US Lacrosse Coaches Conventions. As time went on, we worked hard to branch out with a variety of speakers and my role diminished to emergency duty— 'If we can't get anybody else, we can always ask Hank'—which was fine with me. The different speakers with their different styles and life stories helped keep the regular attendees coming back and attracted new coaches each year."

Gettysburg College Coach Hank Janczyk was one of the founding fathers of FCA Lacrosse and would go on to become second all-time in NCAA men's lacrosse victories.

He also notes, "It was always cool to see who would show up at seven o'clock on a Saturday morning at a lacrosse coaches convention where the Friday nights can go on into the wee hours. I guess you never know what's going on in somebody's life. The speaker would say something about what God had done in his life and, all of a sudden, someone would walk up to Frank or Fred or me to tell us all about their lives."

We know quite a few coaches who started or restarted their faith journeys at one of our FCA Lacrosse Coaches Breakfasts, and many who went back to their schools and started huddles.

Never underestimate the influence of a coach, even on other coaches!

Sports

ward Christian Athletes in '92

Squad' upsets Turtles

. Williams

pposed to be a case of
ns being thrown to the

Vai Lacrosse Sta

Green rdes jump
O tea
Friday
t looked
nter rs p
u reful tion unters d
erunc ences la
de only to c
9-8,
ever po
d to
ation.
A, the
but app d," used a
n as the us defense
ination o

and sheer hustle to shut down the
No. 1 seeded Turtles' potent offense, anchored by Towson State
middie Rob Shek and former
Syracuse All-American Gary Gait,
one of the all-time leading scorers
in the Major Indoor Lacrosse
League.

Gait, who had seven goals in a
22-7 Greene Turtles' shellacking of
the Vail Lacrosse Club in
Thursday's opening round, was un-
able to get into the swing of things
Friday, scoring no goals on six
shots.

"I just wasn't on today," an
Gait said. "(Thursday) everything
was going in, (Friday) nothing was
I'd say it was the altitude, but
think it was the evening activitie

Though David Kelly had ne
game-winning goal at 3:1
second overtime, it wa e

Please see Lacrosse pa

PART V

Growing Pains

CHAPTER 27

Bumps in the Road

"And we know that in all things God works for the good of those who love him,
who have been called according to his purpose."

Romans 8:28

B y 1990, attendance at our FCA Lacrosse Camp and FCA Coaches Breakfasts at the US Lacrosse Convention was starting to take off. The Calvert Hall FCA Huddle was growing, and new huddles were starting in schools throughout the area.

Also by 1990, some unique scenarios were emerging in our family business. By then, I had been in the business four years, and was vice president of sales and marketing. I figured as long as we were bringing in more business than we were losing, we had to be doing ok—right?! I was encouraged with our sales and retention numbers.

My mom had retired from the business about six months after I started in 1986, and since that time I was concerned about who was "dotting the i's" and "crossing the t's." My dad had helped bring in the business, but my mom helped administer and account for it.

It's a long story, but in late 1990, it came to our attention that our accountant, who was a good family friend, and his partner had improperly accounted for some of the premium that we had billed and collected. It affected one of our major association clients, and when we disclosed the error to the client, as well as our plan to fix it, they graciously chose to continue to work with us

Kelly Benefits' third office (corporate headquarters) after my parents started the business in our family home

(and they are fortunately still a client to this day!). Unfortunately, this situation forced us to make major reductions in our staff and other expenses, including our own salaries. We had grown to 30 employees but had to cut back to 20. That was very hard to do when we knew every employee and their families so well.

By this time, my brothers, John, David and Bryan, were all in the business, so we all had to weather this storm together. Fortunately, we each had plenty of experience overcoming challenges and storms from our college lacrosse careers.

John and his Washington College teammates played in and lost three Division III National Championship games, and his senior year, he went temporarily blind due to a degenerative eye condition called Best disease, so his college lacrosse career ended early.

David and Bryan both overcame various injuries and playing time issues as well to help lead their UNC Tar Heel teams to national championships with David as a freshman in 1986, and Bryan as a senior in 1991. These challenges ultimately led them each into a deepened relationship with God, their Creator, as they surrendered their lives to Him through different fellowship experiences they each had while in Chapel Hill as college students.

We were each individually battle-tested, but for this business challenge, we would need each other as well as Big Frank and our mom. At the time, John, David and I were married, so our wives had to step up as well, and each covered the front desk/reception area for a couple of days each week. We needed all hands on deck.

It was during this time that I was made chief operating officer, and all aspects of the business would report to me. I now had sales, marketing, administration, finance, accounting and human resources under my direction. I would be named president a few years later in 1994.

Fortunately, I was equal partners with my brothers, who each did their part to make sure the business continued to grow profitably. The business would provide each of us the flexibility to pursue God's leadings in other areas of our lives as well, which for me included FCA and my various involvements with lacrosse and other community activities.

The Bend in the Road

It was also in 1990 that our father lost his re-election bid to serve a fourth four-year term as a State Senator representing much of Baltimore County. He had taken a strong stance against a poorly written pro-abortion piece of legislation that would allow abortion on-demand through the ninth month of pregnancy with no regulations or limits. That legislative session, he ended up leading an eight-day filibuster, which killed the bill, and also ended up costing him his seat in the Democratic primary that September.

At the "party" the night of his election loss, I stood to acknowledge my dad's faith, courage and conviction and stated that, "We can see to the bend in the road, and only God can see to the end of the road." He had no bitterness or regrets, as he looked forward to the road ahead.

Our dad stood for life and little did he know how much new life God was going to bless him, my mom and our family with in the future.

Despite our challenges with the business and Big Frank's failed re-election, the huddles at Calvert Hall and Navy continued to grow. Although the momentum energized Barry Spofford and me, we had a hard time managing it all as volunteers in our spare time.

FCA Staff in Maryland

Mark Gassman suggested that we explore hiring a full-time FCA staff person for the state of Maryland to help us continue to grow. He explained that FCA operated on a faith-financed model. There's no grant money or government subsidies to pay a salary and expenses for FCA staff. We would have to help raise money through donors and events like banquets.

In the process of trying to formalize FCA in Maryland, we discovered that FCA actually had a full-time staff person in Maryland back in the 1970s, named Bill Lewis. Like Barry Spofford, he was a graduate of the U.S. Naval Academy and had risen to the rank of captain.

After leaving the Navy and joining FCA, his ministry was primarily focused on serving the Baltimore Colts and Baltimore Orioles players and coaches. We learned that Captain Bill didn't do much with school-based huddles or summer camps, but from meeting some of the former pro athletes who knew him, he was well known for always having a car trunk full of books and would give away a book or two—books of truth—to everyone he met.

I loved the idea of giving away truth, so even though I never met Captain Bill Lewis, he inspired me to keep a number of great books in the trunk of my car and in a closet in my office, which I would give to people I met or spent time with, depending on how the Spirit led.

Over the years, many people would cross my path and ask, "Frank, do you remember that book you gave me?" Most of the time I don't, but then they show me the book with the personal note I wrote in it—a word of encouragement that they loved as well. It was fun to add the word "truth" to the giving priorities of time, talent, treasure and testimony that I learned on my summer mission trip in Japan.

By God's grace, Barry and I figured out a way to raise some initial funding, and in 1990, hired a young man who not only had FCA staff experience in another state, but also the faith to move his family to come and serve as our FCA Maryland director. A year later, we decided to host a fundraising banquet at a VFW Hall in East Baltimore featuring Sam Rutigliano, the former Cleveland Browns head football coach, as guest speaker.

Toward the end of the night, we were running behind schedule. It was after 9 p.m., and as I learned the hard way, you always want to end a banquet, especially a fundraiser, before 9 p.m.

We had asked a friend named Sister Ann, a Catholic nun who was passionate about her relationship with God and His Word, to offer the closing prayer. I wanted the banquet to convey an interdenominational spirit, because although FCA is not affiliated with any one denomination, it had a reputation for being more of a Bible Belt ministry.

Over 300 people attended the banquet, many of whom I had personally invited. I wanted FCA to be a bridge to all athletes and coaches, whether they had a Catholic or Protestant faith background, or no faith background at all.

Our new director called a last-minute "audible" the night of the banquet and insisted that a youth pastor he invited from his local church should close in prayer. We had to move Sister Ann earlier in the program to share a few words.

As the youth pastor walked to the podium, I was thinking, *We're fifteen minutes late, but that's not too bad.* The youth pastor began, "I'm here to close in prayer, but before I do..." and proceeded to preach a "fire and brimstone" style message for something like ten minutes. I almost got up three times to remove him from the podium.

Finally, he said, "Okay, let us pray," and began to pray for a bit, then came out of the prayer and gave five more minutes of a narrow, fear-based message. I was infuriated, and firmly confronted our director as soon as the banquet ended.

I thought he had severely tarnished the ministry and goodwill we had been building for three years. I cried myself to sleep that night. The next day I met with Brother René, who was the president of Calvert Hall and had attended the dinner, to assure him that FCA was truly interdenominational, and was fully committed to the core tenets of the Gospel with a focus on God's love, grace, mercy and truth.

It was soon after that banquet that our "first" FCA staff person and state director decided to leave FCA to work with another ministry in another state, which was a better fit for him at the time. For several months, Barry and I were back to doing all the work of the ministry ourselves.

Captain FCA

Barry was also waiting to hear from the Naval Academy about a possible promotion to admiral. When his promotion was denied, he said to me, "Frank, in the Navy, if or when you are a captain and get skipped over for admiral, it's time to move on. I'm upset about it, but I expected it was coming. I believe God has closed this door, and even though I am not a great coach or athlete, I am feeling led to retire from the Navy and possibly take on this FCA Maryland state director position. I'll receive a nice pension, so if we could raise just $1,000 a month from donors to cover my travel expenses and such, I could be our state director. What do you think?"

Talk about a no-brainer. Barry served as Maryland's FCA director from 1992-2000 and never took more than $1,000 a month from the FCA budget. Under his leadership, the ministry exploded. For the first few years, Barry and I did what we could to support all the schools that started huddles, but we had no board of advisors or additional staff to carry any of the load.

"Frank, I want to take my time in building the board," Barry would tell me. He was patient and methodical and after a couple of years, we established an FCA Maryland Advisory Board and he asked me to chair it, which I did for more than a dozen years.

Barry believed in a part-time staff model to start. This way, he could evaluate the staff person and the staff person could decide if FCA was right for them before becoming full-time staff. He hired mostly former teachers, coaches, and business people who loved the Lord and wanted to share His love and truth through sports.

Barry hired part-time staff like Mike McMahon in Anne Arundel County and Kevin Colliton on the Eastern Shore (who are still both on staff as of this writing, more than 30 years later), as well as others in Harford, Carroll and Howard counties to support volunteers who had a heart to share the Good News through school-based huddles and summer sports camps.

Prayer Warrior

Barry was a humble prayer warrior, and under his leadership, FCA Maryland grew to having huddles in dozens of schools, hundreds of kids attending camp, and a good number of new staff joining the team. In 2000, Barry was tapped to become the vice president for the FCA Mid-Atlantic Region, which included Maryland, Washington, D.C., Virginia, Pennsylvania, New Jersey, and New York, so he passed the FCA Maryland state director baton to Rick Conniff, a former West Point football player and businessman who had served on our state board for several years.

To keep the ministry grounded in God's will, Barry hosted an annual prayer and fasting retreat for Mid-Atlantic staff members and volunteers, which started on a Tuesday at noon and ended on Thursday at noon. We met at a church in Harford County, Maryland off of Interstate 95, brought only Bibles and water, and rolled out sleeping bags on the floor to sleep.

Barry would help facilitate times of scripture reading, reflection, discussion, worship and prayer. And because we were all in it together, the time went by quickly. Even if people could only come for part of the retreat, all were welcome. I credit those retreats for establishing a strong spiritual foundation that would lead to significant transformation and growth throughout Maryland and both the Mid-Atlantic and Northeast regions.

In 2008, Barry would become FCA's first, and at that time, only, international staff person on a part-time basis. Once the FCA National Board of Trustees decided to really support and fund the international expansion of FCA, Barry gladly passed the baton to his dear friend, then FCA vice president, and FCA Lacrosse's very own Dan Britton in 2012. As of this writing, Dan is FCA's chief field officer and under his leadership, FCA has grown to more than 400 international staff in 114 countries.

After a faith-filled and courageous multi-year battle with cancer, Barry went home to be with the Lord in 2015. That year, the Barry Spofford Legacy Award was established to be given annually to a Mid-Atlantic staff person who has modeled prayer, humility and service in their relationships and work. Previous winners include Mike McMahon (MD), Harry Flaherty (NJ), Steve Medinger (MD), George Morris (VA), Lynn Kline (VA), Laura Matera (NJ), Derrick Ellison (VA), and Ted Brunner (PA).

It was an honor for me and Rick Conniff (Far Right) to present this painting to Barry Spofford (Left) in recognition of his incredible FCA leadership, impact and influence.

CHAPTER 28

When We Are Weak, He Is Strong

"In the same way, the Spirit helps us in our weakness..."

Romans 8:26

M y platform and recognition in the lacrosse community grew after our MLC team won the USCLA National Club Lacrosse Championship in 1988 and expanded further the following year when The Lacrosse Foundation (which in 1998 became US Lacrosse and today is USA Lacrosse) contacted me with a request.

"Frankie, we're making an instructional video on midfield play and we heard you're not just a good faceoff player, but a really good faceoff teacher and coach as well. We would like you to teach the faceoff segment of our 'Midfield' instructional video," they said.

Vinnie Sombrotto, who played on four U.S. National teams, was going to teach a segment in the same video on shooting, and Jimmy "Darky" Darcangelo, whom I played with at MLC and who played on three U.S. National teams, would cover dodging. I was honored to be even mentioned in the same sentence with Vinnie and Darky, let alone make a video with them. And Steve Stensersen, a great faceoff middie from the University of North Carolina and Mt. Washington Lacrosse Club, would work with me on the faceoff segment.

I agreed, and according to the Foundation, *The Middie* video was their top-selling instructional video and many players and coaches said they bought it specifically for the faceoff segment.

U.S. National Team Tryout Invitations

In 1989, I received another call from US Lacrosse. They invited the 120 best players from across the country—including Fred Opie and me—to try out for the U.S. National Team that would play in the 1990 World Games in Perth, Australia. *Lord, this is amazing!*

I thought I played well in the tryouts and the head coach was Arlie Marshall, who was my coach at MLC. Arlie knew what I could do, loved my game and I thought he would advocate for me, but it wasn't meant to be. I was disappointed that I didn't make the team but grateful that I was at least in

Fred Opie on the wing for a faceoff for Team USA vs. Australia in the 1990 World Games

the hunt. I processed my disappointment with Gayle and my dad, who was still coming to all of my MLC games and had followed the U.S. National Team tryouts as closely as he could.

Fred was selected, which made him the first African American to play on a U.S. National lacrosse team. Fred and Team USA won the gold medal at the World Championship in Australia that next summer.

I continued playing for MLC and in 1992, we won the USCLA Southern Division by beating Mt. Washington in overtime, then won the USCLA National Championship by beating the Northern Division Champions, Brine Lacrosse Club, on Long Island. That was special to win a national championship like that with my brother, Bryan, starting on defense, me starting at faceoff/midfield, and David starting on attack.

After winning the 1992 USCLA National Championship on Long Island, New York with my brothers David and Bryan

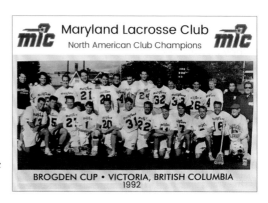

Maryland Lacrosse Club
North American Club Champions

BROGDEN CUP • VICTORIA, BRITISH COLUMBIA
1992

We would later go on to win the North American Club Championship, defeating Victoria Lacrosse Club in a two-out-of-three "Brogden Cup" championship series in Victoria, British Columbia, Canada. It was a great honor when I was named Most Valuable Player of that championship series.

Between the MLC championships and the FCA Miracle in the Mountains team, I was still playing well and at a very competitive level when US Lacrosse invited me to try out for the national team again in 1993. This time they also invited my brother Bryan, who was one of the top defensemen in the country, and I now knew the ropes and had higher expectations. The tryouts consisted of a series of games over a four-day weekend. Again, there were 120 invitees, so they could form six equally balanced 20-man teams to scrimmage each other.

On Saturday night, the last night of games, they usually put the top 40 players they are still considering on one of two teams to play each other in what many guys called "The Game." There were still six teams of 20 guys each, so there were three final games on Saturday night, but one of the three final games was supposedly "The Game." Most players knew if they were still in the hunt to make the 23-man roster.

Based on the guys on my team and the other team, I was pretty sure I was playing in "The Game!" I was thankful to be in it, and even more thankful that I played one of the best games of my life. Afterward, a number of my teammates, including John Tucker, and others who were former U.S. National Team players, came up to congratulate me. "Frankie, you're in! You're going to make it!"

I thought it was going to be between me, Jon Reese, who was a do-it-all middie and faceoff guy from Yale, and Chris Flynn, who had played for that year's U.S. National team coach, Tony Seaman, at the University of Pennsylvania.

But something crazy happened the next morning. Coach Seaman, who had coached against me when he was the head coach at Penn and I was at Cornell, called everyone in for an update. "Gentlemen, the Federation of International Lacrosse (FIL) met this weekend in England and made a rule change," he said. "They capped the rosters at 20 players instead of 23, so we will be carrying three fewer guys than we planned. This will mostly affect some of the specialty positions like long pole and faceoff."

What? Is this the Syracuse game my freshman year at Cornell all over again?

A week later, I was at FCA Lacrosse Camp in Gettysburg. We had over 100 lacrosse campers in attendance so we needed all hands on deck helping coach and lead the huddles. During the week, I was praying and hoping for good news from the US Lacrosse National Team Selection Committee and Coach Seaman.

I was really disappointed when Gayle called me and read the letter telling me I was not selected. Unfortunately, my brother Bryan was not selected either. I had worked hard and played well. But I remembered what my father taught me and prayed, *Lord, this hurts, but through my tears, I praise you. Thank you, Jesus.* I was glad I was at camp because I didn't have much time to mope around.

Jon Reese and Chris Flynn were not selected either as I guess Coach Seaman chose not to use a

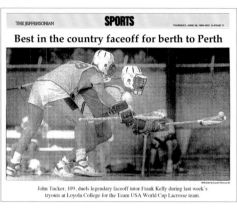

Best in the country faceoff for berth to Perth

John Tucker, 109, duels legendary faceoff tutor Frank Kelly during last week's tryouts at Loyola College for the Team USA World Cup Lacrosse team.

Facing off against my friend John Tucker during the evaluations for the 1990 U.S. National Team

roster spot for a pure faceoff athlete. They did select Tim Soudan, who had been an All-American at the University of Massachusetts and Ryan Wade, who had been an All-American at UNC. Both were great athletes and middies who could faceoff, but I still thought they should have a dedicated faceoff man as well.

A few months later, the FIL reversed its reduced roster decision and allowed each country to add back three players. Coach Seaman picked Chris Flynn as the faceoff specialist.

Flynn was an amazing player, and one of the best two-sport athletes to ever play at Penn, but I thought I was a better faceoff man statistically than him, especially when we went head-to-head at the tryouts. It was painful, but I guess I could understand why Coach Seaman picked his former Penn star over me. And who knows, maybe I wasn't really even in the mix despite my feelings about how I played and what a lot of guys told me. Regardless, it still hurt bad.

To help the national team prepare for the World Games the next summer, US Lacrosse invited a select group of players who had been cut from the National Team to play an exhibition game against them before they left for Manchester, England—the site of the 1994 World Games. I still had a chip on my shoulder and didn't want to play, but the game was in my backyard at Johns Hopkins University so I agreed to do it. I played well, had a lot of success at the faceoff X, and our collection of backups actually beat the U.S. National Team that night.

The pain and disappointment of not making the 1994 U.S. National Team took a while to heal. But years later, I could see that God had used those tryouts and even that exhibition game to plant a seed in me for a different kind of international team—the idea for a team that was focused on greater things than even winning a world championship.

CHAPTER 29

Open Doors

"Praying at the same time for us as well, that God will open up to us a door for the word, so that we may speak forth the mystery of Christ..."

Colossians 4:3 (NASB)

I first met Dan Britton in 1990 when he came on staff with FCA in Northern Virginia. Dan had been a captain and All-Conference attackman at the University of Delaware, so when his dad, Ed Britton (who himself had been a star lacrosse player at the U.S. Naval Academy) connected us, I had a feeling our relationship would become special.

A year after we initially met, we ended up playing on the same professional lacrosse team: The Baltimore Thunder of the newly named Major Indoor Lacrosse League (MILL). I had played for the Thunder a couple of years in the late 1980s and decided to come back, in part because Dan was on the team. Although he was an attackman in college, he played more of a defensive, enforcer type of role in the MILL. He even made the All-Star team one year because of his tenacity.

It was special when the Thunder marketed a Family, Faith and FCA night at the Baltimore Arena after one of our games. Hundreds of people, including a number of the Calvert Hall FCA Huddle members and players I coached hung around after the game to hear each of our faith stories and the exciting opportunities to get involved in FCA.

It was after our Baltimore Thunder season together that we ended up at our fourth year of FCA La-

Getting ready to faceoff (yellow helmet) in an MILL Thunder game at the Baltimore Arena

crosse Camp at Gettysburg College, and we discussed the idea of taking a team to the Vail Lacrosse Shootout, which we did that next summer in 1992 when we had our Miracle in the Mountains experience together.

It was great to have Dan around to bounce FCA ideas off of as it related to camp and our outreach breakfasts at the US Lacrosse Coaches Convention. I helped get things started in 1988 and 1989, but with Dan's energy and experience as an FCA staff representative in Virginia, we were able to take things to another level.

While I was working with Barry Spofford to build FCA throughout the state of Maryland, Dan and I worked together to grow what would come to be known all over the country, and even around the world, as FCA Lacrosse. But in order to really grow and have the greatest possible influence in the lacrosse world, we thought we would eventually have to hire a full-time FCA Lacrosse director to focus on the impact opportunities of future FCA Lacrosse teams, camps and coaches outreach events.

The problem was FCA hadn't done "sports-specific" team ministry like this. Yet!

FCA Lacrosse Staff

Our first FCA Lacrosse staff person would come to us in a very unique way, and not in the exact timeframe we were hoping for.

"The lacrosse world is like a big family," Dan Britton said. "Everybody knows everybody and news travels fast. As soon as we beat the Greene Turtle at the Vail Shootout in 1992, the entire lacrosse community knew what happened.

"That game was a key milestone for FCA Lacrosse. It opened doors for the word to go forth because people loved hearing the story. Frank and I began to think, *Okay, Lord, you allowed this to happen by your gracious hand, and now we want to steward this the best way possible to have greater reach and greater influence for you in the lacrosse world.*"

When we told the Vail story at FCA camps, kids would stand up and cheer like they were at the game itself. Sean McNamara was one of the campers who heard Dan tell it at the Gettysburg College camp the week after it happened. How Sean got to camp was a God story in itself.

In 1992, Sean was a rising high school junior in Rochester, New York. He had saved his money all year to go to the Hobart College lacrosse camp—but his mom forgot to register him. By the time he realized it, the camp had sold out.

Sean asked his next-door neighbor, who coached lacrosse, if he knew of any other camps. "I'm actually going to an FCA Lacrosse camp at Gettysburg College where I will be coaching, and you are welcome to come with me," he said, "but you need to know there is a faith-based component to it and I leave tomorrow!"

"That's okay," Sean said. "I just really want to go to a lacrosse camp."

Sean's neighbor had committed to help set up the camp two days before the campers came, which meant that Sean also arrived two days early. "I sat through the staff training session," Sean recalled, "and towards the end, the leader said all they had left to do was pray for the campers, then they would play basketball. I couldn't wait to play basketball and thought to myself, *I hope they say a quick Our Father so we get out of here soon.*

"But no, the prayer took a while. They handed out sheets of paper with the names of all the campers, and then I listened as these grown men prayed for each name. I was blown away by how much love and passion those men had for names on a piece of paper of people they had never met. Listening to that caused me to ask my huddle leader, Dan Britton, a lot of questions throughout the week. I didn't really understand how personal God's love was for me until Dan and the other speakers unpacked the scriptures."

On the lacrosse field with the great Peter Kohn

Peter Kohn, a man with special gifts (we believe he was on the autism spectrum) who volunteered at the camp as the equipment manager, also made an impact on Sean. "Since I was there early, they asked me to help Peter carry his bags of equipment from the bus station when he arrived," Sean recalled. "During the week, I also helped him knock on doors a couple of mornings to wake up all the campers.

"I sensed Peter's unique and intimate relationship with God, and I had never met anyone with such an extraordinary reverence for God's Word. If he ever found a Bible on the ground, he'd pick it up, hug it, kiss it, and place it up on a table or a bench. All week he constantly reminded me and the rest of the campers about all God's promises in the Bible."

By the time Pat Kelly, the former Baltimore Oriole, spoke on the last night of camp, Sean's heart was open to his message. "God touched me that night, July 8, 1992, and I walked forward to acknowledge my desire to surrender my life to God and receive Jesus Christ as my Lord and Savior," Sean said.

It was crazy to think that we ran from the fields in Vail, barely made it on the flight back to Baltimore, and somehow made it to Gettysburg College in time for the start of FCA Lacrosse Camp. And to think about the influence that camp in 1992 had on the life of Sean and so many others.

Ooh, Gross!

My brother David was one of our most popular coaches and huddle leaders at camp. He understood the game, had played at a very high level, was strong in his faith and was very funny. David would say and do things others would only think about possibly saying or doing, and the kids loved it.

We'll never forget the year David took a couple of brownies from the dining hall and rolled them into an oblong heap and laid it by one of the goals. It looked like a very large dog had relieved itself right there in the crease.

"Coach, look at this!" the goalie shrieked when he saw it. "There's a.... a piece... come here and see this!"

The other kids followed David as he walked over to the brown mound, leaned over, looked at it, picked it up, and sniffed it. He got the reaction he wanted from the kids.

"Ooooh gross!"

Then he took a big bite out of it, and the kids all freaked out.

Everyone knew who "Coach David" was at that camp because he was so goofy and crazy, yet I knew he was really inspired when he heard Pat Kelly speak and saw hundreds of kids, including young Sean McNamara, walk forward to open their hearts to having a personal relationship with God, the Creator, through His son Jesus Christ.

David said, "I liked to have fun and make people laugh, but the year I heard Pat Kelly's message and saw the response of so many campers, I was blown away."

Another highlight for David was when he shared his own faith story and journey for the first time. "My story and message were not nearly as moving as Pat Kelly's, but for me, sharing my testimony was a bold step outside of my comfort zone and an opportunity to point the kids to the Lord while making them laugh."

We're Official

Dan mentored Sean after the 1992 FCA Lacrosse Camp, through high school and over his four years at Randolph-Macon College where he played goalie.

Sean interned at FCA for two summers and, after graduating in 1998, we offered him a full-time position. He laughs about his interview with me and Dan.

"I'll do it, but I'm not going to ask any-body to donate money to me," he told us, after our ten-minute job interview with him.

We had offered him $500 a month to come on board as the first paid staff person working to build an FCA ministry focused solely on the lacrosse community.

"I need it to be a full-time job," he told us.

"It can be full time," we said, "and you

Sean McNamara (Center), Dan Britton (Right) and Peter Kohn (Left) at the 1992 FCA Lacrosse Camp

don't have to ask anyone for money, but we only have $6,000 in the bank account, so we can pay you $500 a month."

Sean graduated from Randolph-Macon College on a Sunday and started work with FCA Lacrosse the following Tuesday, June 1, 1998.

We helped him supplement his income by offering him a part-time job in the file room at Kelly Benefits, and he also coached lacrosse at Messiah College in Mechanicsburg, Pennsylvania, about an hour north of the Kelly Benefits offices in Hunt Valley, Maryland.

Sean recalls, "Every day I drove from where I lived in downtown Baltimore to the Kelly offices in Hunt Valley, then up to Messiah College, then back to downtown Baltimore. It wasn't easy to make ends meet. But since my first FCA camp at age sixteen, I had signed up for everything I could with FCA, led the FCA Huddle at Randolph-Macon, and interned with FCA Virginia for two summers. I loved everyone I had met in the organization and I loved lacrosse, so the job was a perfect fit.

"And although the first lacrosse camp and coaches convention breakfast were in 1988, when I became the first FCA Lacrosse staff person in 1998, FCA created an account number for me and the lacrosse ministry, which would allow us to dream bigger and be positioned for the growth God had planned. FCA Lacrosse was now official!"

Sean was soon reminded of how far the lacrosse ministry had to go when he went to his first staff training meeting at the FCA headquarters in Kansas City, and his nametag said he was from Lacrosse, Wisconsin. That's about as much as anyone at the training knew about the Creator's game, but that was about to change.

CHAPTER 30

Camp Cap Opportunity

"Truly, truly, I say to you, unless a grain of wheat falls into the earth and dies, it remains alone; but if it dies, it bears much fruit."

John 12:24 (ESV)

After the amazing summer of 1992, we were more excited than ever to return with a men's team to the Vail Lacrosse Shootout, and to grow our summer lacrosse camp.

For the next six summers, we took an FCA men's team to Colorado, and although we always seemed to make it to the final four, we never made it to the championship game again. Every year, however, God used the trip to bless the FCA Lacrosse ministry. More and more players and family members came, which enriched the fellowship and sharing times. We enjoyed God's creation while fishing out on the lakes and whitewater rafting on the rivers. The trips were always about playing great lacrosse and sharing God's love and truth with others, while growing in our own relationships with God.

The growth in teams playing in Vail also sparked greater awareness, and thus interest in the FCA Lacrosse Camp at Gettysburg College. In 1994,

We not only played high-level lacrosse, we had a lot of fun whitewater rafting and enjoying God's creation.

around 110 players registered for lacrosse. Barry Spofford, who managed the camps then, called me and said, "Frank, I'm going to call this a good problem, but we don't have room for everyone who registered for lacrosse. Because of space limitations, we need to cap each sport, including lacrosse, at 100 campers."

We were able to finagle a few

more spots and accommodate most registrants. But we solved the "problem" the following year. With Barry's blessing, we eventually spun off a separate lacrosse-only camp under the banner of FCA.

Once FCA Lacrosse was responsible for all aspects of the camp, including coaches, huddle leaders, a worship team, platform speakers, registration, lodging, meals, etc., we had to take our "camp game," to the next level. Many former Calvert Hall Lacrosse players who went on to become reputable college players, my brothers, and other contacts Dan, Hank and Fred had were the key to the success of the camp. We wanted all the boys to have a tremendous experience on and off the field, and most importantly, to see every athlete and coach who attended camp grow in their relationship with God.

After Sean came on staff full-time in 1998, our FCA Lacrosse Camps went to the next level. Because he could focus full-time on building the recruitment of potential campers, coaches, huddle leaders and speakers, the camp ministry grew rapidly.

Through Dan, we were even able to attract great speakers like national best-selling author and platform speaker, Jon Gordon. Jon had played lacrosse at Cornell about eight years after me, and he tells stories about how Coach Moran used to encourage him to go to church, even though he was Jewish.

Jon would tell Coach, "Remember Coach, I'm Jewish."

Coach Moran would say "That's fine, it will still be good for you."

Little did Coach Moran know that he was planting seeds that would years later be a part of Jon's story of coming to a personal faith in Jesus as the Messiah, and the connection to his Creator that he had longed for.

Jon came to FCA Lacrosse camps primarily to support his daughter, Jade, who was playing middle school lacrosse at the time. It was a great time for them to travel together to and from camp, and for Jon to enjoy the same fellowship gatherings as his daughter. Each day, Jon graciously offered to do a post-breakfast message to all the coaches before they would go out on the field for the day. It turned out to have a huge influence on our volunteer coaches, and was a highlight for all who attended these powerful sessions.

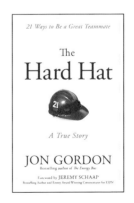

Over the years, Jon has also blessed and encouraged so many in the FCA Lacrosse community through his podcasts and books, including my favorite, *The Hard Hat*, which tells the amazing life, death and lacrosse story of Cornell Lacrosse captain George Boiardi.

We were also fortunate to have men like Mike Jolly from Michigan, literally bringing a busload of boys from Detroit each summer. God was raising up volunteers in so many unique ways, and the Creator's game was being used to connect many to the Creator through these dynamic summer lacrosse camp sessions.

MORE TO THE STORY...

One Divine Connection – Mike Jolly

Dan Britton calls it a "divine connection." I met him and Frank Kelly at a breakfast FCA hosted at a US Lacrosse Coaches Convention in the early 1990s. I coached lacrosse at De La Salle Collegiate High School near Detroit, a Christian Brothers school like Frank's Calvert Hall, and I wanted to learn more about FCA.

Dan and I kept in touch after the convention. He was playing professionally for the Baltimore Thunder and when he came to Detroit to play the Turbos, I took my team to the game.

Dan invited us into the locker room and told the kids about the FCA Lacrosse camps. I was looking for an instructional camp because many of these guys had never played lacrosse before. There weren't many camp options in Michigan or the Midwest at that time, and, knowing Dan, I was confident that the FCA camp would provide both excellent instruction and a meaningful faith opportunity for the kids—who were excited about taking a road trip.

That summer, about a dozen of us drove for two days and pulled up to Gettysburg College in our huge bus.

The kids had a terrific experience. The level of lacrosse was top notch. My players improved their skills and they had fun. I saw a lot of laughter and excitement on the fields. What I didn't see were microscopes—critical examinations of a player's ability with pressure to perform. The coaches were there to teach, not to recruit. They accepted every player at their existing skill level and helped them get better. The positive reinforcement and absence of egos made for a better experience.

Studying the Bible and hearing about a personal relationship with Christ was eye-opening for many of my players. I watched groups of them huddled under shady trees engaged in give-and-take discussions with their huddle leaders.

I listened as one of my players spoke from his heart in front of the entire camp on "open microphone night" about the friendships he had made, the discoveries he had made about his faith, and how grateful he was for his huddle leader and everybody around him. He is now a teacher at De La Salle, an assistant football and golf coach, and a former assistant lacrosse coach.

Though I didn't coach at the camps, the FCA staff let me sit in on the coaches' sessions after lunch. Dan and other staff members led some of the sessions and outside speakers led others. I especially enjoyed Jon Gordon, author of *The Energy Bus* and several other inspiring books. His talks struck a chord with me and I ordered all of his books as soon as I got home.

I applied what I absorbed at the camps back at De La Salle. I began inviting players to offer prayers at the beginning and end of every practice and game. We started an FCA Huddle and, years later, one of the huddle captains became the principal at De La Salle. I set up an FCA camp scholarship fund to help players who otherwise couldn't afford to go.

Dan Britton always says that we should expect every conversation to have a God story on the back end of it, and that is true for us. Players from De La Salle became regulars at FCA Lacrosse camps—hundreds of campers over the years. The impact has been generational, and it all stems from my "divine connection" at a convention.

Special Times – Jon Gordon

FCA Lacrosse camps were some of the most special times of my life, and I was just a parent! I attended several FCA Lacrosse camps so I could hang out with my teenage daughter, Jade, and I was there when she gave her life to Jesus.

The power of the Holy Spirit flows in a huge way at those camps. Young men and women give their lives to God and you see the transformation happen. They weep as they release the heavy weight that they're carrying and their burdens and their pain. Seeing the power of faith in the lives of the campers lifted my spirit.

The camps also gave me an opportunity to recharge and go deeper in my own faith. Dan Britton invited me to speak to the coaches each day, and my conversations with Dan, Frank Kelly, Hank Janczyk, and the other coaches nourished my soul. I felt an incredible connection with God at the evening worship and teaching times. I can't explain it, but both Jade and I experienced it first-hand, and it was special.

CHAPTER 31

Boards and Banquets

*"They devoted themselves to the apostles' teaching and to fellowship,
to the breaking of bread and to prayer."*

Acts 2:42

One of the main tenets of FCA is that it is "volunteer intensive." In many ways, it is the job of FCA staffers to engage, equip and empower volunteers like coaches, passionate parents, and other youth and adult leaders to use sports to share the Good News in a relevant and life-changing manner.

More qualified FCA staff almost always leads to more quality volunteer coaches and leaders.

When I first got involved with FCA as a volunteer in 1987, there was no FCA staff in Maryland and only a few throughout the Mid-Atlantic and Northeast regions.

Over time, it became clear that to hire staff and grow the impact and influence of the ministry, we had to raise money. It has been said that "money is the fuel for ministry," because with no money there is no staff, and where there is no staff, it is hard to reach and mobilize coaches and other volunteer leaders.

In FCA's model, the growth of state and local volunteer advisory boards was the key to raising resources and supporting and encouraging staff.

Before I knew it, I was not only chairing the FCA Maryland Board, I was also functioning as the unofficial board chair and leader for FCA Lacrosse, which I would do for more than a decade, until Sean McNamara came on staff.

Working closely with Barry and FCA Maryland, we knew we had to raise financial resources in order to hire more staff and expand the influence. We determined that the most effective way to do that was through an annual fundraising banquet or dinner. We realized these banquets were a great way to share the FCA story, to make friends, build connections and raise money.

It was our job as board members to get people in the room for the banquet so the attendees could see and hear the vision and be given the opportunity to join the team.

As a local FCA board member, I never looked at it as asking people for money, but as giving people a chance to make a great investment and join a winning team that was helping lives be transformed for eternity.

Barry and I never forgot the first FCA Maryland Banquet we were involved with. In certain ways it was a disaster, and over time we did our best to make each successive banquet better than the last.

We learned that one of the biggest challenges with an annual FCA banquet is securing a top-quality keynote speaker that can help to attract corporate sponsors, guests and potential new friends and donors.

For more than three decades, the FCA Maryland Banquet, or Victory Celebration, which has been renamed several times, has featured professional and college athletes and coaches, and even former Olympic champions. And we have been fortunate to have great Masters of Ceremony, like former Ohio State and Baltimore Colts star linebacker, and local sports radio personality, Stan White. Stan loves the ministry of FCA and has served as an advisory board member for decades.

Ravens and Banquet Favorites

Fortunately, because of a strong relationship with the Baltimore Ravens and their chaplain, Johnny Shelton (who has a long background with FCA), when in doubt, we have been able to secure a top Ravens player or coach, and sometimes their spouse as well. And for many years, we knew if we were in a real pickle, we could always count on multi-time All-Pro kicker and two-time Super Bowl Champion, Matt Stover. Matt played 20 years in the NFL, thirteen with the Ravens, and when he retired in 2011, was the NFL's fourth all-time leading scorer.

Matt had been involved with FCA in high school and college, but his faith really went from his head to his heart, and his relationship with God began to grow in his first year in the NFL with the New York Giants. Matt was humble and could connect with people in a real way. He also had kids who were involved with FCA and FCA Lacrosse, so he could talk about the ups and downs of parenting as well. Everyone in the room could relate.

I've witnessed many incredible moments during FCA banquets. One of my favorites had to be in March of 2012. The November prior, we asked Baltimore Ravens Head Coach John Harbaugh to speak at our upcoming FCA Maryland Victory Celebration and Fundraising Banquet that would be in March at Martin's West (the same location where I got my first trophy as an eight-year-old member of the Orange Crush football team).

The Ravens had recently lost three games in a row and were close to being out of contention for the playoffs. Despite this time of challenge, John graciously agreed. Little did he, or we, know that after he said yes, the Ravens would go on a long winning streak and end up winning the Super Bowl. John and the Ravens defeated the San Francisco 49ers and their head coach at the time (John's brother), Jim Harbaugh, in New Orleans.

A month after their Super Bowl victory, John spoke at our FCA banquet and our normal attendance, which had grown to 700 people at that time, doubled to more than 1,400. Needless to say, we raised a record amount of resources which enabled us to hire additional staff and expand the ministry's impact.

Another banquet favorite of mine was when former Baltimore Raven All-

Interviewing NFL Hall of Famer Ed Reed

Pro safety and NFL Hall of Famer Ed Reed was our guest speaker. Since Ed was not a professional speaker, we thought it would be best for someone to interview him to make sure we heard some of his amazing life and faith stories, especially key questions and insights we wanted to highlight. The staff asked me to interview Ed in front of our nearly 800 guests, which was a lot of fun.

Yet, over the years, the highlights and stories of the greatest impact have been those of the local coaches and student-athletes who have been influenced and transformed by the ministry of FCA. At one banquet, a college student-athlete, who came to a personal faith in Jesus through the influence of FCA Lacrosse, was baptized on the banquet stage. It's fun to be on a team of volunteers and local advisory board members who help support that type of life transformation.

It's amazing to think that one day we would not only have an annual FCA Maryland Banquet, but ten local area banquets as well, together raising more than $5 million each year to support more than 75 staff throughout the state, who would support the student-led FCA Huddles in more than 300 Maryland schools. Our FCA Lacrosse Advisory Board and staff would also eventually raise over $2 million per year through annual contributions and team fees to support more than a dozen FCA Lacrosse staff across the country and around the world.

God was at work, and we were along for the ride!

THE FCA MARYLAND O.J. BRIGANCE COURAGE AWARD

The O.J. Brigance Courage Award was established in 2018 by then-FCA Maryland State Director Shaun Smithson and is presented each year at the FCA Maryland Banquet to a student-athlete or coach who exemplifies faith, focus and fortitude by overcoming adversity in their life, like the award's namesake, O.J. Brigance. O.J. played on the 2001 Baltimore Ravens Super Bowl Team, and six years later, in 2007, was diagnosed with ALS (Lou Gehrig's disease).

In 2008, O.J. and his wife Chanda established the Brigance Brigade Foundation (I was honored to be a founding board member along with my father) to realize a world where people touched by ALS thrive with purpose and passion.

Despite being completely paralyzed from the neck down, and only being able to communicate using his eyes to type out a message on his special computer that is then spoken through a computerized voice, O.J. brings joy, faith and passion to everything he does, including his continued work with the Ravens as the senior advisor to player development. His amazing life story is captured in his book, Strength of a Champion: Finding Faith and Fortitude Through Adversity.

Ravens players and coaches, and all he comes in contact with, love their time with O.J., as he sheds great wisdom and perspective on all of life and the role of the Creator, especially in the times of deepest challenge. FCA Maryland's O.J. Brigance Courage Award winners to date have been Coach Dave McLaughlin, Tayquon Johnson, Miles Taylor, Ashley Whitney, Coach Garrick Williams and All-Abilities camper, Kristen Higgins.

The O.J. Brigance Courage Award is presented annually to the student-athlete or coach who exemplifies faith, focus and fortitude by overcoming adversity in their life.

MORE TO THE STORY...

Seeds of Faith - Matt Stover

Frank Kelly was one of the first people I met when my NFL team, the Cleveland Browns, was moved to Baltimore and we became the Ravens in 1996. It was a uniquely challenging time, but also a great opportunity, especially getting to know people like the Kelly family, who were all passionate football fans and great friends of the ministry that would serve the Ravens players and our families.

Photo by Phil Hoffmann

As I got to know Frank, I quickly learned that he was born to innovate and lead. I don't know if I have ever been around him where he wasn't leading or influencing. I could also see that he was tender and gracious with everyone he met, yet had a deep passion to spread the Gospel and make the world a better place using the platform of FCA and FCA Lacrosse to do it.

I had been involved with FCA since my days as a kicker, punter and wide receiver at Lake Highlands High School in Dallas, Texas, where several of my teammates attended a huddle. At that time in my life, I knew that FCA and going to church were good things, but I didn't yet have a personal relationship with the Lord.

I admired how my FCA classmates lived out their faith, stood courageously and didn't fall into the temptations of the party scene like I had. I aspired to be strong like them, so I attended the huddle, but I kind of had one foot in and one foot out, and I did not have the Holy Spirit in me yet.

The seeds of faith were planted in my heart through FCA, but it would take a number of years before those seeds took root and my relationship with God would become personal, real and life changing.

During our years in Baltimore, I watched Frank take the initiative to connect many people to the Lord and build a team of like-minded athletes and coaches to build FCA Lacrosse in Maryland and eventually across the country, and even around the world.

My wife Debbie and I were thrilled to have all three of our children, Jacob, Jenna and Joe, play for FCA Lacrosse, either on club teams or national teams in Vail and Lake Placid.

Through that experience, they were each able to fellowship with other athletes desiring to grow in their relationship with God, and to play lacrosse and other sports for the glory of God and with his strength, not just their own.

Playing for FCA gave them the freedom to fail. Even our son Jacob, who became an All-American goalie at Loyola University in Maryland had to deal with goals being scored on him and tough losses. FCA Lacrosse taught him to see it as the Lord sees it—as a challenge in the context of His love. Do you still trust Me? Do you still believe I am in control and that I love you? Are you leaning on Me or only on your skill?

For athletes, it's incredibly important to know that they are loved and supported no matter what happens on the field, that they have an Abba Father, who is watching them and enjoying everything they do, regardless of their stats.

I believe in the mission of FCA and the people involved, so whenever Frank or other FCA leaders asked me to speak at the FCA Banquet, I wanted to support them. I was grateful that FCA gave me a platform to share about God's love and grace in my life, and it challenged me to not be ashamed of the Gospel. I was grateful people actually wanted to come to hear my story, and to this day I am encouraged when someone comes up to me and says, "I want you to know that your message at the FCA Banquet really impacted my life and hit me at just the right time." I remind them that it was God hitting or inspiring them, not me.

It's an encouragement to know that resources were raised at each banquet to further grow and expand the influence of FCA to reach more coaches, athletes, their families and friends with the Gospel—to me that's what FCA is all about.

CHAPTER 32

Nothing Is Impossible

"For nothing will be impossible with God."

Luke 1:37 (ESV)

I often look at the 1990s as a decade of foundational growth, not only for FCA and FCA Lacrosse, but for my family and our business as well. In many ways, they all seem connected.

Knowing we could face possible fertility challenges, Gayle and I began trying to get pregnant soon after we got married. We were 23 years old when we got married, and our hope was to have children by our mid-twenties. Realizing the chances of getting pregnant were slim, we felt led to pursue the path of adoption as well.

I'll never forget March 14, 1991. We were scheduled for our final adoption consultation with Bethany Christian Services that evening and would likely have a baby assigned to us within a few weeks. Through prayer and wise counsel, our hearts were prepared for this exciting opportunity. At the same time, we were pursuing fertility treatments in the hopes that Gayle might get pregnant.

That afternoon, I came home from work early to make sure we would be on time for our appointment with the adoption office, which was located in Crofton, Maryland, more than an hour's drive from our home. I walked into the house and Gayle was standing there with a big smile on her face.

"I have great news," she said. "I'm pregnant!"

I knew she had bloodwork that day with her doctor, but I just didn't think that is what I would hear. We hugged and cried and prayed prayers of thanksgiving for the miracle of new life in her. We also hugged and cried and prayed because we knew one of the rules of Bethany Christian Services is if you become pregnant during the adoption process, you will not be eligible for placement until at least one year after the birth of your child.

As we drove to the adoption agency appointment, we cried tears of joy and of disappointment. Our hearts and minds had been prepared for adoption, and we would have to let that go for now. The counselors at Bethany were so gracious, kind and excited for us. As we drove home, we thanked God for His goodness and began to focus and pray for a healthy pregnancy in Gayle.

God answered our prayers, and on October 31, 1991, Francis X. "Frankie" Kelly IV was born. Our second son, Stephen Patrick DeMaine Kelly, would be miraculously born three years later November 21, 1994. We could not have been more thankful to God for these amazing gifts of life.

Women and Children in Colorado

It was special having Frankie as a nine-month-old in Colorado with us for the Miracle in the Mountains experience in 1992, and then a few years later seeing both Frankie and Stephen on Gayle's hips on the sidelines of those Shootout tournament games. It wouldn't be long before they would be playing lacrosse and attending FCA Lacrosse Camp as well.

With Gayle, Frankie and Stephen at the Vail Shootout in 1995

It was during those years while Gayle was on the sidelines with our boys that she caught a vision of her own. "As I looked around the fields and noticed women's teams playing," she said, "I thought, '*Hmmmm, why not an FCA women's lacrosse team in Vail?*'"

First FCA Lacrosse women's team at the 1997 Vail Lacrosse Shootout (Gayle is the first on the left, sitting)

Exciting FCA women's lacrosse game action at the 1997 Vail Shootout

A few years later in 1997, Gayle organized the first women's team in FCA history. God provided a coach from Colorado and players from all over the country.

Gayle recalled, "We all showed up in Vail and *Wow!* We played in the Shootout! There were no sudden death, game-winning shots heard around the lacrosse world, but just being there for the friendship and fellowship was miraculous enough for me."

I got to hang out on the sidelines with Frankie and Stephen and really cheer "Mom" and all the FCA women laxers on. They were awesome!

A Priceless Picture

The following year in 1998, at the age of 34, I played my last Open/Elite Men's division game with FCA. Someone captured a picture of Frankie and Stephen with their precious little hands on me as our team bowed together in prayer after one of our games. That picture is priceless to me!

Our sons Frankie (then six) and Stephen (then three) put their hands on me as our 1998 FCA Team bowed in prayer after my last Elite/Open Division Vail Lacrosse Shootout Game.

It was also during those years that Gayle's doctor felt that in light of her medical condition, we should not try to get pregnant with another child, so our hearts and minds began to turn back to the idea of adoption. We decided to hold those thoughts and feelings loosely, and did our best to stay open to God's leading and direction, which He would confirm in the not-too-distant future.

CHAPTER 33

Blessed to Be a Blessing

"Do nothing out of selfish ambition or vain conceit.
Rather, in humility value others above yourselves, not looking to
your own interests but each of you to the interests of the others."

Philippians 2:3-4

I will never forget the day my longtime Kelly Benefits assistant, Mary, buzzed me to announce that Dal Shealy, the president of FCA, was in our lobby to see me.

Dal had coached college football for many years before becoming president of FCA in 1992. One of his first big decisions was allowing our 1992 Miracle in the Mountains lacrosse team to wear the FCA name and logo on our uniforms for the Vail Lacrosse Shootout—the first team in any sport to do so.

Now, five years later, he traveled all the way from Kansas City to ask something of me.

"Frank, the Governance Committee of our Board of Trustees has asked me to invite you to serve on the FCA National Board of Trustees (NBOT)."

"You have done a great job as a volunteer leader and advisory board member and chair helping to grow FCA in Maryland, the Mid-Atlantic and Northeast region, and through FCA Lacrosse, and we believe you would be a great asset to our NBOT as well."

Wow! I was more passionate about local hands-on ministry, and my heart was more in the field than in the board room, but after prayer and a lot of discussion with Gayle, I called Dal to tell him I would be honored to serve a three-year term.

Sitting With Legends

On my right sat the legendary Dallas Cowboys head coach, Tom Landry. On my left, the University of Nebraska's three-time national champion head coach and future congressman, Tom Osborne. Across the table, LPGA Hall of Fame golfer, Betsy King.

I thought to myself, *What am I doing in this room?*

It was fall of 1997, and I was in Boston attending my first FCA National Board of Trustees meeting.

It didn't take long before a highly controversial subject came up and an intense discussion followed as to whether or not FCA should keep or sell a large camp facility and property that they owned in Indiana. Some board members wanted to sell it because it was struggling financially. Others thought FCA should keep it because people had donated money to the camp in other peoples' names that were profiled prominently at the camp.

I could feel the wisdom and strength emanating from Landry and Osborne, but they didn't say a word. I slowly raised my hand and asked a few common-sense questions to better understand the situation. Then Dal said, "Frank, you obviously have some interest in this," and the next thing I knew, I was on the Camp Evaluation Committee. No one invited Landry or Osborne. So that's how it works!

A Second Term

I was asked to remain on the National Board of Trustees for a second three-year term, and during that time was honored to chair the Governance Committee, which oversees the selection process for new board members.

A woman named Chris Steckel was a perfect candidate—a former athlete, bright and articulate in her interview, the mother of three athletes, and the wife of Les, an NFL Super Bowl offensive coordinator and former head coach. Chris accepted our invitation to join the board.

The FCA board has the unique practice of inviting the board members' spouses to every meeting. Spouses don't vote, but the board welcomes their participation in the discussions. Les Steckel couldn't ordinarily come with Chris because of his coaching schedule, but at a meeting in 2001, he showed up.

The saying in professional sports is that coaches are hired to be fired and that it's not a matter of "if" you will be fired, but "when" you will be fired. Les had been let go by the Tampa Bay Buccaneers—by his friend and spiritual mentor, Tony Dungy—despite being the offensive coordinator of a team with a 10-6 record, the highest-scoring season in Tampa Bay's history at that point, and a trip to the playoffs.

I often sat next to Chris at these board meetings, and now I was next to Chris and Les. Les had been involved with FCA since the 1970s as a camp coach, huddle leader, and event speaker, and brought "instant offense" to the meetings.

Les would soon after be invited to be an official voting board member, and in 2005 would succeed Dal Shealy as president.

Every person on that board brought a humble, servant's heart to each meeting, which was a blessing for all in attendance. In many ways, I felt like I had been adopted or welcomed into a family of amazing sports and faith-based servant leaders and influencers.

The Spirit of Adoption

In 1997 during my first year on the FCA NBOT, the spirit of adoption became clear in our family in other ways as well. Gayle and I both felt that God had blessed us in so many tangible ways with Frankie and Stephen, and our growing business, that we were supposed to open our family and home to adopting a child.

Our sense was that we should pursue adopting a baby girl from China, since at the time, China had a "one child" per family policy. We learned that because most Chinese couples wanted their one child to be a boy, to carry on their family name, they willingly put their baby girls up for adoption, or worse. We would be thrilled to receive and care for an unwanted Chinese girl.

During the Catholic Charities Adoption Services training classes we had to attend in order to be eligible for an international adoption, we discovered that we were not eligible for Chinese adoption because we already had two children.

Fortunately though, through several unique circumstances from our session, we believed God was leading us to adopt from South Korea, which was open to our family status and also had significant needs.

In December, we received an assignment from Holt International Adoption Agency in Seoul, Korea. Our baby daughter, Lee Yoo Me (we renamed her Jacqueline Lee Kelly), who had been born prematurely on September 12, 1997, would be ready to be picked up in March.

Gayle and our sister-in-law, Melissa (my brother David's wife), went to Seoul to get Jackie and bring her home, while I stayed with Frankie and Stephen.

On March 15, 1998, Gayle came walking down the airplane jetway with Jackie sitting in her arms, her little ponytail sticking out the top of her head, and her facing all of us as they made their way through the gate.

We were only supposed to have a few of us at the gate, but our entire family of more than 30, and many friends, showed up in force to welcome her into the Kelly family.

Gayle and I knew we had been "blessed to be a blessing" with our family, our roles with FCA, my work as president of Kelly Benefits, and soon enough, with opportunities to coach our children and many of their friends in youth sports. Exciting, challenging and very busy days were ahead.

Frankie, Stephen and I were thrilled to grab baby Jackie Lee from Gayle after their long flight home from Seoul, South Korea.

CHAPTER 34

Breakfast of Champions

"Instruct the wise and they will be wiser still;
teach the righteous and they will add to their learning."

Proverbs 9:9

T he FCA NBOT was exciting, but I was more focused than ever on continuing to grow FCA in Maryland, having our FCA Lacrosse teams competing at a high level, increasing our FCA Lacrosse Camp attendance, and improving our outreach to high school and college coaches.

At future US Lacrosse Coaches Conventions, we also started more proactively promoting our FCA Lacrosse Coaches Breakfast. We printed flyers, and Dan and I handed them out to coaches as they lined up at the various registration tables to sign in and pick up their materials. Some years, we placed a flyer on each of the 5,000 chairs set up for the Friday night plenary session. I'm not sure we were allowed to advertise like that, but we went with the idea of asking for forgiveness rather than permission, and nobody stopped us.

Attendance at our convention breakfasts increased from a few of us around a couple of tables in the lobby of the hotel in 1988, to 20 then 40, then over 80 in 1991. Later in the 1990s, over 400 came to hear former Baltimore Colt and Syracuse football and lacrosse player, Joe Ehrmann. Joe spoke powerfully about the concept of transformational "Inside Out" coaching through a life-changing relationship with Jesus Christ.

God blessed our outreach efforts even when the logistics worked against us. One year, the convention came to the Baltimore Convention Center but we had trouble booking a room for our coaches breakfast. We switched to a luncheon offsite about a mile away at Fleming's Prime Steakhouse.

Our speaker was Baltimore Colts Hall of Fame wide receiver Raymond Berry, a man of faith who played thirteen seasons and won two NFL championships with the legendary Johnny Unitas. After his playing days, he coached in the NFL, including six years as head coach of the New England Patriots.

Bill Kirwan, who played goalie at Johns Hopkins in the late 1950s and early 1960s, and who served on our FCA Lacrosse Advisory Board, helped us organize the luncheon and invited two of his former teammates who had long and illustrious coaching careers.

One was Bob Scott ("Scotty") who coached at Hopkins and led them to seven national championships. Scotty was one of the most revered, respected, and loved coaches in all of lacrosse. His players would run through a wall for him, and he was a perfect gentleman off the field.

I met Coach Scott years later when his grandson played on the youth team I coached through our local recreation council. I spoke with him after many of the games and he was always gracious with his advice and perspective.

The other coach Bill invited was Jerry Schmidt, an All-American player at Hopkins and the only lacrosse player to ever appear on the front cover of *Sports Illustrated* magazine. He coached at Calvert Hall and as an assistant at Cornell before taking the head coaching job 45 miles away at Hobart College, which sparked a fierce rivalry with Cornell. He led Hobart to three Division III National Championships.

Bill believed that Scotty and Jerry would be open to a message from Raymond Berry—someone from their generation who had similar success as both a player and a coach.

About 100 guests squeezed into Fleming's, and you could hear a pin drop as Berry gave an incredible message. Both Scotty and Jerry indicated on their response cards that they had made a commitment to the Lord, and both remained friends of FCA for the rest of their lives.

We have had many amazing coaches and athletes speak at FCA Lacrosse breakfasts and lunches over the decades, including FCA Presidents Dal Shealy and Les Steckel, and lacrosse legends like Frank Urso, the four-time first-team All-American from the great 1970s University of Maryland teams.

That's the special way of FCA—coaches and athletes influencing other coaches and athletes.

MORE TO THE STORY...

FCA Lacrosse Came Up All the Time – Les Steckel

Although I never coached lacrosse, I did have 25 years of experience as an NFL coach, including being the head coach of the Minnesota Vikings in 1984, so when Frank asked me to speak at the US Lacrosse Coaches Convention, I was happy to do so.

Having served on the FCA Board of Trustees with Frank, and in my role as president of FCA, I saw up close Frank's love and passion for lacrosse and the coaches and athletes who played it.

I knew he loved FCA's mission and he wanted to support the growth and development of lacrosse around the country and the world.

I knew his teammate in this mission was one of our top staff executives, Dan Britton, who had also played lacrosse in college and professionally. Dan and Frank are two peas in a pod, two fireballs, so when they asked me to speak at the FCA Lacrosse Coaches Breakfast at the US Lacrosse Coaches Convention, I was honored to be there and encourage those lacrosse coaches in their personal faith journeys.

I realized that a number of the coaches came for the free breakfast, but many left wanting to grow in their relationship with God and to get more involved with FCA because they could see it was a tool to help kids fulfill their potential and grow in their faith as well.

When I first got involved with FCA in the early 1970s, most people saw it as a football ministry. But when I traveled the country as president, FCA Lacrosse came up all the time. People around the country knew about it, coaches and athletes were impacted by it, and it has been exciting to see and hear about FCA and the Creator's game working together to change so many lives.

From a Mess to a Messenger – Dr. Frederick Douglass Opie

My friend Frank Kelly often says that, "lacrosse is a great game, but a terrible god." I can relate, as lacrosse also became an idol for me growing up.

I transferred from Herkimer Community College to Syracuse for one reason—I was in search of winning a national championship.

Wins and championships can become idols for coaches also. In my talks at the FCA Lacrosse Coaches Breakfasts, I asked them, "What's your first ministry? What is your relationship like with the Lord? Are you praying with your wife? How is your relationship with your kids?" If those relationships aren't a higher priority than coaching, the wins won't matter.

I played in back-to-back national championship games against Johns Hopkins and lost both, so I know a little bit about the vanity of idols.

Because of my master's and doctoral studies, and working toward a tenured teaching position, I couldn't play on any of the FCA teams in Colorado with Frank. But when I had windows of time, I spoke at FCA Lacrosse Coaches Breakfasts at the US Lacrosse Convention, and worked and spoke at FCA Lacrosse camps.

There is a lot of sick masculinity in lacrosse that leads to dysfunctional behavior. When I spoke to the coaches and players, I was open about the times in my life when I was performing well as an athlete or coach but not as a Christian, and how I learned the degree of sacrifice it takes to live, play and coach for the glory of God. The bottom line of the Christian life for me is: if you've had a mess, you can be a messenger about that mess, and the grace and power of God redeeming that mess, for His glory and for the good of others.

Many of my special moments were unplanned, and that's the beauty of the FCA Lacrosse experience. During Bryan Kelly's freshman year at the University of North Carolina, he wasn't playing as much as he wanted and was struggling with his identity, not only as a lacrosse player but as a person. Frank asked me to meet with Bryan when he was in Baltimore for a game. I was able to encourage a fellow defenseman and now he is mentoring and encouraging dozens of kids every year as a top-level high school lacrosse coach.

Mentoring moments like that, and influencing current and future coaches, are a big part of the FCA Lacrosse ministry, and the reason I wanted to be part of the movement as much as I could and whenever I could.

Sports

ward Christian Athletes in '92

Squad' upsets Turtles

Williams

posed to be a case of
s hair brown to the
the he with ered
2 Lacrosse she
Greene turtles jump
0 lead the all
Friday with
the with
m let
rcross she
a rreful weer a ter of
u cond s
the oup of the last
-8, even though se
ever rcross br et for
d to he u s
ation.
y the fit its first
ut app ed become
as the ous defense
nation of us

and sheer hustle to shut down the
No. 1 seeded Turtles' potent offense, anchored by Towson State
middie Rob Shek and former
Syracuse All-American Gary Gait,
one of the all-time leading scorers
in the Major Indoor Lacrosse
League.

Gait, who had seven goals in a
22-7 Greene Turtles' shellacking of
the Vail Lacrosse Club in
Thursday's opening round, was un-
able to get into the swing of things
Friday, scoring no goals on six
shots.

"I just wasn't on today it up,"
Gait said. "(Thursday) everything
was going in, (Friday) nothing was.
I'd say it was the altitude, but I
think it was the evening activitie."

Though David Kelly had the
game-winning goal at 3:14 the
second overtime, it was the

Please see Lacrosse pa

PART VI

Young Guns

CHAPTER 35

One Way 2 Play

"Don't let anyone look down on you because you are young, but set an example
for the believers in speech, in conduct, in love, in faith and in purity."

1 Timothy 4:12

When Sean McNamara came on staff with FCA Lacrosse in 1998, he looked at the fruit of our men's teams playing in Vail every year and asked a question that moved FCA Lacrosse into a whole new sphere of influence: "Why do we wait until players are in college or later to start providing that kind of experience for them?" He wanted to put together a high school team to travel for games and tournaments along the Northeast coast and build a retreat around it.

"Let's take the model of what we're doing with the elite adult teams and apply the same concept to high school players," is how Sean pitched the idea. "Let's see if we can find 20 players from our network of friends and coaches."

I wasn't sure it would work, but in 1999, Sean and Brian Hubbard, who was in the original huddle at Calvert Hall and played at Michigan State, formed a team, rented a bus, and drove up to the Avalon Shore Showdown in New Jersey.

"God did something special that weekend," Sean said, "but whatever could go wrong, did go wrong." And it started before the first faceoff. FCA players were coming in from up and down the Northeast—Baltimore, Northern Virginia, Long Island, and the Buffalo, Rochester, and Syracuse areas. On the way to the fields for the first game, Sean spotted a broken-down car on the side of the road—with a couple of FCA players in it. Sean pulled over and squeezed them into his car.

"The tournament directors from New Jersey had no idea what FCA was, and even called us the 'Fellowship of Catholic Academies.'" On our first day there, somebody drove their car across the field and ran over FCA's equipment. We had some discussion about their driving skills and the need to pay for the equipment," Sean remembered.

The best news and the worst news was how FCA "messed up the whole tournament," according to Sean.

"They organized the Showdown for one reason—so that two New Jersey state championship teams from different school-size divisions could ultimately play in the championship game to determine who was better. We showed up with barely enough players, most of whom met each other for the first time when they arrived at the field. But we had talent and an exceptional coach in Jon Torpey, who later became head coach at High Point University. We busted the brackets by beating one of the New Jersey state champions to get to the Showdown championship game. The other New Jersey team was so disappointed they didn't even bother playing us—they forfeited the championship game to us!"

Sean recalls one final mishap. "We had the guys all pumped about driving go-karts after the games, but when we got to the track, we found out you had to be eighteen to drive them." Out in Colorado, the FCA men's team always did amazing group activities like whitewater rafting and horseback riding, so I didn't even think that a group activity like that would be limited by their age.

"But God packed a lot of fellowship into that short weekend," Sean added. "Some of the guys developed good friendships, and any time you could be with Peter Kohn, who came as our equipment manager, it was special. And we put together something that FCA Lacrosse never had before—a high school team."

But the biggest miracle to Sean was that "parents would trust Brian, Jon and me—three single guys in their twenties—with their teenagers for a weekend."

Sean and Brian were thrilled with the results of the high school experiment and wanted to keep it going, but less than thrilled with how poorly the Showdown tournament was managed. "Next year, we'll run our own tournament," they decided.

The next summer, in 2000, they organized a high school tournament under

Carey Casey

the banner of FCA's "One Way 2 Play" initiative, a national program led by former UNC football star and FCA vice president, Carey Casey, which encouraged players to commit to playing—and living—alcohol- and drug-free. It also recognized that a relationship with God is a "two-way" relationship between God and each person. God always gives us the opportunity to accept, neglect or reject Him, so we have to choose if we want to "play" or connect with Him as well.

Brian directed the tournament, which started small and really grew over the years. Sean coached the FCA team in the tournament, which proved to be a great joint approach to serving. This further solidified Sean's vision of forming a high-level FCA Lacrosse National High School Team, to travel and fellowship together, while competing in top tournaments in the Mid-Atlantic and Northeast.

FCA Lacrosse's future with high school and youth teams and tournaments would blaze a new trail full of twists, turns and wild rides.

MORE TO THE STORY...

Faith, Commitment and Accountability – Brian Hubbard

At our first-ever FCA One Way 2 Play Lacrosse Tournament, players, coaches and parents all appreciated the quality of the lacrosse as well as our Saturday night message on living and playing drug- and alcohol-free through Faith, Commitment and Accountability (FCA). We never had a parent say, "Nope, I'm not interested in my teenager hearing that."

Reaching coaches was the key—coaches like Andrew Gerard. Andrew helped coach the 1992 FCA team in Vail, but we lost touch with him over the years while he was coaching at C. Milton Wright High School in Harford County, Maryland. I invited him to our tournament, and he brought his team, not because he needed more games to play, but because of the relationship we had previously forged through FCA.

"I had no idea it would be this good," he said, and continued to bring his teams year after year. As we poured into Andrew, he went back and poured into C. Milton Wright—a school with 1,400 students. Andrew went on to become a top high school and youth lacrosse official, bringing integrity and positive influence to the game in his essential role.

I talked with many other coaches at our tournaments who wanted to learn more about FCA Lacrosse and start FCA Huddles at their schools and Bible studies with their assistant coaches. It was exciting to see new doors of influence opening in the lacrosse community.

National Teams – Drew Wardlow

Andrew Stimmel and Peet Poillan were fifteen-year-old high school students in 2004 when I recruited them to play in one of the FCA Lacrosse One Way 2 Play tournaments that Sean McNamara and Brian Hubbard organized.

Sean had asked me, after I had just finished my freshman year at Grove City College north of Pittsburgh, to bring a team from the area. Andrew and Peet's names popped up in my online search of top recruits in Western Pennsylvania. I looked up their numbers in the phone book and called them out of the blue, and I was so glad they agreed to play. I had no idea how talented they really were and that Andrew would someday be a team captain at Ohio State and head coach at Marquette, and Peet would become a four-time Major League Lacrosse All-Star and offensive coordinator at Marquette.

Our team from Pittsburgh, called the "Steel City All-Stars," surprised Sean and everyone else at the tournament by finishing third, losing the semifinal game in overtime against the eventual champions, a team with Paul Rabil and Kevin Huntley, both of whom went on to be superstars at Johns Hopkins University and then professionally.

My experience recruiting and coaching that team really planted a seed in my heart that would lead me to eventually come on staff with FCA Lacrosse when I graduated in 2007, and take on the role of national teams coordinator.

Our goal with the FCA national high school teams is to create a special experience that players can't find on any other team. It begins off the field. Over the five days of a tournament weekend, the players live in the same dorms as the coaches. They eat meals together, run out for ice cream, play miniature golf, sight see the local attractions, pray, and study the Scriptures.

I knew "the huddle leaders were the key." The huddle leaders are usually somewhat older guys who have played competitively in college and who, when they were the players' ages, were in the same situation, facing the same challenges and opportunities. When the huddle leaders share their stories—the good, the bad and the ugly—the kids can relate to them and, because of the leaders' achievements and stature in the lacrosse world, respect them.

Each day after the games, usually in the evening, the huddles follow a proven sequence. After an ice breaker, the leader will read a passage of scripture and then ask penetrating, open-ended questions—*Who is God to you? Was there a time when you felt the presence of God in your life? What does it mean to have a posture of gratitude?*—questions no one has ever asked them in a lacrosse setting or possibly any setting before in their lives.

We want the kids to understand that lacrosse is what they do, it's not who they are. Our heart's desire is that they will experience and receive God's love, grace and truth and choose to follow Him. The discussion often reminds the players that this is not about religion, but a personal relationship with their Creator.

A Ten-Day Tour – Jeremy Sieverts

Although I was blessed to be a captain on the 2009 University of Maryland team, and to play eleven years of professional lacrosse, I will never forget our ten-day FCA national high school team tour in 2004 that began with a college recruiting tournament in Pennsylvania.

We played three games on Saturday and three more on Sunday in front of dozens of college coaches. Guys from all over the country played on our team—from Maryland, Virginia, Upstate New York, even a kid from Denver.

Next stop, the FCA Lacrosse Camp in Gettysburg. We coached and led huddles for five days, even though we were barely older than some of the campers. I woke up early to shoot lacrosse balls with the other camp counselors and huddle leaders, then worked with the campers from 7 a.m. to 9 p.m., stayed up and played silly card games until 11, then got up and did it all over again.

From Gettysburg, we drove an hour to the Genesee Valley Outdoor Center fields in Parkton, Maryland for what was planned as part training camp, part retreat, and part outdoor nature experience, which meant sleeping in tents. We got more nature than we bargained for—it rained for a day and a half, which put a damper on lacrosse practice and made for soggy sleeping. But the rainouts gave us extra time for rest, devotionals, and Bible studies with the coaches.

We took it all in stride—just part of the experience—but by the end, the coaches wanted to reward us for our patience so they ran out to Costco and bought steaks for dinner.

On to Annapolis, Maryland for the FCA One Way 2 Play tournament. We upgraded from tents to piling into our host families' basements, which we thought was fun—the way big families do it. No hotels. You stay with family.

All fun stuff and fond memories. When you share ten days like that with guys who love lacrosse and who are open to growing in their relationship with the Lord, you forge strong friendships. A number of the guys have remained in my life, and we still lean on each other to this day.

CHAPTER 36

Let the Children Come To Me

"Jesus said, 'Let the little children come to me, and do not hinder them,
for the kingdom of heaven belongs to such as these.'"

Matthew 19:14

M y first coaching experience was in 1988 at Calvert Hall, yet my first
time coaching one of my own children, some of their cousins and
their friends would come about ten years later.

By 1998, Gayle and I had three children, and my brothers and their wives
had eight children between them. Eventually, we would end up with 21 children
between us, and the cousins would play on many teams together over the years.

For me, deciding to coach our kids was a no-brainer. I loved being with our
children, loved sports, and really wanted to help all the kids on the team have
fun and fulfill their potential.

I also loved spending time in the car with our kids driving to and from practice and games. It gave me a captive audience, and we had many amazing conversations along the way. And, if I was the head coach, I could control the practice
schedule, which made life more manageable for me and Gayle.

I remember our son Frankie's and my nephew David Jr.'s first 7-8 lacrosse
team. I coached it together with my brother David and we had so much fun sharing the Creator's game with these wide-eyed seven- and eight-year-olds.

Soccer and Football

For a number of years, I ended up coaching Frankie and Stephen in soccer, football, basketball, baseball and lacrosse, primarily through the Luther-
ville-Timonium Recreation Council (LTRC).

I had never even played soccer before, but I knew how to organize, encourage
and motivate kids, and even ended up coaching a few championship soccer teams.

I'll never forget the year I was the head coach for Stephen's 9-10 LTRC travel soccer team, and the assistant coach for Frankie's 11-12 LTRC football team. Because I was the head coach of Stephen's soccer team, I could plan his practice schedule so as to not conflict with Frankie's football schedule. We were about three weeks into the season when I got a call from the LTRC football commissioner that our head coach had been permanently suspended for getting in a fight with a referee after one of his son's games, and that I was now the head football coach for that team. What?!

As I look back, I don't know how I got through that season, but I was able to coordinate our soccer team practices on Tuesdays and Thursdays from 5:30 to 7 p.m., and our football team practices on Tuesdays and Thursdays on the next field over from 7 to 9:00 p.m.

I literally ran from one field to the next and shifted from a soccer mindset to a football mindset. Both teams made it to the playoffs that year, and our soccer team won multiple tournament championships.

One of my favorite football coaching memories was the year when Cam Cameron was the offensive coordinator for the Baltimore Ravens, and I was coaching the 11-12 LTRC Blue Knights.

Because his son was a year older than our son Stephen and played on the LTRC 13-14 team, Cam would end up watching the second half of all of our Saturday games. As an NFL coach, he was busy coaching on Sundays, and every other day of the week except Saturdays. He would have to bring his son early to "weigh in" one hour prior to his scheduled game time and have nothing to do but watch our games while he was waiting for his son to play after us.

We had a very good team, and did some fun things on offense, so Cam would often comment when I would see him after our games about how much he liked our offense and my play calling.

He was probably just being nice, but he always made me feel pretty good. It was cool that we both also shared a background with and love for FCA.

An FCA Youth Lacrosse Team?!

In late summer of 2004, I got a call from my childhood friend Dan "Louie" Llewellyn (the one who, in 1977, said he could see me playing lacrosse at Cornell, when I had not yet ever played organized lacrosse).

That past spring, I had coached our son Stephen and my nephews Johnny (my brother John's son) and Patrick (my brother David's son) and their LTRC Lightning (age 9-10) lacrosse team, and Dan had coached the Kelly Post Lightning Team. We were two of the top teams in the state of Maryland, along with Fallston Recreation Council.

"Frankie, there's this Fall Brawl Pumpkin Tournament at The Haverford School in Philadelphia coming up. Why don't we put together an FCA team of '9-10 age' players to go play?"

"I don't know, Louie," I said. I thought the boys were too young for an FCA team and that kids should play fall sports like football and soccer in the fall, and lacrosse and other spring sports in the spring. "All the kids on my team will be playing soccer and football then and that should be their priority and focus," I told him.

It was a blessing to coach and have our sons play for LTRC—a lot of Kellys on the Lutherville fields back in the day.

God used Dan to push me.

"That's okay, it won't conflict," he said. "It's just a one-day tournament on a Sunday. I think we should take six or seven of the top players on your team, I'll bring six or seven of my top guys, and I know the coach of Fallston and we can get six or seven of their guys. It will be an FCA All-Star team."

"Okay," I said, "but here's the deal. For me, it can't be just about lacrosse. It will have to be faith-based. We'll pray before and after every game, have a short scripture-based devotion between games for the players, and some fellowship time with the parents."

"No problem, Frankie. No problem."

The kids meshed so well that it was hard to believe they had never played together before. We didn't see it then, but that team would become the foundation of something special that God was going to do. It was the first time we ever did an FCA Lacrosse youth team. We won the tournament in Philadelphia, and with

It was fun coaching our first-ever FCA "youth" lacrosse team.

such a good team, many of the parents said, *Let's keep this thing going!* I was reluctant, but we agreed to play a tournament or two together the next summer, and the team kept winning.

Little did we know what the Creator had in store for this young group of pioneers.

MORE TO THE STORY...

Released to Drop My Facades – Dan Llewellyn

I played on one or two FCA adult teams and fell in love with the concept of adding a spiritual dimension to a lacrosse experience. In a sport better known for partying, it was a blessing beyond words for me to play in an environment where I could share my heart spiritually with other guys.

What a gift that would be to give to my son and the rest of the kids on my team!

One day while I was in my office, an email popped up from John Nostrant (a star player at Washington College where he played with Frank's brother John), who was then the varsity lacrosse coach at The Haverford School in Pennsylvania, with information about his Fall Brawl Pumpkin Tournament. *Here's our chance!*

I called Frankie, and although he was reluctant at first, he agreed to lead the team.

Playing in the tournament wasn't all smooth sailing. Our opponents were older on average and had played together as teams longer than us—which was never. We didn't have time to get uniforms so the kids had to wear hand-me-down FCA adult uniforms which looked more like lacrosse dresses than lacrosse jerseys on them. Also, we found as we had in the past that when you openly express your faith, some people will take potshots at you.

But the kids and the parents all had a blast. *Let's keep doing this!*

When the kids, coaches, and parents shared their life experiences, it brought tears to my eyes. I felt released and strengthened to drop my facades and open up about the mistakes and bad choices I had made that led me to spending a year in prison for a white-collar crime I committed only two years prior. I felt comfortable with my band of brothers willing to forgive me and stand with me and Frankie reminded me and others often that we are not the Fellowship of "Perfect" Athletes and Coaches, but the Fellowship of "Broken and Forgiven" Athletes and Coaches. I was so thankful for that grace extended to me.

Coach Frank Made Me Feel Special – Kacy Kapinos

"We'd love to have you play for us! I think you can really help the team!"

That's how Coach Frank invited me to join the team. I was only ten years old when our first FCA youth team was established. He made me feel special, like I was meant to be there, and that's why I wanted to play for FCA.

Coach Frank believed in me and all the players he coached, and he did all he could to make us better. He believed that we could compete at the highest level and could always find a way to accomplish what we set out to do, and we believed it too. He made lacrosse fun.

But Coach Frank always set aside time for sharing the Word of God, with both the players and the parents, to point us toward the Lord. Coach Frank and the huddle leaders—who were high school or college athletes I could relate to and look up to—always tied Bible passages back to sports in some way, which helped us understand the message. The overarching theme came from "God's Game Plan."

Once he stepped on the field, Coach Frank wanted us to win more than anybody out there. But not at all costs. We learned even as young boys that when you wear a jersey with "FCA" on it, you're open to being judged and mocked when you let the competitive spirit get the best of you. "You're supposed to be Christians and you do something like that?," we would sometimes hear from opposing players. But Coach Frank would remind us that we were the Fellowship of "Forgiven" Athletes, not the Fellowship of "Perfect" Athletes.

Over the following summers we played in various local and regional tournaments, and somehow, we won most of them, but the real win for me was growing in my relationship with God.

Coach Frank has always been there for me. Even today, as a young adult, with as busy as he is, he still makes time to meet for breakfast and offer advice when I ask him. I pray I can be more like him as he strives to be more like Christ—committed to my faith, my family, and to helping others grow in their relationship with God too.

CHAPTER 37

Loaves and Fishes

"'How many loaves do you have?' [Jesus] asked. 'Go and see.' When they found out, they said, 'Five – and two fish.' ... Taking the five loaves and the two fish and looking up into heaven, he gave thanks and broke the loaves... He also divided the two fish among them all. They all ate and were satisfied and the disciples picked up twelve basketfuls of broken pieces of bread and fish. The number of men who had eaten was five thousand."

Mark 6:38-44

I t was 2009 when our FCA U15 Lacrosse Team played in the inaugural US Lacrosse U15 National Championship. It had been five years since the core of this team first played together as ten-year-olds at the one-day Fall Brawl Pumpkin Tournament at The Haverford School in Philadelphia. That was FCA Lacrosse's first-ever youth team, and although they won a lot of tournaments over the years, this would be the biggest tournament of their lives to date.

After a crazy late come-from-behind victory in the first-round game against New England Select Lacrosse League (NESLL), our team continued to win and earned a semifinal berth. We were down 7-2 at half-time of the Sunday morning semifinal when some bizarre things occurred. We kept turning the ball over against the aggressive ten-man ride that Next Level, a team from Washington, D.C. and Northern Virginia, was playing against us. As discouraged as I was, during my halftime speech, I did my best to stay positive and encourage the team to keep their heads up and never quit.

"Hey, Coach Frank," said Kacy Kapinos, our tough two-way midfielder and leader on our team, "we have to remember the devotional Bible story you shared with us this morning." I had shared a story prior to the game from the Gospel of Mark, where Jesus and his disciples were faced with the challenge of feeding thousands of people, yet the only resource they had access to were from a little boy who had five loaves of bread and two fish, and Jesus multiplied them. "Remember the five loaves and two fish. We are only down by five goals, and we've scored two goals. God can do this! We can do this!"

"Wow! Great reminder, Kacy. God can do anything," I said, though I was not feeling very optimistic.

We made a few adjustments and put in our other goalie, Brian Rasinski, who always liked to run with the ball whenever he made a save. Normally, we yelled at Brian to stay in the goal, but in this game, maybe we needed to try a different strategy.

Sure enough, to start the second half, Brian makes his first save and takes off running. He makes it to our defensive restraining line free and clear. He reaches the midfield line and two defenders double-team him.

My assistant coach, Jeremy Sieverts, who had just finished his senior year as a team captain at the University of Maryland and would go on to be a future all-star and all-pro in Major League Lacrosse, turns to me and says, "Coach Frank, shouldn't we call time out?"

Normally, that's the right call, but we had so much trouble clearing the ball in the first half, and I'm so mesmerized by a goalie who could run that fast, I decide to let it play out. He beat the double-team and is now on our offensive side of the field near our offensive restraining line.

"Coach, don't you think we should call time out?" Jeremy asks again. Again, normally the right call for this situation.

My gut was telling me to let him go. "Let's just see what happens," I said.

Then we watch Brian make a play I had never seen before or since at any level of lacrosse. He ends up taking the ball all the way behind their goal. They are still trying to double-team him, but he somehow splits the defenders, runs around the crease to his right, dives, shoots, and scores with his big goalie stick to cut their lead to 7-3.

I glance over at Next Level's coach, whom I had met briefly once or twice. He looks at me with an "Oh my gosh, what just happened?" look on his face. I see something in his eyes and something in the situation that makes me think, *We are going to win this game!*

We come all the way back to tie the score with less than two minutes left. Garrett Flannery, one of our defensemen, has the ball and clears it over the midfield line. I scream at him, "Give it up! Pass the ball!"

Next Level is shutting people off and pressuring Garrett.

"Don't shoot! Pass the ball!" I continue screaming.

Garrett takes one step over the restraining line, shoots, and pings the upper corner.

"Great shot Garrett," I yelled as I shook my head in disbelief. FCA wins!

Now I'm the one with the "Oh my gosh, what just happened?" look on my face.

God's ways are definitely higher than our ways.

After the game, we pause for a time of prayer to thank the Lord and marvel at the miracle of the five loaves and two fish and we rename one of our key offensive plays "52" in its honor.

A couple of hours later, we're playing in the US Lacrosse Youth Under-15 National Championship game on the stadium field.

Instant Classic

The championship game against For Love of the Game (FLG), a team from Long Island, was the complete opposite of our semifinal game. We jump out to an early lead and have a 7-3 lead at halftime, but they make a run to tie the score at 8-8 with less than two minutes left in the fourth quarter.

In overtime, my son Stephen wins a clean fast-break faceoff and takes off downfield with his cousin Patrick, who set up at the point to Stephen's right. They're both left-handed and we were running a leftie break. I have seen it before many times, Stephen to Patrick for a fast-break goal, so I am thinking the game is over. Stephen looks at the goal and thinks about shooting but throws a pass to Patrick. A defenseman for FLG takes a risk and jumps the pass and just barely tips it and ends up scooping the ball for a fast break in the opposite direction.

Yes, the game could be over in a few more ticks of the clock, but not the way I wanted. The defenseman clears it, draws a slide, and hits an attackman who shoots a rocket. The ball hits the lower pipe and ricochets out of bounds. A player from each team dives toward the end line as the player closest to the ball when it goes out of bounds gets possession for his team. It's close, and the referee calls possession in our favor.

We clear the ball and this time Jeremy and I both agree to call timeout. In the huddle, I call for one of our favorite plays out of our 3-1-2 formation that positions Stephen, a left-handed midfielder, at the top right corner and our right-handed midfielder Kacy at the top left corner with my nephew, Patrick, starting with the ball from behind the cage, coming to his left. As was my practice as a coach in tight, late-game situations, I like to ask the players if they have any other thoughts or suggestions.

Kacy piped up. "Coach Frank, I think you should flip me and Stephen."

That adjustment did not make complete sense to me at the time, but I trusted Kacy's instinct as one of the key leaders of our team. We end up getting a wide-open shot from our crease attackman, Matt Verderamo but he misses the cage, so Patrick picks up the ball on the end line, comes around with the ball to his left and draws a slide and throws it to Kacy on a little "V" cut who is in perfect shooting position as a righty—he would not have been there with my play. He shoots and scores.

Jim Verderamo, Matt's dad, and our team videographer captured it all on camera, including the crazy dogpile on Kacy as Jim ran onto the field shouting over and over, "FCA wins the National Championship! FCA wins the National Championship!"

"Instant Classic" shouted the headline in the two-page article about the game that appeared in *Lacrosse Magazine*. "I thought I missed," Kacy admitted in the article. "I turn around to see my teammates coming to hug me. What an unbelievable experience."[1]

Four FCA players—Kacy Kapinos, Stephen Kelly, Garrett Flannery, and Thomas McBride, our other goalie—made the All-Tournament team.

Kacy's shot was heard around the youth lacrosse world and put FCA on the youth and club team map. The *Lacrosse Magazine* article talked about "FCA standouts fast-tracked for powerhouse high school programs" and "whom you might find one day tearing up NCAA competition."[2] Several of our players would go on to lead their high school teams to MIAA and state championships and a couple of NCAA Division I National Championship games as well.

The 2009 Lacrosse Magazine *article titled "Instant Classic" captured the excitement of our FCA Lacrosse team winning the inaugural US Lacrosse U15 National Championship. Scan to see the game-winning overtime goal.*

With that kind of exposure, more of the top youth players in the country wanted to play for FCA. We added national teams in different age groups and started taking multiple teams to tournaments in Vail, Lake Placid, New York and Tampa, Florida, all with a desire to play great lacrosse and share God's love and truth, in relevant ways through our team dinners, huddle times and pre- and post-game messages. Players knew that during our time together, we would be talking about our faith and what it meant to have a relationship with God, and they were very open to hearing what we had to share.

We were very competitive on the field and won our share of championships along the way, but more importantly, we were winning off the field with the FCA message and excellent volunteer coaches and huddle leaders. Several college players who had been part of the Calvert Hall and other huddles came back to help coach our FCA youth teams and lead huddles. As successful college players and even some pro players, the kids wanted to be around them.

We were reminded again that if there were one word to define FCA, it would be "Influence."

MORE TO THE STORY...

A Challenging Time in My Life – Kacy Kapinos

The summer of 2009 was a challenging time in my life, with both family and personal struggles. No one on the team really knew the personal and family issues I was dealing with, so before the championship game, I asked God to please let something go my way, to please let me do something big.

It had to be 95 degrees every day of the tournament. We played six games in the two days leading up to the semifinal against Next Level, who was stacked with players from the Washington, D.C. and Northern Virginia area. We fell behind, 7-2, and just seemed flat. Our goalie Brian Rasinski completely changed the momentum of the game when he overcame some of the crazy checks and went the length of the field to score an incredible goal. We were fortunate to win that game.

When I made the game-winning shot in overtime of the championship game, my teammates dog-piled me and I could hardly breathe, but it was a special experience. The joy of victory and the celebration even brought my family closer together that day for which I was most thankful.

Be Prepared – Patrick Kelly

What coach of ten- and eleven-year-olds knows the strong hand of every player on every opposing team, and shows up to every game with a three-page scouting report and a written game plan? I only know one—my Uncle Frank.

He coached me on every FCA team I played on into high school and put us up against some stiff competition. He managed to get us into the first-ever US Lacrosse U15 National Championship tournament the summer after my freshman year. I remember thinking, *This is so cool! There are a lot of guys here who are going to be playing top-level Division I and eventually professional lacrosse.*

I look back now and laugh about how prepared Uncle Frank was and how well he prepared his players, but to him, it was only natural. He was also always prepared to share God's Word in a way that we could understand and receive it. And our assistant coaches, like Jeremy Sieverts, were also prepared and focused on sharing their lacrosse experiences and personal faith stories in ways that impacted all of us.

In all those years, I think our FCA team lost only three or four games when Uncle Frank was coaching, but more importantly, we each grew in our personal relationships with God because of our time together as a team.

Why I Coach – Jeremy Sieverts

Why did I coach for FCA Lacrosse?

As a twelve-year-old, I lived in separate worlds. Religion and faith were Sunday morning things. Sunday afternoons were for sports. On weekdays, I went to school and afterwards, played roller hockey, lacrosse, soccer, and whatever else. Saturday was for soccer games, lacrosse games and watching sports all day.

Until I played for FCA Lacrosse, I had never heard a lacrosse player talk about God. I had never seen a lacrosse player read the Bible. But my FCA Lacrosse coaches and huddle leaders played for Division I schools, where I dreamed of playing. They were colorful, exciting, fun guys, the kind I wanted to be around. And, by the way, they loved Jesus. I could tell that their faith was as much a part of who they were as lacrosse. They opened my eyes—my separate worlds were meant to be all one.

They cared more about me as a person than about how many goals I scored. Whether we won the championship or got thumped, the scoreboard was never the main thing. More important was obedience to Christ, competing hard and the brotherhood we shared.

I loved my FCA Lacrosse experiences and appreciated the impact they had on my life. When I was playing at the University of Maryland, I just felt like there were a lot of younger versions of me out there in the youth lacrosse world, and I wanted to show them what my coaches had shown me that opened my eyes. I coached for FCA Lacrosse because I enjoyed being a part of it and wanted to pay it forward.

I've coached high school lacrosse for many years, and I can hear my former coaches from McDonogh, Butler, Maryland, and FCA coming out of me. From my FCA Lacrosse coaches, I've tried to adopt the perspective that kids will stop being lacrosse players at some point—some sooner than others—and to ask myself, *What am I teaching them other than how to pick up a ground ball and shoot overhand? I try to genuinely invest in who they are and their well-being.*

I really enjoyed coaching the FCA 2009 Under 15 National Team with Frank Kelly. As one of the founders of FCA Lacrosse, I looked up to him, and now here we were coaching this team together. And to win that championship in overtime was really special.

In the grand scheme of life, it's about much more than winning championships. We're here to enjoy the Creator's game and the community and the bonds that the game creates.

It was an honor for Jeremy Sieverts and me to coach this amazing team, which would have players go on to star at colleges like North Carolina, Ohio State, Maryland, Johns Hopkins, Virginia and Hobart.

Sports

ward Christian Athletes in '92

Squad' upsets Turtles

Williams

posed to be a case of
s b... thrown to the
... the h... fa... red
... Lacrosse Sho... d
Greene ... jump...
... y ... ... with
athle... ...
... high ... quarter... d
... s la...
... ... the w... ted
... ... club
-8, ... was
... ... bra... et for
... to ... tion.
... the t... its first
... app... become
as the ... d," used a
... nation of ... us defense

and sheer hustle to shut down the
No. 1 seeded Turtles' potent offense, anchored by Towson State
middie Rob Shek and former
Syracuse All-American Gary Gait,
one of the all-time leading scorers
in the Major Indoor Lacrosse
League.

Gait, who had seven goals in a
22-7 Greene Turtles' shellacking of
the Vail Lacrosse Club in
Thursday's opening round, was un-
able to get into the swing of things
Friday, scoring no goal ... six
shots.

"I just wasn't on to... y a...
Gait said. "(Thursday) everything
was going in, (Friday) nothing was
I'd say it was the altitude, but ...
think it was the evening activitie...

Though David Kelly had ... ne
game-winning goal at 3:14 ... ... e
second overtime, it wa... ... ...

Please see **Lacrosse** pa...

PART VII

I'm Retired!?

CHAPTER 38

The Masters

"I can do all things through him who strengthens me."

Philippians 4:13 (ESV)

I got a call from Marc Hoffman and Dale Kohler about playing on some "Masters" Team that was going to the Vail Shootout in the summer of 1997.

"What's a Masters team?" I asked.

They told me it was primarily for guys that were 35 and older, but the Vail tournament was allowing each Masters team to have two players between the ages of 33 and 35. They had done their homework and knew I had recently turned 33, and they felt that I could really help them at the faceoff X.

As far as I was concerned, my playing days were winding down and I was looking forward to retiring, but since Dale (who was in his forties, and had been a legend at Calvert Hall and then at Hopkins in the 1970s) asked me, I felt like I had to say yes.

I also liked the idea that the team was being sponsored by and playing as "Lax World," which was the name of the store founded by my good friend and MLC teammate, Jimmy Darcangelo.

I liked playing with different guys and thought it would be fun to play in Vail with a team other than FCA. I wanted to be in the world but not of the world, to be an encourager, a light and a bridge to the Good News. Besides, FCA did not do Masters teams so it was a great chance to get to know more guys that obviously loved the Creator's game if they were playing into their forties.

Speedy Gonzales

Before the championship game, one of my Lax World teammates, Peter Schaffer, made me an offer. He held up a pair of beautiful, white and red Nike cleats in my exact size and said, "Frankie, I'll give you this brand-new pair of Barry Sanders cleats if you go 100% at the faceoff X today."

Neither of us thought I had much chance of going home with the prize. I hadn't been playing much competitive lacrosse the last several years, and I was going up against a tough couple of faceoff guys in the championship game. But because I was 33 years old, I actually had two things going for me: youth and speed.

Since I was one of the youngest players on the field, and I had trained to get into shape, and despite thoughts that I was too old to be playing competitive men's lacrosse, for some reason, compared to the other "Masters" players, I felt like "Speedy Gonzales."

Peter was a sports agent who represented football Hall of Fame running back Barry Sanders and other NFL players, and had been the general manager, head coach, and a top player for Team Colorado for many years. He was also the guy who, in 1992 when FCA played Team Colorado in the semifinal of the Vail Shootout, brought in the Detroit Lions' chaplain to pray for Team Colorado before the game.

Someone must have been praying for me at the Masters tournament that day because I caught fire at the X and won 22 of 22 faceoffs, my first and only perfect game.

We won the championship and I was named co-MVP of the tournament alongside Gerry Byrne, the do-everything (including faceoff) long pole, who single-handedly almost beat our team. Gerry went on to be an amazing defensive coordinator at Notre Dame and head coach at Harvard University.

"Thanks, Schaff, these are awesome," I said when Pete handed me the cleats. And I still have those cleats to this day.

Maybe I had a few more games left in me. Little did I know...

The 1997 Lax World Masters Vail Shootout Champions

CHAPTER 39

His Ways Are Higher

*"'For my thoughts are not your thoughts, neither are your ways my ways,'
declares the Lord. 'As the heavens are higher than the earth, so are my ways
higher than your ways and my thoughts than your thoughts.'"*

Isaiah 55:8-9

B y 1998, our business had grown to more than 85 employees, and we moved into our sixth office since our parents started the business in our family home in 1976. We were now marketing to and through other insurance agents and brokers, and we began to attract larger clients with hundreds, and even thousands, of employees.

We moved into this new office building in the summer of 1998.

We thought for sure this building we bought and renovated would be our office space for many years to come, since our new 33,000-square-foot facility could house up to 150 people.

Sean McNamara and FCA Lacrosse were also working out of our new facility, and our growing Communications and Marketing Team was supporting various FCA Maryland and FCA Lacrosse communication projects. We loved FCA's values of integrity, serving, teamwork and excellence, and we wanted everything we did with and for FCA to reflect those values.

I was still helping to lead the FCA Huddle at Calvert Hall, but only coaching lacrosse there part-time. My brother Bryan was now the head varsity lacrosse coach at The Hall, as well as working in the business, and together with my brothers John and David, we were working to grow the business and they were supporting the growth of FCA as well. We were fortunate to have wives and growing families who supported our collective work in the business, our community and passion for FCA and the Creator's game, even at the international level.

International Origins

Team Canada beat us badly, and that's how it started.

When the World Lacrosse Championship came to Baltimore in 1998, we pulled together a team of local FCA players and asked Team Canada, featuring former Syracuse superstars Paul and Gary Gait, if it would benefit them for us to scrimmage them. Since I had played well in the Masters tournament the year before out in Colorado, I figured I could take some runs and we could help give Canada a good look, a sparring partner, if you will. They enthusiastically took us up on the offer. They wanted live competition to help them prepare.

Though my dreams of playing internationally for the U.S. National Team in 1990 and 1994 were dashed, I still had a little itch for international competition. And even more so, I never lost the vision or desire to share God's love and truth with all the lacrosse community. Since the international lacrosse community was coming to our backyard, it seemed like the natural thing to do.

Our goal was to serve Team Canada, and they appreciated the opportunity to practice under game-like conditions. They crushed us but we didn't feel too bad about it—we played hard. In the World Games, Team Canada played great and ended up in the championship game, where they lost to Team USA in double overtime in what many have called "the greatest lacrosse game of all time."

The experience was all part of God allowing FCA to broaden its experience with international competition and build favor in the lacrosse world.

Down Under

In a way I never expected or had even considered, God gave me a chance to play at the next World Lacrosse Championship in 2002 in Perth, Australia. Marc Hoffman, who invited me to play on my first Masters team in 1997, and was really a men's lacrosse league legend, called me out of the blue with an invitation.

"Frankie, we're taking a USA Masters Team to Australia to play in the World Championships. We really need a strong faceoff middie and would love it if you could play with us. Are you interested?"

I was 38, which was still on the younger side for the 35-and-older Masters category. I was still in decent shape, but I wasn't sure I wanted to go. I hadn't played competitively for a couple of years and again thought my lacrosse career was over.

Gayle really encouraged me to do it. I think she wanted to see me have the joy of playing internationally and sensed that this was of the Lord. She was adventurous and loved to travel so this was a win-win in her mind. After some prayer and reflection, I decided to go for it. It would take a lot of hard work to get back into faceoff shape, especially knowing we would play seven or eight games in a two-week period.

Gayle helped organize our family's travel plans. Our sons Frankie and Stephen, and daughter, Jackie, joined us, along with our nephew, John Martin Lombardi, whom we brought as a special guest and occasional babysitter when Gayle and I attended the evening team functions.

We have many special memories of koala bears and kangaroos, but something we laugh about to this day is how I constantly opened Gayle's passenger door for her on our rental car, mainly (I hate to admit) because the passenger's side was on the left side of the car and the driver's side was on the right side of the car, or opposite U.S. cars. Out of habit, I continually opened her passenger-side door first. Gayle often jokes about what a gentleman I was in Australia.

Are You Frank Kelly from the Faceoff Video?

Japan sent their first-ever team to the games that year. Lacrosse was still in its infancy in Japan then and they brought an exhibition team, not to compete for the Championship, but to play practice games against other teams to find out what the World Championship competition was like.

They asked if our USA Masters Team would play an exhibition game against them, and our team organizers happily obliged. Even though they were much younger than us, we beat them pretty badly, but their two faceoff men were very good and had amazing technique.

After the game, the teams lined up to shake hands and exchange mementos. I then made my way over to their two faceoff men, as is customary (like opposing quarterbacks after a football game who look to congratulate each other). I tried a little of the Japanese I remembered from my 1986 AIA Japan summer missions trip on them.

"Kon'nichiwa! Watashi no namae wa, Frankie desu."

In their broken English, they replied, "Frankie? You Frank Kelly of faceoff video?"

"What?" I asked

"Are you Frank Kelly from faceoff video?"

"Yes, I'm Frank Kelly from the faceoff video."

They were so excited they began yelling and screaming and pulled their whole team over and started hugging me. "Frank Kelly! Faceoff video!" They had actually learned how to faceoff from watching the faceoff video I made six years earlier for the US Lacrosse Foundation with Gordon Purdie and Andy Kraus.

Gordon was a five-time Australian National Team Player, a member of the 2002 Australian National Team, and a good friend who had been involved with FCA. Andy Kraus was a former University of Virginia first-team All-American and the faceoff specialist who beat me and others out for the U.S. National Team in 1990.

The faceoff guys from Team Japan told me they watched our video many, many times and worked hard on the technique I/we taught. Unlike many Americans who would ask me the keys to facing off and concentrate for maybe 20 minutes, these guys listened and put in the many hours needed to refine their faceoff techniques and skill. God had to take me to Australia to meet two of my best faceoff students, who were from Japan.

My teammates were wondering what the heck was going on out there, and pestered me for the rest of the tournament with, "Is that Frank Kelly from the faceoff video?"

To this day, I still see friends from that 2002 USA Masters Team who greet me with, "Is that Frank Kelly from the faceoff video?"

God is amazing! His ways are higher! Not only did he give me a chance to play on an international team on another continent, and bless my family and me with a really fun trip, and connect me with Japanese players I had helped through a six-year-old video, but our team won the 2002 World Game Masters championship!

Gayle, Frankie, Stephen, Jackie Lee and me after winning the 2002 World Lacrosse Masters Championship in Perth, Australia

This was so cool, I thought. *But I doubt I will ever do anything like it again.* This would be the perfect time to end my crazy lacrosse career.

FCA Down Under

This summer the World Games took place in Perth, Western Australia and some familiar FCA faces had strong showings during the games! Here are the highlights:

➤ Gordon Purdie (right) of team Australia competed in his record 5th World Game!

➤ Frank Kelly III (left) helped lead USA/Team Toyota to the World "Masters" Championship.

➤ Doctor Bill Kirwan (right) is the oldest goalie in the game of lacrosse and had a strong showing in the games playing for the USA Eagles in the International Grand Masters competition.

A feature in the 2002 FCA Lacrosse Newsletter (that our Kelly Benefits Communications Team helped create) celebrating FCA laxers Gordon Purdie and Bill Kirwan, and includes a fun picture of me with the two Team Japan faceoff men

MORE TO THE STORY...

I'll Cherish Our Friendship Forever – Gordon Purdie

As much as I felt back in 1991, *This is cool! I'm making an instructional faceoff video,* I sat in awe as Frank shared all of his secrets about winning faceoffs. It was inspirational, and a joy to be a part of. That video went on to be viewed and embraced by thousands of coaches and faceoff athletes across the country and around the world.

Frank has always been a friend and a mentor to me, someone I've looked up to, both on and off the field. We connect on a spiritual level, which takes our friendship to a higher place—no hiding our true feelings about anything. We're comfortable calling each other at any time and talking about anything, from faceoff rule changes to life and faith issues we're going through.

I feel so blessed to have a friend like Frank and I'll cherish our friendship forever.

CHAPTER 40

Gideon's Army

"The Lord said to Gideon, 'You have too many men.
I cannot deliver Midian into their hands, or Israel would boast against me,
"My own strength has saved me."'"

Judges 7:2

I definitely thought my competitive lacrosse days were over after the 2002 World Games in Australia, when I got another random call. This time it was my former Cornell teammate and friend, Timmy Goldstein. He was two classes behind me and played on the 1987 team that was undefeated until losing by one goal to Johns Hopkins in the National Championship game.

Timmy was putting together a team of former Cornell "Big Red" lacrosse players, called Rusty Red, and they were going to play in the 2003 Lake Placid Masters Division Tournament in honor and memory of Cornell Lacrosse legend, Eamon McEneaney, who had died in one of the Twin Towers in the 9/11 attack on our country. He said they really needed a top faceoff guy, and I was it. How could I say no to that? I would have to get back in faceoff shape, and there is no way we could lose this tournament.

We won it, and although I got a concussion in the championship game, I somehow finished strong. Although we won in honor of Eamon and it was a great experience, this time I was certain that my playing days were over. I did not need to be getting concussions at the age of 40.

Yet the following year, Lake Placid came calling again. Am I crazy?!

I played with the 2003 Rusty Red Masters team in Lake Placid to honor Cornell lacrosse legend Eamon McEneaney (Above) who died in one of the Twin Towers on 9/11/01. We had to win that tournament in honor of Eamon, and we did!

Masters in Lake Placid

Sometimes God wants to show us that He is in control and we are not, and that His ways are better than our ways. Sometimes He shows us by accomplishing big things with small numbers.

I don't know if it was the concussion I received in the Lake Placid Rusty Red Masters Championship game or what, but for some reason I started feeling a strong impression in my mind that God wanted us to put together a first-ever FCA "Masters" team to play in the 2004 Lake Placid tournament. Seriously?!

I had a great time and learned a lot with the Rusty Red Masters Team the summer before, and even though I would be 40 years old, I was feeling like this might be a great chance to reconnect with some former FCA teammates and possibly expose some of my older friends to an FCA Lacrosse experience.

By 2004, the Masters tournament in Lake Placid had grown to one of the largest in the country and there were actually two divisions, so I thought, *Why don't we put together an FCA Masters team to play in the division Rusty Red isn't in?*

The guys I called were for the most part excited about playing and we had about 20 who said they would come. I had to beg a few players, like my brother David, to play and unfortunately, as the tournament date approached, one after another dropped out for various reasons. By the time we got to Lake Placid, there were only fourteen of us. Fortunately, Dan Britton, Steve Paletta and my brother David, who all played on our 1992 Miracle in the Mountains team, were there, but how could fourteen older guys survive four lacrosse games in four days?

We met for the first time as a team at the field 30 minutes before our first game for a time of introductions and re-introductions and prayer. Standing in the circle, God brought the Old Testament story of Gideon to my heart and mind. Gideon had planned to lead 32,000 Israelites into battle against the Midianites, but God whittled his army down to 300. How could 300 warriors defeat an army described as "...numerous as locusts; and their camels were without number, as numerous as the sand on the seashore?"[1] Only by believing that God's work, done God's way, will not lack God's supply. In Gideon's case, God's way was an unusual battle plan to attack by blowing trumpets and smashing pitchers. After reflecting on the story, we dubbed ourselves "Gideon's Army."

Our first-round opponent was a team with about 30 players aptly called Team Tsunami. One run after the opening faceoff, Kevin Frank, who hadn't played lacrosse since our days at Cornell, pulled a hamstring, which left us with thirteen players standing.

Our best player was the five-time Australian National Team midfielder, Gordon Purdie, a crafty, younger player (if you call a 38-year-old a younger player) with incredible stamina. Gordon loved that we had a smaller team and encouraged us to devise an unusual game plan around him. Gordon could run all day and would continually induce defenders to foul him so we could play a man-up much of the game.

We would work the ball to get a little rest, then feed the ball to the crease where my brother, David, who hadn't played much the prior decade (but his middle name was still Eugene and his nickname was still "Eugene the Scoring Machine") could still catch anything and put the ball in the goal.

Gordon loved it! With that strategy and our wives and kids on the sidelines cheering us on, we managed to beat Team Tsunami and then win our second-round game, which landed us in the semifinals.

It was exciting to have my former Cornell teammates and their Cornell wives be a part of our FCA Lacrosse team and family in Lake Placid. (L to R): Kevin and Emily Frank; me and Gayle; Steve and Christine Paletta; and Tim and Kirstin Vivian. (Not pictured: Paul and Patricia Kuehner)

Although we had only fourteen players on our 2004 Lake Placid "first-ever" FCA Masters team, we had an amazing cheering section of family and friends.

MORE TO THE STORY...

Family and Fellowship – Kevin Frank

After Cornell Lacrosse and our AIA Bible study that we led, I left the whole athletic scene and immersed myself in urban ministries in Syracuse. Frank and I had kept in touch and always supported each other, but when he asked me about playing on the FCA Masters team in Lake Placid, I reminded him that I hadn't touched a stick in almost 20 years and had no healthy ligaments left in my ankles.

"You don't even have to play if you don't want to," Frank said. "It would be great if you suited up and got in a couple of runs, but bring the family and just come for the fun and the fellowship."

"Okay," I said. "I have no interest in lacrosse, but I love you guys and what you're doing, so I'll come."

I was amazed at how good everyone could play. They were better than they were in college and every bit as competitive. At that stage of life, my only athletic goal was to climb mountains with my future grandchildren, and anything that might jeopardize that, I didn't need to do.

That's why, when I tweaked my hamstring on my first run in 20 years trying to beat a guy to a ground ball, my first thought was, *This is perfect!* I was so glad! I did not need to be playing with those guys. I wasn't helping them, and I wasn't helping myself.

Since I didn't have to play, I could enjoy even more the beauty of Lake Placid, the time my family spent with Frank's family, the fellowship and discussions about the Lord and life, and watching my friends play for a championship. That was a special experience.

Crying for Your Mommies – David Kelly

We were short-handed on players and didn't look very intimidating but that didn't stop me from mouthing off at the other team. My good friend Pat Reed (aka "Steiner") played for Team Tsunami and we always liked to joke around. They were loaded with talent and numbers (over 30 guys on their team) and expected to kick our butts. They strutted out on the field in their fancy uniforms, looking like a real team in a single-file line.

As they ran by us and prepared to warm up, I yelled, "Hey Team Tsunami, after this game you're going to be crying for your mommies."

"What did you say?" grunted one of their players.

"You heard me!"

Thank God and Gordon that I scored a bunch of goals and we beat them.

CHAPTER 41

Searching for Something More

"Come to me, all you who are weary and burdened, and I will give you rest."

Matthew 11:28

I had invited Glen Miles—my childhood friend and a former U.S. National Team member and first-team All-American midfielder at the U.S. Naval Academy who went on to be a top-gun fighter pilot—to play with us in Lake Placid for our first-ever FCA Masters Team in 2004, but he had already committed to another team.

Glen hung out with us though, because, as he explains:

"My life looked successful on the outside—I was 40 years old, happily married with great kids—but I was struggling on the inside, addicted to approval and popularity, as well as to pleasure and thrills. I tried to find all that again in lacrosse but it left me empty and searching for something more.

"Throughout my life, I had a lot of Christian influences. Frank Kelly is at the top of the list. Two friends at the Naval Academy—one in my fighter squadron and one fellow athlete, NBA Hall of Famer David Robinson—were also role models who pointed me toward God, but I was never willing to follow the path they showed me.

"I had caught up with Frank in Vail in 1993 when I played for Team Texas but was more interested in partying than joining his FCA fellowship huddles. But in 2004, as I approached mid-life and struggled with my identity, I was more open to hearing God's Word and asked Frank if I could hang out with the FCA team. They welcomed me like a brother, and I stayed with them at the Gauthier's Motor Inn—a complete dump that proved I was willing to search anywhere to find God—ate meals with them and attended their fellowship times.

"In the second game with my team, I remember vividly leaning into our team's huddle during a timeout and hearing nothing but 'F-that guy' and 'F-the ref' and laughter over various exploits with women the night before. During the timeout, I felt my spirit lifted outside of my body. I looked down at myself in the huddle and sensed that *I thought I wanted back into this but this is not who I am anymore. This is not where I want to be anymore.*

"After that game, I asked Frank, 'Can I finish the tournament playing for FCA?' Frank and the rest of the team were cool with the idea. Frank cleared the roster switch with the tournament director and the other teams, and I suited up with FCA for the semifinal game.

"Two plays, one from each of my games with FCA, summarize my experience that led to the transformation in my life that occurred in Lake Placid.

"In the semifinal game, I had just subbed onto the field when Gordon Purdie, who I had played against in the 1990 World Lacrosse Games in Perth, Australia, starts streaking downfield with the ball. He turns to throw it and he sees me, a guy he has never played with before, and he decides, *Nah, I'm not going to give you the ball.*"

When I saw that play, I thought, *Gordon, you just blew off a legend! A former U.S. National Team player, Glen is not some hack we added to have another warm body. He can catch!*

"Maybe I did look Glen off," Gordon remembers, "but faking passes is part of my game—to open up the passing lanes. It wasn't because I didn't think he could make a play."

"I had to earn my stripes on the team," Glen said.

Gordon adds, "Frank, Glen, and I have been reliving that moment for almost 20 years. If I could go back in time and do it over, I would save all the debating and throw the ball to Glen—even though he may or may not have been as open as he thinks he was!"

We won the semifinal and played the next day for the championship, which is where the other play that Glen referenced occurred. The game went into overtime and Glen recalls how the situation, and play, that unfolded would change his life forever:

"We're in the championship of the Masters, and the game goes into sudden-death overtime. I'm struggling in lacrosse and really playing poorly by all measures. I'm searching for my identity. I'm struggling to be who I want to be and who God created me to be.

"Frank wins the faceoff to start the overtime period, and I'm running down the field ahead of him. Frank's about ten yards inside the midfield line with the ball. I'm about five yards above the restraining line. Frank throws me the ball. In that very moment, with the ball in the air coming at me, glowing,

I prayed, *God, you are unbelievable. I cannot believe you would take this moment to reach out to me.*

"The ball comes to my stick. I awkwardly switch to my right hand to make sure I don't drop it. I catch the ball, take two steps to the restraining line, switch to my left hand, and throw an ugly shot at the goalie, talking to God in the middle of the whole shot. *I can't believe you're doing this. I can't believe you're doing this.*

"The ugly shot bounces between the goalie's legs and into the net. The three players on our bench raise their arms in celebration and sprint out onto the field. All the kids in the stands burst into cheers and jump up and down. I sit down on the grass and give my life to Christ. I will never forget that moment."

When God whittled down our roster, it was not only to teach us about His power to overcome long odds but, more importantly, about His power to change a heart and a life, forever.

Kneeling (L to R): Dan Britton, Gordon Purdie, Tom Hall, Frank Kelly III, David Kelly, Jason Levinson
Standing: Tim Vivian, Paul Foreman, Dave Hall, Ben Anderson, Chuck Knudsen, Steve Paletta
Glen Miles, Big Frank (BF), Paul Keuhner   *Not Pictured: Kevin Frank*

MORE TO THE STORY...

Catching and Shooting – David Kelly

"This place is disgusting. I don't even want to sleep in here," my wife and daughter said when we walked into our room at the Gauthiers Motor Inn. I can't say I blame them.

But there was a great diner across the street, and one day when I was hungrier than usual, I ordered a hot roast beef sandwich with fries and gravy for my pre-game meal. Frank walked in.

"Eugene,"—Frank liked to call me by my middle name—"are you eating all that right before our game?"

"Yep."

"Gener (short for Eugene), there's no way you can play after eating that."

"We'll see how it goes."

At one point during the game, Frank called a timeout. We barely had enough guys to field a team so, at times, we had to play out of our normal positions. Frank looked at me and said, "Eugene, I need you to play some midfield."

"There's no way I can run up and down this field with all the french fries and gravy sitting in my stomach," I said. "I'm only good for catching and shooting, and remember, the Gener doesn't do groundballs." Frank shook his head and smiled in disbelief.

I did plenty of catching and shooting throughout the tournament and was actually named the tournament's offensive MVP. I think I only had two groundballs in four games, and I owed most of my goals to Gordon Purdie. He was our true MVP because the defensemen left me open to double-team him. Gordie did all the work, found me, and I scored the goals. Not bad considering I didn't even want to go to Lake Placid at first.

A real highlight was spending time with Glen Miles. He was a childhood friend of Frank's and used to spend the night at our house a bunch of weekends. Glen was an amazing athlete who hit the party scene hard in high school, college and beyond, and used to laugh at our early FCA teams in the 1990s. His game-winning goal in overtime of the championship game was special, but the most significant thing that happened that weekend was witnessing Glen's surrender and commitment to Christ.

CHAPTER 42

Chosen

"For he chose us in him before the creation of the world to be holy and blameless in his sight. In love he predestined us for adoption to sonship through Jesus Christ, in accordance with his pleasure and will..."

Ephesians 1:4-5

We took an FCA Masters Team back to Lake Placid in 2005, but no championship overtime goals were to be had. I continued coaching Frankie and Stephen and our new FCA youth team, but the highlight of our year as a family was our trip to Seoul, South Korea as a family the week after Christmas in 2005 to pick up our new son. He was two and a half years old, named Kim Joo Yung, and had experienced a lot of transition in his young life.

We decided to rename him Joseph Kim Kelly. "Kim" was his Korean surname, "Joseph" was close to Joo, and we loved the "Josephs" we read about in the Bible. It didn't take long before we all started calling him "JK."

I will never forget the meeting we had a few months earlier when we had to decide if we would adopt this "needy" young boy from another country into our family. Gayle and I prayed about the decision a lot and one day decided to have a family meeting with our three children in the treehouse in the backyard of our home. We had never all been up in the treehouse together before (or since, by the way), but I thought it would be a more relaxed type of place to have such a serious discussion.

Frankie was fourteen, Stephen was eleven, and Jackie Lee was eight years old at the time. Gayle and I were both open to the idea and thankful for our adoption of Jackie Lee when she was six months old.

We were in a great place as a family; out of the diaper and car seat stage, but I used to make half-joking, half-serious comments during quite a few of our family dinners. For years, we had dinner around our rectangular wooden country table, which had two seats on each long side, and one seat at each head of the table. I always sat at one head and Gayle at the other, while the kids sat with two on one side and one on the other. Very often after saying grace, or while eating, I would see the one empty seat, and say "I feel like someone is missing." I had been doing this for years when we mistakenly received a call from Catholic Charities Adoption Services about a need they had. That call ultimately led to this unique and unexpected opportunity.

Perched in the treehouse, I started with our oldest. "Frankie, what do you think?"

He quietly replied, "Do what you think is best, but I really like our family the way it is."

"Thanks, Frankie," we replied.

Then I went to Stephen, who at that time and age was probably the most self-focused of our crew. To Gayle's and my surprise, Stephen said, "He can have my bed! I will sleep on the floor. I definitely think we should adopt him." Wow?! What a bold response.

Then we turned to Jackie Lee. As our youngest, she was kind of shy, and by nature an introvert. With little tears in her beautiful black Korean eyes, she said, "I like our family the way it is too. But who am I to say no to adopting this boy when you didn't say no to me?"

Wow! By then, we were all in tears. It was a Thursday afternoon and that night, I decided I would pray and fast over the weekend since we had to give Catholic Charities our answer by Monday morning.

I had learned through prior experience, and more importantly, God's Word, that He often confirms important decisions in "threes."

Gayle and I were just not sure, as this decision would significantly impact each of us, our family dynamic, and our future.

I decided to fast for three days (fasting was not a discipline I practiced very often, but when I did it before I experienced real clarity) and asked God to please confirm the decision beyond a shadow of a doubt.

I fasted all day on Friday, and that evening took Frankie, Stephen and Jackie to our community pool. Very few people were there when a woman came up to me out of nowhere and started asking me about our kids, who were all swimming together in the shallow end of the pool.

She noticed Jackie and asked if she was adopted.

I said, "Yes, we adopted her from South Korea."

She said, "Wow, that is great. We actually have two adopted children. First, we adopted a little girl, and then we adopted a boy."

"Wow!" I said, "How is it going?"

She said it was great and then made her way back to her friends.

That was interesting, I thought, but didn't even mention it to Gayle that night when we got back to the house.

The next day, I ended up at the pool in the late afternoon. Again it was not crowded and I was talking to the lifeguard, who was also a family friend, when another woman I didn't know or recognize came up to me to ask about Jackie.

"Is that your daughter?" she asked. "She is beautiful, where is she from?"

"Thank you," I said, "She's from South Korea."

She got all excited and told me she had a good friend who adopted two children from Korea. She said, "First they adopted their daughter, then they adopted their son."

"Wow!" I stated, then asked her, "How is it going for them?"

"Great!" she replied, "The best decision they ever made."

This time when I went home, I had to share it with Gayle. Was God confirming this?

The next day, our family was invited to a cookout at another pool (I hadn't been to a pool three days in a row since I was a young boy). Even though I wasn't eating, I was walking around the pool when I saw a friend in the pool holding her newborn baby. I knew it was her fourth and yelled out "Congratulations!"

She yelled back, "Hey Frank, now we have four children, just like you!"

I said, "We don't have four, we only have three!"

She then said, "I thought for sure you had four children. All I know is when I see you and Gayle, I see four children."

I couldn't believe it! I offered another congrats and made my way right over to Gayle. I told her what happened—three crazy confirmations in three days.

In South Korea, on our first official day as JK's family

I said, "Call Catholic Charities in the morning. Let's adopt this boy."

The first couple of weeks after we returned from Korea were very difficult. JK was very distraught and despondent. At two and a half years of age, he spoke no English, loved Korean food, and had never seen so many white people in his life. Eventually, he settled in.

Rusty Red, White and Blue

When we returned from Korea, the Creator, God, again had plans to increase my international lacrosse experience. As usual, I didn't see it coming. In 2006, the year of the next World Lacrosse Championships, which were being held in the city of London in Ontario, Canada, I got another call from Timmy Goldstein.

"Frankie, we are taking our Rusty Red Masters Team to the World Championships in Canada. We really want and need you as a faceoff man."

For this tournament, Timmy and Joe Lizzio, who had founded the Cornell Masters Rusty Red Team, were adding former U.S. National Team players and other top Masters players from other colleges to the roster to play in the Masters Division as "Rusty Red, White and Blue." It was a phenomenal team and after more prayer, reflection and conversation with Gayle, I felt that God wanted me to represent Him and join them.

Gayle planned another family adventure—trips to foreign countries for lacrosse tournaments were becoming a habit for us. This time we had a fourth child to take. JK had now been with us six months, was starting to settle in, and was nearly three years old.

My favorite memory was the day I noticed the Korean National Team playing on an adjacent field. After our Rusty Red, White and Blue game, I walked over to watch Team Korea, holding JK in my arms. By chance, I struck up a conversation with their team captain, Won Jae Park, and he was kind enough to hold JK and let me take a picture of him with the Korean team. Little did I know that our paths would cross again with Won Jae, twelve

Our newly adopted son, JK, pictured with the Korean National Team at the 2006 World Lacrosse Championships in Canada

years later at the World Championships in Israel.

Our Rusty Red, White and Blue Masters team was really talented, with the likes of former U.S. National Team members Lindsay Dixon, Tim Schurr, and Timmy Goldstein, and former All-Americans Bobby Cummings, Steve Sombrotto and Gerry Byrne, just to mention a few. And we won the championship, which made me 2-for-2 in international World Games "Masters" tournaments.

God was graciously turning the pain and disappointment I felt from not making the U.S. National Team more than a decade earlier into joy in ways I never could have imagined, another example and reminder that "We can see to the bend in the road, only God can see to the end of the road."

Our Rusty Red, White and Blue 2006 World Masters Team was loaded with "old" talent.

CHAPTER 43

Transitions

"...one thing I do: forgetting what lies behind and reaching forward
to what lies ahead, I press on toward the goal
for the prize of the upward call of God in Christ Jesus."

Philippians 3:13-14 (NASB)

Transitions can be challenging for any person, family or organization. Not long after we returned from the World Lacrosse Championship in Canada, our FCA Lacrosse Advisory Board received some exciting, yet challenging news. A unique opportunity was being offered to our FCA Lacrosse director, Sean McNamara, in the form of an invitation from FCA's new president, Les Steckel.

I appreciated the way Dal Shealy, who was president of FCA from 1992 to 2005, passed the baton to Les, who had decided to retire from coaching football. Both were great supporters of our FCA Lacrosse outreach efforts, and both were guest speakers at our FCA Lacrosse Coaches Breakfasts on more than one occasion.

Although Dal had never played or coached lacrosse, he could really connect with lacrosse coaches, or any other coaches for that matter. One thing Dal did during his message that I still can't figure out to this day, is he would bring the sports page of the local newspaper (if the convention was in Philadelphia, it was the sports section of the *Philadelphia Inquirer,* etc.) and he would spread it wide open as if he were about to read it.

He would then talk about how things in life can tear us up—mistakes we've made, things we've said, ways we have neglected and disobeyed God. While he was talking about the effects of our mistakes and sins tearing apart our lives, he would be tearing the sports section into 20 pieces. Once the paper was shredded, he would crumble it into a ball and then talk about how Jesus Christ lived, died and rose from the dead to restore us, to forgive us, and if we let him, make us whole again. He would then unfold what had been a shredded newspaper into its original, whole, functional state.

It was an incredible illustration of the Good News and helped many lacrosse coaches in attendance take that next step in their relationship with God.

Les was an amazing speaker as well, and one of the things I think he came to realize by being around our FCA Lacrosse outreaches is that different sports have different cultures. He was impressed with our focused passion and commitment to love and serve the lacrosse community in unique ways, and he was getting questions from other sports leaders around the country who wanted to do the same for their sport.

Les decided to approach Sean McNamara, our FCA Lacrosse director, about possibly moving to the FCA Support Center (or headquarters) in Kansas City to lead a new initiative to support and grow sports-specific ministry efforts for other sports like we were doing for lacrosse.

Les Steckel speaking to coaches and other centers of influence

We didn't like the idea of losing Sean, but we loved the idea of a new paradigm for FCA that allowed people most passionate about their specific sport to be full-time ambassadors to their sport community and culture.

Some of our FCA Lacrosse Advisory Board members were angry about Sean leaving and actually wanted us to leave FCA and become our own lacrosse ministry, but I encouraged them to see the big picture—that God was taking one of us (a lover of the Creator's game) to bless and multiply the overall ministry and kingdom influence of FCA.

I reminded our board that "We need to put the Kingdom first, and if we give FCA our best, God will bless us. He tells us in the Gospel of Luke that if we give, it will be given to us, a good measure pressed down shaken together it will pour into our laps, for by the standard of new measure that we give it will be measured to us in return. We can't outgive God, and we need to trust Him in this transition."

A Big Move

In 2007, Sean and his young family moved to Kansas City to help establish and support this new FCA sports-specific ministry vision. It wouldn't be long before Sean was helping to encourage and support new focused ministry efforts in wrestling, ice hockey, soccer and even motocross and surfing.

It took more than a year to find a new FCA Lacrosse director after Sean left, but fortunately, we had a strong FCA Lacrosse Advisory Board, made up of about a dozen volunteers who loved lacrosse and the mission of FCA. We also had two new staff members whom Sean had hired and could help fill the leadership void.

Drew Wardlow came on staff with FCA Lacrosse in 2007 after graduating from Grove City College, where he was a two-time captain on the men's lacrosse team, and a two-time All-Conference player. He joined Scott Hodgson, who came on staff with FCA Lacrosse in 2006 after being the volunteer assistant at Ohio State University, and prior to that serving as offensive coordinator at his alma mater, Susquehanna University. These guys did everything in their power to keep the camp and national teams going.

It was a long two years, but we finally found our next FCA Lacrosse director when a young man who had spent five years as a consultant at Booz Allen responded to an online ad we posted. It was a great day in 2008 when Ryan Horanburg (with the support of his new wife, Kate) accepted our offer to become our next director, especially realizing that he, like most FCA staff, would be responsible for raising his own salary through faith-based contributions.

Ryan says, "I was making money but not making a difference. That's why the national director position at FCA Lacrosse appealed to me when I was leaving my business consulting job. Working for FCA Lacrosse would combine my desire to present the Good News to people with the sport I loved. God could use me to impact players, coaches and families."

As the new director, Ryan sat down with his staff and our advisory board, and asked a typical consultant question: "If resources weren't an issue, what are some big, outside-the-box ideas we can dream about?"

Over the next decade, we would watch God provide the resources we needed to grow the ministry and influence of FCA Lacrosse beyond our wildest dreams.

Early FCA Lacrosse staff, (L to R) Drew Wardlow, Jen Noon, Josh Hoffman, Lauren King, Scott Hodgson, Merissa Bogdanor and Ryan Horanburg, filled the leadership void left by Sean McNamara after he moved to Kansas City to lead FCA's sports-specific ministry outreach.

Sports

...ward Christian Athletes in '92

...Squad' upsets Turtles

...Williams

...posed to be a case of
...being thrown to the

and sheer hustle to shut down the
No. 1 seeded Turtles' potent offense, anchored by Towson State
middie Rob Shek and former
Syracuse All-American Gary Gait,
one of the all-time leading scorers
in the Major Indoor Lacrosse
League.

Gait, who had seven goals in a
22-7 Greene Turtles' shellacking of
the Vail Lacrosse Club in
Thursday's opening round, was un-
able to get into the swing of things
Friday, scoring no goals on six
shots.

"I just wasn't on today,"
Gait said. "(Thursday) everything
was going in, (Friday) nothing was.
I'd say it was the altitude, but I
think it was the evening activities.

Though David Kelly had the
game-winning goal at 3:14 ... the
second overtime, it was ... the

Please see Lacrosse pa...

PART VIII

Family Affair

CHAPTER 44

I Am Second

"...'If anyone wishes to come after Me,
he must deny himself, and take up his cross daily and follow Me.'"

Luke 9:23 (NASB)

In 1997, Gayle and I moved from our townhouse in Loveton Farms to a house we had built that was closer to the city. By then, Gayle was no longer teaching but had a small educational consulting business, which gave her the flexibility to focus most of her time on our boys and our home.

My only requirement for our new house was that it had a flat backyard with enough space to play around with any kind of a ball as I confirmed with Gayle that one of the rules of our new home was "you are allowed to play ball in our house!"

I used to play a lot of "divers" with Frankie and Stephen, where I would throw a small football or tennis ball on their bed and they would dive and catch it. We played a ton of "knee" football in the hallway, where you had to be on your knees as you tried to get by the other guy and score. I definitely wanted them to be comfortable with physical contact, and joked around a lot about roughing them up—they loved all the games we made up, and so did I.

It wasn't long before Frankie was playing travel soccer, basketball and lacrosse, and high school was rapidly approaching. As an eighth grader at Calvert School in Baltimore City, he looked at a number of high schools in the area but when it was decision time, he wanted to go to Calvert Hall. I think he wanted to continue the tradition my brothers and I started, play lacrosse for his Uncle Bryan (whom he always referred to as Coach Kelly when at school or on the lacrosse field), and be a freshman with his cousin David Jr.

Frankie was a solid athlete; not the biggest and fastest, but very smart and a total team player. He ended up playing two years of basketball and four years of football and lacrosse at The Hall, and he was very involved in our FCA Huddle

there, even becoming president of
the huddle his senior year.

A real FCA Lacrosse highlight
came his sophomore year, when
Frankie was invited to be on the
2008 FCA Lacrosse National High
School Team, which was being
coached by Glen Miles, Andrew
Stimmel and FCA Lacrosse staffer, Drew Wardlow.

The 2008 FCA Lacrosse National High School Team in Toronto, Canada (see the famous CN Tower or Space Needle in the background)

After surrendering his life to
the Lord in 2004 with the FCA
Masters Team in Lake Placid, Glen went back home to California and followed
His lead to become a high school and club lacrosse coach. He was even named
Southern California High School Coach of the Year a couple of times, so he
was the perfect person to lead FCA's first "international" National High School
Team.

The FCA team ended up winning our self-proclaimed North American
Cup Championship, defeating the Ontario Edge at the University of Toronto
in Canada.

It was very special for me to see Frankie take the first faceoff for FCA Lacrosse's first-ever competition outside of the United States. It was even more
exciting to see the fellowship and message of God's love and truth being shared
with such amazing high school players from all over the country, many of whom
would go on to have stellar college careers.

In August 2008, Frankie (#18) took the first faceoff for the first-ever FCA Lacrosse competition outside the United States at the University of Toronto, helping lead the FCA National High School Team to a North American Cup Championship.

Hall in the Family

Frankie's senior year, he was recognized as Calvert Hall's National Football Foundation Scholar-Athlete (I was blessed to receive the same award 28 years earlier to the day). He was also fortunate to help lead the Cardinal football team to a win over their archrival, Loyola Blakefield, in the annual Thanksgiving Day game, breaking a nine-year losing streak, one of the longest in the more than 100-year history of the Turkey Bowl.

In the spring, he was selected as a captain of the lacrosse team, and would help lead a team that included his brother Stephen and cousin Johnny (both freshmen), and cousins David Jr. (a senior) and Patrick (a sophomore). The *Baltimore Sun* did a fun article about the five Kelly cousins all playing on the same, nationally ranked high school lacrosse team for their Uncle Bryan (Coach Kelly) titled, *Hall in the family for Kellys.*

Unfortunately, that team did not make the playoffs, but had some exciting wins and created some fun memories for our family. This was only the beginning of Kelly cousins playing together at Calvert Hall.

Frankie (Left) as a senior and Stephen as a freshman at the 2009 Thanksgiving Day Turkey Bowl game. That spring, Frankie and Stephen would team up with their cousins David Jr., Patrick and Johnny on the lacrosse field.

6 THE BALTIMORE SUN | **SPORTS** | FRIDAY, APRIL 30, 2010

VARSITY

BOYS LACROSSE

From left, Patrick, Frankie, Stephen, David and Johnny Kelly all play for uncle Bryan on Calvert Hall's varsity. "It's been a great experience," Bryan Kelly said. "They are very respectful of the boundaries I set here as their coach and outside of school as their uncle."

MATT ROTH/PHOTO FOR THE BALTIMORE SUN

Hall in the family for Kellys

Cardinals coach has five nephews on this year's team, with more on the way

By Nelson Coffin
TOWSON TIMES

As youngsters following their uncle's 2003 Maryland Interscholastic Athletic Association A Conference championship team, Frankie, David Jr., Patrick, Johnny and Stephen Kelly dreamed of the day when they, too, would play for Calvert Hall.

"We did the math," said Frankie, the school's student body president, who's headed to North Carolina, where his uncles, Bryan and David, won national championships with the Tar Heels. "We figured out that there was only one year when all of us could be on the same team."

After some calculations, 2010 was the year the youngsters decided the Cardinals would become decidedly Kelly-centric.

"We always dreamed what it would be like to get all five of us on the same team," said Frankie's brother, Stephen.

Of course, everything had to fall into place.

Although senior midfielders Frankie and David would be virtual locks to earn roster spots, Stephen and Johnny had to play their way onto the team as freshman middies. David's brother, Patrick, filled a need on an attack unit that lost Patrick Fanshaw (Loyola) and Jason McFadden

(Georgetown) to graduation.

"I recused myself from [making decisions on] cuts," said Calvert Hall coach Bryan Kelly, who coaches the sons of his siblings Frank III, David and John. The four Kelly brothers are all Calvert Hall alums.

Besides, it's not that unusual for freshmen to contribute to the current Cardinals, considering three other rookies — midfielders Tom Hollenback and John Betz and longstick Garrett Epple — are on this year's squad.

The coach has made good use of his nephews' talents for a team that has had an up-and-down ride in 2010, posting a 4-5 conference mark after beating St. Paul's, 9-8, on April 23 and losing to Gilman, 14-6, on Wednesday. Patrick had a goal and three assists — including the game-winning feed to sophomore Carter Brown with nine seconds remaining — while Frankie gobbled up 14 of 17 faceoffs in the victory over St. Paul's.

Still, there's more to the experience than statistics for the Kelly crew, who are never on the field at the same time, because Frankie and Stephen share faceoff chores.

"Wins and losses won't determine how much fun we've had this season," said David, who will attend Rutgers in the fall.

"And the season's not over yet," added Patrick, who leads the Kellys in goals this spring.

Nor is the influx of future Kelly stars likely to end anytime soon. Bryan's sons Jacob, David, Joshua and Caleb will join cousins Timmy, J.K., Micaiah and Boaz to give the Kellys a potential presence at Calvert Hall through 2029.

Uncle Bryan, however, tries to keep family ties out of all important team business.

At practice and school, he insists on being "Coach," not "Uncle Bryan."

"I don't know of many guys who have the opportunity to coach [so many of] their nephews," the coach said. "It's been a great experience. They are very respectful of the boundaries I set here as their coach and outside of school as their uncle."

Moreover, he's more interested in treating them as Cardinals — not Kellys.

"I think sometimes I can be harder on them" than on other players, he said. "I was really on Patrick's case [last week]. And they know that no Kelly is bigger than the team. They're no more important than anyone else on the team, that's for sure. But I'm also very glad they're on our team."

ncoffin@patuxent.com

Red, Orange or Blue

Beginning September 1st of Frankie's junior year, he started getting recruited by colleges for lacrosse. I thought that was way too early, but that's the way the system worked then.

Because Frankie was a good student and athlete, and because of his various leadership roles (including being president of the student body), he was recruited by some amazing coaches and universities, including a number of Ivy League schools.

He sorted through his options, which was very exciting, and narrowed it down to Cornell (my favorite option—I wonder why?), Princeton (Gayle's favorite option), Harvard University (just like one of my options nearly 30 years earlier) and the University of North Carolina at Chapel Hill. Which would Frankie choose?

One day he announced that he would make his decision by the upcoming Sunday. "It's your decision," I told him, "and I'll pray and fast for you before Sunday."

Over breakfast at Bob Evans, he told Gayle and me, "I've made my decision. I don't see myself at Harvard. I could definitely see myself at Cornell, and I think I would really like Princeton, but I just can't imagine saying 'no' to the University of North Carolina. If I could, I would do a year at each school, but I think I'm supposed to go to UNC."

We celebrated his decision, and although it was a little bittersweet for me, God, in His sovereignty, confirmed the wisdom of Frankie's choice during that August weekend in 2010 when Gayle and I dropped him off at school.

The lacrosse athletes arrived on a Friday, and UNC Head Coach Joe Breschi hosted an Italian dinner for everyone at his home. Saturday morning, we all moved Frankie into his dorm alongside his roommate Will Campbell and Will's fun and friendly parents, Jim and Debbie from Ohio. On Saturday night the lacrosse team families met for dinner at the Top of the Hill restaurant on famous Franklin Street. A lot of excitement and laughter was shared by all of the new teammates from around the country and their family members who were in attendance. On Sunday, it was time to say goodbye.

As Gayle and I stood with Frankie in front of his new dorm, Avery, and prayed with him, releasing him to the Lord, my phone, which was in my back pocket, started buzzing, but I wasn't going to answer in the middle of the prayer. After our goodbye hugs, kisses and a few tears, Frankie walked back into his dorm and Gayle and I walked over to our car. I looked at my phone and saw the missed call was from North Carolina's 919 area code and figured it must have been from one of the Tar Heel lacrosse coaches.

I called the number and it wasn't one of the coaches. It was my old friend from Athletes in Action, Mike Echstenkamper (a.k.a. Mike "X").

I immediately flashed back to the time I met Mike at the AIA Ultimate Training Camp in Colorado in 1985 after my junior year at Cornell. Mike had played baseball in the New York Yankees organization for a number of years and told me at the camp that he had recently decided to let go of baseball, join the AIA staff and was assigned to the University of North Carolina.

I told him, "My brother David will be a freshman there next year, maybe you can meet him someday."

UNC won the National Championship in David's freshman year in 1986, and my brother Bryan joined him there in 1987. Bryan struggled his freshman and sophomore year with some injuries and getting little playing time (I could relate to that story), and he ended up needing back surgery. I remember calling Mike X then as well.

"Hey Mike, it's Frank Kelly. Do you remember me from the AIA camp in Colorado?"

"Oh yeah, Frank. I remember you."

"My brothers, David and Bryan, are down there at UNC. Bryan is having a tough year and needs some encouragement. Could you possibly get together with him?" Mike ended up having a huge impact on Bryan's life.

Now, some 25 years later, Mike calls me while I'm at UNC praying with Frankie as he gets ready to start his career and experience as a Tar Heel.

"Hi Frank, it's Mike Echstenkamper," he said when I called him back. "I understand you dropped your son Frankie off at school today."

"Yeah, Mike, we're just leaving," I said.

"I'm calling to get his number. I'd like to invite him to our AIA 'Welcome to UNC' Cookout, which we are hosting for new freshman athletes this afternoon."

Gayle and I couldn't believe it. At the very moment we were praying over our son and releasing him to the Lord, Mike X was in my back pocket calling me. God in His goodness had a plan for Frankie.

Frankie had a solid career and was a true team player and a spiritual leader on the team. His brother Stephen would also choose UNC three years later and they played together during Frankie's senior year when he was recognized as a UNC Scholar-Athlete.

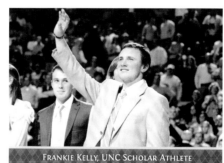

FRANKIE KELLY, UNC SCHOLAR ATHLETE
Maryland/UNC Basketball Game, 02/04/14

Frankie stayed a fifth year as a graduate assistant on the team and completed a Master's of Accounting at the Kenan-Flagler Business School. He actually coached Stephen and the other faceoff middies, which was fun to watch.

AIA at UNC

During Frankie's junior year, AIA selected him to be filmed for a segment of their video series called *I Am Second*, in which athletes tell the story of how their relationship with God became personal and real and how they came to put God first in their lives, and themselves second. In his video, Frankie summarizes how his experience at UNC impacted his spiritual life:

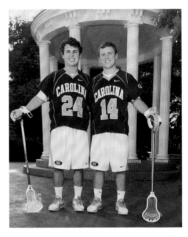

It was special to watch Frankie (Right) as a senior and Stephen as a freshman play together for the Tar Heels.

Scan to watch I am Second.

"Growing up in Baltimore, I was blessed to have a loving and godly family, and faith was instilled in me at a young age," he said in the video.

"That created some really dangerous attitudes in my heart. I was doing good things in my life so that people would look at me and say 'what a good kid.' That was coming out of selfishness. I didn't appreciate God for who He was, but for what He could get for me, and how my faith could elevate me.

"Through some great connections I've made here at UNC with AIA and the Summit Church and different influences that people have had on my life, I've come to discover that I can obey God because I desire to obey God.

"Now, I want people to look at me and say, 'what a great God he serves.'"

God's plan for Frankie at UNC included much more than school, lacrosse and fellowship. In Mike X's AIA group, he met another athlete, a gymnast named Acacia Cosentino, who would ultimately become his wife and the

Mike Echstenkamper officiating Frankie and Acacia's wedding in July 2017

mother of our first grandchild, Francis X. "Quin" Kelly V.

You never know who God will put in your path, as you choose to follow Him, even when it means wearing Carolina blue rather than Cornell red.

MORE TO THE STORY...

Fan, Player and Coach – Frankie Kelly

I was on the field where it happened—the Miracle in the Mountains in Vail, 1992! I'm in the team picture—the baby in the back row that one of the players is holding up.

My summers as a young child were defined by traveling with my family to FCA Lacrosse events—Vail and Lake Placid several times, and once to Australia. People tell me the Gauthier's Motor Inn in Lake Placid was a dump, but I was too young to notice and just treasured the eight-hour car rides watching the same three movies over and over on the TV with a videocassette recorder duct-taped between the front seats, the waffles, the pool, the lake and the canoes.

As an FCA Lacrosse camper, I had a blast meeting kids from different states, playing tons of lacrosse, eating ice cream for lunch and staying up late. The huddle leaders were significant role models for me. They were star lacrosse players at their high schools and colleges, so I couldn't write them off as "uncool."

I got to know some of them even better at the college tournaments I attended with my family in Ocean City, Maryland. I would watch them play, then hang around at their pizza dinners and Bible studies after the games.

Hearing the older players talk about living differently, living for the Lord, made me think, *If they can do it, so can I.*

FCA didn't regularly field a team in my age bracket, but in 2008 when I was a rising junior in high school, I was a player on one of FCA's first national high school teams and we ended up winning the first-ever North American Cup Championship in Toronto, Canada. It was cool to travel to a new country where they play a different style of lacrosse. That was my first experience on a team with Division I recruits from across the U.S. The late-night conversations could get pretty intense, but bonded us as a team. I'm still friends with a handful of those guys now, more than a decade later.

I credit the quality and commitment of those FCA coaches—like Andrew Stimmel who went on to become the head coach at Marquette University—and huddle leaders for helping prepare me for the college game and college life. Even while I was playing at the University of North Carolina from 2011-2014, I played two summers on the FCA men's team in Vail. We all stayed together at a big house in the mountains, which created a fertile environment for impromptu discussions about God, the Bible, and life while we were grilling steaks or playing cards. Those organic fellowship times beyond the formal Bible studies and huddles took our friendships to new levels.

My experiences as an FCA player sparked in me a passion to coach FCA teams and recreate those experiences for younger guys. I had a special heart for the Under-19 age players. I knew the pressures they faced graduating from high school and preparing to go to college because I had just gone through it myself—the pressure of the expectations of parents and coaches, handling the freedoms and responsibilities of fending for themselves, worried about how much playing time they'll get and what will happen if they get injured or their grades drop. Standing on the brink of big changes like that gets a kid's wheels turning.

Not all the players took it to heart, but I encouraged them to plug into a campus ministry and a local church, to be a light and not just go along with the flow of what everybody else was doing. I tried to help them anchor themselves in God and His Word, not in lacrosse, so that if something they were worried about did happen, their world wouldn't collapse.

I've grown up with FCA Lacrosse as a fan, a player and a coach. I've seen how it has taken the Gospel to families and campers like me, to players and coaches across the U.S.—I counted about 40 former FCA guys on recent NCAA Division I final four teams—and to the nations, one late-night conversation at a time.

CHAPTER 45

Rising Son

"Delight yourself in the Lord and he will give you the desires of your heart."

Psalm 37:4 (NASB)

I'll never forget our son Stephen's first lacrosse game. It was early one Saturday morning in the spring of 2000, and as we drove to the field, I looked in the rearview mirror and he had all of his equipment on, including his helmet. He was ready to go, and he was only six years old.

I was helping coach his team and we only put seven guys (two attackmen, two midfielders, two defensemen and a goalie) on the field at a time. Stephen ran to the center of the field and really wanted to take the first faceoff.

Stephen's first lacrosse game and goal off of the opening faceoff

The whistle blew to start the game and off he went. He clamped the ball, pushed it forward, scooped it up, went right down the center of the field, shot the ball and scored. Little did we know it then, but that would be one of many faceoff-related fastbreak goals in the future.

Just like God chose to bless our 1992 FCA team in Vail to give credibility to FCA Lacrosse, I think God chose to bless many of our youth players with on-the-field success to help grow the FCA Lacrosse youth ministry. It started with our first 9-10 youth team in 2004, then our first U15 National Championship in 2009, which Stephen was a big part of.

It's in His Bones

Stephen decided to follow his brother Frankie and cousins David Jr., Patrick and Johnny to Calvert Hall. They all played together on the "Hall in the Family" team in 2010.

As a sophomore, Stephen had a great year, being recognized as one of the top faceoff men and midfielders in the state and being named first-team All-Metro in the *Baltimore Sun* (which is a big deal in the lacrosse world in Maryland).

His success led him to getting an invitation in 2011 to try out for the U.S. Men's U19 Team that would represent the USA at the U19 World Championships in Turku, Finland the following summer.

Only a rising junior in high school, Stephen was one of the youngest U19 players invited to try out as one of the top 120 players in the country. In some ways, it was similar to the invitation I

Two FCA Lacrosse teammates and brothers in Christ, Kacy Kapinos (blue) covering Stephen (white) in a 2012 high school game when Calvert Hall was ranked #1 and Loyola was ranked #2 in the country

had received to try out for the U.S. Men's U19 Team two decades before. We both had our doubts that he would make the cut, first because of his age—most of the other players were already in college or going into their freshman years—and second because of his performance in "The Game."

He played well enough over the first few days of tryouts when they broke the 120 players into six different teams to be evaluated during all the games they played on Thursday, Friday and Saturday, and made it into what some folks called "The Game"—the final test for the top 40 players from whom the team would be chosen—similar to what I experienced in 1993.

The tryouts were held at the University of Maryland Baltimore County (UMBC) in Baltimore, so it was easy for me to go and watch. On my way to the stands that Saturday night, I ran into John Tucker, whom I had played with in what I thought was "The Game" in 1993. John made the USA team for a second time that year and went on to a Hall-of-Fame career. That night, John's son Ryan was playing on Stephen's team (he was certain to make the team like his father before him). We sat and watched together reminiscing about old times playing together for MLC, and even about those 1993 tryouts, when John told me I was going to make it.

Stephen did not have his best game as a faceoff middie that night. They put two other top faceoff specialists on the opposing team, both of whom ultimately made the U.S. Men's U19 Team, and they got the best of him. After the game, I took him out for a quick bite to eat and to offer a little encouragement.

"Look, you didn't have your best game," I said, "but the main thing now is to finish strong tomorrow. Most likely, you won't make the team. You are the youngest guy out there and all things being equal they will probably take an older, college-experienced player. It would be easy to pack it in, but God is in control. There's one more game and you never know what will happen."

I arrived about an hour before the game that Sunday morning and we went to a side field and worked for about 20 minutes on a flaw I had noticed in his faceoff technique. Stephen gave it his best. He went out and played a great game, and with 20 seconds left, in 95-degree heat, he took another faceoff, sprinted downfield on a fast break, fired a shot, and scored. It reminded me of his first faceoff and goal nearly a dozen years earlier as a six-year-old at LTRC.

I was so proud of him for finishing strong. A few days later he got the call that he made the team—the youngest player to ever make the U.S. Men's U19 Team. Ryan Tucker received good news also.

A number of months later, Gayle and I walked into the house from a weekend away watching Frankie and UNC play an early season game. Laying on the kitchen table was the latest *Lacrosse Magazine*. On the cover was Stephen in his Calvert Hall uniform, facing off with the sun coming up over his shoulder and the big caption: *Rising Son*. I don't know how they came up with that headline, but I could not help thinking about the ultimate Rising *Son*.

The article inside the magazine, which included a great picture of Stephen in front of the Calvert Hall scoreboard and "Kelly Field" signage (Big Frank and our family did a lot to raise money for the turf field, so Calvert Hall named it Kelly Field), was titled "It's in His Bones."

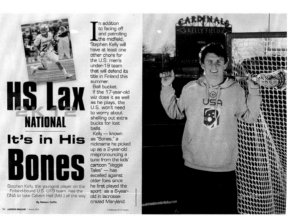

He picked up the nickname "Bones" as a young boy, when he kept singing a *Veggie Tales* video song about an evil king in the Bible, named Nebuchadnezzar, whom the show renamed "The Bunny" for the sake of their young audience.

Everyone would laugh when Stephen would sing "The Bunny Song," but it sounded like he was calling himself "The Boney," which everyone jokingly called him for a while until it evolved to "Boney" and then "Bones," which is a nickname that would stick, especially in the lacrosse world, even to this day.

Finland

Before leaving for Finland, Stephen was blessed to win an MIAA high school lacrosse championship together with his cousins Patrick, Johnny and Timmy. They were coached by their Uncle Bryan and ironically, the head coach for the opposing team was Jack Crawford, who was going to be an assistant coach for the U.S. Men's U19 Team in Finland. Calvert Hall had a great day and defeated Loyola by a lopsided score.

My parents with their sons and grandsons (L to R) John and Johnny, me and Stephen, and David with Patrick and Timmy after the 2012 MIAA Championship game (Not pictured is Uncle Bryan/Coach Kelly)

In the line after the game, as Stephen and Coach Crawford shook hands, Stephen said, "Coach, let's go win a world championship!" In Finland, Jack mentioned to Gayle and me several times what encouraging words those were after that disappointing loss.

Although the U.S. Men's U19 Team was upset twice losing pool play games against the Iroquois or Haudenosaunee National Team and Team Canada, they later beat Canada 10-8 in the championship game to win a gold medal and the World Championship.

Representing the United States and Team USA and playing in Turku, Finland against teams from around the world was a huge honor for Stephen and his lacrosse career, and it made me smile that he got to experience something that I never did.

It was also an open door and another opportunity for us to better understand and witness first-hand true international competition and the World Games structure and format. I met and spent time with several of the leaders of the Federation of International Lacrosse during our two weeks in Finland, which would ultimately help prepare us for taking FCA Lacrosse overseas in the future.

We spent two weeks in Finland cheering on Stephen and Team USA.

From Calvert Hall to Carolina

After winning a World Championship in Finland, Stephen finished his high school lacrosse career at Calvert Hall as a two-time high school All-American, an Under Armour All-American and three-time *Baltimore Sun* first-team All-Metro selection.

He had also been fortunate to help Calvert Hall win an MIAA Championship in football his sophomore year—Calvert Hall's first football championship in 28 years. I thought Stephen was an even better youth and high school football player than lacrosse player and he was recognized twice as a *Baltimore Sun* High School Athlete of the Year finalist. I never came close to receiving any honors like that.

Stephen chose to play his college lacrosse at the University of North Carolina, over a number of great schools that recruited him, including Virginia and my beloved Cornell, where he could have played football as well.

One of his main reasons for committing to UNC was to play with his brother Frankie and his cousin Patrick. Patrick was a year older than Stephen and, in 2012, they were named Co-Players of the Year in a local paper after they led Calvert Hall to only its second lacrosse championship in the previous 35 years. They were then hoping they could help bring a national championship back to Chapel Hill, since the Tar Heels

Stephen scoring what turned out to be the game-winning touchdown in the 2010 Turkey Bowl. That win sealed Calvert Hall's first MIAA football championship in 28 years.

had not won one since 1991 when their Uncle Bryan (Coach Kelly) was on the team.

But before heading south, Stephen would head north to Lake Placid to play for the FCA National High School Team, under Coaches Glen Miles, Jeremy Sieverts (who helped coach our 2009 U.S. National Championship Team), Greg Bice, Drew Wardlow and me. The team had a great experience on and off the field and was fortunate to win the Lake Placid Summit U18 Championship. Many of these players would go on to play at amazing schools like Maryland, Johns Hopkins, Duke, Syracuse, Princeton, UNC, Ohio State, Jacksonville and Towson University.

FCA Lacrosse was hoping to influence the influencers, and these national teams were a big part of that. With volunteer coaches and huddle leaders like those named above, you can see why the movement and influence continued to grow.

The 2012 FCA National High School Team and Lake Placid Summit U18 Champions

MORE TO THE STORY...

The Rock of My Faith – Stephen "Bones" Kelly

My earliest FCA Lacrosse memories are watching my father play in Lake Placid. They were the best lacrosse players in the world to me as a six-year-old. The other kids and I would rock the sidelines with chants of "God is on our side! God is on our side!" Maybe not the best theology, but we loved cheering for our dads.

I was always excited about the long drive up and the inn where we stayed. The diner across the street was the coolest place in the world to me!

I also sat in on some of the prayer and Bible study times that my father and others led, and I could tell that some of the guys' lives were changed on those trips because I had many of them as coaches, including Glen Miles, who became an impactful coach and mentor in my life. I actually committed my life to Christ when I was eight years old after one of Dan Britton's evening messages in Lake Placid.

My first overnight camp was at the FCA Lacrosse camp in Gettysburg. I remember being a nervous nine-year-old when I first got there, but I also remember how much fun I had with hundreds of other kids around. The huddle leaders and worship times also made a huge impact on me.

God worked in major ways in 2004 at the Pumpkin Fall Brawl tournament in Philadelphia. How cool it was to play and pray with the best nine- and ten-year-old players from the different Baltimore-area recreation councils, dominate the tournament, and generate interest in FCA youth lacrosse.

Everyone left that day saying, "Wow, we need to continue making teams like this and playing as much as we can," and over the next several summers, we played in two or three tournaments each year, including the big ones in Vail, and won a bunch of them.

We also grew together as a community in our faith. It was great to pray and study the scriptures with big-time college players like Jeremy Sieverts, who coached and taught us that lacrosse and sports weren't the most important things in life. I always loved seeing my friends who didn't have a faith background or any interest in it come to their first FCA experience and after a while say the closing prayer after a game. I thought that was the coolest thing in the world.

Our success set the stage for the first-ever US Lacrosse U15 National Championship in 2009. After we won the championship game in overtime, people came up and asked us what FCA was all about. Kids from all over the country started thinking that FCA was a really cool team to play for.

Stephen's FCA youth teams that I helped coach were fortunate to win the Vail Shootout a couple of times.

I continued to play on FCA national teams through high school, which took me back to the place where my relationship with God and my FCA Lacrosse memories began, Lake Placid—*Wow, I'm playing here now!*—and brought me full-circle with some of the men I had watched play ten years before, like my father and Glen Miles, who coached the team.

Although we learned a lot through some of the tough losses we experienced together, we won a lot of big tournament championships in Vail and Lake Placid, which further elevated the awareness and stature of FCA Lacrosse to the point where kids were almost begging to be on the team.

The only requirement to play on an FCA team was to love lacrosse and be open to growing in your relationship with God. My dad and our other coaches and huddle leaders always tried to create an environment that was fun, authentic and a safe place to discuss the things of God, no matter what a player believed coming in.

In college, I began coaching and leading huddles at FCA camps and coaching FCA youth teams, which included my brother JK and cousin Micaiah. The main message I wanted the kids to grasp was the same one that had made such a difference in my life—that the most important thing in their lives is not lacrosse, it's having a relationship with and being a follower of Jesus.

I encouraged them to be thankful every time they were able to step out on a field. I told them about the times I had struggled in life and how those struggles shifted my perspective on what's important and prepared me for success. I wanted them to know that even if God blessed them with victory, winning would not give them lasting happiness and peace in life. Only God could do that.

What I've valued most about my FCA Lacrosse experience is becoming close with players from around the country and creating a community of guys who talk freely about life, about God, and about relationships.

From those long-ago days of watching my father play at Lake Placid until now, FCA Lacrosse has always been a rock and place of encouragement for my relationship with God.

It was very cool to see Stephen speak at FCA Lacrosse Camp when he was a college player at UNC since he attended that same camp as a young boy.

CHAPTER 46

Shield of Faith

*"In addition to all this, take up the shield of faith,
with which you can extinguish all the flaming arrows of the evil one."*

Ephesians 6:16

Despite popular belief, not everyone in our extended Kelly family has loved the Creator's game. With the 21 Kelly cousins (fifteen boys and six girls), everyone has played a bit, but not everyone has embraced it as a passion.

When our daughter Jackie was about seven years old, and her older brothers were starting to play a ton of lacrosse at a high level, she came to me one day after her lacrosse season ended. She was on the "Pink Team," and her coaches were really nice.

Jackie and her "Pink Team" teammates

"Dad, I have terrible news," she said. "It's really bad, just terrible news."

Uh oh. What terrible news could my seven-year-old have for me? Should I go get Gayle?

"I don't like playing lacrosse," she said.

"Is that it? Is that your terrible news?"

"That's it, Dad. I know you won't be happy about that."

"Actually, Jackie, I'm totally fine with it. I think it's great if you don't play. I'm kind of tired of lacrosse anyway."

Jackie ultimately tried gymnastics and really liked it, but watching her flip around on a balance beam was scary for me. Her greatest gift is actually her

artistic talent and ability to draw almost anything, which is a lot safer than lacrosse or gymnastics.

Jackie gave lacrosse another try in middle school at Calvert School after a couple of her friends talked her into it. I was excited for her, but didn't make a big deal of it or ask a lot of questions. I just showed up at the first game. I arrived a little late and the game had already started. I looked out at the girls running up and down the field. Where's Jackie? I couldn't have missed her because they weren't wearing helmets. I looked over at the bench. Was she sick and not here?

The other team took a shot and...there's Jackie! She's the goalie! Apparently, no one on the team played goalie, so the coaches asked if anyone would be willing to serve the team and volunteer to play in the goal. Unbeknownst to Gayle and me, Jackie had stepped forward. Since she didn't really like lacrosse anyway and didn't really have a favorite position, she agreed to be the goalie. Who knew?

She was pretty good! In a big game a couple of weeks later, Jackie had around a dozen saves, which is a lot in a youth girls' lacrosse game—seven in the fourth quarter which sealed a one-point win for Calvert. Her secret: she never flinched. She stood her ground in the

Jackie is the only Kelly to have ever played goalie.

goal and let the shot hit her body if she couldn't get her stick on it.

In the car after the game, I couldn't contain myself. "Jackie, that was amazing! You played great and really, really helped your team."

"Oh, thanks," she said. "Did we win?"

"Yes, Jackie, you won!"

But she didn't really care about winning or losing. What I think she loved about playing goalie was that after every game all her teammates would run to her and jump up and down and give her some love and encouragement. Win or lose, they ran over to congratulate their goalie because they knew how hard it was to play in goal—and they knew that none of them were willing to get in there and do it.

I think we as Jackie's parents helped end her lacrosse career the following year. We took her for an eye exam. She was nearly legally blind and started wearing contact lenses. I immediately noticed something different

It was really fun to watch Jackie (far left) play goalie for FCA in Vail, with her cousins Grace (second from right) and Natalie Paletta—my Cornell teammate Steve Paletta's daughters.

about her goalie play. Now that she could see the ball better, she flinched when shots came at her and didn't save nearly as many as the year before. After that eighth-grade season at Calvert and a trip with FCA Lacrosse to Vail—where she won the championship playing with her cousins Grace and Natalie Paletta—she hung up her stick.

Jackie was the first and still the only Kelly to ever play goalie, and I give her a lot of credit for giving it her best.

MORE TO THE STORY...

Struggles and Strength in My Faith – Jackie Kelly

I've watched FCA Lacrosse up close since I was young and can attest that my father, the staff, and coaches have never strayed from their original vision to influence the lacrosse world for Christ.

FCA Lacrosse is special in so many ways. I don't think everyone realizes how inclusive the teams are. Kids from all faiths and all stages of faith—even no faith—are welcomed and loved by the coaches and players.

There's also a place for athletes like me for whom lacrosse is not their first

Jackie has always marched to the beat of her own drum. We took a picture of each child on this ledge overlooking the Grand Canyon. Frankie, Stephen and JK each faced the camera; Jackie faced the canyon. No wonder she was willing to play goalie.

love. I grew up competing in gymnastics and didn't pick up a stick until middle school. I picked up a goalie stick because, while I was strong and agile from my gymnastics training, I didn't like running up and down a field—they don't call lacrosse "the fastest game on two feet" for nothing!

I played in tournaments around Maryland, but my trip to Vail was the most impactful experience for me. We won every game, which didn't really matter to me, but exploring around town with my mom and the girls from all over the country, and our fellowship at the huddles and team dinners are what made the week memorable and meaningful.

FCA Lacrosse teams seem to win a lot, but winning is never the end goal. It's more about building community and relationships, and that's what made the difference in my life. Over the years, I have struggled with my faith, but it was always stronger when I played with FCA Lacrosse.

CHAPTER 47

Thumbs Up

"Rejoice with those who rejoice, and weep with those who weep."

Romans 12:15 (ESV)

Although Frankie and his Tar Heel teammates were fortunate to win an ACC Lacrosse Championship his junior year in 2013, UNC just could not get by the first round of the NCAA Playoffs. As Coach Joe Breschi's first official recruiting class, their team steadily improved, but it took a while to change the culture after he returned to his alma mater from being the head coach at Ohio State for nearly a decade.

During Frankie's senior year, with Stephen as a freshman sidelined after he broke his wrist in a game against Harvard and Patrick getting limited playing time as a sophomore, the Tar Heels lost again in the first round to Denver. Frankie had a great game and finished his senior season and Tar Heel career strong, but the disappointment of losing lingered.

**UNC MEN'S LACROSSE
2013 ACC CHAMPIONS**

Things changed in 2016 when UNC had a chance to get back to the NCAA Tournament Final Four for the first time in 23 years. The 2016 team featured fourteen players who had played on an FCA Lacrosse Team before college, including three Kellys: our son Stephen, a junior, and my brother David's sons Patrick, now a senior, and Timmy, a freshman.

After defeating Marquette 10-9 on a snowy May day in Milwaukee, Wisconsin in the first round of the NCAA Playoffs, to advance further, UNC would have to beat Notre Dame in the second round. *Oh no, not those guys again*, I thought. There was no love lost between the teams. Only three weeks before, UNC came back from five goals down in the fourth quarter to beat them after Stephen's game-winning goal off of a fast-break faceoff in the last couple minutes of the game. The season before, Notre Dame scored three goals in the last minutes for a come-from-behind victory over UNC.

This second-round game would be played in Columbus, Ohio at The Ohio State University in their football stadium, known as "The Shoe"—a neutral site for the players and fans, but an emotionally charged site for UNC's head coach, Joe Breschi.

Breschi's son Michael was born in Columbus when he was the head men's lacrosse coach at Ohio State. Their bedtime ritual always ended with Michael saying, "Hey Dad, thumbs up!" as they flashed each other the thumbs-up sign.

Michael was tragically killed in a parking lot accident in 2004 at only three years old.

The Ohio State community mobilized support for the Breschi family, and my brother Bryan called or texted Joe several times a week for the next year. They had been teammates at North Carolina from 1988 to 1990 and were together for the 1991 National Championship season when Bryan was a senior and Breschi was an assistant coach. "I watched Joe's faith evolve and grow," Bryan told *FCA Magazine*.[1]

The annual Ohio State vs. North Carolina "Thumbs Up" fall ball game, played at Calvert Hall, attracted thousands of fans and the Kelly family, who in the picture above were there to cheer on my nephew Johnny (#10 in red) and our son Stephen and nephew Timmy (both back row in blue).

Bryan helped organize the annual "Thumbs Up" Fall Ball scrimmage between UNC and Ohio State that was played at Calvert Hall for years and raises money for the Michael Breschi Scholarship Fund at Ohio State, awarded to the player "who exemplifies the spirit of Michael." FCAer Kacy Kapinos received this prestigious award in 2016 and my nephew Johnny received the award in 2017.

An Emotional Return

It was very emotional for Coach Breschi to return to Columbus where he had coached for ten years, and where Michael was buried. My nephew, Team Captain Patrick Kelly, brought Coach Breschi and the team to tears with his address before the game against Notre Dame. "We know Michael is with us. We're going to play as hard as we can to honor your son," Patrick said.

"Patrick was a leading voice on that team," according to Scott Hodgson, the FCA campus director at UNC. Scott had been on staff with FCA Lacrosse in Maryland for eight years before moving to Chapel Hill to lead the FCA ministry there. "Patrick rallied the entire team to agree to rest and recover as much as possible throughout the playoffs, which meant abstaining from alcohol and staying off their feet as much as possible."

Patrick had taken over leadership of the team's Bible study from Frankie after he graduated. He was also on the joint FCA-AIA student-athlete leadership team. Mike Echstenkamper and Scott from FCA met regularly with Patrick and other athletes and coaches from lacrosse and other teams.

Throughout the game, whenever the situation got tight, the players flashed the thumbs-up sign. But after the score was tied at 2-2, the game didn't have many more pressure situations. Stephen was on fire at the faceoff X and North Carolina jumped ahead 10-2 and won the game 13-9.

"That's the best game we've ever played in my time at North Carolina," Breschi told *FCA Magazine*.[2]

The Tar Heels would move on to their first Final Four in more than two decades.

MORE TO THE STORY...

Michael's Backyard – Patrick Kelly

As soon as our plane landed in Columbus, I could tell that Coach Breschi wasn't his usual, upbeat self. On the morning of the game against Notre Dame, he visited his son's grave, only ten miles from "The Shoe" where we were playing, and I could see that he was down.

A lot was riding on the game. Coach Breschi had never made it to the Final Four as a head coach, and though we hadn't had a great season record-wise, we were only one win away.

Before our team breakfast, I stood up and gave a speech similar to the kind that Coach Breschi gives us before the Thumbs Up games in the fall:

"We've had some great games this season and for many of them, we were playing for others. That's what this team is about. It's not about playing for ourselves, but playing for that guy to the right and left of you.

"Some particular games, though, stand out. The Duke game when we played for Del and the other injured guys who couldn't go out and fight on the field with us, and against Notre Dame a few weeks ago when we played for our seniors.

"And now we're in Ohio, where coach Breschi started his head coaching career. We're all at UNC because Coach Breschi gave us the opportunity to play for this awesome school, and we all strive to be more like him because he models hard work and strong character for each one of us.

"But this game, and the location of this game, is something special. Coach's son, Michael, is buried only miles away from where we're playing. So, I ask for all of us to play for Coach Breschi today, and let's do it in Michael's memory. I have a feeling if Michael was with us today, he would really want to see his dad get to his first Final Four as a head coach. We have the opportunity to make that happen in Michael's backyard.

"So let's play for coach Breschi today and let's honor Michael's memory by getting a win. I love all of you guys, and as always, thumbs up."

You could hear a pin drop. Everybody's anxiety was high, and all I did was put into words what everybody was already thinking. By getting it out in the open, everybody was able to take a deep breath and let it go.

I saw Coach choking up a little toward the end, and we rallied behind his raw emotion. "This is big," he said. "Let's go out there and take it to them."

God is Amazing! – Joe Breschi

When my young son, Michael, passed away in 2004, there were only a few people I could talk to about it, and Bryan Kelly was one of them. When you suffer a loss like that, you gravitate toward people who will wrap their arms around you and help you understand the big picture through faith. Bryan Kelly was that man for me.

He was a rock. Bryan assured me that Mike was in a better place and helped me strengthen my relationship with God through the tragedy. He helped me better understand the "why," and that God had His arms around our family.

We spoke several times a week after it happened, and we still stay in touch today. Bryan never forgets Mike's birthday; never forgets the anniversary of his death.

Bryan has been an integral part of the Thumbs Up game at Calvert Hall, and the wider Kelly family also supports the game and the Michael Breschi Foundation. Gayle Kelly is on our volunteer staff, and Senator Kelly (a.k.a. "Big Frank" or "BF") has always provided phenomenal support to my family and me. When he hugs me, I can tell he means it.

On our run to the Final Four in 2016, the day before we played Notre Dame in Columbus, Ohio, where Michael is buried, I asked my former assistant, Coach Nick Meyers (who took over after me at Ohio State), to take me to the cemetery to visit Mike.

At the team dinner that night, I said, "Guys, all I have to say is 'thank you.' Thank you for giving me the opportunity to come back and visit Michael. You guys did it. The fact that we're in the quarterfinals playing Notre Dame, here where I started my head coaching career at Ohio State, and also had the chance to come back and spend time with Mike—I'm beyond grateful. I want you to go out there and enjoy it."

My eyes teared up and you could have heard a pin drop in that room.

At a typical pregame breakfast, we eat, I go over a few final details of the game plan, and we get on the bus. But the morning of the Notre Dame game, Patrick Kelly stood up and did something no one had done before.

"Coach, I have something to say," he said.

"Go for it," I said.

He told me how grateful all the players were to my wife, Julie, and me for bringing them to Carolina, and told me they were going to take me to my first Final Four, in memory of Michael, who was with us on our journey.

Guys were crying, guys were fired up, and I was a mess.

In every huddle throughout the game, the players held their thumbs up and I was so thankful.

God is amazing!

CHAPTER 48

Final Four – Here We Come!

"The thief comes only to steal and kill and destroy;
I have come that they may have life, and have it to the full."

John 10:10

After the big quarterfinal win over Notre Dame, the Tar Heels were thrilled to be going to the Final Four in Philadelphia. Coach Breschi called my father a few days after the big win to make good on a promise. When Coach Breschi came to North Carolina from Ohio State in 2008, UNC was coming off another average season and hadn't won an ACC game in four years. After Frankie arrived in 2010, they began to win some games against Duke, Virginia and Maryland, but again kept underperforming and not going far in the post-season.

After several years of this, and after Patrick, Stephen, and then my nephew Timmy started playing for UNC, my father would joke with Coach Breschi. "Joe, you have or have had four of my grandsons play for you, so when you guys get back to the Final Four, like UNC used to when you, David and Bryan played here, you have to put Big Frank on the sideline."

"Dad, please don't talk to the coach," my brother David and I would say, but my father, half joking, persisted and got Coach laughing, so he finally agreed, "I'll tell you what, Big Frank," he said one year, "if and when we're in the Final Four again, I'll do everything I can to get you on the sideline."

Sideline Pass

"I worked it out," Coach Breschi called and told my father during the week leading up to the Final Four weekend. "Big Frank, I have a sideline pass for you, but it is very important that you don't say anything to any of the players during the game because there is a strict limit on the number of coaches you can have. We don't want anyone to think you're an extra coach on the sideline."

His grandsons Stephen, Patrick and Timmy all called before the big game. "Pop Pop, we heard Coach Breschi invited you onto our sideline for our Final Four game up in Philadelphia. We think that it is great but please don't talk to us during the game. Not a word." They knew it would be hard for Pop Pop to contain himself once he was there.

So there was my father, on the sidelines at Lincoln Financial Field in Philadelphia, beaming as he watched three of his grandsons play in the NCAA Final Four.

Unseeded UNC jumped off to a fast start, and even scored three goals in an eleven-second span, as Stephen had back-to-back fastbreak faceoff wins and assists that led to quick goals by Chris Cloutier, then Luke Goldstock. The Tar Heels beat seventh-seeded Loyola University 18-13 in the semifinals, setting up a match with the University of Maryland—the number one ranked team in the country that was riding a sixteen-game win streak—in the championship game on Memorial Day.

That day had special historical significance for my family. It was the 25th anniversary of UNC's undefeated 1991 national championship team that my brother Bryan started on. He and his UNC teammates were being honored at halftime. It was also the 45th anniversary of Big Frank's father's, my grandfather's, sudden death from an infection after surgery in a Philadelphia-area hospital. And here was Big Frank on the sideline watching three of his grandsons play in a national championship in Philadelphia.

In the Maryland game, Stephen won the early faceoffs and North Carolina jumped out to a 4-0 lead. But Stephen had taken 35 faceoffs in the semifinal game against Loyola just two days earlier, and Maryland's starting faceoff man took only eight in his semifinal game because he was struggling and was

Stephen won the early faceoffs in the National Championship game, and UNC jumped out to a 4-0 lead.

replaced, but now he was fresh in the championship game. By the second half,

Stephen seemed fatigued, and Maryland started winning faceoffs and mounting a comeback.

Going Out in Style

North Carolina is down by two late in the fourth quarter. My nephew Patrick has the ball. My father looks up to the sky and prays on the sideline, *Lord, maybe I shouldn't be asking for this, but this is Patrick's last game. Please let Carolina win, but if that's not in Your plan, please let Patrick go out in style.* Patrick promptly throws a high pass that sails out of bounds, but instead of stopping and pouting, he sprints off the field to let a long-pole defenseman into the game who hustles into the hole and causes a Maryland turnover. The ball comes back to Carolina.

Patrick comes back onto the field, catches a pass on the right wing and threads the needle with a pass through three defenders to Luke Goldstock who makes an amazing catch and shot for a goal! Carolina trails by one. Stephen wins the next faceoff, and 30 seconds later, Patrick takes the ball to the cage and scores the tying goal.

Both teams have chances to score in the waning seconds of the fourth quarter but never convert. A UNC defenseman picks up Maryland's errant shot and throws the ball downfield as time expires in regulation. But wait, there are flags on the field. *What happened?* The referee calls an unsportsmanlike conduct penalty on Luke Goldstock, Carolina's attackman.

I'm standing next to Luke's dad, Lenny, and after the official announcement of the penalty over the loudspeaker, he storms out of our section to walk off some steam. (If you watch the replay, you'll see a Maryland defender cheap shot Luke in the back, then see Luke turn and push the Maryland defender. The referee only saw Luke's push.)

Because of the penalty, there is no faceoff and it's Maryland's ball as overtime begins. They're a man up and they get the shot they want. Maryland's Connor Kelly (no relation), who has already scored four goals, has the ball and he's in his spot on the left wing, ten yards out. If you give him a hundred shots from there, he's going to make 98 of them.

But Carolina defenseman Zach Powers dives towards Kelly. Zach is laid out straight six feet off the ground like Superman with his stick extended just enough to alter the shot. It bounces off UNC goalie Brian Balkam's leg and Carolina clears the ball.

Coach Breschi calls timeout and puts his top offensive unit into the game, which includes my nephews Patrick and Timmy, the freshman. Timmy finds himself matched up on a short-stick defender behind the goal. He dodges and beats his man to the right, draws a slide and feeds the ball to a cutting Chris Cloutier, who had scored nine goals in the semifinal game against Loyola and has already scored four goals in the championship game.

Carolina is about to win but Maryland goalie Kyle Bernlohr makes one of the greatest saves in NCAA National Championship history with his body going one way, and his goalie stick the other way to stop the shot. But after the save, there's a scramble for the loose ball in front of the goal, and a referee throws another flag high into the air. This time, the penalty is on the Maryland defenseman who had cheap-shotted Luke Goldstock just a few minutes earlier. This time he gets caught.

The UNC extra-man offense unit comes on the field. UNC moves the ball quickly and Michael Tagliaferri has the ball in his stick. His father, John, and I were fraternity brothers and football teammates at Cornell. Michael has a wide-open shot but makes the extra skip pass to Chris Cloutier who catches it and shoots it left-handed, sidearm, low and away and the ball hits the net just inside the pipe. He scores! UNC wins in overtime and the Tar Heel fans go crazy!

National Champs!

With Big Frank on the sideline hugging the coaches, Stephen, Patrick, Timmy, and their teammates piled on top of each other on the field, and the rest of the Kellys go crazy in the stands. Michael Breschi and my grandfather Kelly, whom I never met, watch from on high. The dream of a National Championship victory becomes a reality.

The ultimate "Thumbs Up!"

Big Frank on the field with his grandsons (L to R) Stephen, Timmy and Patrick after their Tar Heel team won the 2016 National Championship 14-13 in overtime

MORE TO THE STORY...

The Carolina Kellys – Joe Breschi

After such an emotional win against Notre Dame, the pundits thought for sure we wouldn't be emotionally stable enough to take on Loyola in the semifinal game. But instead, the Notre Dame win took the monkey off of our back and lifted the pressure off getting to the Final Four.

I was fortunate to have not only Patrick Kelly on the team, but also Stephen Kelly, a junior, and freshman Timmy Kelly. I wanted Big Frank with us on the sidelines at the Final Four so he could watch up close three of his grandchildren play for the National Championship. It was my way of thanking him for helping the Breschi family survive.

Joe Breschi was featured on the front cover of the October 2016 issue of FCA Magazine, *which included a story entitled "Tragedy, Tears and Triumph."*

We came out against Loyola with all guns blazing and dominated from start to finish. Once again, we felt Mike's spirit, and the thumbs were up in the huddles and the guys were loving each other and having the times of their lives.

Throughout our run, Patrick talked about God's hand on our team, and we felt quiet confidence and unbelievable peace. God's hand, the spirit of Michael, and the spirit of Steve Muir were all present in our overtime victory over Maryland for the championship.

As I reflect on that championship season, I flash back to the 1980s when I first learned of the Kelly family from playing against David and Bryan in high school. Our schools are archrivals—their Calvert Hall vs. my Loyola Blakefield. But I didn't really know the Kelly family until David, Bryan and I played together at North Carolina and attended the Athletes in Action Bible study together. That's where I built upon my childhood faith and dug deeper into who God is and my relationship with Him.

Over the years, as I got into coaching and the Kellys got into FCA Lacrosse, my connection with the family grew bigger and bigger in every way. I coached Frankie, Patrick, Stephen, Timmy, and Jacob Kelly (Bryan's son, who came to Carolina when Timmy was a senior). Cut from the same fabric, the five of them are not only outstanding lacrosse players, but they were also each multiple-time All-ACC Academic Team selections, and most importantly, they are men of faith and servant leaders who show love in their relationships.

When I arrived as head coach at UNC in 2008, my assistant coach, Brian Holman, and I started a Bible study for the players. For the first couple of years, I'd lead the study using my FCA Bible and two or three players would show up. Then Frankie Kelly came to UNC. He brought more guys to the group and took over leading it.

Patrick, Stephen, Timmy and Jacob followed Frankie in taking over the reins and for years, over 20 kids would come regularly. The "Carolina Kellys" have opened the doors for more kids to come, eat pizza or Chipotle, and explore the Word of God. The team Bible study changed the lives of many players who came through our program. I could tell you the same kinds of stories about each of the Kelly men. They not only led the team in pursuing faith, but they also led as players and as individuals on the field and off the field. That's what makes the Kelly family so special—they have faith and life in perspective.

Sports

THE BALTIMORE SUN | SATURDAY, MAY 28, 2016

MEN'S LACROSSE NCAA FINAL FOUR

Always 'another Kelly'

Three family members on team are continuing a Tar Heels dynasty

UNC ATHLETICS PHOTOS

"I knew it was something I wanted to be a part of," junior faceoff specialist Stephen Kelly, right, says of North Carolina lacrosse.

Freshman Timmy Kelly looked around for another program before telling Tar Heels coach Joe Breschi, "I can't really resist."

Patrick Kelly is a senior midfielder for North Carolina. He's Timmy Kelly's brother and Stephen Kelly's cousin.

The Baltimore Sun *article from the Final Four weekend was fun and the QR code below captures an all-access look at UNC's 2016 National Championship victory and game-winning overtime goal. Go Heels!*

SEEING GOD IN THE NUMBERS

Throughout history, God has shown Himself in a burning bush, a pillar of cloud, and through various dreams and visions. And we know that numbers matter to God. He even has one book of His Word to us, the Bible, named "Numbers." At times, He speaks through numbers as well.

There was a lot happening on Lincoln Financial Field (The Linc) in Philadelphia that Memorial Day afternoon, Monday, May 30th, 2016, when UNC became the first unseeded team in history to win the NCAA Division I Men's Lacrosse Championship, beating undefeated Maryland 14-13 in overtime, but more impressive than those numbers were other numbers that rang true after the final whistle sounded.

Many have replayed this game in their heads, rewatched the highlights and relived the thrills with family, friends, Coach Breschi and anyone else who was remotely interested. For those who have watched most closely, it would appear that the Creator, God, showed Himself present through numbers that day. What do you think?

My grandfather Kelly died over Memorial Day Weekend 45 years prior. Isn't it interesting that Chris Cloutier, who scored the winning goal, wore jersey number 45?

When Bryan and his 1991 UNC championship teammates came out on the field at halftime for their celebration and recognition, they all wore polo shirts with a 25th-anniversary logo and the number 32 on their sleeves, the jersey number of their missing teammate and FCA Miracle in the Mountains midfielder, Steve Muir, who died of cancer the year before. Isn't it interesting that Cloutier scored the game-winning goal with 32 seconds off of the man-up penalty on UNC's 32nd shot of the game?

Maybe some are reading too much into it, but pondering how everything played out, Tar Heel fans might say of The Linc; "What an awesome place, like the house of God, at least for that day."

CHAPTER 49

The Thrill of Victory and The Agony of Defeat

"Rejoice always, pray continually, give thanks in all circumstances;
for this is God's will for you in Christ Jesus."

1 Thessalonians 5:16-18

After the 2016 National Championship campaign, expectations were running high for the Tar Heels the following year.

It has been said, "to the victor goes the spoils," and after the season, a number of UNC players received All-American honors, including Stephen and Patrick. Stephen was also named All-ACC and Co-MVP of the Championship team.

Many of Carolina's top players were returning, so there was a lot of buzz in the air about a repeat. Unfortunately, the 2017 season brought some unexpected challenges that sadly resulted in some painful losses. The

Although UNC won the 2017 ACC Tournament Championship, they got knocked out of the NCAA Tournament in the first round.

Tar Heels would have to win the end-of-the-season ACC Tournament, which was being hosted at Duke, to even have a shot at an NCAA playoff bid.

Stephen and the other captains really challenged the team, and they ended up upsetting Syracuse in the semifinal and Notre Dame in the championship game. So as ACC Tournament Champs, they would definitely get an NCAA Tournament bid, and hopefully a home game, which would be great since the first round of playoffs were on UNC's graduation weekend, and there would be numerous festivities on Saturday, and the actual graduation ceremony on Sunday morning.

We were all very disappointed to hear the ESPN Tournament selection committee announce that UNC would be playing at Albany on Saturday night. We were even more disappointed to sit in torrential rain, with a raucous Albany crowd, to watch the Tar Heels lose, playing their worst game of the season. Needless to say, it was a long flight back to Chapel Hill, and we got there just a few hours before graduation.

Fortunately, my nephew Johnny and his Ohio State Buckeyes team got hot and made a run all the way to the NCAA National Championship game on Memorial Day at Gillette Stadium in Foxborough, Massachusetts. Ironically, they lost a close game to Maryland, the team UNC had upset the year before.

It was amazing to see Johnny and a good number of his teammates circle up, take a knee and bow in prayer after that painful loss. Like UNC, Ohio State had a lot of guys on their team who had played for FCA and who attended their team Bible study, which was supported by their head coach, Nick Myers.

Coach Myers was Joe Breschi's assistant at Ohio State when Joe's son Michael died, so they went through a lot together, including each growing in their relationships with God.

We were all continuing to learn that life is full of ups and downs, wins and losses, new life and death, and our challenge is to see the Creator's hand at work in all those situations, and to give thanks, not for all circumstances, but in all circumstances.

FCA Lacrosse was committed to sharing these truths with young and old, and all who pick up the stick. Exciting days were on the horizon.

Johnny Kelly (#10) and his Ohio State Buckeyes made an amazing run to the 2017 NCAA National Championship and members of their team Bible study chose to circle up and give thanks after each game, win or lose.

MORE TO THE STORY...

A Space to Be Vulnerable – Johnny Kelly

I've had the opportunity throughout my life to be involved with FCA in
multiple capacities, and each has had
its unique impact on my life.

My Uncle Frank asked me to play
on FCA's first youth team in 2004,
when I was ten years old, and growing
up I always attended the FCA Lacrosse
camps in Gettysburg. I'll never forget
Dan Britton standing up and sharing
his faith story. For me as a ten-year-
old, that was profound and compelling to hear. I made friends with guys

*FCA staffer Drew Wardlow with my son
Stephen and nephew Johnny (front row when
they were ten-year-olds) leading a huddle at
FCA Lacrosse Camp at Gettysburg College*

whom I also played with on FCA club teams and national teams, and I still keep
in touch with many of them today.

FCA staffers Drew Wardlow and Josh Hoffman led the huddles. We took
deep dives into the Scriptures, and I leaned on them for help in understanding
how they applied to my life. I loved hearing the different perspectives of teammates from all over the country, all different walks of life, and different places in
their faith journeys. Drew and Josh walked us through God's Word with empathy and were never judgmental.

To see the dedication that Drew, Josh, my dad, and my uncles had to the
Lord and His will was just incredible. They modeled for me what a walk with the
Creator looked like.

Josh also helped with the FCA Huddle at Calvert Hall when I was there.
High school is that stage of life where guys' neurons aren't always firing correctly, but Josh would listen and let us get out whatever was in our heads without
being condescending.

He created a space to be vulnerable, which is rare in athletic settings. Older
guys would speak at the huddles and share their struggles—the good, the bad
and the ugly. They were real about how they reached the end of their rope and
leaned on the Lord to learn how to love themselves and love others in the right
way.

I'll never forget when Kevin Buchanan, a former Major League Lacrosse
and Premier Lacrosse League all-star, shared his journey with my huddle. I had

always looked up to him because I was following in his footsteps at Calvert Hall and Ohio State. He told us how the Lord helped him persevere in high school and college, and then overcome the learning differences and other issues he had to deal with in getting a job.

When I got to Ohio State, I would often remember Kevin's words. Little did I know

The Kelly family with Johnny (back row center, with black OSU jacket) after the 2017 National Championship game

that one day I would be a Buckeye lacrosse captain just like him.

Although we lost to Maryland in the 2017 National Championship, it was an honor to battle with my Ohio State brothers and teammates, many of whom had been influenced by FCA, and to share the experience with the entire Kelly family in the stands.

Not Alone – Kevin Buchanan

When I arrived at Calvert Hall in 2001, I was battling obsessive-compulsive disorder, which, as with other members of my family who also struggled with OCD, sometimes included bouts with depression.

When coach Bryan Kelly told all the guys trying out for lacrosse about the FCA Huddle—he offered it to us, but never pressured anyone—it was natural for me to go. My parents had instilled a strong faith foundation in me, and I relied on my faith to help me through my trials.

Frank Kelly and Brian Hubbard led the weekly huddles and Bible studies before school and on occasion, Brian led some at his home. Brian's uplifting, non-judgmental style made us comfortable talking about what was on our hearts and minds, and I was encouraged to know that I was not alone. I was not the only guy working through issues, and I appreciated how Brian ministered to us as our sounding board and advisor.

I hit another speed bump my freshman year when I was the last player cut from JV and moved down to the freshman team. *Am I no good? Do I have any future in lacrosse?* My faith told me not to give up, that God had a good plan for me, and getting cut from JV turned out to be the best thing that could have happened for my lacrosse career by far. My game reached a new level under Coach

Mike Thomas, who had coached varsity lacrosse at The Hall for many years, and after retiring, was coaching the freshman-sophomore team.

I played varsity my next three years at Calvert Hall and got good enough to play at Ohio State University, where I was honored as Conference Player of the Year and Second-Team All-American in 2008.

My FCA Huddle and Bible study experiences at Calvert Hall were so impactful that I wanted to find something similar at Ohio State. I joined a Bible study with my teammates that we called "Goodfellas," which kept me consistently in fellowship and God's Word.

Over the summers while in college, I played on a couple of FCA Lacrosse tournament teams, but my passion was leading huddles at the FCA Lacrosse camps at Gettysburg College. I wanted to share the life lessons I had learned navigating the high school and college lacrosse experiences and guide the kids through their challenges the way Coach Kelly and Brian Hubbard had helped me. God blessed me as I served the kids, like Johnny Kelly and a number of the Kelly cousins and their friends, not only by the way they responded but by how much I learned because I had to reflect and think deeply on God's Word if I was going to explain it.

After college, I played professionally for twelve years, made the U.S. National Team in 2014 and the U.S. Indoor National Team in 2011 and 2015. I finished my career in 2020 with the Chaos Lacrosse Club in the Premier Lacrosse League.

As I traveled for games, I had many opportunities to connect with local FCA Lacrosse huddles in the cities where I played, and I've continued to speak at FCA Lacrosse camps when I can.

My message to the kids reflects my experience with FCA Lacrosse: No matter what you're going through physically, psychologically or spiritually, you're not alone. You have brothers and sisters in Christ ready to help you, so stay the course and work hard. God has a plan for you, and faith in Him is the way to a healthier mindset and a better path.

CHAPTER 50

Refreshing the Blessing

*"May the Lord show mercy to the household of Onesiphorus, because
he often refreshed me and was not ashamed of my chains. On the contrary,
when he was in Rome, he searched hard for me until he found me."*

2 Timothy 1:16-17

After following Stephen and UNC's up-and-down 2017 season, and coaching JK and our FCA "2022" (high school graduation year) Club Team through the spring league and early summer tournaments, I was both excited and nervous about heading back to Vail.

That summer, 25 years after the Miracle in the Mountains, we thought it would be special to put a team together in Vail to celebrate the anniversary and see what God might do this time. Six of us from the original team made the trip.

Most of us were over 50 years old, but because others, like Brian Hubbard, were just out of high school back in 1992 and had not yet reached the "50" milestone, we had to enter the Super Masters division for ages 40 and above. We filled in the roster with as many 40-somethings as we could find, mostly guys who had played on FCA teams over the years.

"The Originals," 25 years later (L to R): Steve Mason, Steve Paletta, Gregg Langhoff, Dan Britton, me and Brian Hubbard with the actual scoring sheet and box score from the 1992 Miracle in the Mountains game

Our team dedicated the weekend to Steve Muir, who was a huge contributor to our victories in 1992 and had died of cancer in 2015, leaving a wife and three children.

Dan Britton set the tone for the week after a morning practice with his devotional on VDPs and VRPs. "Are you familiar with VDP Disease?" he asked. "It stands for Very Draining Person Disease. It's spread by people who exhibit repetitive negative, pessimistic, complaining, and life-sucking behaviors. They criticize, complain, whine, make excuses and find faults.

"The cure is called VRP—Very Refreshing People. When VRPs are around, you feel like a million bucks. They breathe encouragement, blessing, and hope into your soul and remind you that nothing is impossible with God."

Dan used the example of Onesiphorus, one of the Apostle Paul's VRPs, when Paul wrote "May the Lord show mercy to the household of Onesiphorus, because he often refreshed me and was not ashamed of my chains." Dan explained that the word "refreshed" means "to brace up or revive by fresh air." "And this was not a one-and-done refreshing," Dan said, "Onesiphorus poured out encouragement time and time again."

Then he challenged us. "Are you a Very Refreshing Person? Do you bring life to people? To your spouse? To your children? To the people you lead?" That message set the tone for a special yet challenging weekend together.

I was 52 and had "retired" from playing lacrosse at least five times over the last 20 years, and definitely did not want to be taking a ton of faceoffs. We recruited two stud faceoff guys in their forties, so I thought, *Perfect! We've got these young bucks, so I can take a few midfield runs and maybe a couple of faceoffs, and then kind of hang out on the edges of the action.*

Wrong! In the first game, both of the young bucks pulled their hamstrings. I guess they were not really that "young" being in their early forties, but they were a lot younger than me, and I was the only faceoff guy standing. *You gotta be kidding me!* But I played pretty well, and we won. I got hot in the second game and was winning faceoffs and starting fast breaks, and we won again.

Old Goats and Elder Statesmen

We faced the Navy Old Goats in our next game. Two former Navy lacrosse players played on our team—Glen Miles and his good friend and former Navy teammate Buddy Garland, who was on our FCA Lacrosse Advisory Board—so there was some good fun, camaraderie and fellowship around that game.

Buddy was a spiritual leader on the Navy team in his collegiate days and asked the Old Goats if they would like to gather on the field after the game for a brief prayer and reflection time. "Sure," they said.

We beat them in a close game, which put us in the semifinals, but my back began to stiffen.

In our joint huddle after the game, Glen and I said a few words about FCA Lacrosse, then as a group we thanked God that, even in our forties and fifties, we could still play the Creator's game and enjoy the mountains and the beauty of the creation that He gave us.

I was excited for the semifinal game because we were playing on Ford Field, right next to the main field where we beat Greene Turtle 25 years before. Our opponent was the Elder Statesmen, one of the top Super Masters teams in the country—the Greene Turtle of the 40 and over teams—coached by Peter Schaffer, who had coached Team Colorado and hired a chaplain for the game against us 25 years before.

I ran into Peter before the game. We were chatting about 1992 and I mentioned that we were playing in honor of our former teammate, Steve Muir, who had passed away.

"You're not going to believe this," Peter said. "We're playing in honor of our teammate, Steve Pelado. He died two weeks ago."

"Looks like we're both mourning a loss," I said. "How about we pray together for their families after the game."

"Let's do that."

In the game, we got off to a quick start. I won the opening faceoff and ran down on a clean fast break, passed the ball to Gregg Langhoff who threw it to Alvin Bowman who shot and scored. But it was downhill from there. After taking almost every faceoff for three straight games my back was killing me. *What am I doing out here?*, I thought.

A lot of us were hurting, but Dan had taught us in his VRP devotional earlier in the week that refreshing people are relentless. "Onesiphorus searched hard for Paul. He did whatever it took to bring a big dose of refreshment to him," he said. We all hung in there because we couldn't let each other down, but there was no miracle comeback. We lost, 13-7.

After the game, we joined with the Elder Statesmen to remember the bigger picture. Peter said a few words about Steve Pelado's life, career and family, then we told them about Steve Muir. We were all trying to figure out what to do with our emotions. A few FCA teammates and I closed our time with prayers for both of their families.

"That was awesome, thank you for doing that," the Elder Statesmen players said afterward.

After the game, my back hurt so bad I almost had to crawl off the field, but I wasn't going to miss our excursion that night to a nearby resort called 4 Eagle Ranch.

4 Eagle Ranch

Dan had pointed out that the act of refreshing can be risky. "As a former slave," he said, "Onesiphorus risked his life by going into prison to refresh his brother in Christ. Sometimes we need to step out of our comfort zone to refresh others."

After dinner at the Ranch, we sat around a bonfire and asked people to step out of their comfort zones and refresh each other by sharing where they were in their faith journeys and the roads that had brought them to that point. The miracles we witnessed on this trip were those that the Lord had worked in people's lives through the FCA Lacrosse ministry over the last 25 years.

I told my story. Glen Miles, Brian Hubbard, Steve Paletta, Steve Mason and Gregg Langhoff all stepped out and shared from their lives. Marc Hoffman, in his sixties, talked about his blossoming faith. Alvin Bowman gave us the "spitting" version of his story, which was off the charts.

Tom Hall reminisced about playing on our Lake Placid Gideon's Army Masters team with his brother Dave, how his son, Matt, served on FCA Lacrosse staff for several years and about the opportunity to play for the first time in Vail on the same team with his nephew Josh.

And Don Knobloch, who was the oldest player on our team at age 65, spoke about the ripple effect of FCA and the power of an invitation. I invited Don to come and play with us, even though he had never played before.

Don remembers, "I couldn't believe Frank asked me to play on the FCA 25th Anniversary Vail Team in 2017. Although I had never played lacrosse growing up, I had coached a lot of youth lacrosse in the Denver, Colorado area once my sons started playing as young boys. Even though I had a stick in my hand a lot of the time as a coach, I had no real playing experience and so I was really honored to be included and a little nervous about playing with all these great former players."

I first met Don about ten years earlier when I coached against him in the Vail Lacrosse Shootout with my son Stephen's U15 team. We were losing to Don's team by three goals with only a couple of minutes left, and somehow, we beat them, sending Don into shock. Our teams ended up playing before or after each other on the same fields throughout the tournament, so we got to know each other coming onto or getting off the field. We faced each other again later in the tournament and beat them pretty good, yet Don and I became friends.

Later that summer, he brought a team to that first U.S. U15 National Championship tournament in Bel Air, Maryland. We didn't play each other that week, but when FCA advanced to the semifinal game, Don brought his whole team to the game to cheer for us. They literally stood behind our bench and practically joined our team in our huddle during time-outs. They listened to every word we shared during those tense game-time situations. After we won, he wandered over to our huddle. "I always wanted to know what you do in those huddles," he said.

After that tournament, Don went home to Denver and soon after, formed six FCA Lacrosse teams that impacted hundreds of kids and their families' lives over the next decade. And his son, Blake, played on a bunch of our FCA National Teams that I was fortunate to coach.

After hearing each other's stories around the bonfire, we all had an opportunity to publicly commit or recommit our lives to the Lord, surrender any area of concern to Him or request prayer for something. As each person shared what was on their heart, Dan Britton challenged them to toss a stone into the fire as a visible symbol of their commitment or surrender to God, our Creator.

Around the bonfire at 4 Eagle Ranch

Welcome to the Family

It was very emotional for me when Michael Cummings got up and approached the fire. I knew Michael through his brother, Bobby, who I had played with at Cornell. Michael also played and had a great career at Cornell—including playing in two national championship games—but I never played with him because he came the year after I had graduated.

After Cornell, Michael made a killing as a bond broker on Wall Street but lost it all living fast and loose. Over the years, we played pro indoor lacrosse against each other and saw each other at different tournaments in Vail and Lake Placid. We ended up running into one another at the funeral of a former teammate, Paul Schimoler. Paul was a four-time All-American at Cornell and U.S. National Team goalie. He died of brain cancer in 2013 and at the reception in Paul's memory and honor, Mike and I reconnected and really shared on a deep level. He poured out his heart about some of his struggles, and I shared about God and His Word, which I explained is living, active and powerful enough to change our lives no matter what mistakes we have made.

After Paul's memorial service, we stayed in pretty regular contact with a few calls a year to each other. As we were putting the team together, the Lord kept putting Mike on my heart, so I reached out to him. He was living in Arizona and when I called, he was really excited, as he had recently started attending a church and was growing in his faith and relationship with God.

Now Michael was here, and when he dropped his stone in the fire, he quietly and with tears in his eyes, shared his story:

"Just a few months ago, in the spring, I was struggling with a huge hole in my heart that I had been trying to fill with all kinds of things since my college days 30 years prior. I felt like a failure and didn't know if I wanted to live anymore. But God had heard the cries of my heart, and in His plan, miraculously reached out to me and began the transformation of my life in a matter of a few days.

"It started when a friend invited me to Cornerstone Church near my house in Chandler, Arizona. I walked in, heard the music, read the words of the song on the screen, and immediately began to cry. *Oh my God, I've found something here.* I sat down in the front row. All of my pent-up fear and anxiety instantly drained from my body, and I gave my life to Christ that day.

"But the spiritual warfare began almost instantly. The next day, while soaking my sore muscles in the bathtub after a workout, a frightening image flashed past me. I felt like I was outside of my body, looking at myself from above. *It's the devil trying to take me out. He doesn't want me on the path following Jesus.*

"The following evening, my phone rang. I'm a New Yorker and very skeptical about phone calls coming in at eight o'clock at night. I thought it was probably somebody asking for money, but it was a person from Cornerstone Church. My first thought was, *Here we go; what do they want?*

"'Hello, Michael. I just wanted to touch base with you since you came to our church. Is there anything we can pray about for you?'

"I've attended Cornerstone ever since.

"A day later, Frank Kelly, who is one of the most caring people I know, called to check in on me, as he often did over the years. After we talked about my experiences of the previous three days, he said, 'Listen, Mike, we're putting a Super Masters 40+ FCA Lacrosse team together to play in Vail this summer. I'd like you to come. Can you make it?'

"I didn't have to think twice. Knowing Frank's faith, and coming on the heels of what had just happened to me, I viewed Frank's invitation as a serendipitous road sign pointing to the next step on my spiritual path, so I'm very thankful to be here."

My heart was pounding as Michael spoke. I could feel the pain of his prior mistakes, yet I was excited about his new openness to the Lord. I was also excited that my former Cornell football teammate and Bible study leader, Jeff

Caliguire, and his wife, Mindy, had driven up from their new home in Boulder, Colorado to be a part of our fellowship.

After Michael shared his story at the bonfire, Jeff walked over to him to say, "Welcome to the family." That sparked a friendship, and Michael entered Jeff's life coaching program to learn more about following Jesus and navigating life. Since that time together, Michael met and married his wife Maya, and, in 2021 at age 53, became the proud father of their son, Patrick.

God's Game Plan tells us that when we get right with our Creator through his son Jesus Christ, we experience a spiritual birth, and all who make that commitment to Him become spiritual brothers and sisters. Although our physical family is important and a real priority for me and most others, our spiritual family and connection can be much broader and over time become even more significant in our lives.

Dan had taught us in his devotional on Onesiphorus that our words can unlock God's greatness in others. "When you are refreshing, you are a blessing," he said. To refresh and bless was our purpose in coming to Vail in 1992 and 2017, and the goal of every FCA Lacrosse team that came all the years in between and since.

"There's a level of camaraderie on FCA Lacrosse teams that frees guys to open up about their journeys," Jeff observed. "Frank and all the coaches and leaders let everyone be themselves. They are never judgmental, and that creates a 'let's talk' environment when the games are over."

Dan closed his devotional with a prayer that he challenged us all to say, and it remains our prayer today:

Father, there is fresh power at the foot of the cross. Thank You for loving us and refreshing us all the time. We want to be used to pour out Your goodness to others. Help us to be VRPs—Very Refreshing People—every day.

Although there were no miracle wins on the field in 2017, we were blessed and refreshed to hear many miraculous stories of hope, healing and transformation around the bonfire that night.

FCA teams and families often huddle up and share personal faith stories and pray together when they visit beautiful 4 Eagle Ranch.

MORE TO THE STORY...

A Transformed Life - Michael Cummings

I had played in Vail frequently in the late 1980s and early 1990s—as much for the nightlife as for the lacrosse—so my experience with FCA was dramatically different. I made fast friends with my new brothers and sisters in Christ and felt strengthened by their support.

The night of the bonfire at 4 Eagle Ranch, Frank asked me to share with the group what had happened to me a couple of months earlier. I wasn't used to talking publicly about my faith, but it was a powerful, touching experience when I said it out loud.

I developed a relationship with Jeff Caliguire, and for the next year, he coached me on how to give my fear and shame over to God and helped me through some tough spots in my employment.

Sharing my story in Vail fueled me to go and tell it to college lacrosse players, and so far, I've spoken to the Duke, Maryland and Penn State teams. I told them, "Hey, I was just like you guys, sitting in your seat, believing I was impervious to bullets and bad decisions in life." Then I told them about my successes and

Michael Cummings with his wife Maya and son Patrick

my mistakes. People liked me because I was a good lacrosse player, then people liked me because I made a lot of money on Wall Street. But there are a lot of false pits you can fall into out there. I had low self-esteem, and people with low self-esteem make bad decisions because they're either trying to impress people or trying to be someone who they're truly not.

My life today is 180 degrees from where it was in 2017. The brotherhood in Vail ignited a big growth period for me. Frank did for me what he does all the time for people: he picked me up. And then Jeff helped me work out a lot of issues in my life.

It's been a good road. I met a wonderful woman, Maya, whom I'm now thrilled to call my wife. In 2021, we welcomed our beautiful newborn son, Patrick, into our family—a family I don't think I would have if I hadn't played with FCA in Vail.

FCA Lacrosse 25th Anniversary Team
2017 Vail Lacrosse Shootout – Grand Masters

Kneeling Left to Right: Marc Hoffman, Dan Britton, Frank Kelly III, Brian Hubbard, Gregg Langhoff, Steve Mason, Stephen Paletta, Billy Corbett

Standing Left to Right: Mike Shannon, Marty Stadelmaier, Glen Miles, Don Knobloch, Dean Curtis, Dan Kesselring, Mike Frederick, Josh Hall, Tom Hall, Jason Streeter, Mike Fitzgerald, Buddy Garland, Luke Griemsman, Alvin Bowman, Paul Wayne Mahlow, Mike Cummings, Ben Anderson, Sean Guildener, Shane Twomey, Steve Reed

Sports

...ard Christian Athletics in '92

...Squad' upsets Turtles

...Williams

...posed to be a case of
...s being thrown to the
...the he will...ed
...Lacrosse Shel...t
...Greene...s jump
...lead the...
...Frag...swing
...he...pocket
...umpte...
...ters...CA
...school masters...
...ucrew Shel...
...ic people...
...8, was...club...
...over...ket for
...d to...
...tion.
...the t...its first
...become
...ut app...ed," used a
...as the...us defense
...nation of...

and sheer hustle to shut down the
No. 1 seeded Turtles' potent offense, anchored by Towson State
middie Rob Shek and former
Syracuse All-American Gary Gait,
one of the all-time leading scorers
in the Major Indoor Lacrosse
League.

Gait, who had seven goals in a
22-7 Greene Turtles' shellacking of
the Vail Lacrosse Club in
Thursday's opening round, was un-
able to get into the swing of things
Friday, sc...goals on six
sho...

"I just wasn't on tod...ell,"
Gait said. "(Thursday) everything
was going in, (Friday) nothing was.
I'd say it was the altitude, but...
think it was the evening activitie...

Though David Kelly had...e
game-winning goal at 3:14...e
second overtime, it wa...

Please see *Lacrosse* pa...

PART IX

Lacrosse the World

CHAPTER 51

Lax on Lake Victoria

"...No eye has seen, no ear has heard,
and no mind has imagined what God has prepared for those who love him."

1 Corinthians 2:9 (NLT)

Since the mid-1990s, Kelly Benefits and its employees have partnered with World Vision to sponsor children in Ethiopia to help provide for their basic food, clothing, education and health care needs. The employees contribute half of the monthly amount, and Kelly Benefits contributes the other half for each child sponsored. It's part of our corporate commitment to giving, having been inspired by Jesus' call in Acts 1:8 to be His witnesses locally, regionally, nationally and to the remotest parts of the earth. This was our primary international giving initiative.

As we continued to give locally, regionally, nationally and internationally, our business continued to grow as well. We actually outgrew our relatively new corporate headquarters that we moved into in 1998 with almost 85 employees. Nearly ten years later, we had grown to more than 300 employees and had to lease additional office space in two separate buildings that were across the street.

In 2007, I was named CEO of Kelly Benefits, Big Frank became chairman of Kelly & Associates Insurance Group, and my brothers were presidents of the different entities and divisions they ran. Each had major responsibilities outside that as well. Not that titles matter that much in family businesses, as we were still equal partners in everything, looking to use each other's strengths and gifts to grow the business.

A Vision Trip

Since Kelly Benefits and our People were now sponsoring more than 200 children primarily in Gurage, Ethiopia, I wanted to arrange a "Vision Trip" for any employee who wanted to meet their sponsored child or children and see the impact of their support firsthand.

Because of wars on the borders of Ethiopia and Eritrea, we were advised not to go for about a ten-year period. It was a long wait, but our World Vision representative, Steve Krentel, did a great job laying a foundation for me to go on my first Vision Trip in 2012. To make sure everything was safe, our family decided it was best for me to go alone before bringing any of our co-workers.

Two months before I was scheduled to leave, Steve called me. "Frank, World Vision always takes groups of sponsors on these Vision Trips, so there will be others traveling with us. The final itinerary just came out and we are scheduled to stop in Uganda for five days before we go to Ethiopia for another five days," he told me.

What? I had no interest in Uganda. I didn't even know where it was, and the only reason I had even heard of it was because of Idi Amin, its brutal president in the 1970s. But if a five-day layover in Uganda was what it would take to get to Ethiopia, I guess that is what I would have to do.

The weekend I was leaving for Africa was jam-packed because it was the same weekend in January as the US Lacrosse Convention in Philadelphia. I drove up on Friday for our FCA Lacrosse Advisory Board meeting and dinner, and then we hosted our annual FCA Lacrosse Coaches Breakfast on Saturday morning. After more than 20 years of hosting this free breakfast, we usually had a couple hundred coaches in attendance.

This breakfast was not easy to pull together since we had to raise about $20,000 each year to cover the cost, line up speakers and promote the breakfast to make sure the room of prepaid seats was filled.

That year, our speaker was Frank Urso, the former four-time, first-team All-American, who had played in and won two national championships at the University of Maryland in the 1970s. His story of success (one of only four four-time first-team Division I All-Americans in history), then pain and failure and ultimate redemption with and through Jesus was incredibly inspiring. The fact that he was the head lacrosse coach at Garnet Valley High School in Pennsylvania only added to his credibility with the other coaches in the room.

Most years I would have gone home after the breakfast, but this year the U.S. U19 Men's National Team asked our son Stephen and three of his U.S. National Team teammates to put on a midfield and faceoff clinic that afternoon at 3 p.m., so I was going to stay and watch.

You're Going to Uganda Tomorrow?

Since I was there, I agreed to work our FCA booth in the Exhibit Hall from 11 a.m. to 2 p.m., then had an hour to kill. I wandered around the exhibition hall. A booth called "Fields of Growth" caught my attention because the pictures looked like kids from Africa, which was where I was headed the next day. I introduced myself to the person at the booth, Kevin Dugan.

"You're Frank Kelly?" he said. "You're with FCA, right?"

"That's right…I think I know you from somewhere," I said.

"I played on an FCA team once," he said.

"Really?" It took a while, but then I remembered that Kevin had played and coached lacrosse at Notre Dame and had been the head coach at the University of Scranton. "Yes, now I remember you, Kevin!"

"What is Fields of Growth about?" I asked. "These pictures look like they're from Africa."

"They are from Africa. We actually started lacrosse there two years ago in Uganda," he said.

"Uganda? What?! I'm going to Uganda tomorrow!"

"You're going to Uganda tomorrow? That's incredible! You've got to meet our players, and all the guys and girls playing lacrosse. They would love to see you."

The deluge of war orphans and AIDS orphans in Uganda led Kevin to set up a non-profit called Fields of Growth, which brought college students there for short-term trips to help serve and care for them. A lot of the students who signed up for the service trips happened to be college lacrosse players, and while they were there, taught the kids how to play lacrosse.

"That sounds great," I said, "but I don't even know where I'll be. I'm going with a guy named Steve Krentel from World Vision, and I have to go wherever he goes."

"Do me a favor," Kevin said. "Can you just email your itinerary to me?"

"Alright, I'll email it to you."

I met Steve bright and early the next morning at Dulles International Airport in Washington, D.C. and together we enjoyed our fifteen-hour flight to Uganda's Entebbe International Airport. As we came off the plane and down the walkway, we saw a small woman in the distance holding a sign with the orange World Vision logo that read: "Welcome, Mr. Kelly. Welcome, Mr. Krentel."

We expected to see someone from World Vision, but behind her stood eight Ugandan lacrosse players banging a drum and holding up a huge "Welcome Kelly" banner attached to and spread out by two lacrosse sticks.

"What the heck is that?" Steve asked. "Do you know people in Uganda?"

"No one," I said. I didn't know anything about Uganda until I spoke with Kevin Dugan yesterday and I read about its history on the plane ride over.

The World Vision woman greeted us, then the Ugandan lacrosse players told me that Kevin Dugan had emailed them my itinerary and told them I was a lacrosse guy worth meeting. They started hugging me and asking when they could see me again. I looked at Steve.

It was incredible being greeted by Ugandan lacrosse players when we landed in Uganda's Entebbe International Airport.

"Well, Frank, today would be the only day. Our itinerary is packed, but we set aside the first day as a rest day. So, it's 10 a.m. now and we don't have anything planned until dinner at 6."

"Can they come over to our hotel?"

"Sure," Steve said. "Most people take a nap, but you do whatever you want."

I didn't even know the name of our hotel, let alone where it was located, but I learned that World Vision usually makes sure your first hotel is the nicest of the trip, to provide decent rest after many hours of travel. Our hotel happened to be located right on Lake Victoria, which was beautiful, and I ended up hanging out all afternoon playing lacrosse on Lake Victoria with about a dozen Ugandan players, mostly in their late teens and early twenties.

"Mr. Frank, we're coming to the World Lacrosse Championships in the U.S. in 2014 and we are going to win it all!" they boasted.

An unexpected surprise was spending my first day in Uganda playing the Creator's game on the shores of Lake Victoria. Fortunately, I had some FCA Lacrosse and Kelly Benefits shirts to give away.

"Okay," I said, shaking my head. "But I didn't even know anyone played lacrosse here until yesterday. How are you going to do that?"

"Mr. Kevin Dugan and Miss Aimee Dixon are helping us," they said.

Aimee played lacrosse at the University of Louisville and was a student-athlete who came to Uganda through Fields of Growth for a three-week trip. She ended up staying for six months, captivated by the Ugandan people, culture and needs.

What a crazy start to my trip. But the rest of my time in Uganda was much more sobering. At World Vision's child soldier rescue rehabilitation center in Gulu, I saw up close the trauma caused by an evil Ugandan rebel group led by Joseph Kony that, over a period of more than 20 years, had kidnapped tens of thousands of children from various villages, and forced the boys to fight in their army and turned the girls into sex slaves.

Five days before, I knew nothing about Uganda. Now, God was turning my heart towards its oppressed children.

The rest of our trip through Ethiopia was also amazing. No lacrosse, but I had the opportunity to meet some of the children our family and the People of Kelly Benefits sponsored, and to see the water wells, school buildings and small medical centers our gifts help build.

I had no idea how impactful a "Vision Trip" would be, or that I would see some of those Uganda Lacrosse players again, much sooner than I thought.

CHAPTER 52

International Vision

"For God so loved the world that he gave his one and only Son,
that whoever believes in him shall not perish but have eternal life."

John 3:16

T he Ugandans were serious about playing in the 2014 World Lacrosse Championship in Denver, but they needed help. Late in 2013, Aimee Dixon called me from Uganda.

"Hello, Frank, this is Aimee Dixon from Fields of Growth. I understand you met some of our players in Uganda a year or so ago, and they suggested I call you. I am trying to raise $150,000 to get the Uganda National Team to the World Championship in Denver. Can you help me?"

My first thought was, *Wow, they said they wanted to come, but this is wild.*

"What are you thinking?" I asked.

"I need a couple of anchors, two or three $10,000 sponsors. Would your company consider being a $10,000 sponsor?"

"I like the idea," I said, "but I'll have to talk to my dad and my brothers and call you back."

"In exchange for your sponsorship, we'll put your company logo on the sleeve of our uniforms and all of our other things as well," Aimee added.

We discussed it as a family and with a little encouragement from me, we agreed to sponsor them. Aimee raised the full amount she needed, and the Ugandan National Team would become the first African team to ever play in an international lacrosse competition.

Around the World

While God was showing me how the World Lacrosse Championship tournaments worked and how lacrosse was growing in unexpected places like Uganda, He was also opening FCA's eyes to what He was doing through sports ministries across the globe.

In 2007, Dan Britton and four others from FCA attended the International Sports Coalition conference in Thailand, along with 700 other leaders from over 100 countries. People from other continents constantly came up to him and told him things like, "I was in the U.S. ten years ago and saw your sports camps. I came back and started doing camps here in Africa." Or, "I have a friend in the U.S. who sends me copies of FCA's Athletes Bible that helps us reach athletes and coaches here in Europe."

While FCA's leadership was focused on ministry to the 4% of the world's population living in their U.S. backyard, God was using FCA without them even knowing it to help reach the other 96%.

Dan discovered a vast grassroots movement through a network of sports ministry leaders around the world that was opening the door for FCA and FCA Lacrosse to possibly step in and help. He spoke to people like Pastor Gary Visitacion, who had a sports ministry in the Philippines, and Reon Tay, who played on Singapore's national lacrosse team, who told Dan how much they were "waiting and dying" for FCA to help them build interest in lacrosse by possibly bringing teams and coaches to Singapore to support their camps and outreaches.

"If you can bring some high-level coaches and athletes, you can come in and do whatever you want," they said.

Although Barry Spofford was FCA's first staff person focused on international ministry and outreach, he was only working part-time and the needs and opportunities around the world were so significant. In 2007, FCA conducted five camps in five countries, with a total of 760 campers. By 2013, FCA ran 87 camps in 26 countries, with over 13,000 campers.

Amazed at what God was doing around the world and sensing His calling to a new type of ministry, in 2013, the FCA Board of Trustees created a new division, FCA International, and named Dan Britton as its first executive director.

That same year, I got a call from Les Steckel asking me if I would be open to rejoining the FCA Board of Trustees. It was no longer the "National" Board of Trustees, since FCA was now fully on board with international ministry.

I talked and prayed about it with Gayle, and we both thought I should do it. She would join me at the semiannual board meetings when she could. Although Gayle was also serving on several boards herself, including the Community Bible Study (CBS) board, an international ministry she had been involved with since 1992. Between the boards and all that was going on with our children at home, we would have to do our best to juggle our schedules.

With Gayle's support, I was thrilled to get back to Les with my decision and would end up serving two more three-year terms alongside an amazing group of leaders from across the country and around the world.

MORE TO THE STORY...

Energy and Passion – Les Steckel

When you say the name "Frank Kelly," the first thing that comes to my mind is energy and passion. That's what he brought to our FCA Board of Trustees. He doesn't know any other speed but 100 miles an hour.

My wife, Chris, and I have traveled the country and met hundreds and hundreds of wonderful people. We would try to go to dinner with each Trustee candidate and their spouse to see where their marriage was. In my role as president of FCA, we wanted to make sure we had strong men and women of integrity and humility in FCA leadership roles. Frank and Gayle jumped out at us.

Frank had served on the FCA Board of Trustees from 1997 to 2003, but I thought, you know what? It's 2014, Frank's had a break, there is so much now happening internationally, and he has a passion for that, I'm going to ask him to come back for another term.

Watching Frank in our board meetings made me smile. He was a blazing notetaker like me and I loved that about him. He would collect all the information, then sit quietly and wait for the right moment to share his thoughts. He wasted no time zeroing in on the bottom line. He sugarcoated nothing, and he was always right on target.

I appreciated Gayle's input as well. She didn't vote but attended a number of the board meetings with Frank and brought the same level of wisdom and energy. They're just a go-getter couple.

Frank's advice challenged some board members, but he said what we needed to hear. He helped FCA advance in many areas, and the direction he offered regarding international and inner-city ministries was especially inspiring to all of us.

CHAPTER 53

Team Serve

"Serve wholeheartedly, as if you were serving the Lord, not people, because you know that the Lord will reward each one for whatever good they do..."

Ephesians 6:7-8

With everything that was happening in the international lacrosse arena with me personally and with FCA, I believed that God wanted FCA Lacrosse at the 2014 World Lacrosse Championship in Denver. Our FCA Lacrosse staff, who were already overworked, weren't as convinced.

"We have our camp that week," they said.

"We have camp every year," I answered. "The lacrosse world is coming to Denver and we need to be there." The last time the World Games were hosted in America was in 1998. Instead of traveling to dozens of countries to play lacrosse and share the Good News, dozens of countries are coming to us, right here in America.

"We can't afford it," they said.

One of my strengths is persistence, and I continued to challenge them.

"I feel strongly that we must be there. Let's put a fleece before the Lord like Gideon did in the Old Testament, to ask for a clear confirmation if we should do this.

"Let's meet with the Federation of International Lacrosse (FIL—now called World Lacrosse) leadership and ask if they will let us come. They might not, but if they give us their blessing, we'll look at it as an open door, then we'll go to the US Lacrosse leadership team to see if they'll support our efforts. We'll need their permission also since they're the hosting organization in Denver. If we get approval from both organizations, we'll look at it as a sign to go for it."

I'll never forget our meeting during the US Lacrosse Convention in January 2014 in the huge sitting area in the middle of the lobby of the Philadelphia

Marriott. Three representatives from FIL were there, including Stan Cocker-ton, a former Canadian National Team player who was the president of the FIL, Tom Hayes, the former coach at Rutgers who had worked tirelessly as a volunteer to grow the game of lacrosse around the world since the mid-1970s, and Ron Balls from England, who was on the FIL Board for decades. With me was Ryan Horanburg, our FCA Lacrosse director, and Josh Hoffman and Drew Wardlow who were both FCA Lacrosse men's ministry staff leaders.

"Gentlemen, thank you for your time," I began. "I believe you are famil-iar with FCA Lacrosse, and that our goal is to serve the lacrosse community. What we would like to do is bring a team of 20 to 25 players, mostly post-col-legiate and high-level athletes, to Denver and serve the FIL and as many teams as possible during the World Championships.

"We are willing to do anything you might ask—fill water bottles, string goals, clean up trash—but our real passion would be to scrimmage against some of the developing countries. We would like to come and make ourselves available as practice dummies and to provide some free position instruction for any team.

"But in the spirit of full disclosure, we would also want to share with them about why we are doing what we're doing and what FCA is about. And, ideally, we would like our FCA team, which we are calling 'Team Serve,' to live in the dorms with the teams."

Awkward silence. The FIL representatives looked around at each other.

Then Tom Hayes spoke. "Frankie, I like it. I think it's great."

Stan Cockerton agreed. "I fully support it. Great idea."

And Ron Balls nodded in approval as well.

They then told us that US Lacrosse was looking for a bunch of volunteers as the host country and that they would love to hear from us.

I smiled and glanced over my shoulder at Ryan, Josh and Drew, who were smiling and rolling their eyes.

We left the lobby and I arranged a meeting with US Lacrosse.

"You can bring 25 volunteers? That would be great," they said.

"And what we would really like to do is stay in the dorms with the other teams," I said.

"I think we can make that happen," they said.

We received God's confirmation and although Ryan and Drew stayed back to lead the FCA Lacrosse Camp, Josh and I helped pull together the 25 players and raise the needed funds. We went to Denver as Team Serve.

The Darling of Denver

God is so gracious. He arranged for us to stay in the same dorm as the Ugandan team, which my nephew David Jr. was helping coach. He had played at Rutgers and met some other lacrosse players who had been to Uganda with Fields of Growth. One thing led to another, and he visited Uganda and was invited to be a part of the team's coaching staff. He was staying in the same dorm with the Uganda team as well.

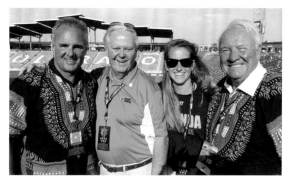

I love this picture with Coach Richie Moran (the GM for Team Ireland), Aimee Dixon (the GM of Team Uganda) and Big Frank (whom the Ugandans called "Jajja" or "Grandpa").

We bonded closely with them, which would sow the seeds for a possible future FCA Lacrosse ministry there.

God also arranged the schedule so that Uganda's first game was against Ireland, whose general manager (GM) was my former coach at Cornell, Hall-of-Famer Richie Moran.

Uganda was getting thoroughly thumped by Ireland, 17-0 in the third quarter, but I could see them playing better as the game progressed. Late in the third quarter, Castro David Onen, who had fled Northern Uganda as a young boy to escape possible abduction by the LRA terror group, had the ball behind Ireland's goal. He dodged hard to his right around the crease and dove, and I mean near-ly six feet off the ground, perfectly parallel, shooting and scoring the first goal ever by an African player in international competition. His new nickname "Air Onen" was born.

The crowd goes wild, chanting "U-gan-da! U-gan-da!" like they just won the tournament.

The first ever African goal scored in international competition by Castro David "Air" Onen vs. Team Ireland

"The most beautiful goal I've ever seen,"[1] said

Kevin Dugan in *Lacrosse Magazine's* September 2014 issue, which featured three Ugandan players on the cover and an eight-page story about the team.

A picture of Onen shooting in mid-air went viral on the internet and became the signature photo of the 2014 games, and in the photo, plain as day, is the Kelly Benefits logo on his sleeve. My phone rang non-stop. "Dude, what is your company logo doing on the Ugandan team jersey?"

"It's a long story."

I never knew it but there is a large Ugandan population around Denver. Suddenly hundreds, sometimes thousands of fans showed up at their games. One local woman who had never heard of lacrosse but saw the Ugandan team on the local television news made bagged lunches for them.

"Uganda has become the darling of Denver; the *envy of every selfie-seeking fan and player*," wrote *Lacrosse Magazine*. "An unlikely beacon," the writer called the team because they were from a country "with poverty and disease on its doorstep."[2]

My daughter Jackie designed Uganda "Crane" (the country's mascot) T-shirts for the Ugandan team and we made about 100 extras to sell as a fundraiser. They were sold out in just a few hours.

Team captain, Patrick "Pato" Oriana made history again three days later in Uganda's game against South Korea. Down by five goals, Uganda fought back to tie the score 9-9 in the fourth quarter. With 36 seconds left, Pato scored the game-winner off a faceoff to give Uganda its first victory. Later in the tournament, Uganda defeated Argentina and finished with two wins and five losses.

Opened Doors

Team Serve helped US Lacrosse with odds and ends like stringing goals and lining fields and helped any team in any way they wanted. My son Frankie, who had played with the FCA National High School Team in Canada back in 2008, got another taste of international lacrosse competition. He did work with faceoff guys from each of the national teams we scrimmaged. He coached Team France on their man-down defense, though he admitted that "it was a little hard to explain 'rotate' in my broken French. We didn't go over lacrosse terms in my French classes."

Our first FCA Team Serve had a great time scrimmaging and practicing with Team Uganda and seventeen other countries.

We ran drills with teams. We worked with goalies. We scrimmaged eighteen countries, including Uganda, which was special. After every practice or scrimmage, we shared handouts with the other teams that explained what FCA was about and what it meant to be a three-dimensional athlete (mental, physical and spiritual) and to be personally connected to the Creator of life and the Creator's game. One of us would lead a brief devotional and share about God's position, Man's condition, God's provision and Man's decision. We would usually close with prayer and a blessing over the team.

Dan Britton remembers that "they were so blessed and encouraged by how we made ourselves available to them and by what we shared that it led to further conversations."

We lived in the dorms with teams from more than 30 countries. Every day we ate breakfast, lunch and dinner with all the different teams and players from around the world. God literally brought the lacrosse world to us, and we got to know them and share the Good News with them when appropriate.

"God opened doors for us to be the hands and feet of Jesus to the lacrosse world," Dan noted.

I was learning and seeing more and more what God meant when he impressed the word "lacrosse" on my heart during that summer mission in Japan in 1986. What an incredible way to help connect the lacrosse world to the Creator through the Creator's game.

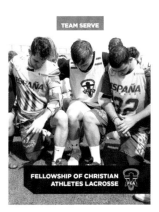

One of our FCA Team Serve players praying with the Team Spain players

Since Team Canada beat Team USA in the championship game, US Lacrosse decided to not make the main feature of the cover of their monthly magazine about either of those teams, and instead made "For Uganda, For Africa" the headline, and put three Ugandan players—Patrick Oriana, Allan Amone, and Ronald Otim—on the cover. And of course, our Kelly Benefits Exchange business name and logo are shown on Patrick's sleeve. "Give and it will be given to you" shows itself true again.

MORE TO THE STORY...

I Was Living a Dream – Michael Bahiizi

I couldn't believe it was happening. My parents didn't believe it was really happening until they saw my plane take off for Denver.

The flight to Denver was the first time most of us on the Uganda team flew on an airplane. We were exhausted after flying six hours to our first stop in Qatar, where we learned what *layover* means, and we didn't like it at all. We overslept and Coach Boston had to race up and down the hotel hallway pounding on our doors and shouting at us to wake up. We almost missed our flight out.

After flying another 20 hours we walked off the plane in Denver to the cheers of Kevin Dugan's friends who welcomed us. Kids asked for our autographs. Parents wanted pictures of us with their kids. I was living a dream.

Most of what I saw in Denver—the huge airport, wide roads, big cars, the Rocky Mountains—was all new to me. I couldn't believe I was actually walking on the same soil as the sights I had only seen before in movies.

"Drink plenty of water," everyone warned us. "Keep hydrated." We didn't pay any attention because we thought we could handle the weather. But it was a different kind of hot and a different kind of air than we were used to, and when we all woke up the next day with headaches, we started drinking water.

In the dorms and dining halls, we were excited to meet and talk in person to players we had been watching on YouTube. All the teams were friendly to us, but we hung out mostly with Team Mexico and FCA Team Serve.

Frank Kelly's father, who we called "Jajja" ("Grandpa" in Uganda) treated us to an all-American dinner. I loved the pizza, but my mouth wasn't ready for the buffalo wings I chomped into—a different kind of hot than I was used to. But the ice cream we had for dessert cooled me off.

We were surprised to see so many fans at our games waving Uganda flags. After our first win of the tournament against South Korea, we ran over to the stands where our fans had erupted into cheering, waving flags, beating drums, and jumping up and down. The whole mob of us broke out into singing and dancing on the sideline. That was a highlight for us, like a scene from a movie.

And little did I know what God had planned for me with FCA in the future. Each day was full of new surprises.

CHAPTER 54

Unless the Lord Builds the House

"...Unless the Lord builds the house, they labor in vain who build it..."

Psalm 127:1 (NASB)

As we continued to give our time, talent and treasure to those in need locally, regionally, nationally and internationally, God continued to bless and grow our business. It was not without a ton of hard work and dedication, as well as the incredible skill and efforts of our people, that we overcame significant challenges along the way.

In 2014, my brother David found a potential new home for our rapidly growing business, but it would take a significant investment to buy and renovate it. My brothers and I would each have to sign personally for the large mortgage we would need if we chose to move forward, and we would have to put our personal homes up as collateral.

We knew we really needed to pray about this decision and seek God's confirmation and blessing. We decided to do a prayer walk with our parents, wives and our 21 children between us, who ranged from four to 23 years old at the time.

We all met at the multi-acre property in the parking lot of the existing 100,000-square-foot building. It was a cold, blustery day in December and we walked around the building three times together, while quietly praying. At the end, we would gather and just ask if there was a clear sense or confirmation of what we should do.

When we finished walking, we gathered in a circle in front of the building on the cracked cement. One of us asked, "Does anyone have an impression or clear sense of what God wants us to do?"

Silence.

For a couple of minutes, no one said a word, until one of us looked down and saw a beautiful white flower growing out of the cracked and broken cement.

This flower should not have been there in those conditions. A couple of us felt that God was speaking to us through that flower about redeeming this building and bringing beauty and life back to it, like the Creator does when He redeems our broken lives and makes something beautiful out of them.

We sensed that was the confirmation we were looking for, and decided to buy the building, which had originally been a Farmers Bank, and then became the corporate headquarters for FILA USA—an Italian sportswear company.

My brother David oversaw the project, which involved completely gutting the building, redesigning the inside flow and front entrance, and installing all new windows and doors.

In June of 2015, the more than 400 People of Kelly Benefits moved into our seventh corporate headquarters since our parents had started the business in our family home nearly 40 years earlier.

The ribbon-cutting of our new headquarters with the People of Kelly Benefits in June 2015

World Vision

The following summer, after we had settled into our new corporate head-quarters (at 1 Kelly Way—pretty cool having our own street name!), we planned another trip to Africa with World Vision, this time with my wife Gayle, our daughter Jackie, and our youngest son, JK, to visit our sponsored children in Ethiopia and northern Uganda as well. My Kelly Benefits coworkers Javy Diaz and Brian Hubbard, who both sponsored children in Ethiopia, joined us, and

Brian brought his 13-year-old daughter Leanna.

This trip we would start in Ethiopia, so we had to drag our golf travel bags (which were full of lacrosse sticks and equipment) with us for about five days before we could give them to our lacrosse friends in Uganda.

While in Ethiopia, we got to visit with our sponsored children and their families. One day, we had a lunch in a park, where our daughter Jackie's sponsored child, Alima, was present. It was exciting to see them meet for the first time, since they were close in age. We also met Alima's mother, Katima, who told us the incredible story (through an interpreter) of how she found her daughter as a baby, abandoned in the bush, and took her into her family and raised her.

Our daughter Jackie and Gayle, with Katima and her adopted daughter Alima, in Gurage, Ethiopia

So here we are in Gurage, Ethiopia, where we have two beautiful, adopted girls and two beautiful adoptee moms connecting in a deep and emotional way. Only God could coordinate this type of meeting.

Brian and his daughter, Leanna, got to meet one of their sponsored children as well—a young boy named Nezif. We were also able to visit some of the communities where the People of Kelly Benefits' contributions help dig wells so clean water is accessible to families.

Back in Addis Ababa, the capital city of Ethiopia, Brian and I made sure to

visit Calvert Hall's "brother" school, St. Joseph's, in the hopes that we might convince them to start playing the Creator's game there. We felt like we were lacrosse missionaries!

After our time in Ethiopia, our World Vision leaders, Steve Krentel and Robin Folkerts, took us on a two-day safari in Murchison Falls National Park (right on the Nile River in northern Uganda, which was full of God's amazing creation), before we made our way to Kampala, the capital city of Uganda. There we were greeted by many of the Uganda lacrosse players we met in Denver in 2014, and other friends and supporters of their newly established Uganda Lacrosse Association (ULA). This time, I was ready for their enthusiastic welcome at the airport.

FCA/Kelly Cup in Uganda

Since we were going to be in Uganda for five days, we decided to sponsor a lacrosse tournament.

Ibra Makanda (then president of the ULA), and Michael Bahiizi (who played defense on Uganda's National Team) worked with Sarah Nambawa (a Ugandan by birth who ran track at Middle Tennessee State and was now on staff with FCA—one of FCA's first staff members in Africa and the very first in Uganda) to plan a lacrosse tournament that they would call the "FCA/Kelly Cup," which Kelly Benefits would help financially support. The tournament would be played at Makerere University Business School in Kampala.

It turned out to be an amazing day with four youth teams, four high school teams, four men's teams and two women's teams all competing in separate divisions of the tournament.

Talk about tough faceoff men, playing in the FCA/Kelly Cup Lacrosse Tournament with no shoes on (like many of the other Ugandan players)

The games began around 10 a.m. and ended at dusk. It was really fun to see JK and Leanna each play in one of the youth games. Brian and I even took a few shifts in one of the men's games! I had to be able to say, "I have taken a faceoff and played some midfield on African soil."

There was quite a crowd watching, including some folks from Kenya and Rwanda who wanted to learn more about lacrosse.

At the end of the tournament as the sun was setting, we pulled everyone together and a few of us spoke about the joy of the Creator's game and how we could have a personal relationship with the Creator, God, through His son, Jesus Christ. Sarah spoke, as did some of the players, who were followers of Jesus, and they let me close out the day with a blessing and a prayer.

Who could have even imagined us hosting a lacrosse tournament in Uganda, and laying the foundation for a possible FCA Lacrosse ministry in Africa? What a joy! What a blessing!

The weather was beautiful for the FCA/Kelly Cup Lacrosse Tournament in January 2016 in Kampala, Uganda.

MORE TO THE STORY...

A 13th Birthday Celebration – Brian Hubbard

My wife and I had sponsored a child through the Kelly Benefits matching gifts program with World Vision for over 20 years. When our two children were young, we sponsored two more in their names, and as our children grew, they became pen pals with their Ethiopian friends. So when Frank invited me on his World Vision trip to Ethiopia and Uganda in 2016, I was all in.

My daughter, Leanna, was turning thirteen that same year and we told her we would do something extra special for her birthday. "Would you like to go to New York and see a play? Or how about Disney World?"

One night she overheard me talking to my wife about the World Vision trip—the long flights, the vaccinations, the packed schedule—and broke into the conversation.

Leanna with one of the Hubbard family's sponsored World Vision children, Nezif

"Can I go with you to Africa for my thirteenth birthday trip?"

My initial reaction was, *not a good idea.*

"Leanna, you don't want to go over there," I said. "This isn't going to be a vacation."

"I really want to go," she said, so I looked into it, prayed about it and decided it wasn't any riskier than driving on the Baltimore Beltway, and that a father-daughter trip to Africa with World Vision was probably a once-in-a-lifetime opportunity that I shouldn't pass up. I felt even better when I found out that Frank was taking his two youngest children, Jackie and JK, so I told Leanna, "We're going!"

It was amazing that Frank somehow helped support and coordinate an FCA/Kelly Cup Lacrosse Tournament with more than a dozen teams right there in Kampala, Uganda. The tournament in Uganda brought back memories of our first FCA One Way 2 Play tournament in 2000. Nothing like it had been done before. Back then, we had twelve teams, we had some dirt fields, we rolled out some balls and after playing lacrosse, came together to pray and hear a word from the Scriptures.

This was the same thing, only now we were on another continent.

We had a blast at the tournament. Frank and I even suited up and took a couple of runs in the seniors' games, and Leanna, Jackie and JK suited up and played in the youth games. What an experience!

We left behind ten golf bags of lacrosse equipment for Michael Bahiizi. It was an honor and a privilege to help promote lacrosse in Uganda. This is unbelievable, I thought. *Now I've been a part of sharing the Gospel through lacrosse at home, throughout the Mid-Atlantic region, in Colorado, and now on the world stage in the middle of Uganda. And my daughter is with me.*

What a blessing to see God build the influence of FCA Lacrosse around the world!

On our trip, Brian Hubbard and I met with some leaders of the Uganda Lacrosse Association (ULA) and some FCA volunteers to discuss ideas for growing the Creator's game in East Africa.

CHAPTER 55

"The Cross" in Kenya

*"'He himself bore our sins' in his body on the cross, so that we might die to sins
and live for righteousness; 'by his wounds you have been healed.'"*

1 Peter 2:24

Kenya, Uganda's neighboring country, embraced boys' lacrosse soon after the Uganda National Team returned from the 2014 World Championships in Denver, Colorado. In 2016, Uganda invited a Kenyan team and a U.S. team to Kampala to play in the first-ever East African 7s Lacrosse Championship tournament.

Fred Osore had been running a successful soccer-based sports ministry in Kenya when he discovered lacrosse.

"When I found out about this sport called lacrosse, it made me forget about soccer," Fred said. "I saw my first game when Coach Storm Trentham and DBA Sports from England came to Kenya and started girls' lacrosse. Lacrosse was new, it was different, it was exciting to play and watch, and when I showed it to schools around the village of Mumias, in western Kenya, everyone was keen to play it."

"It's called lacrosse," Fred would tell people.

"What did you say? Sucrose? Is that some kind of sugar food?"

"No, it's a sport. Lacrosse. The word means, 'the cross' in French," Fred would explain.

"What does that mean, 'the cross'?" some often asked, which opened the door for Fred to turn the conversation to Christ and his death on the cross, explaining that by his wounds we can be healed.

Fred said the new game took off quickly in Kenya. "The students bonded around the new game. When players got together in a group and held their sticks and passed the ball around and caught it in their pockets, it somehow sparked camaraderie and friendship and they didn't want to stop playing. It was like they were pulled away from every other sport and wanted to be known as lacrosse players."

Fred was excited about the opportunity to have a Kenyan team play in the first international lacrosse games in Africa but told the tournament organizers he would need financial help to get U19 boys and girls teams there. "You should contact Frank Kelly," they told him.

"Who is Frank Kelly?" Fred asked.

"He's with FCA Lacrosse."

"What is FCA Lacrosse?" he asked.

The Ugandans explained the role that FCA Lacrosse had played in helping grow lacrosse in Uganda and that we were sponsoring the tournament. When Fred emailed me about his hope for taking a Kenyan team to Uganda, I asked if there was anything I could do to help.

"We're raising money here in Kenya," he told me, "and we are trying to get others outside of Kenya to support our efforts. Can you possibly help us the way you and others have helped Uganda?"

"Let's talk some more. I know that I and others really want to see lacrosse grow across the continent of Africa, and Kenya's participation is essential," I said.

The Kenyan boys and girls teams entered the tournament as huge underdogs against Uganda. The boys' game finished true to expectations, a 9-3 loss. But the girls surprised everyone with a 3-1 upset victory.

The tournament showed Fred the potential of a lacrosse ministry in Kenya. He recalls, "At the tournament, I was so amazed at how someone could use a little-known sport to influence so many lives in Uganda that I decided to put aside soccer and focus my sports ministry on lacrosse. I also emailed Frank again about establishing FCA Lacrosse in Kenya."

I set up a Skype teleconference and introduced Fred to Dan Britton, Ryan Horanburg, and other leaders at FCA. They were excited about what he was doing and invited him to meet them in the U.S. After that trip, the encouragement Fred received and after praying with his wife, Esther, he decided to join the FCA Lacrosse staff.

In 2019, the pieces were in place for Coach Storm Trentham to take the first-ever African women's team to the World Lacrosse Championship in Canada. Fred wanted to do whatever he could to help. The roster of the U19 Kenya National Team was made up of a wide range of Kenyan girls, a number of whom Fred had recruited and encouraged to play. Kelly Benefits and FCA Lacrosse were happy to be sponsors to help the team get to Canada.

Kenya finished in 18th place out of 22 teams, but "the nineteen girls on the

Kenyan team have captured the hearts of everyone in the host city of Peterborough, Ontario with their strength, resiliency, and positive attitudes" wrote a local reporter.[1]

The publicity from the Kenyan Girls' National Team generated more local interest in lacrosse and more schools

Fred Osore from Kenya spoke at our Calvert Hall FCA Huddle (Fred is second row, fourth from left).

contacted Fred asking to play. Fred's challenge is getting enough equipment. There is no place to buy lacrosse equipment in Kenya, and no equipment is produced on the continent of Africa, so he depends on people and teams from other countries to bring equipment for them when they come to Kenya to visit or play.

"We've had teams from Messiah College in the U.S., from England, Uganda, and World Lacrosse visit so far," Fred said.

Fred shares his excitement about the fruit of FCA Lacrosse. "After our FCA Lacrosse practices and clinics, which have averaged nearly 50 players, we share a lesson from God's Game Plan, and I am thankful that people are open to the Good News. I invite those who have become followers of Jesus to meet for an additional Bible study, and members of this group are now sharing their stories with the larger group."

"One young man who was into drugs said to me, 'Coach Fred, I'm happy that I met you because through meeting you, I gave my life to the Lord.'"

I'm grateful to God that He is drawing young men and women to Himself as I engage them on the newly established lacrosse fields in Kenya."

Fred Osore (in red shirt) praying with coaches and referees before taking the fields and leading the growth of FCA Lacrosse in Kenya

MORE TO THE STORY…

Hopes and Dreams – Fred Osore

In 2017, I made my first trip to the United States. I stayed at Frank's house and felt an instant connection to all when I met my brothers and sisters in the FCA family who were using sports to share the word of God.

I had been trying it on my own, but I had not been very deliberate about it. I was casually playing sports with kids and sprinkling in a bit of faith and Jesus here and there. FCA Lacrosse was serious and intentional about coaching the kids to become better players, and even more serious and intentional about sharing the Word of God.

Everyone I met was not only enthusiastic about what they were doing and the impact of their ministries through lacrosse, but they were also excited to help me. "We think we can put some training and support behind what you're doing," they said.

I returned to Kenya and prayed about joining the FCA Lacrosse staff. Frank continued to work with me to raise support while I made up my mind. I returned to the U.S. again in 2018 to meet more FCA staff members and more potential donors.

When one brother said he would invest a fairly significant one-time gift in my ministry and others offered to join my support team with online monthly contributions, I sensed that God was leading me to join FCA Lacrosse. I wanted to wake up in the morning and go to sleep at night thinking about how to use sports to spread the Word of God and not have my day taken up by other concerns. On a leap of faith, I left my full-time job to join the FCA Lacrosse staff and reduced my expenses to live on the amount of support God had raised.

After returning to Kenya from the U.S., I took all the lacrosse sticks and balls I received from my FCA Lacrosse friends in America and went to schools that had an interest in playing the Creator's game. I taught a few players and coaches and left them with sticks and balls to share and practice with.

I also began organizing weekend camps for additional instruction and practice, and have encouraged all coaches and players who really want to learn to check out a number of excellent lacrosse instruction videos on YouTube.

My hope is to share God's love and truth with as many people as possible through the Creator's game, and my dream is to see Kenya take a men's and women's lacrosse team to the Olympics in 2028. I want to do my part to make those hopes and dreams a reality.

CHAPTER 56

YouTube and Ukraine

"Then I heard the voice of the Lord saying, 'Whom shall I send?
And who will go for us?' And I said, 'Here am I. Send me!'"

Isaiah 6:8

In 2010, Vova Demediuk made a comfortable living as an engineer at a nuclear power plant in Ukraine, but in his heart, he felt the desire to do more for God.

"I was restless and sensed God wanted to do something unique through my life. I got to a point of surrender where I prayed, *Here I am, take me.* Then I stumbled across a YouTube video of a lacrosse game, a sport I had never seen before. It looked strange and crazy, but something drew me to want to play. The urge was so strong I couldn't sleep for a couple of nights."

Lacrosse videos on YouTube, *Wow!* Technology had come a long way since *The Middie* video I made with The Lacrosse Foundation in 1989. Back then, coaches had to lug out a television, a physical VCR tape and VCR machine, and hook up a web of cable wires so that one group of players in one room at one time could watch it.

After seeing lacrosse on YouTube, Vova searched the internet for lacrosse teams in Ukraine and found none. He searched his neighboring Eastern European countries and discovered teams in Poland. He called the Polish teams and asked if he could play for their clubs.

"Have you ever played before?" they all asked.

"Never," Vova said, but one team invited him for a tryout.

"I knew only one person in Ukraine who owned a stick and a ball," Vova recalled. "Someone I found on Facebook who had played in the U.S. and lived six hours away." Vova drove the six hours to meet him so he could learn how to throw and catch and learn the rules.

"We had only one stick, so we took turns," Vova said. "I'd throw a ball to him by hand so he could show me how to catch it with the stick, then he'd show me how to throw the ball with the stick and I'd catch it in my hand. Then he gave me the stick to try throwing and catching. He gave me the stick and two balls to take home, and everything else I learned about lacrosse, I learned from YouTube videos."

Vova made the team in Poland, and for the next three years, he rode fifteen hours to Poland on a bus, played two games, then rode another fifteen hours on the bus back home. Vova explains how God answered his prayer to "do more for Him" through lacrosse:

"In 2012, I asked a person at my church, Andriy Kravtsov, who was on staff with this faith-based organization called Fellowship of Christian Athletes and had led an FCA camp I had attended, to meet me for coffee so I could tell him about my love for lacrosse. In the middle of our conversation, I reached across the table and grabbed Andriy's shirt. 'I want to be part of FCA! I want to start a lacrosse ministry in Ukraine!'"

Vova and me in front of "The Creator's Game" statue at the USA Lacrosse Headquarters and National Teams Training Center in Sparks, Maryland

Andriy was puzzled why anyone would want to start a ministry in a sport that nobody in the country played, but told Vova that his FCA director back in the U.S. had played lacrosse "many, many years ago" in college and professionally.

"What's his name?"

"Dan Britton."

Through Vova's contact with Dan, FCA supplied him with ten sticks and ten balls—but had no helmets or gloves—and he began giving lacrosse presentations to ten- and eleven-year-old boys. God blessed him with a cluster of kids who wanted to play, and also blessed him abundantly beyond anything he had asked or thought—he met his first wife, Sveta, at one of the presentations.

Breakthroughs

By 2014, Vova had developed lacrosse to the point where he was ready to hold the first lacrosse tournament ever played in Ukraine. Three teams from

Kyiv played in a round-robin format. None of the teams had a full roster, and they had to share equipment, but it was a historic and breakthrough moment for lacrosse in Ukraine.

Vova joined FCA Lacrosse's full-time staff the following year. "My parents thought I was crazy to leave my engineering job, but all I knew was that God wanted me to do it and I would trust Him," Vova said.

In 2017, FCA translated into Ukrainian the Miracle in the Mountains documentary about the improbable victories of the first FCA Lacrosse team in Vail, Colorado in 1992. Vova shows it at all of his camps "because it inspires the hope in our coaches and players that God will make something big out of our small beginning in Ukraine," he said.

In 2017, Dan Britton and others helped Vova establish the Ukraine Lacrosse Federation. Vova serves as president, and Dan is the Ukrainian National Team's head coach. We all worked for Ukraine's official recognition and membership in World Lacrosse, which was effective in 2018.

Today, lacrosse is growing across the country of Ukraine, including their indoor leagues and tournaments.

Victory and Loss

The March 2018 issue of *FCA Magazine* featured an incredible article about Vova and his family titled *Victory and Loss in Ukraine*, and noted that Vova's lacrosse ministry paused when, eighteen months after his wedding day in 2013, and three months before their first baby was due, his wife Sveta was diagnosed with leukemia.[1]

The Ukrainian doctors gave Sveta just two weeks to live. Even if she did live long enough to give birth, the baby, according to doctors, would almost certainly have problems. The doctors recommended an abortion, but Sveta refused. "Our God is strong. Our God is big. He's going to take care of us," she told Vova.

FCA Ukraine Director Andriy Kravtsov sprang into action. He found a Polish hospital willing to try to save both Sveta and the baby. He mobilized churches in Ukraine and Poland to cover the bulk of the expenses. People randomly showed up to help, including one man who single-handedly covered the $100,000 needed for Sveta's bone marrow transplant. An additional $30,000 came from FCA supporters in the United States.

"I saw Jesus in them," Vova said.

After doctors removed Sveta's tumor, her blood would not clot. She went into labor and the baby was born, weighing just one pound. Vova and Sveta named their girl Nicole, which means "victory."

For the next year, Vova swung back and forth between two hospitals in Poland, watching the two loves of his life fight for theirs. In one hospital, Sveta was undergoing chemotherapy. In the other, Nicole was under the watchful eye of ICU doctors and nurses.

"The pain," Vova said, "was bottomless."

Nicole weathered the storm, and Sveta went into remission. But three months after receiving a clean bill of health, her cancer returned. Less than two months later, she passed away. More than 3,000 family members, friends, and neighbors attended her celebration of life.

"Vova is one of my heroes of the faith," Dan Britton said. "Even though he has been through so many trials, he has grown in his faith as a result and continues to shine for Jesus. Vova always has the joy of the Lord in his heart, and his big smile always gives you the assurance that God is in control of his life. His vision to spread lacrosse and the Good News throughout Ukraine and impact coaches and athletes gives him a foundation of purpose and hope to overcome the trials."

At the end of his long grieving process, Vova met a woman named Marichka. "They were made for each other," Andriy said. They fell in love and got married in October 2016. Nicole now has a sister, Naomi, and a brother, David.

"There is faith when it seems like you've lost everything you're standing on—the faith that can

Vova and his family in 2023

take you through the hardships of life, the faith of that person is stronger than the faith that can move mountains," Vova said.

That faith would also soon lead Vova into an international lacrosse experience that he, and each of us involved, would never have imagined and would never forget.

MORE TO THE STORY...

The Power of Coaches – Vova Demediuk

I have learned so much through my involvement with FCA and lacrosse, particularly about the power and influence of coaches in players' lives. In a war-struck country like Ukraine, there is a lot of pain and suffering, and one must wonder what difference can a coach make? I saw that difference with a player I coached named Dima.

Dima was ten when he came to one of my first lacrosse demonstrations and continued to come to our camps and clinics. His life took a turn for the worse when at age thirteen, his parents divorced, his mother moved to Italy for a better job, and his father was called to fight in the war against Russia. Dima lived with his older brother, an alcoholic who physically abused him. I spent a lot of time trying to encourage Dima not to give up during this dark time, and he placed his faith in Christ and endured.

When Dima was 20, his father returned from the war but was soon struck with cancer and passed away. I understood the pain of losing someone you love from cancer and drove four hours to be with Dima at the funeral. I was the only adult there to comfort him, which helped me understand the ways God uses coaches to love people, and the need to share the Gospel with every coach and every player.

Sports

ward Christian Athletes in '92

Squad' upsets Turtles

Williams

posed to be a case of
... being thrown to the
... the wise ... red
... Lacrosse ...
Greene ... jump-
... on the ...
... the ...
... the ...
athlete ...
... team ...
... current ... afternoon
... seems ... and
... le could ... wanted
... club
... was
... ever ... you ...
... to ... bracket for
... tion.
... the tournament its first
... but appe ... d become
... as the "... ... used a
... ation of ... us defense

and sheer hustle to shut down the
No. 1 seeded Turtles' potent offense, anchored by Towson State
middie Rob Shek and former
Syracuse All-American Gary Gait,
one of the all-time leading scorers
in the Major Indoor Lacrosse
League.

Gait, who had seven goals in a
22-7 Greene Turtles' shellacking of
the Vail Lacrosse Club in
Thursday's opening round, was un-
able to get into the swing of things
Friday, scoring ... goals on six
shots.

"I just wasn't on to ...,"
Gait said. "(Thursday) everything
was going in, (Friday) nothing was.
I'd say it was the altitude, but ...
think it was the evening activitie...

Though David Kelly had ...e
game-winning goal at 3:1... ...e
second overtime, it wa... ...e

Please see Lacrosse pa...

PART X

From Ithaca to Israel

CHAPTER 57

Fight, Finish, Faith

"I have fought the good fight, I have finished the race, I have kept the faith."

2 Timothy 4:7

I could never forget my sophomore year on Cornell's Schoellkopf Field in Ithaca, New York, when I thought for sure that my lacrosse career was over. Now here I was, nearly 35 years later, still involved in the game and on a flight to Israel for the World Lacrosse Championships.

World Lacrosse oversees men's and women's lacrosse championships on a four-year rotation, which includes Men's Field, Women's Field, Men's U19 Field and Women's U19 Field.

Our family was thrilled to watch our son Stephen and his U.S. U19 Men's teammates win a gold medal at the U19 Men's World Lacrosse Championships in Turku, Finland in 2012. Our FCA Lacrosse "Team Serve" was fully present at the Men's World Lacrosse Championships in Denver, Colorado in 2014. And my nephew Timmy played on the U.S. U19 Team in 2016 in British Columbia, so we had an idea of what to expect with the 2018 Men's Championships that were being hosted by the Israel Lacrosse Association (ILA) in Netanya, Israel.

We were excited that the ILA (whose leadership team included good friends from my old club lacrosse days, including Mark Greenberg, whom I played with at MLC, and Bill Beroza, whom we played against from Long Island Lacrosse Club) wanted our FCA Team Serve to be there to help however we could.

Like in 2014, we hoped to "serve" as many national teams as possible by practicing with and scrimmaging against them to help them prepare for their opponents. It was definitely tougher to get a group of 25 to 30 guys to come to Israel for two weeks than it was to get guys to play on Team Serve in Denver four years earlier.

Although it took a lot of time and effort, Team Serve finally came together,

FCA Team Serve's oldest player, Marc Hoffman (62), with its youngest player, JK Kelly (14), both "shut down" defensemen

and was made up of more than two dozen guys who ranged in age from fourteen to 62. Fortunately, we had my son Frankie helping recruit and build the team, so most of the guys were in their twenties and thirties. Dan Britton and I were also part of our servants team of coaches and lacrosse players, including four sets of fathers and sons (like Dan and his son, Eli).

A number of us were also fortunate to have our wives there, and most of them jumped right in with a servant's heart as well.

Of course, Big Frank was there to support us and see me and four of his grandsons (Frankie, Stephen, JK and my nephew, Timmy) all play together. Unfortunately, my mom couldn't make it, as she was focused on her seventeen grandchildren who were still back in the States, but we knew she was praying for us morning, noon and night.

Father/son combos on FCA Team Serve in Israel (L to R Standing: the Quiggles, the Hoffmans and the Brittons. Kneeling: the Kellys)

Jerusalem on Thursday?

The first Tuesday after we arrived in Netanya, I got a call from Scott Neiss, director of operations for the 2018 World Lacrosse Championships. "Frank, we really appreciate you bringing your FCA Team Serve to Israel to help with the World Games. I know you want to serve and scrimmage national teams to help them get ready for their games, so we were wondering if you guys could help us out and practice with and play several countries in Jerusalem on Thursday?"

"Great. We will be there," I said.

FCA Team Serve was staying with other national teams at the Hadassah Neurim Boarding School in Netanya, a beautiful Mediterranean city north of Tel Aviv, about two hours from Jerusalem. Per Scott's invitation, we were scheduled to scrimmage Scotland at 9:30 a.m., Uganda at 11:30 a.m., Russia at 2:30 p.m., then return to Netanya to play South Korea at 6:30 p.m.

We loaded up our four rental vans and nervously made our way to Jerusalem. We had no guides so we weren't exactly sure where we were going or how we would get there. When we got to Jerusalem, I couldn't help but wonder at the historic landscape surrounding us. It was a stark contrast to the modern, synthetic turf sports complex that New England Patriots owner Robert Kraft had built right there on the outskirts of Old Jerusalem.

Team Scotland, their head coach, Brian Silcott, and their assistant coach, Mike Paletta (my Cornell friend Steve Paletta's younger brother) appreciated how we practiced anything they wanted—man-to-man and zone defense, man up/man down, as well as pressure rides and clearing situations.

After practicing and scrimmaging together, both teams lined up and as we shook hands, we gave each of their players a FIGHT-FINISH-FAITH wristband we had made for the trip. It is customary in the international lacrosse "friendly" games to give a token of appreciation that represents your country or team. Our light blue rubber bracelet was based on FCA's Summer Camp Theme "Strong" and the Scripture where the Apostle Paul, as an old man, wrote to Timothy, a young man that he mentored, "I have fought the good fight, I have finished the race, I have kept the faith."

We then asked if we could speak with their team about why we were there and what it meant to "fight," "finish" and have "faith."

With their coaches' blessing, I referenced the wristband and reminded the guys, "You each had to fight and compete to make your national team. Now you need to fight and battle here against the best competition in the world. You need to finish what you started. You are going to play seven or eight games in twelve days. You might want to quit, but we want to encourage you to finish strong. You need to fight and finish to the end!

"And you need faith! Faith in your teammates to be there for you; faith in your coaches and their preparation; and most importantly, here in the Holy Land, we want to talk about considering faith in our Creator and heavenly Father, who loves you so much that His only begotten son, Jesus Christ, died on a cross just a few miles from here, and according to tradition and scripture, He rose from the dead, defeating satan, death and sin. Through Him, Jesus, your sins can be forgiven, and you can be rightly connected to God, the Creator of the universe. You can actually meet and know the Creator, through playing the Creator's game, right here in Jerusalem and Israel."

It was special for our FCA Team Serve and the Kelly family to exchange small gifts with Team Scotland's coaches— Brian Silcott (R) and Michael Paletta (L), pictured on either side of me—after our scrimmage.

Faceoffs in Israel

After our time of sharing and getting some fun pictures with Team Scotland, on came Team Uganda. Many of their players recognized us from four years prior when our Team Serve scrimmaged them at the World Games in Denver. They also knew me from my time in Uganda in 2012, and Gayle, Jackie and JK from our time together at the FCA/Kelly Cup Lacrosse Tournament we sponsored and attended in Kampala back in January 2016.

They ultimately bee-lined straight to my father, whom they remembered from their time in Denver in 2014 when he treated them to monster-sized ice cream sundaes at Cold Stone Creamery—they had never seen or tasted anything like it. Ever since then, they called him "Jajja," which means "grandfather," so they were excited to see him again.

I was not a grandfather yet but, at 54 years old, I was not very interested in playing any more lacrosse. However, there in Jerusalem, on the field with Team Uganda seemed like the perfect setting for me to suit up and take just a couple faceoffs. I wanted to say that I faced off in Israel, against Team Uganda, the first African team to ever play in an international lacrosse competition. Besides, when would I ever be able to play again with all three of our sons?

I lined up at the faceoff X with my sons Frankie, age 27, on one wing, Stephen, 24, on the other wing, JK, 14, down on defense, and my nephew Timmy, 22, on attack. I told Stephen I would try to clamp the ball and push it back behind me for him to pick it up.

Adrenaline pumping, I moved before the whistle blew.

"Foul on FCA!"

"Redo! Redo!" I pleaded. "It's only a scrimmage. Give the old guy a break!"

Uganda showed mercy and we faced off again.

The whistle blows. I clamp the ball and put it behind me. Stephen scoops it up and we run downfield. We work the ball around and a pass back to me flies by my head, as I miss the perfectly placed ball.

Uganda picks up the loose ball and heads downfield. Their player dodges to the goal, Frankie strips the ball loose, and JK comes up with the groundball. He passes to Stephen, who passes upfield to me (I was still back by the midfield line, cherry-picking) and I throw the ball to my nephew, Timmy, down on attack, who shoots and scores.

A Kelly-to-Kelly-to-Kelly-to-Kelly-to-Kelly goal against Team Uganda in Jerusalem with my wife and father in the stands watching—only the Creator could orchestrate that!

The Ugandans loved Big Frank (blue shirt), whom they called "Jajja," and it was powerful to pray together with Team Uganda on a lacrosse field in Jerusalem.

MORE TO THE STORY...

Like 48 Missions Trips – Frankie Kelly

With 48 countries coming to Israel, going to the World Lacrosse Championship was like going on 48 missions trips at once! We recruited my good friend Dan Carson to help coach our team and my job was recruiting players and raising funds to help offset the $4,000 cost for anyone unable to pay their whole way. I knew plenty of FCA lacrosse players, but the bigger questions were: who was willing and able to fly thirteen hours to play? And who was still in shape?

One of the names not on my original list was a goalie whom I had played with at the University of North Carolina, Bradley Dunn. It was getting down to the wire and we still needed a goalie. I hadn't been in close touch with Bradley since graduation, and he hadn't been interested in FCA in college, but he lived in the Atlanta area where I lived, so I took a chance.

"Bradley, would you want to come with us to play lacrosse in Israel three weeks from now?"

"Well, my wife is seven months pregnant, but I was going to be on a fishing trip then and it was canceled, so, yeah, I'm in!"

When Bradley landed in Tel Aviv after the overnight flight, a stream of text messages from his wife popped up on his phone. "I think I'm going into labor!"... "I'm at the hospital!"..."No, false alarm!"

Bradley played great, but more importantly, while we were there, he took a huge step in his relationship with God and asked me to baptize him the day we visited the Sea of Galilee as an outward expression of his inward commitment and decision to become a believer and follower of Jesus.

By God's grace, he returned home in time for the birth of his child. Through the generosity of donors who love the Lord and love lacrosse, the Creator's game, like my grandfather, God provided enough funding so that finances didn't prevent anyone from going.

Frankie (Right) and Dan Carson helped coach and lead Team Serve on the field and off.

CHAPTER 58

Peace in Jerusalem

"But I tell you, love your enemies and pray for those who persecute you..."

Matthew 5:44

Russia was up next. This scrimmage had special significance for one of our players, Vova, who was on staff with FCA Lacrosse in Ukraine. Growing up in Ukraine, Vova spoke fluent Russian and lived through the political and military conflicts between Ukraine and Russia.

My father was struck by the wonder of God when he observed that there we were, Americans, in Israel, playing with teams from around the world, including Turkey and Russia. And there was Vova, from Ukraine, the country Russia invaded in 2014 (and then again in 2022). Where else have people from those nations come together in peace?

Earlier in the day after our scrimmages with Scotland and Uganda, during our lunch break in the beautiful new Kraft Fields locker room, Vova shared his powerful story of how God rescued him out of drug addiction and the pain of the untimely death of his first wife, leaving him with a young daughter with special needs. By this time, he had remarried and was the proud father of another daughter, only seven days old.

As I shared earlier, most of what Vova knew about lacrosse he had learned from watching YouTube videos, and in his first few games, his skills were pretty rough. My nephew, Timmy, took a real

Vova (far right, standing) from FCA Ukraine sharing his story during a rest period in one of the Kraft Family Sports Complex locker rooms... Incredible!

liking to Vova and since they were playing together on attack, he decided to spend hours with him practicing attack moves and shooting around the goal. "Vova," Timmy encouraged him, "I think you're going to score a goal against the Russians!" Timmy was wrong. Vova scored three.

After the game, we gathered with Team Russia and gave them our wristbands. Vova translated my message on FIGHT-FINISH-FAITH and what it means to have a relationship with God. "Do you mind if Vova prays for you now?" I asked. They nodded with approval.

As the sun was setting behind us, Vova prayed blessings in Russian over the Russian team, and prayed about embracing a personal relationship with the Creator and heavenly Father, through His son, Jesus Christ. God showed us how He could use a lacrosse field to break through political and cultural barriers and unite people who might otherwise be considered enemies.

Gayle noted that, "Everything just kind of stopped when Vova prayed over Team Russia. It was almost like the birds stopped chirping. I didn't understand what he was saying, but I felt it was a powerful, spiritual moment—an example of the impact that FCA Lacrosse was having on players and coaches from around the world."

I wondered if this is part of what God envisioned when His Word, the Bible, says in more than 30 different places to "Pray for the peace of Jerusalem"?

We definitely felt a special peace in Jerusalem that day!

We scrimmaged Russia in Jerusalem... and Vova had a hat trick before he prayed with and over both teams in Russian.

MORE TO THE STORY...

Lacrosse United Us – Vova Demediuk

As soon as I heard about FCA Team Serve going to the World Lacrosse Championship, I started praying that I'd be able to go. I hung a poster of Netanya Stadium on my refrigerator to remind myself to pray throughout the day.

Frank and Dan helped make it happen for me financially, and in Israel, my eyes were opened to what it would take for Ukraine to compete on the international stage. It was a blessing for me to be around such talented athletes.

I also saw the big picture of FCA Lacrosse—reaching the world with the Gospel through lacrosse. God gave me opportunities to contribute, once by sharing my personal story with Team Serve, and especially at our scrimmage against Russia.

I hated that Russia had invaded Ukraine and killed and displaced so many people. I wanted to score a goal against them, and all of Team Serve wanted me to score against them. The Kelly cousins—Frankie, Stephen and Timmy—all coached me on playing attack, and Dan told everyone to "keep feeding Vova." I was thrilled when I scored three goals, but my Kairos moment—a moment of grace and life transformation—came after the game when Frank asked me to pray for the Russian team.

I knew some of the Russian players. I had contacted them in my search for lacrosse players and teams near Ukraine and had spoken to them through video calls over the years. I hated that Russia had invaded my country, but I believed that the Russian people were God's creations.

I felt the power of the Holy Spirit speaking through me as I prayed God's blessings upon them. Lacrosse united us, and the Holy Spirit helped me choose to love, not to hate.

CHAPTER 59

"Soul" Korea

"This was so he could redeem those under the Law so that we could be adopted. Because you are sons and daughters, God sent the Spirit of his Son into our hearts, crying, 'Abba, Father!'"

Galatians 4:5-6 (CEB)

After scrimmaging Scotland, Uganda and Russia in Jerusalem, we drove the two hours back to Netanya, and somehow mustered enough energy to practice with and scrimmage Team Korea at a nice field near the Championship Stadium.

Gayle and I were really looking forward to this practice and scrimmage time because of how much we loved South Korea. Ever since we adopted our daughter, Jackie Lee, and later our son, Joseph Kim (JK), Korea had a special place in our hearts and souls.

We could remember back to 2006, when we were in Canada for the World Lacrosse Championships and I played with the Rusty Red, White and Blue Masters Team and ended up getting pictures with JK and the Korean National Team after one of their games. JK was not even three years old yet and had only been with us for about six months. At that time, he still understood Korean, so he smiled when the guys started speaking to him in their native tongue.

It was exciting for me to share our FCA Team Serve "Fight, Finish, Faith" message with Team Korea.

the guys started speaking to him in their native tongue.

I struck up a conversation with one of their players, Won Jae Park, and he was kind enough to hold JK and let us take a picture of him with the rest of the team, surrounding them.

Now, here we were in Israel twelve years later, and JK, a defenseman, would be covering Won Jae, an attackman (and also the captain of their team). It turned out that Won Jae also knew the Creator, was a follower of Jesus and loved the mission and vision of FCA.

We had a great session together. Frankie and Stephen worked with their faceoff guys, and when we scrimmaged, I actually took a midfield run or two myself. When would I ever again get a chance to say I played lacrosse against Team Korea in Israel?

Gayle had ordered some pizzas and drinks to be delivered to the fields, so we could all enjoy dinner and fellowship together after the scrimmage. Gayle came to me in a panic just before we were all getting ready to come over and eat together, to tell me that a swarm of ants got into the pizzas. *Uh oh—what were we going to do?!* Fortunately, it didn't faze the guys.

"Extra protein!" they said.

We ended up having another dinner together later in the week at a nice hotel on the beach in Netanya, and there we got to share more about the meaning of FIGHT-FINISH-FAITH and other stories of connection with our Creator.

We were also able to recreate a picture or two from 2006. It wasn't so easy for Won Jae to hold JK anymore!

MORE TO THE STORY...

A Special Experience – JK Kelly

Yes, it was the World Games, but it still seemed to me—fresh out of eighth grade—a long way to go to play lacrosse. But playing with my brothers, my dad, my cousins, and many of my former FCA Huddle leaders and coaches was something special that I had never experienced before.

I was the youngest player on the team by far, but my teammates—guys I had watched since I was eight years old—treated me like a true peer. And we didn't go all that way just to play lacrosse. Walking where Jesus walked brought the Bible to life for me. It all really happened; it's not just a collection of stories.

And it was powerful when we shared the Scriptures and prayed with players from around the world, including my birthplace, South Korea. Pretty cool!

Team Korea captain Won Jae Park and JK 12 years after the World Lacrosse Championships in Canada (2006) when JK (then three years old) was embraced and lifted by Won Jae and his Korean teammates

An All-Time Experience – Stephen Kelly

It was exhausting, but it was worth it.

On Saturday before I left for FCA Team Serve in Israel, I played in a Major League Lacrosse game with the Chesapeake Bayhawks against the New York Lizards in Annapolis, Maryland. On Sunday, I flew the 12 hours and landed in Tel Aviv before joining the team in Netanya.

For most of the next eight days, I played in three or four scrimmages a day and ran drills and clinics for faceoff guys from around the world, including the faceoff man from Team Korea, which was incredible.

Frankie and Stephen (#24) worked with faceoff guys from multiple countries, including Team Korea, which was very special because of our family's unique connection there.

I flew home on a Tuesday, went back to work, and played a game with the Bayhawks on Friday against the Charlotte Hounds, so that was a crazy two weeks for me.

It's hard for me to say no to any FCA experience, especially the opportunity to play on the same field with my father and brothers in the Holy Land. It was an all-time life experience for me, and I still hear others raving about its impact on them to this day.

CHAPTER 60

Where Jesus Walked

"Therefore go and make disciples of all nations, baptizing them in the name of the Father and of the Son and of the Holy Spirit..."

Matthew 28:19

Throughout the tournament, we also played against teams from Israel, Italy, Luxembourg, Mexico, the Netherlands, the Philippines, Spain and Turkey. We also helped with other odds and ends—stringing goals, lining fields, putting up shooting nets behind goals—anything the tournament directors needed. We even did a half-day lacrosse clinic one day for about 50 kids at a small school in Jerusalem.

On the days we had no scrimmages or clinics, we scheduled tours to some of the historic sites in the area. Friends from FCA, Kimberlie and Sahar Saado, who lived in Israel, took us to actual places where Jesus walked. We toured Bethlehem, the birthplace of Christ. We went to Nazareth, where Jesus grew up as a child. We also visited the ruins of Caper-

(Above) We did a one-day FCA Lacrosse camp at the Anglican International School in Jerusalem. (Below) Jackie Lee getting in on some coaching action. Ground balls win games!

naum, a town right on the Sea of Galilee, and saw the ruins of the synagogue where Jesus taught and the area where Jesus lived as an adult. I envisioned the fishermen on the water.

We climbed the Mount of the Beatitudes overlooking the Sea of Galilee where Jesus shared parables with thousands of people. Later that day, we even went swimming in the Sea of Galilee, where Marc Hoffman, the oldest player on our team at age 62, asked his son, Josh, to baptize him. Incredible!

Bradley Dunn, a former teammate of my son Frankie at North Carolina, and Connor Lesman, a player of Jewish heritage, then asked Frankie to baptize them. Each of them had come to Israel to be on Team Serve, but none of them had taken the steps of being baptized and publicly expressing their inward commitment to follow Jesus. It was a very powerful and emotional experience witnessing these baptisms right there in the Sea of Galilee—The very water Jesus had walked on!

FCA Team Serve in the Sea of Galilee after witnessing and celebrating the baptisms of Bradley Dunn, Connor Lesman and Marc Hoffman

MORE TO THE STORY...

I'd Like to Get Baptized – Joshua Hoffman

He's not a pastor, and he's not a theology major, but my father, Marc Hoffman, loves God and is always loving people. He came to know Christ largely through the influence of my mom and his friendships with Dan Britton, Frank Kelly, and other FCA teammates. He also loves the Creator's game, so I'm not surprised that God gave him a heart for the lacrosse community, including the rough cases.

"Hoffie," or "Big Hoff," as friends call him, has probably played more lacrosse games than anyone on the planet. He coached varsity lacrosse at Gilman School for 23 years and is a member of the Greater Baltimore Chapter of the US Lacrosse Hall of Fame. Even now in his sixties, he'll play in the Open (any age),

Masters (40+), and Grand Masters (50+) divisions—all in the same tournament! He wasn't going to miss the chance to play in the Holy Land beside me, Frank and Dan, and their kids.

On non-game days in Israel, as we toured the Mount of Olives, Capernaum, and other biblical sites, Frank and Dan would pause to share Bible stories and messages related to each location. One day, as we stood in waist-high water in the Sea of Galilee, Frank and Dan asked if anyone wanted to be baptized.

All of a sudden, I hear my dad say, "I'd like to get baptized." As he waded forward, I walked over to him and put my arm around his back. Dan, who might know more about my father's wild and crazy past than anyone but me, let me take the lead and stood beside us as my father took the plunge and publicly declared his faith in Jesus.

My father's baptism was a key step in the maturation of his faith, and a beautiful moment that bonded our father-son relationship like no other ever could.

Josh Hoffman baptizing his father Marc in the Sea of Galilee

Lord, My Life is Yours - Bradley Dunn

My connection with FCA Lacrosse was brief, but it changed the course of my life.

In high school, I stepped away from my faith and focused on being "the guy." I was an All-State lacrosse player and graduated with a 4.0 GPA. I felt pretty good about myself when I arrived at the University of North Carolina. Then reality hit.

As a freshman, I decided to "walk on" and try out for varsity lacrosse but didn't make it. I was determined to make the team my sophomore year but got cut again and started to realize, *okay, maybe I'm finding something out about myself.* Maybe playing Division I lacrosse was a childish dream. But I wasn't ready to shelve the game altogether, so I played for the club team.

In my junior year, I was sitting on the couch playing video games in my fraternity house when an email popped up from Stephen Toomy, the director of UNC men's lacrosse operations. The email said that three goalies had gone down with injuries and asked if I was interested in playing goalie for the Tar Heels.

I thought the email was a scam; that my friends were messing with me. But I called Steve, and he told me it was for real. The next step was a visit to the physician where they poked and prodded me with a bunch of needles and took an EKG. Ten days later my name appeared on the active roster. I don't think I fully believed I was on the team until I sat in Coach Breschi's office and Steve asked me what size cleats I wore.

Looking back now, I realize that God very much wanted me on that team, but freshman and sophomore years were not the right time. I had no delusions about my place on the team—backup goalie, carry water bottles or buckets of balls—and I knew my time on the team could end at any moment, but I thought, *Hey, this is cool. I get to play on this team for a while.*

A few weeks later we played at Hofstra on Long Island, New York, near where my extended family lives. A season-high crowd of over 5,000 fans filled the stadium, and I think probably 10% of them were related to me and had come just to see me in a college lacrosse uniform. I was starstruck.

We caught fire in the second half and led 14-5 with about three minutes left in the game when Coach Breschi looked down the sideline and called out, "DUNN, START WARMING UP." I thought, *Wait, wait, are you serious right now?*

With 1:51 left, a Hofstra midfielder fired a shot on goal. I made the stop—no one is sure if my eyes were open or not—and "set off the biggest celebration of the night on the Carolina sidelines," according to the game recap article. With my family going bonkers in the stands, it looked like a scene from the movie *Rudy.*

I made the team again my senior year and can say with certainty that I finished my career with the highest save percentage in NCAA lacrosse history—100%—though going 3-for-3 in five games isn't enough chances to qualify me for an official record.

There was something different about one player on the team, Frankie Kelly. He was a good guy, an excellent player, academically accomplished, and an unashamed Christian. He led our team Bible study and invited me no less than 100 times. Every time, I was too busy, but I continued to observe and admire him from a distance.

We went our separate ways after graduation in 2014, but we both landed in Atlanta. In 2018, my wife, Bri, was pregnant with our first child when Frankie called me out of the blue. "Hey dude, we're fielding an FCA team to play at the World Championships in Israel this summer, and we need a goalie. Would you want to come and play?"

It so happened that I was supposed to be away for my "Dadchelor" party the same week of the games, but the trip fell through, so I already had the time off planned. I expected Bri, who would be nearly seven months pregnant when I left, to say she'd rather I not go, but she said, "Absolutely! You have to do that!"

A few weeks later, I took off for Israel. While I was in the air, Bri went into labor. When I landed, I saw her flood of text messages: "I'm going into labor." "I'm on my way to the hospital." "I'm here at the hospital." I expected the last text to be a picture of my prematurely born son, but no. The doctors dialed back the labor in time.

Frankie and the whole team wrapped around me. They prayed with me and for me. Everyone was genuinely concerned for what I was going through but also thankful and happy that I didn't miss the birth of my child.

Each day I slowly but surely weaved in with all these genuinely nice dudes who, oh, by the way, were all very good lacrosse players as well. We'd stay up late playing Mafia and have a blast—with no alcohol. Then we'd wake up the next morning and scrimmage Russia or South Korea or Scotland or whoever, absolutely thump them, then pray with them after the game, give them gifts, and make sure they had enough Gatorade. The thought dawned on me, *Maybe I've had the wrong perception, and not all Christians are Bible-beating, self-righteous people.*

I had sensed a nudge back toward my faith over the four years since I had left UNC, but my interactions with the guys on Team Serve were a major impetus that climaxed at the Wailing Wall, the site of the Jewish temple that was destroyed in 70 A.D. As most visitors do, I wrote a prayer note and slipped it into a crack in the wall. On my note, I wrote, "Lord, my life is Yours, and I want You to do with it what You will."

The Wailing Wall is a quiet, reverent place, but fifteen seconds after I placed my note in the wall, I heard someone clear as day shout my name. "BRADLEY!" I turned around—I was going to chastise them for their rudeness—but I saw no one.

We left the wall and boarded the bus to go to Capernaum and the Sea of Galilee. Along the way, Coach Frank asked if anyone would like to be baptized in the Sea of Galilee and if so, to let him know. At that point I thought, *Okay, I think I get the picture. I understand now that faith isn't what I had assumed.* It would only be fitting for Frankie Kelly to baptize me.

Frankie baptizing Bradley Dunn in the Sea of Galilee

After Frankie lifted me from under the water, I watched another baptism and then swam by myself over to a pier and dove repeatedly off the pier. I felt like the whole weight of the world had lifted off of me.

When I got back home, my son, Grayson, was born on schedule. I gradually lost my desire for dipping tobacco, a potentially harmful and addicting habit. About six months after Grayson was born, I was watching Billy Graham on television—something I would have called ridiculous a year before—when I heard a voice tell me, "Put down that Truly you're drinking, and I'll replace it with something better." I set the can on the kitchen counter and haven't touched alcohol since.

For sure, my faith and sobriety have enabled me to succeed in ways I could not have beforehand or on my own. I can say with 100% certainty that it all started at UNC with Frankie Kelly, and came to fruition in Israel.

My second son, Trainor, was born in 2021. Our family is growing in our faith and we're active at church.

I'm good friends with Frankie, and he's the common thread throughout my story. At UNC, I don't think he was on a project to save my soul. He was just going about his life the way he knew how, and I took notice probably more than he realized. I think about Frankie's example a lot and ask myself, "How do I conduct myself? How am I living my life? Who's taking notice of me?" If I follow the Lord and do well in all my endeavors, maybe I'll impact someone.

That's the enchantment of FCA Lacrosse. They're followers of Jesus who are down-to-earth, very cool, who beat you on the lacrosse field and then treat you so nicely afterward that you enjoy your encounter with them. They make you wonder what they've got cooking.

Picture of Team Serve in front of the Wailing Wall, where many of us, including Bradley Dunn, put our handwritten prayers in the cracks of the wall

CHAPTER 61

The Dead Sea to The Mount of Olives

"After he said this, he was taken up before their very eyes,
and a cloud hid him from their sight."

Acts 1:9

Another day when we had no scrimmages or practice sessions, we decided to drive the three hours to the Dead Sea, which is more than 400 feet below sea level and full of the saltiest water anywhere in the world. On the way, we stopped for a hike through the desert up to the Falls of En Gedi.

The landscape in Israel can change from one extreme to the other in no time. One minute we were trekking through the desert, the next minute we were swimming in the waterfalls of En Gedi, where David hid from King Saul in Old Testament times.

Two of our players, Myles Cohen and Kyle Gilliam, said after seeing the guys get baptized in the Sea of Galilee a few days earlier that they wanted to publicly acknowledge and profess their faith and get baptized as well. It was incredible as they each asked me to baptize them in one of the pools created by

Myles Cohen (left picture) and Kyle Gilliam (right picture) asked to get baptized in one of the waterfalls of En Gedi, in the desert area on the western shore of the Dead Sea where David hid from King Saul around 1000 B.C.

one of the waterfalls, right there in the desert. About a dozen of us celebrated with Myles and Kyle as they emerged from the cleansing waters.

We later went and floated in the Dead Sea, surrounded by the mountains where archaeologists discovered ancient Old Testament manuscripts, called the Dead Sea Scrolls, which did a lot to confirm the authenticity of many parts of the Book of Isaiah and other sections of the Bible.

Two Seas

After floating around in the Dead Sea, I took a minute to pull our group together and remind everyone that the water in the Dead Sea was nearly ten times saltier than the ocean, and that the salinity of the water was such that plants and animals could not live or flourish there, hence its name. I also pointed out that the water in the Dead Sea actually came from the beautiful Sea of Galilee, where Jesus spent a lot of time (and where we had visited and swam earlier in the week), and where his disciples often fished in the fresh, clean water that was teeming with life.

I pointed out that the Jordan River, where Jesus was baptized, flows down from the mountains and into the top, or north, end of the Sea of Galilee (which is really more like a freshwater lake than a sea). It then runs out the bottom, or south, end of the sea for another 104 winding miles into the Dead Sea, which had no outlet. The water flowed into the Dead Sea and stayed there, stagnating and ultimately eliminating all life in it.

It was a reminder that if we receive without giving, we'll stagnate like the Dead Sea, and nothing good will grow in or around us. The contrast reminded

Nothing like a "mud bath" in the Dead Sea followed by drinks at the "Lowest Bar in the World." Gayle, Jenna Porter, Acacia and Jackie did not have to worry about any fish or creatures bothering them as they sought to revitalize their skin, since nothing lives in that water.

all of us on Team Serve about why we were there—to give, serve and watch God multiply our efforts for His glory and honor and the well-being of all we met.

The Mount of Olives

The highlight of our tours for me was ascending the Mount of Olives overlooking Jerusalem.

"This is where Jesus stood before he ascended into heaven 40 days after his resurrection," our tour guide, Sahar, told us.

"Hold on a minute," I said. "So, you are telling me this is where Jesus shared his final words before ascending into heaven, when he said, "...you will receive power when the Holy Spirit comes on you; and you will be my witnesses in Jerusalem, and in all Judea and Samaria, and to the ends of the earth?"[1]

"Yes, right here."

My heart welled up in awe as I contemplated how God had brought me to the exact place where Jesus stood and spoke the words recorded in Acts 1:8. The verse God used in Japan to call me back to Baltimore, my Jerusalem, in 1986 to serve in some way with and through business, schools, lacrosse and friends.

I had experienced the power of the Holy Spirit. I loved being a witness and telling others about the great news of Jesus and here we were in Israel—experiencing Jerusalem, Judea and Samaria, as well as connecting with and serving lacrosse teams from more than 40 countries around the world.

We paused, and I shared with the group my reflections on that scripture, its influence on my life, and the amazing work, ministry and influence God had done and was doing through FCA Lacrosse.

It was an incredible experience for me to share with Team Serve on the top of the Mount of Olives overlooking the Old City of Jerusalem, where Jesus spoke the words recorded in Acts 1:8 before He ascended into heaven.

MORE TO THE STORY...

My Life is Nothing Without Him – Myles Cohen

I was in the middle of my summer internship with FCA Lacrosse when Ryan Horanburg asked if any of us would be interested in going to Israel with Team Serve. A week later, I was on my way.

It was so cool to interact with athletes from around the world, including Africa, Asia, Australia and Europe, and to visit biblical sites in the Holy Land. On a hike through the desert, we came upon the falls of En Gedi and couldn't resist taking a dip to refresh. When our coach, Dan Carson, asked if anyone lost the "backpack" he had found, Mr. Kelly, being a little hard of hearing, thought he asked if anyone wanted to get "baptized" in the falls, so he repeated what he thought was Coach Dan's question. One of our teammates, Kyle Gilliam, stepped forward and said, "I would like to get baptized."

As I watched Kyle and thought about the guys who got baptized a few days earlier in the Sea of Galilee, a wave of emotion swept over me. *This is something I really need: to recommit my life to Jesus. My life is nothing without Him.* I stepped forward and Mr. Kelly baptized me.

Mr. Kelly is a role model who welcomes and loves everybody. My entire experience in Israel will live in my heart for the rest of my life.

Teamwork – Jackie Kelly

My father was in his element, that's for sure! He loves lacrosse and loves God even more, and it was cool to see him so excited to combine his loves in the Holy Land.

Acacia, Jackie, Gayle and Jenna filling water bottles with Gatorade mix to bless and serve the national teams that we played

While my dad, brothers and cousins served mainly on the field, my mom, my sister-in-law Acacia and I made lunches and snacks, filled Gatorade bottles, and organized dinners for Team Serve and some of the international teams, including South Korea, my birth country.

It was amazing to tour and visit some of the sites you read about in the Bible, and to even go swimming in the Sea of Galilee and Dead Sea. The Sea of Galilee was much nicer, but I was thinking the mud from the Dead Sea might be better for my skin.

The entire trip was a team effort, and it was fun to watch God use Team Serve to spread the Good News and the game of lacrosse.

CHAPTER 62

Netanya to Uganda

"How beautiful on the mountains are the feet of those who bring good news, who proclaim peace, who bring good tidings, who proclaim salvation..."

Isaiah 52:7

W hoever thought that leaders of national lacrosse teams from 48 different countries, and every continent across the globe, would come to the Holy Land, Israel, to play the Creator's game? It was encouraging to meet players, coaches and team leaders in the dorms and at the hotel, as well as in the dining facilities and on the fields of Netanya.

One of the teams we spent the most time with was Uganda, because of my history with them from my visits there in 2012 and 2016, and from Team Serve's time with them at the World Lacrosse Championships in Denver, Colorado in 2014.

Their leaders were honest about their struggles at home and their challenges to growing the game due to a lack of sticks and equipment. We committed to collecting more sticks and gear, and getting it to them one way or another, and we have done so regularly for years now.

One of the Uganda Lacrosse Association (ULA) leaders we spent the most time with was Michael Bahiizi, a defender on the Uganda National Lacrosse Team, who had also played in Denver four years earlier. He was fascinated with our Team Serve vision and mission and

It was nice to have FCA Lacrosse leaders meet with Uganda Lacrosse leaders, including Michael Bahiizi (far right in the picture) during the 2018 World Games in Israel.

couldn't believe how we were integrating our faith with the sport we loved. He began to ask a lot of questions about FCA—how it worked, and if there were opportunities to bring FCA Lacrosse to Uganda on a full-time basis.

Michael notes that, "Most Christians in Uganda think that ministry only takes place within a church building. In 2014 in Denver and then again in Israel in 2018, I discovered that I could potentially minister and serve the Lord through the sport I loved and do it on a lacrosse field."

We explained to Michael that the FCA model typically requires staff to raise their own financial support through donations to FCA, and that there was already a full-time staff person in Uganda, named Sarah Nambawa, who was not only the first FCA staff person in Uganda, but all of Africa.

Sarah was born in Uganda but went to college in the U.S. on a track and field scholarship at Middle Tennessee State University. Although she was a track and field star, an injury caused her to reevaluate her life and led her to involvement with FCA, which helped her grow in her relationship with God. She was so excited about this unique ministry to coaches and athletes that she decided to pursue a staff role with FCA and was now back in Uganda and on staff with FCA full-time.

Michael had a strong sense that God was calling him to full-time ministry with FCA Lacrosse back in his home country as well, so when he returned to Uganda from Israel, he met with Sarah, which led to discussions with Dan Britton and ultimately the go-ahead for Michael to pursue his dream.

Michael called me and we discussed a plan for him to come to the January 2019 US Lacrosse Convention being held in Philadelphia. Michael had been saving money for an airplane ticket and praying for the opportunity to visit our FCA Lacrosse offices and staff in Maryland. We would also develop a plan for Michael to meet with other FCA staff and potential donors.

Believe it or not, when Michael landed in Philadelphia, he had no place to stay and no money in his pocket, but he had faith that God would provide. He had recently graduated from college and traveled with his friend and Uganda National Lacrosse Team teammate, John Paul Okura, who was coming to the US Lacrosse Convention to represent the ULA at the international lacrosse meetings happening there.

His friend John Paul was able to get them a ride from the airport to the hotel, where he caught up with me, FCA Lacrosse Director Ryan Horanburg, and former Uganda National Lacrosse Team General Manager Aimee Dixon.

"Where are you staying?" Aimee asked.

"I don't know," Michael said, and explained his situation.

"What were you thinking, coming to the U.S. without a place to stay and with no money in your pocket?" she asked.

He was thinking that he knew enough people that he wouldn't have to sleep on the streets, and he had faith that if he took the steps of obedience to get here, God would take care of the other details for him.

God was faithful. Peter Ginnegar, Team Uganda's head coach at the time, offered to let Michael stay in his room.

Michael would also need a place to stay after the convention, since Ryan and I could not host him those days due to prior travel and family obligations. We were planning to host and network Michael the following week.

Again, Coach Ginnegar came through.

"Where are you going and where are you staying after the convention?" Coach asked.

"I don't know yet," Michael replied.

Fortunately, Coach Ginnegar had extra airline miles, and offered to fly Michael to California for the week to stay with him. Michael had been in the U.S. for about 72 hours, had experienced sub-freezing temperatures and snow for the first time in his life, and now he was getting ready to fly to California, where Coach Ginnegar would take him to Hollywood, and even golfing for the first time ever, in Palm Springs. *Are you kidding me? Talk about God providing!*

Coach Ginnegar let Michael use more of his airline miles to return to Philadelphia, where I picked him up the following weekend. After enjoying some famous Philly cheesesteaks, which he had never experienced in Uganda, we drove back to my home in Baltimore. Michael stayed a few nights with me, Gayle and our family, then a few nights with different FCA and FCA Lacrosse staff, before we coordinated some networking opportunities with potential donors. Everything was falling into place, and you could sense Michael's excitement.

Michael notes, "When I returned to Uganda, I thought it would take only another week or two for FCA International to set up my organization number and bring me onto the FCA Lacrosse staff, so I did not look for other employment. But my timing was not God's timing.

"While I waited for my account to be established and my support to start coming in, I volunteered with FCA Uganda, prayed and fasted, and asked God to equip me with the tools I needed to grow the FCA Lacrosse ministry. I moved back home with my parents to save money. Then my father was in an accident, hospitalized and couldn't work, which made me the only source of support for my parents and sisters. *God, what am I going to do?*

"God answered my prayer on September 1, 2019, when I received the email that I was officially on the FCA Lacrosse staff. I could now focus full-time on sharing the Good News across the hills, valleys and fields of Uganda, like I experienced watching FCA Team Serve in Israel.

Frank and Gayle Kelly were the first to join my home team of supporters. Frank introduced me to many other people who joined my financial support team and had a passion for FCA and lacrosse to grow in Uganda and across the continent of Africa."

Michael worked hard to recruit and train coaches and young players, and to grow the Creator's game throughout the country. He could often be seen on the back of a motorcycle taxi, (called a "boda boda" in East Africa) carrying lacrosse sticks, lacrosse balls and at times, even a goal or two, going to various fields between the Ugandan cities of Kampala and Jinja.

Interest in lacrosse and FCA was growing rapidly, with ever-increasing participation and enthusiasm, when the COVID-19 pandemic hit. Michael continued to meet with coaches and players in small groups until things settled down and the fields were full again.

Unfortunately, more challenges came Michael's way in early 2022. As he notes:

"After the death of my grandfather (my mother's father), even more family responsibilities came upon my shoulders, and after much prayer, I decided to take a leave of absence from FCA to care for my family.

"I continue to seek discernment on a best way forward. I still love FCA and lacrosse, and hope to be back on staff when the time is right.

Michael (Right with gray t-shirt) training potential new lacrosse coaches in a local Ugandan village

"I am grateful for the lacrosse coaches and players I was able to recruit and share God's love and truth with. I believe that the seeds that have been planted will continue to support the growth of FCA and lacrosse in Uganda, as I desire to see some of the coaches and players I recruited and trained someday be a part of future Uganda National Lacrosse teams."

Together, we still believe that the best is yet to come in Uganda and across the continent of Africa.

Michael preparing some young Ugandans for their first introduction to the Creator's game

CHAPTER 63

Olympic Dreams

"Everyone who competes in the games exercises self-control in all things.
They then do it to receive a perishable wreath, but we an imperishable."

1 Corinthians 9:25 (NASB)

E ver since God put the word "lacrosse" on my heart and mind as an arena for service, I have kept my eyes and ears open on ways to serve and help grow the game. God's blessings on my playing career and on FCA Lacrosse—locally, nationally and internationally—opened the doors for me to serve on the two major governing bodies for lacrosse.

As a member of the US Lacrosse Foundation Board, I co-chaired the campaign to raise $15 million to build the new US Lacrosse Headquarters, Hall of Fame, and National Teams (hoping someday to be U.S. Olympic Teams) Training Center that opened in Sparks, Maryland, only a half mile from our corporate headquarters, in 2016.

I was also invited to join the Olympic Vision Committee of The Federation of International Lacrosse (FIL), whose name was changed to World Lacrosse in 2019. We were tasked with doing everything possible to help lacrosse become an Olympic sport. It became obvious that the FIL model of operating on a shoestring budget and an all-volunteer staff was not sufficient to get the job done. It was clear that we needed a high-profile executive director focused full-time on the task.

To hire someone like that, we needed to raise money. Some members of the FIL board helped coordinate a meeting with Joe Tsai, the wealthy co-founder of the Chinese tech giant, Alibaba, "the Amazon of China." The dinner meeting was scheduled during the 2016 U19 Men's Championship in the city of Coquitlam in British Columbia, Canada.

The FIL asked me and another volunteer, John Urban, to be part of the team to represent the Olympic Vision Committee and meet with Joe.

"Sure, I can do that," I said. The bonus for me was that I could watch my nephew, Timmy Kelly, who had starred at Calvert Hall and North Carolina, and was now on the U.S. Men's U19 Team.

In the course of doing my homework, I discovered that I had played lacrosse against Joe in college—he was Yale 1986 and I was Cornell 1986. He grew up in Taiwan but came to the U.S. for his education.

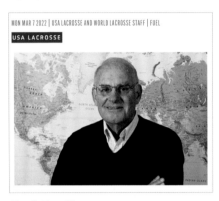

Coach Tom Hayes

Two longtime volunteer leaders from the FIL, Tom Hayes and Bob De-Marco, would be leading the meeting with John and me. The four of us discussed our strategy. Tom and Bob, representing the rest of the FIL board, thought we should ask Joe for a smaller amount than I thought we needed to attract and hire the kind of talent and experience we would need to grow the game around the world and to help lacrosse become an Olympic sport. Any contribution was going to be helpful, but I figured we could wait and see how things unfolded in the meeting.

Joe had brought his two young sons with him, both lacrosse junkies, but they did not join us for the dinner meeting.

After exchanging greetings and sharing some fun lacrosse memories and stories, we got down to business.

"We really want to see lacrosse become an Olympic sport," we said.

"I do too," Joe said, perhaps thinking about the future of his boys.

"To make that happen, we need to hire a full-time director," I said.

"That definitely makes sense," Joe said. "How much do you think that is going to cost?"

I said, "Well, some have suggested a budget of approximately $100,000 a year, which would be a huge step in the right direction, especially after 45 years of being a passionate and dedicated, yet volunteer-run organization, but I think it will take at least $250,000 a year to get the right person."

Joe said, "I agree. It will take at least that much." And then without hesitating, before we even asked for any dollar amount, he said "I will commit $250,000 a year for ten years."

All John, Bob, Tom and I could do was look at each other and under my breath I thanked God, the Creator, for this incredible gift.

"And when the time is right," Joe continued, "I'll give more for the marketing budget because you'll need that also." Game changer! Joe was so humble and generous, and his commitment changed the international trajectory of the game of lacrosse forever.

I asked Joe if there was anything we could do for him. He said, "My sons would love to meet some of the U.S. Men's U19 Team players."

"Would they like to have breakfast with the U.S. team?" I asked.

"That would be awesome—they would love that!"

I texted the U.S. head coach, Nick Myers, whom I knew because he coached my nephew Johnny at Ohio State, and my nephew Timmy was playing for him on the U.S. Men's U19 Team. "Nick, a number of us from the FIL board and Olympic Vision Committee just met with Joe Tsai, a huge lacrosse fan and generous donor. Is there any way his two young sons could come to breakfast tomorrow and meet the team?"

"No problem, Frank."

The next morning, the Tsai boys sat down to breakfast with Timmy, who played at the University of North Carolina, and Ryan Conrad, who played at the University of Virginia. True hard-core fans, they knew exactly how many goals, assists, and ground balls Timmy and Ryan had their entire high school and college careers including the current World Championship tournament. They had a blast, and with their encouragement, the U.S. Team went on to win a gold medal by defeating Canada in an unbelievable come-from-behind one-goal victory in the championship game.

Thanks to Joe Tsai's support, World Lacrosse hired Jim Scherr in May of 2017 as their president and CEO. There could not have been a better candidate—an All-American wrestler at Nebraska, with extensive experience as an Olympic athlete, former president and CEO of both USA Wrestling and the United States Olympic Committee—Jim knew all the key players in the International Olympic Community and specifically at the International Olympic Committee (IOC).

Tom Hayes and the FIL board had been working on an Olympic bid for decades, had overcome many hurdles and

World Lacrosse CEO Jim Scherr (pictured between me and Dan Britton at the World Lacrosse Championships in Israel) was key to lacrosse being recognized as an Olympic sport.

were really close, so it didn't take long for Jim's leadership and relationships to pay dividends. In 2019, the International Olympic Committee (IOC) granted lacrosse provisional recognition which would allow it to be included as an "exhibition" sport in an upcoming Olympics starting possibly as soon as 2024 in Paris. In July 2021, the International Olympic Committee granted lacrosse full recognition as an Olympic sport, which paves the way for lacrosse to hopefully be played as an official sport in the 2028 games in Los Angeles.

Our Olympic dreams were becoming a reality!

MORE TO THE STORY...

Getting Lacrosse in the Olympics – Joe Tsai

I did not know Frank Kelly at the time, but we first crossed paths on a college lacrosse field, when I played at Yale and he played at Cornell. We both graduated in 1986.

It was 30 years later in 2016 when I officially met Frank at the U19 Men's World Lacrosse Championships in British Columbia, Canada. I supported the teams from Hong Kong and Taiwan, and I brought my two young sons who played lacrosse and wanted to see the best U19 players in the world.

Frank impressed me as a man who is earnest, honest, open, all heart, and an absolute gentleman.

I was invited to a dinner with Frank and representatives from the FIL who were on the committee that was raising funds to make lacrosse an Olympic sport. At the dinner, I agreed to contribute financial support toward a CEO position with the specific purpose of getting lacrosse into the Olympics.

Another highlight for me was the morning after our dinner when my sons ate breakfast with Frank's nephew, Timmy Kelly, mid-

Joe Tsai (Right) and his sons Dash and Jacob with Hong Kong head coach Scott Browning at the 2016 Men's U19 World Lacrosse Championships in British Columbia, Canada

Dash Tsai (with his father Joe) would six years later play for the Hong Kong National Team at the 2022 Men's U21 World Lacrosse Championships in Limerick, Ireland.

fielder Ryan Conrad, and the rest of the U.S. Men's U19 Team. My boys were thrilled to get autographs and some swag from the players.

Through his work with FCA Lacrosse, the FIL and now World Lacrosse, Frank Kelly has been instrumental in growing the game around the world. He helped develop lacrosse in Uganda and Kenya, and lacrosse's growth on a new continent, Africa, made it a truly global sport—an important factor in World Lacrosse CEO Jim Scherr's effective pitch to the International Olympic Committee.

Expanding the Map – Jim Scherr

I met Frank for the first time at a breakfast meeting in 2017, a few months after I became CEO of FIL/World Lacrosse. He was the fundraising co-chair on our board and had helped bring our most prominent donor to the table. My first impression was that Frank was passionate about lacrosse, and a mature and effective leader with a strong personal presence.

I saw his passion and leadership shine forth up close at the 2018 World Championships in Israel. Frank and his teammates on Team Serve were a competitive bunch that enjoyed playing at a high level. The teams they played against appreciated having a quality opponent to scrimmage.

I sat in on some of Team Serve's players' meetings—a rewarding experience for a guy who was involved with FCA and wrestled with Athletes in Action in college. I attended a special event where Frank and others from the team shared their testimonies with players from around the world and explained the mission of FCA Lacrosse. I've heard nothing but good feedback from players who have attended FCA Lacrosse events.

Frank was instrumental in helping the Ugandans raise the resources they needed to participate in the games, and I saw the hope that the international lacrosse experience infused into the lives of the Ugandan players. Playing on a team provided an organized activity and a structure that not only allowed them to travel but also helped many of them to stay in school and in a better economic situation. For those who were interested, FCA Lacrosse offered the opportunity to pursue a relationship with Christ and fellowship with like-minded athletes.

Uganda's presence, which showed that a team from the continent of Africa could play lacrosse at the elite level, expanded the map for the game. Uganda opened the doors for forming teams in Kenya, South Africa, Nigeria and Rwanda, and for establishing a continental federation. Such a strong African program greatly enhanced our opportunity to get and keep lacrosse in the Olympics because it added another team sport on the continent with a sizeable number of players.

Following the success in Africa, we have tapped into FCA's network to grow the game in Eastern Europe and other countries around the world.

Frank is a confidant of mine and other leaders of our teams. We appreciate his friendship, his expertise and support. Frank, the entire Kelly family, and FCA Lacrosse are part of the fabric of the game. They are a positive influence on the World Lacrosse organization and our teams. They have earned great respect, and I am happy to support their endeavors.

We Breathed on Each Other – Steve Stenersen

Frank Kelly and I didn't just play against each other, we breathed on each other.

After playing on the 1981 and 1982 University of North Carolina National Championship Teams, I came back home to Baltimore and was one of the first employees hired by The Lacrosse Foundation. I also continued playing lacrosse, as a faceoff midfielder for the Mt. Washington Lacrosse Club and battled Frank head-to-head,

Steve Stenersen (#36) and me (battling at the faceoff X), are long-time friends in working to grow the Creator's game in the U.S. and around the world. In the picture above, you can see why I was running away from him.

where we breathed on each other for eight years when he faced off for the Maryland Lacrosse Club. Both were excellent clubs, but MLC usually got the best of us. We only beat them twice while Frank and I were both playing.

We connected again as Frank was launching FCA Lacrosse and I was the CEO of The Lacrosse Foundation, the organization that evolved into US Lacrosse in 1998 and is today known as USA Lacrosse. I was happy to give him the time and space to hold breakfasts and set up booths at our conventions when he requested it. FCA Lacrosse was all about advancing the game, which was completely in sync with my aspirations. I strived to create a culture of belonging, and we had organizations of all shapes and sizes and areas of focus already involved in the convention.

In 1998 Frank asked for a more formal venue at the convention to present the FCA Lacrosse Peter Kohn Service Award. I didn't hesitate to say yes. I first met Peter in 1982 when he served as the equipment manager at the North-South

All-Star Game played at Hobart College. He served in the same role for many U.S. men's national teams, which fell under my purview at The Lacrosse Foundation and US Lacrosse.

Peter was a special man who represented the essence of giving back to the sport and everyone who played, coached, and officiated in it. I was honored and humbled when Frank called me in 2014 and congratulated me as that year's FCA Peter Kohn Service Award recipient, in recognition of my then 30 years working for the growth and advancement of the game.

When FCA Lacrosse launched its club program and my son Cole and I found out that Frank Kelly, Bryan Kelly, and other coaches with stellar reputations were coaching, we wanted to be a part of it. Bryan and I share a special UNC Tar Heel bond. He played on the National Championship team in 1991, and I played on the back-to-back National Championship teams in 1981-82.

In youth sports, it's all about the coaches. I wanted good people and knowledgeable people for Cole, and FCA Lacrosse had quality coaches up and down every sideline. Cole played multiple years for FCA Lacrosse and loved his experience.

Frank and I also worked closely together after we recruited him for the US Lacrosse Foundation Board, which works with our staff in the key area of philanthropy.

Frank was a natural for our board—experienced in the game and passionate about the transformative opportunities lacrosse provides for kids and a business leader experienced in a variety of philanthropic endeavors who could address our philanthropic priorities and help generate resources to fuel the mission.

Alongside three others, Frank co-chaired our $15 million capital campaign that raised funds to build a new 45,000-square-foot national headquarters and national training center in Sparks, Maryland—a campaign that surpassed its goal.

As a couple, Frank and Gayle gave generously to the cause, reached out to others to ask for their support, and provided helpful counsel to evolve the organization. Their vocal support spoke volumes about the integrity of US Lacrosse.

FCA Lacrosse players and coaches have contributed significantly to the sport's domestic development, but maybe even more importantly, to its international growth and development. Frank served on the Olympic Vision Committee of the Federation of International Lacrosse, now known as World Lacrosse, and was a big part of helping lacrosse, "the Creator's game," become recognized as an Olympic sport.

Frank was not a young man in 2018 when he ran up and down the field in Israel in the name of building relationships and fostering lacrosse in other nations. Frank and his team worked an exhausting schedule supporting the players and coaches of fledgling teams. They embodied passion and commitment to the sport's global growth.

FCA Lacrosse represents the best of the sport. They are a microcosm of what sport provides—a community of people who believe in the value of team sports and benefit from the fellowship that such unity provides. FCA Lacrosse is all about creating fellowship around the game while practicing the golden rule: "Do unto others as you would have them do unto you."

PART XI

Baltimore and Beyond

CHAPTER 64

The Saints Go Marching In

"In the same way, let your light shine before others, so that they may see your good works and give glory to your Father who is in heaven."

Matthew 5:16 (ESV)

Although doors were opening around the world for the Creator's game and FCA Lacrosse, my heart always came back to Baltimore, where so much got started.

I remember when I sensed the call to start my post-collegiate life in my "Jerusalem" (Baltimore), I wasn't necessarily thinking too much about the inner-city impoverished parts of Baltimore. I was thinking in more global terms, like the greater Baltimore area, and all those who cheered for the Baltimore Orioles, our former Baltimore Colts and our current Baltimore Ravens.

It didn't take long for me to get connected to former Baltimore Oriole, Pat Kelly (no relation), and a former Baltimore Colt named Joe Ehrmann, both of whom loved God and had huge hearts for at-risk Baltimore City youth.

I first met Pat and Joe and a number of other professional athletes, most of whom turned out to be followers of Jesus, through a Baltimore nonprofit called Pro Athletes Against Drugs. The organization recruited pro athletes in the Baltimore community to meet together for a breakfast and training session, and then go into a number of different Baltimore City schools to do assemblies and speak with kids about living drug- and alcohol-free.

Since I was playing lacrosse professionally for the Baltimore Thunder, I was invited to be one of the speakers and would be assigned to a specific school where I would present.

One year, I invited Gayle to join me, and during the breakfast and training, they announced that one of their scheduled speakers, the famed Harlem Globetrotters basketball star, Meadowlark Lemon, was not going to make it and another athlete was needed to go and speak to the kids at Lombard Middle

School in East Baltimore.

Out of desperation, they asked (begged) Gayle to fill in and speak as a former three-sport college athlete. Gayle was ready to kill me, but she did it.

Gayle says, "Can you imagine what those kids were thinking when they were expecting the world-famous Meadowlark Lemon and instead got me—a white woman who had played a few years of field hockey, lacrosse and cross country at Mary Washington College?"

We still laugh about that one!

One day, Pat asked me to speak and serve at his summer camp, and he graciously spoke at many FCA dinners and our 1992 FCA Lacrosse Camp where Sean McNamara "walked the aisle" and surrendered his life to Jesus, the Creator, as he understood Him.

Joe, who had an all-pro football career with the Colts, had also played lacrosse at Syracuse University, so after he started a unique faith-based community center in East Baltimore called The Door, he asked me if I would help put together a first-ever youth lacrosse team for them. I convinced my brother Bryan to help, and for a couple of years, our "Door" lacrosse team practiced and scrimmaged in some very unique places and on some very unique fields in East Balti-

The Door lacrosse team, which my brother Bryan (standing left) and I (kneeling left) coached for a couple of years in the early nineties

more. It was not uncommon for us to carry our lightweight goals and some equipment up to half a mile to find the best place to practice and play.

Seeing where those children came from and what they had to overcome planted seeds of compassion and empathy in my heart that would shape my thinking about sports ministry and lacrosse in our city for decades to come.

Coach G and Park Heights

The west side of Baltimore had challenges as well. I was fortunate to meet Garrick Williams in the late 1990s at Dr. Roland Patterson Sr. Middle School, near Sinai Hospital in West Baltimore. For a number of years, our FCA Maryland ministry was growing and earnestly seeking to effectively serve student-athletes and coaches in underserved parts of our city. I just couldn't get those prior experiences with Pat Kelly and Joe Ehrmann out of my mind or off of my heart.

We hired our first Baltimore City FCA representative—her name was Carmen Reece, and she had been a cheerleader at the University of North Carolina before moving to Baltimore with her husband, who was a pastor at a city church. After a couple of years working to make inroads, Carmen and her husband moved out of state to pursue another pastoral position.

We ended up hiring former Baltimore City (Northwestern High School) and University of Wisconsin football and basketball star Ray Sydnor as our next FCA Baltimore City staff person. Together, we decided to start an FCA youth basketball program and huddle, and our FCA Baltimore City Board chairman at the time, Roland Patterson Jr., knew we could get the school named after his father to host this unique outreach. We would provide sandwiches for the kids after school, then oversee a weekly basketball clinic and games followed by a huddle time of teaching from God's Game Plan.

Garrick Williams was a volunteer mentor there and was helping to lead the huddle times. He was humble, hardworking and really knew how to connect with kids, so when he talked about wanting to start a new football team in his neighborhood, Park Heights, I encouraged him. God brought other supporters his way as well, and the Park Heights Saints were born—triplets—Garrick filled three youth teams.

Garrick and Teresa Williams

Poverty, violence, gangs and drug dealing are rampant in Park Heights, the neighborhood where Garrick and his wife, Teresa, raised their three children. Garrick wanted to shine the light of the Gospel there through sports with a focus on youth football.

"Coach Garrick" (also known as "Coach G" and "Brother Garrick") had worked as a community liaison and youth outreach worker at Sinai Hospital. He's also an ordained minister, a violence-prevention mentor at area schools, and has won various community service awards. He knew that coaching football could open doors for the Good News and that "the kids follow the coaches."

"I thought I could use this as a ministry. They want to know football, I want them to know Christ and life,"[1] he told *Baltimore* magazine in February 2020.

Today, Coach Garrick and his 45 volunteer assistant coaches, including former drug dealers and gang members as well as current and former Baltimore City police officers, are working together to reach over 200 kids on nine football

teams and a cheerleading squad, offering a safe environment, mentor-
ship and a structure wherein they
can develop physically, socially, in-
tellectually and spiritually.

Garrick often praises the dedication of his assistant coaches.
"Look at brother Jay Steimetz,"
Garrick said. "He's been with me
for 20 years. He sold his house in
the suburbs and moved to Park
Heights. That's commitment."

*Coach Garrick (Left) with Coach Jay Steimetz
(Second from Right) and other friends of the Saints
at their annual Father's Day cookout*

When I started coaching my sons Frankie and Stephen in football at Luther-
ville-Timonium Recreation Council (LTRC), I would take their teams down to
Park Heights to scrimmage the Saints. They were always tough games, and a bit
of an eye-opener for my players and parents, who were used to the comforts of
the suburbs. After the scrimmages, Coach Garrick would share a message from
God's Game Plan, the Bible. He always had a small gift for each of my players and
I would bring FCA Bibles for his teams.

An FCA Umbrella

When Garrick's church, Agape Miracle Church, fell on hard financial times
after the death of its founding pastor, Rev. Eleanor Graham Bryant, it could no
longer support the Saints' football team.

"Coach G., would you want to partner with FCA?" I asked. "FCA could be
an umbrella structure for financial support, encouragement, and accountability for you." He agreed, and the Park Heights Saints joined the FCA family in
2008.

"Coming under the FCA umbrella has given the Saints access to more resources and opportunities," explains Garrick. "The kids can apply for scholarships to summer camps, and the football teams can travel—we've won multiple
national championships at youth tournaments in Florida. One of our favorite
outreaches continues to be our annual FCA Park Heights Saints Father's Day
Cookout, which is held the Saturday before Father's Day," notes Garrick.

Hundreds of family members show up to support the players and coaches,
and to enjoy the free burgers, hot dogs, drinks, ice cream and even free pony
rides. A real highlight is that a number of the boys' fathers, who are not typically in their lives, show up to the welcoming atmosphere as well. In some cases,

families are reconciling and being healed, and the love of God is being shared with everyone.

Football is Coach G's favorite sport, but God was soon going to open a door for the Creator's game to be played in Park Heights as well. And a special place for the players and coaches to congregate off the field would not be too far behind.

Scan to see an amazing video about the FCA Park Heights Saints.

Coach Garrick (Back Right) with one of his nine FCA Park Heights Saints football teams

CHAPTER 65

A City on a Hill

"You are the light of the world. A city set on a hill cannot be hidden."

Matthew 5:14 (ESV)

As the influence of FCA and FCA Lacrosse continued to grow, so did Kelly Benefits and the different ways my brothers and I and our wives were involved in the community.

Between us, we serve or have served on more than 40 different nonprofit boards. It has been an honor to serve on boards like the Living Classrooms Foundation, the Cal Ripken Sr. Foundation and the Greater Baltimore Committee, and help lead various fundraising efforts and capital campaigns for Calvert Hall, USA Lacrosse and Helping Up Mission (HUM).

The HUM campaign was special since Gayle and I worked together to co-chair their $60 million "Inspiring Hope Campaign" to build a facility in East Baltimore that would house up to 200 women battling addiction and homelessness, as well as up to 50 of their children. This would keep mothers from being separated from their kids while they sought help, hope and healing in HUM's amazing, free, 365-day spiritual recovery program.

I have also enjoyed helping pull together different groups of business leaders, primarily presidents and CEOs of local, Baltimore-based organizations in both a faith-based CEO Advisory Forum that meets monthly to discuss business leadership and management challenges from a biblical perspective, and a separate Balti-

Helping Up Mission Women's and Children's Center

more Business Leaders Prayer Circle, that connects high-level CEOs and executives to meet once a month for an hour to fellowship and pray for our city.

God's Word reminds us that, "...our struggle is not against flesh and blood, but against... the spiritual forces of evil in the heavenly realms."[1] Our battle, even for our city, is a spiritual one and we believe that the prayers of people coming together are powerful and effective.

Influence and God's blessings can be shared in a variety of ways, yet in a city like Baltimore, there are almost always obstacles that want to prevent them.

Did You Know Jesus Loves Sports?

The FCA Baltimore City area representative staff position was full of challenges. Over a fifteen-year period, a lineup of talented, persistent, and pioneering leaders stood in the gap: Carmen Reece, Ray Sydnor, George Hopkins (who had played football at Morgan State University), Patrick Gaines (who had head coached championship high school football teams in Texas), and Wayne Lee (who had a pastor's heart and ultimately became one). But the many transitions made it difficult to gain much traction and credibility with FCA in the city.

Fortunately, our FCA Baltimore City Leadership Board was persistent and continued to pray for the right person to be raised up to effectively lead what we knew could be a ministry of hope, healing and light in our city.

In 2011, our prayers were answered when God tapped the shoulder of a former Baltimore City St. Frances Academy basketball star, and then young mother of a middle school-aged son. Her name was Sirena Alford. Sirena would become a Baltimore City FCA volunteer, then board member, then part-time staffer before being named our Baltimore City FCA metro area director.

Sirena recalls how God used her son, Steven Jr., to connect her with FCA:

"We'd like to offer Steven a scholarship to our 2011 FCA leadership camp up at NorthBay," Janet Zorn and Rachel Heggins, who led Steven's huddle at Roland Park Middle School.

"I had first heard of FCA only a couple of months before when I saw their table at the school's clubs and extracurricular activities fair.

"'You should check them out,' I suggested to Steven, and he began attending the huddles.

"But Steven had never been away for a weekend before, NorthBay was over an hour away, and I didn't know much about FCA, so my husband—'Big Steve'—insisted that Steven could go to the camp only if I went with him.

"I volunteered to work on the kitchen crew so I could stay at the camp for the weekend and make sure Steven was okay. We were delayed in arriving at

NorthBay and when I walked into my dorm room, I saw four bunk beds. A group of college girls, who were also volunteer leaders, had already settled into the bottom bunks, leaving the old lady in the room to climb up and down all weekend. *The things a mother will do for her son!*

"Like a typical middle-schooler, Steven didn't pay much attention to me the whole weekend, but I could tell that he loved the camp. Our church is small and there aren't many kids Steven's age there, so for the first time in his life, he was part of a large group of young people playing sports and praising God.

"When Steven asked me, 'Did you know that Jesus loves sports?' I knew that he and God had connected over the weekend.

Sirena Alford with her husband, "Big Steve" (Left) and son, Steven Jr.

"I was so touched by everything I saw at the camp—especially the young men praying with Steven before we left—and the impact it had on my son, that I accepted an invitation to join the FCA Baltimore City Advisory Board in 2012, came on staff part-time in 2013, and would eventually become the full-time Baltimore City FCA metro area director.

"Neither of us missed another camp until Steven graduated from high school."

Hearts for the City

During this same time frame, we saw the FCA Maryland state director position transition from Rick Conniff to Mark Stephens in 2012.

Mark had been a high school and college wrestler at Salisbury University (he likes to call Salisbury, "the Harvard of the Eastern Shore of Maryland") and was blessed with four daughters, so he would soon after trade in his wrestling singlet for girls' lacrosse sticks, which turned out to be a real blessing for our growing FCA Lacrosse ministry.

Mark worked closely with our FCA Lacrosse director, Ryan Horanburg, to support the growth of FCA Lacrosse in Baltimore City, throughout the State of Maryland, the Mid-Atlantic region and around the world.

In 2017, Mark would pass the mantle of leadership for the state of Maryland to Shaun Smithson (a former honor guardsman and chaplain for the D.C. United professional soccer team), and Mark would assume a role with FCA focusing on international ministry efforts and expansion in East Asia.

Both Mark and Shaun had a real heart for Baltimore City, so working together with Sirena and a growing army of volunteers, including Sirena's "Dream Team," stories of FCA impact and transformation continued to roll in.

FCA Huddles and Fields of Faith outreaches were started at the most historic and prestigious public high schools in Baltimore City, including Dunbar, Frederick Douglass, City College, Polytechnic and Western, just to name a few.

Sirena and Shaun's partnership with Coach Garrick and the FCA Park Heights Saints would also take things to a whole new level and shine the light of influence in one of the most challenged communities in West Baltimore.

Sirena Alford and her Baltimore City FCA "Dream Team" with Coach Garrick

Baltimore City FCA leaders, coaches and friends at a Fields of Faith night at Paul Laurence Dunbar High School

Watch God Do It

"For we are God's handiwork, created in Christ Jesus to do good works,
which God prepared in advance for us to do."

Ephesians 2:10

"On September 30, 2015, at one o'clock in the morning, the Lord allowed me to dream," Coach Garrick told *Baltimore* magazine. "This is what He showed me. A living room with a white leather sofa and chairs. A big TV. A nice kitchen. Upstairs, a computer room and a bedroom, should it be needed. And a weight room in the basement and a deck out back."[1]

Garrick was dreaming about the dilapidated rowhouse on Reisterstown Road where Reverend Eleanor Graham Bryant had discipled him and many others from the Agape Miracle Church congregation. The home had been previously owned by Rev. Bryant's mother. Garrick dreamed of rebuilding it into a safe place where Saints players could come to do schoolwork, meet for prayer and Bible study, work out, and hang out to eat a meal and watch a game.

"We can make this house a great beacon of light again, in a dark place," Garrick said.

He dreamed of a food pantry that fed the surrounding community and a classroom where players' parents worked on their GEDs and accessed resources to find jobs. It was a big dream, but Garrick believed that "God doesn't give you something great that you can do without Him. I can't do it alone. I need an army."

Sirena Alford, our Baltimore City FCA metro area director, Shaun Smithson, our FCA Maryland state director at the time, and I worked with Garrick to raise the $250,000 in cash and gifts-in-kind to make his dream a reality.

This is My Sandbox

We recruited Wayne McPartland, a former three-time All-American defen-

330   BALTIMORE AND BEYOND

seman at Loyola University who had rehabbed over 250 homes in the city, to oversee the entire buildout. I remember Wayne making fun of our FCA Lacrosse team back in his playing and partying days, but he later came to faith through the influence of FCA and was willing to volunteer for a year and give his time and tremendous experience as the general contractor. Wayne recalls:

"When Frank Kelly connected me to Garrick Williams to look at the run-down townhouse he wanted to transform into a community center, I instantly connected with his vision.

"I grew up in half a dozen different foster homes in the borough of Queens, New York, so I know what it's like not having parents or anybody that cares about you. At age nine, a family told me they were going to adopt me.

"'What does that mean'? I asked.

"'It means you are going to live with us. We're going to raise you.'

"'You mean I won't have to leave?'

"I understood the huge impact the Community Center was going to have on the kids in Park Heights. The Community Center is not going to leave. Brother Garrick and all the people there who care about the kids are not going to leave.

"The house was gross, tangled with cobwebs, and rodents were everywhere. Parts of it were burned out. The roof was caving in. People were afraid to step inside. They were overwhelmed by the task. But I had seen it all before and I was excited to dive in. *This is my sandbox, man!*"

"God Did It!"

When Garrick shared his dream with me, he probably could have been talked out of it. But I was adamant that "if God said it, we could do it."

The house was owned by Agape Miracle Church, and when he told Pastor Cynthia about his dream, she asked him to write down his vision for transforming the house back into a place of ministry. Garrick wrote a letter describing everything that God showed him in his dream and closed it with "Watch God Do It!"

Under the piles of rubble in the house, Wayne uncovered an old Bible. In the front was a date—1964—and a name—Eleanor Graham Bryant. To Garrick and the rest of us, that reminded us that one of the only things that lasts in this world is God's Word.

Wayne noted, "There are robberies, drugs and shootings all through the streets of Park Heights, but we didn't have one issue the entire year we put that place together. God works in tremendous ways. He had us all working for Him and His glory. It made my heart burst to be a part of it."

We were all blessed to be surrounded by people who had a heart for God and a heart for others. Watching the restoration of the house come to pass strengthened all of our faith. At the ribbon cutting, Garrick closed his prayer over the new community center in praise of the One who moved mightily in Park Heights and shouted, "God did it!"

Four years after Brother Garrick's dream, the Park Heights Saints Community Center opened in March 2019.

It was awesome to see the Baltimore business and faith community come together to build the FCA Park Heights Saints Community Center. Special shoutout to Wayne McPartland (far left standing with black sweatshirt), Pastors Tae Pae and Mitchell Lee of Grace Community Church and then-FCA Maryland state director Shaun Smithson (Mitchell and Shaun center front row) for their extraordinary dedication and effort in helping to make Garrick's dream from God a reality.

MORE TO THE STORY...

Building a Foundation – Wayne McPartland

I always joke with Frank, "I know that one person plants the seed and other people water it. But you need to start using Miracle-Gro because the seed you planted in me took 30 years to sprout!"

After I graduated from Loyola University in 1987, I played a year for the Maryland Lacrosse Club with Frank, David and Bryan. I was in my early twenties and did not have my head straight on my shoulders. I had grown up in the foster care system in New York before I was adopted and ended up attending St. Mary's High School on Long Island in Manhasset, New York. Frank reached out and shared God's Word with me, but I was more interested in parties.

I moved on to play for Greene Turtle and was on the losing side of the mountain where the miracle happened. We considered FCA a ragtag bunch that couldn't afford real jerseys and thought we would destroy them.

The game felt like it started early in the morning, but I think it was a noon game on the famous Ford Field. FCA trotted out on the field all bright and shiny; we were out at the bars the night before and staggered through our warmups. After they beat us in double overtime, we walked off wondering, *What the heck happened here?*

After Vail, I got into real estate development and lost touch with the Kelly brothers until eighteen years later. By August 2010, I was still living in the Baltimore area, and after three years of feeling kicked in the gut by one circumstance after another, I raised my eyes to the heavens and cried out, *Why am I here?*

I thought I was going crazy. Who was I looking up to?

At the warehouse I was working in at the time, I crossed paths later that day with a guy named Kevin Couser, who happened to be a pastor in Baltimore City who rented space there. He noticed the distraught look on my face and asked, "Wayne, what's going on?"

I told Kevin honestly what was going on. He took hold of my hands and prayed for me. At that moment, my life started turning around. It was hard for me as an athlete to say, "God, I can't do this without You." It was humbling for me as a man to surrender to someone whom I had never met, but the day I fully surrendered was the best day of my life.

A few weeks later, I ran into David Kelly and told him about my experience.

"Wayne, I think you're ready," he said.

"Ready for what?"

"We are starting a Bible study in our office with a few guys. I'd like you to come."

"Man, you've been trying this for years!" I said. "All right. I'll give it a shot. But can you set me up with a Bible so I don't look like the dumb guy in the smart class?"

I showed up the first week and David handed me two books with sportspeople on the covers.

"What are these?" I asked.

"These are Bibles," David said.

"Are you sure? There's no leather and no tassels. They look like comic books."

"They're FCA Bibles," David said.

"Ok, well...can you tell me which is the Old Testament and which is the New Testament?

David looked at me like I had something growing out of my forehead.

"Really? The Old Testament is the front half, the New Testament is in the back half."

In our Bible study, I could ask the guys to explain the passages to me and in a short time had learned more than I had learned in my whole life up to then. With the FCA Bible, and through David, Matt Stover from the Baltimore Ravens, and the other athletes in the group, for the first time in my life I heard Jesus speaking to me in a tongue I could understand—sports.

I was a sponge for the Scriptures. I never missed a week of Bible study. I sat next to the leader so I wouldn't get distracted. After acting like a fool for so many years I opened my heart and let Jesus pour in. It wouldn't have happened without FCA.

A year later, Bryan Kelly asked me to coach an FCA club lacrosse team of third graders. That's a big commitment, I thought, but I dove into it and learned something about how God works.

I had never quite understood how to "serve the Lord." I couldn't go get Him a cup of coffee; I couldn't wash his feet. But as I was teaching lacrosse and sharing God's Word with the kids, it dawned on me. *I'm a conduit between God and His children. This is serving the Lord!*

Not only that, coaching forced me to go deeper into my faith because if I was going to teach, there was more I had to learn.

After a tournament in Vail with my FCA team, I came back to the Bible study and said, "Guys, you all said that God had a plan for me. I really, really enjoy coaching these kids and I see that this is how I'm serving Him. I just don't know why He waited this long to get me into this."

"I'll tell you why," Stover quipped. "Because He didn't want you anywhere near his children before this year!"

Now that the players I started coaching ten years ago are teenagers and some even in their twenties, I see the importance of pouring into kids at a young age. Some of them might take a bite of the apple in high school or college, but most seem to return to the foundation that the Lord used FCA coaches to set for them. When the dust settles, they see what's right and what's wrong. God's Word will not return void. I've seen that happen a lot.

CHAPTER 67

Lax in "The Hood"

*"And provide for those who grieve in Zion—to bestow on them a
crown of beauty instead of ashes, the oil of joy instead of mourning,
and a garment of praise instead of a spirit of despair..."*

Isaiah 61:3

Coach Garrick never calls Park Heights, or the community where his teams practice and play, "The Hood," even though most of his coaches and players do. He looks at his community as a place of healing, hope and restoration, and he doesn't like the negative connotations associated with the slang term.

It didn't matter to John Harbaugh, NFL Super Bowl champion head coach of the Baltimore Ravens, what they called the community the evening he came to the fields to meet Garrick, Sirena and the FCA Park Heights Saints coaches, players and cheerleaders. He just wanted to bless and encourage all the young football players and coaches in attendance.

Coach John Harbaugh with Sirena Alford at an FCA Park Heights Saints football practice on Lucille Park Field

Because of our family's and business' support of the Ravens, as well as Coach Harbaugh's long association with FCA and his love for Baltimore City, I knew him well enough to invite him to Park Heights where he led football drills and enthralled us all with an uplifting and motivating message. He and Coach Garrick—who had never been a big follower of professional football until that day—became fast friends and have been known to text back and forth even on Ravens game days.

When Coach Harbaugh met Sirena, he turned the subject to lacrosse because he's not only a football coach—he's a lacrosse dad. His daughter, Alison, had played since second grade and was playing in college at the University of Notre Dame. "Is there anything going on with the FCA Park Heights Saints and lacrosse in the city?" he asked.

Sirena told him about the clinics and camps that FCA Lacrosse had been doing at Lucille Park, home field of the FCA Park Heights Saints, and explained the potential for significant growth of the Creator's game in Park Heights and throughout the city.

We also told him that to build a lacrosse program in Park Heights, it would be a good idea to convince some of the Saints' football coaches to help coach lacrosse. I decided to host around 30 coaches for dinner and assured them that coaching lacrosse wouldn't be that hard because of all the ways that the two games complement each other.

"What I'd like to do," I told the football coaches, "is set up a coaches' clinic for you and teach you the game." It rained the day before the clinic and the field was a muddy mess, but we decided to go for it. We taught them how to catch, throw and scoop—with a tennis ball so no one got hurt. After a few drills, they felt confident and their competitive juices started to flow. "Can we play a game?"

We set up the goals and picked teams. The only problem was that we had no helmets, pads or gloves, and had to call the game off when somebody got slashed and a wild fight broke out.

Things did not go as planned, but a few coaches agreed to help when their schedule allowed, and Coach Harbaugh's interest to support the growth of lacrosse in areas like Park Heights was a real encouragement.

Kacy Kapinos and me running a lacrosse training session for the Saints football coaches. It did not go as well as we hoped!

An Amazing Job

Coach John Harbaugh notes, "Sirena does an amazing job in Baltimore City. Kids love to play sports, so FCA and FCA Lacrosse are natural vehicles for introducing young people to Christ. But starting a lacrosse club is hard to do. By supporting Sirena and FCA Lacrosse, we can get the equipment, find the fields, and get lacrosse growing in the city. I want to help as much as I can."

Sirena notes, "With Coach John Harbaugh's contribution to Baltimore City FCA, we have awarded dozens of FCA Lacrosse Camp scholarships, and it has been a joy for me to see the kids' faces light up and to witness the growth in lacrosse's popularity in Baltimore City. The list of players who attended a camp and play in high school and college continues to grow."

Whether through football, cheerleading or lacrosse, our goal is to give more kids more opportunities to hear the Good News of the Gospel. As Coach Garrick says, "The big trophy comes when the kids and coaches realize that God loves them and has a plan for their lives. My plan is always to help them meet the Real Champion—Jesus Christ."

FCA Park Heights Saints lacrosse clinic

MORE TO THE STORY...

You Would Be Perfect – Sirena Alford

In 2013, I joined the Baltimore City FCA staff as a part-time outreach representative. I worked solo for several years after the metro area director position became vacant, and I kept thinking about applying for the director job. At an FCA meeting, I asked Frank and Gayle Kelly what they thought of the possibility. "You would be perfect," they said.

I passed a series of job interviews and began raising my financial support, but my big break came when Frank, Ryan Horanburg and Shaun Smithson invited me on a Zoom call with Baltimore Ravens Head Coach John Harbaugh who has a passion for expanding the game of lacrosse in Baltimore City. I didn't know anything about lacrosse, but I knew plenty about the city.

On the call, Shaun asked if I would share my story with Coach Harbaugh. When I finished, Coach Harbaugh asked, "What's your budget?" I threw out a number, and Coach Harbaugh offered to cover it. I was shocked. A month later, I presided over my first board meeting as the Baltimore City FCA metro area director.

When I speak at various sports and faith-based events, I often say, "I thank God for Jesus Christ, my husband, and Frank Kelly!" Without Frank, his father and the entire Kelly family's support, I don't know how I would have had the opportunity to serve as the Baltimore City FCA metro area director. I would not oversee FCA Huddles in fourteen Baltimore City public schools, provide character coaches for four girls' lacrosse teams in the city, or fund scholarships for inner city boys and girls to attend FCA Lacrosse camps. Frank and the influential supporters he has introduced me to have sparked the growth of lacrosse in Baltimore City.

"The Godfather" of Baltimore City Youth Lacrosse - Donnie Brown

At one of its Victory Celebration banquets, Baltimore City FCA honored Coach Donnie Brown for his decades of service to FCA and the city of Baltimore. Many call Donnie "The Godfather" of youth lacrosse in the city.

"I've been involved in everything lacrosse for decades," Donnie says, "as a player, coach, referee, board member and now as the executive director of Charm City Lacrosse."

Donnie played on the famed "Ten Bears" lacrosse teams in the 1970s and 1980s at Morgan State University—the first historically Black college or university to play NCAA Division I lacrosse. His playing career claim to fame is scoring the game-winning goal in Morgan's overtime victory over Notre Dame in 1981.

Donnie has been passionate about introducing African American boys and urban youth to the great game of lacrosse—the Creator's game. He knows the game helps instill discipline, hard work, teamwork, perseverance, and other values that are essential. He has been a champion for Black youth for decades in Baltimore and realized FCA could help him accomplish his mission.

Donnie called me in the early 2000s about entering his Warriors club team in FCA's One Way 2 Play tournament at Messiah College.

"The FCA tournament would be nice," Donnie told me, "but we don't have the budget to get there."

We helped Donnie raise the additional funds he needed for the trip, and while he was at the tournament, Sean McNamara told him about the FCA Lacrosse summer camp in Gettysburg and suggested that a couple of his players could benefit from the camp. Donnie had reservations, especially about one player that he knew had "anger management" issues, but he talked with the players' parents about the camp, and they all signed up.

Donnie drove up to camp one afternoon and describes what he saw and how it changed his future summer plans: "I went up to make sure my players hadn't burned the place down, and I couldn't believe the change I saw in them. The atmosphere was so different than any other camp and I could only stop and think, *What's going on here? This is good. This is really, really good!*

"The next summer, I passed up working for pay as I always had at the Loyola,

UMBC and Hopkins summer lacrosse camps and volunteered at the FCA Lacrosse Camp. The spirit of the camp keeps me coming back every summer. I see the impact the FCA camps have on the players—athletically, socially and spiritually—and on their character and the kind of people they become."

Coach Donnie Brown in action

REMEMBERING COACH DIPPER

Garrick Williams Jr.
September 7, 1982 – March 1, 2021

Tragedy struck the Williams and FCA families on March 1, 2021, when Garrick Williams Jr., known as "Coach Dipper," was walking across the Mondawmin Mall parking lot and was intentionally hit and killed by a car. He was 38 years old. Dipper had played for the Saints growing up and had coached the Saints for ten years.

"Dipper was more like a mentor to his players," assistant coach Jay Steimetz told WMAR-TV news. "He not only taught the kids about the game of football but also about the Xs and Os on how to succeed in life. It wasn't a matter of what can you do to win a game. It was what can we do to help you grow and be better in life."

The Park Heights Saints and FCA communities rallied in support. The day after Dipper died, Baltimore Ravens Head Coach John Harbaugh and Ravens Chaplain Johnny Shelton visited Garrick and his wife, Teresa, spending a couple of hours in their Park Heights row home to comfort them.

The 40 other volunteer coaches, made up of former drug dealers and gang members, Baltimore City police officers, and other men and women of faith, are as committed as ever to carry on the legacy of "Coach Dip" and share the love and influence of the greatest coach of all time, Jesus Christ.

"The kids loved him. The community loved him. This is a hurting time," Coach Garrick told WBAL-TV news. "I want them to understand the main thing my son stood for: God is good, all the time. What I would say to my son is that you did all you could and we'll handle it from here."

This mural was painted on a warehouse wall that is located right next to the FCA Park Heights field in honor and memory of Coach Dip (Garrick Williams, Jr.).

CHAPTER 68

Keeping It Alive

"Having so fond an affection for you, we were well-pleased
to impart to you not only the gospel of God but also our own lives,
because you had become very dear to us."

1 Thessalonians 2:8 (NASB)

In 2012, my brother Bryan and his wife, Heidi, returned from the Vail La-crosse Shootout having had a great experience with their young FCA National Team, which included a good number of local area boys, but with only one regret.

"A number of the young kids and their families come back to Baltimore from that mountaintop experience, and we have no way to continue learning and expanding the impact on an ongoing basis," they said.

Heidi felt strongly about starting a local FCA Lacrosse club team as a way to water the seeds of faith that were planted in the various summer tournaments. Jimmy Page, who was the FCA Mid-Atlantic vice president at the time, and had experienced Vail, agreed. "We gotta have club teams to keep the Colorado and summer experiences alive," he said. "It might be messy, and we might make mistakes, but this is our opportunity for a ten-times multiplier of influence on coaches and athletes at the top level of lacrosse competition. And we already have a core group of athletes

Jason McFadden, who played at Calvert Hall ('09) and Georgetown University ('13), taking in the beauty of Piney River Ranch, was one of many amazing coaches and huddle leaders for various FCA Lacrosse youth teams at the Vail Lacrosse Shootout.

and coaches engaged. *Let's do it!*"

Bryan and Heidi continued to pray about the idea.

"Our oldest son, Jacob, was in eighth grade, so high school was on the horizon," Bryan recalled. "As a high school coach, I knew how much kids are challenged with drugs, alcohol and peer pressure. They need to hear the truth and the Good News that FCA conveys on a regular basis to help muster the courage to live for the Lord and do what's right. I couldn't think of a better way for them to hear than an ongoing club team that had young college-age huddle leaders who the younger guys could look up to as they talked about the importance of their relationship with God."

I agreed with Bryan and Heidi about the impact an FCA Lacrosse club team could have on the kids, but I also had a couple of concerns.

First, our goal was to reach the entire lacrosse community and for FCA to support and encourage every club team, and I thought that competing against other club teams could create an overly competitive or adversarial relationship with other clubs and thus their players, coaches and parents. And second, in club lacrosse, you might have 100 kids try out for a 20- to 25-player roster. I didn't like the idea of cutting 75 to 80 kids.

But Bryan and Heidi pushed forward and suggested we field three teams. I was still anxious because we could have to cut a large number of kids and I didn't want a kid's or family's first experience with FCA to be getting "cut" or "rejected." The Creator loves everyone, and I wanted all who registered and tried out for an FCA Team to be welcomed and experience God's love and grace in a personal way. Bryan decided to schedule a tryout and see what God would do.

My brother Bryan coaching an early FCA Maryland Club team

"The response blew my mind," Bryan said. "We formed six teams—three A-teams and three B-teams."

That meant more than 120 young lacrosse players would hear the Good News in the huddle times after their practices and weekend games and at their summer and fall tournaments.

Bryan coached a team and I agreed to coach one of the B-teams with our son JK and some of his friends, who would be the youngest players on our 9-10 team. We agreed to offer scholarships to our FCA Lacrosse Camp for any player who did not make one of the FCA Club teams. We wanted everyone interested in FCA Lacrosse to have a positive, life-changing experience.

Retreat!

After the FCA Maryland Club Lacrosse program and teams were established in 2012, and played a full summer and fall tournament schedule, we decided to hold an overnight winter retreat on a weekend in early December at a local facility called River Valley Ranch (RVR).

Since there were six club teams then, each with approximately 25 players per team, all 150 kids were invited, and fathers were welcome to attend to help monitor the boys and participate in the fellowship.

The boys had a blast with all the amazing activities at RVR, including paintball, ziplining, dodgeball and other fun and competitive games. The retreat always featured a gifted platform speaker, like Steve Fitzhugh, the former Denver Bronco, who could make the kids laugh and cry and really understand the Good News, and a great group of current and former college lacrosse players, who would lead the breakout and huddle times.

Steve Fitzhugh is a former Denver Bronco and an all-time favorite FCA camp and retreat speaker.

Not only were the kids growing in their relationship with God, the Creator, but so were many of the dads in attendance who had never experienced anything like it before.

MORE TO THE STORY...

Influence Multiplier – Jimmy Page

When I took over the leadership role of the Mid-Atlantic region for FCA, I began working with Frank, Bryan and Heidi Kelly, and others to get club lacrosse going. They put their Kelly name on the line to recruit more coaches and players. Their reputations assured coaches and players that FCA Lacrosse would deliver high-level lacrosse with a higher purpose.

Bryan and Heidi rolled up their sleeves and took point, and they were off the charts with their level of engagement and financial support. Frank, with Gayle's full support, was a force of nature with his tenacity and persistence, as well as his passion to involve the parents and siblings who would often travel with our teams.

I believed that competing at the highest levels with club teams would create a sustainable FCA Lacrosse ministry. We could attract and develop talented players, disciple them in their relationship with God, and send them off as leaders to their high schools and colleges. Some of them would come back and serve as huddle leaders in our camps and coaches on our teams. Some of the huddle leaders and coaches would come full circle and later serve on staff.

As our club teams competed, we could see our influence on the wider lacrosse world spread and increase. Some players, parents and coaches from other teams would see us huddle before and after games and come over and ask, "Hey, what are you doing?"

After we explained, many said, "That's so awesome!" People are attracted to a program that is competitive on the field yet keeps something more important at the center of it.

We're not the Fellowship of "Perfect" Athletes, and there are times when a player or coach loses their cool and says something or acts outside of our value system. But those situations provide a different kind of opportunity—to ask for forgiveness, make amends, and show people what humility, grace and mercy look like. It's all about modeling a relationship with God in the best moments and the worst moments.

The influence multiplier extends to the parents and siblings who travel with our teams. Frank and the FCA Lacrosse staff developed studies and devotions for family huddles, and when we're away overnight for a tournament, we offer more extended talks at larger-scale team dinners. We've seen family members come to faith, and we've seen families engage or re-engage with churches back home. That's generational influence.

The first FCA Lacrosse team that shocked Vail in 1992 showed the lacrosse community, over one week, what it looks like to compete as seekers and followers of Jesus. The club teams would demonstrate week after week and season after season that they compete as hard as anybody and have a guiding set of values that hopefully strengthens each player's relationship with God and determines how they do it.

Have You Ever Been in a Bible Study? – Todd Garliss

I had heard good things about this relatively new FCA club lacrosse team program, and as a parent decided to have our son Charlie try out for one of the younger teams.

We weren't strong in our faith at all, but I thought it would be good for Charlie to be around coaches and people who were at least trying to prioritize character and values.

I was standing along a fence at Calvert Hall watching the tryouts with some of the other parents, when one of the coaches, Frank Kelly, came over and asked me about how things were going and who my son was.

"I'm Todd Garliss, and my son is Charlie. He is trying out for midfield," I said.

Without hesitation, Frank made a positive comment about Charlie's speed and hustle (which he needed to overcome his small size) and pointed out that the kids, who were now broken into small groups on the field, were having a "huddle time" and discussing things about life and faith.

Frank then asked me, "Have you ever been in a Bible study or small group before?"

"Huh? No, I haven't," I replied, and then Frank asked me if I would have any interest in joining with some other guys he knew who were meeting together on Tuesday mornings for breakfast.

After an awkward pause I said, "Yeah, that would be great."

I can't explain it, but I believe divine providence was at work that day. I think the Lord was just moving in both of our lives, as I was feeling a hollowness in my life at that time, and that conversation was exactly what I needed. For some reason, I felt drawn to wanting to learn more about God. That small group men's Bible study would change my life.

Charlie made the team and played several years for FCA before becoming passionate about squash, and I have been a part of a great local church and a number of small groups, including one with Frank, to this day.

Frank inviting me to my first Bible study pushed me in the direction of engaging in a personal relationship with the Lord. I'll always be grateful to my friend and brother in Christ for that.

CHAPTER 69

Godly Women

*"Charm is deceptive, and beauty is fleeting; but a woman who fears the Lord
is to be praised. Honor her for all that her hands have done,
and let her works bring her praise at the city gate."*

Proverbs 31:30-31

O n Ryan Horanburg's second day on the job as national director of FCA
Lacrosse in 2008, a mom called him and asked, "Do you run any lacrosse camps for girls?" My wife, Gayle, had taken an FCA women's
team to Vail in 1997, but Ryan had to tell the mom that there were no FCA Lacrosse summer camp opportunities for females at that time.

Two years later, FCA Lacrosse hired its first women's director, Merissa Bogdanor, added a Fellows Internship for women, and entered a women's college
team in a tournament in Ocean City, Maryland. Four of the players on the team
told Ryan they were interested in running a lacrosse camp for girls. Ryan asked
them, "If I commit to getting 30 girls to come to the FCA Lacrosse Gettysburg
camp, will you commit to working at the camp?" All four said yes, and 27 girls
signed up. Close enough.

In 2011, we formed our first national women's high school team. And when
Merissa transitioned off of staff to focus her time on being a mom, we were
fortunate to have Lauren Iacoboni fill the women's director role. Lauren came
from a big lacrosse family, having played herself in high school and college, and
having coached at Dulaney High School (Gayle's alma mater). Lauren also had
cousins who played at a high level, including her nephew Mikey Wynne, who
starred at Notre Dame, so she knew and understood the game.

All In

Lauren ended up passing the baton to Meg McKnelly in 2017 after Meg graduated from the University of Delaware, where she played goalie on their wom-
en's lacrosse team.

Whether in a small group or a large huddle, FCA Lacrosse Women's Maryland Club and National Team Director Meg McKnelly was all in.

Meg's first experience with FCA Lacrosse left her with a very positive impression of the leadership team and the families involved. It started with her younger brother, Michael, who loved his experience on an FCA National youth team in Vail, and then with his FCA Maryland club team.

After meeting Ryan Horanburg and the other FCA Lacrosse staff at the annual fall ball "Thumbs Up" game between North Carolina and Ohio State at Calvert Hall (where her brother attended and played), Meg knew she wanted to get involved with FCA Lacrosse, so she decided to jump in with both feet.

Meg agreed to coach and lead huddles at the FCA Lacrosse Camp and for the FCA Women's National High School Team in Lake Placid. And in the fall of 2017, she ended up coaching the first-ever FCA Maryland girls club team. It wasn't long after that Ryan asked her to consider coming on staff. Meg considered a couple of college coaching offers, but ultimately felt she could have a greater impact on the game and in the lives of hundreds of female lacrosse players that were now involved with FCA Lacrosse each year. Soon after joining the FCA Lacrosse staff in 2018, Meg would become the director of the FCA Maryland girls' club and FCA National teams.

Meg went to work right away recruiting and training women huddle leaders and coaches. She notes that: "FCA training can be transformational, as it was for me as a college athlete serving at FCA Lacrosse Camp when Frankie Kelly was a part of the camp leadership training team and spoke about 'owning my faith—not my parents' faith—and pursuing Christ on my own.' His message penetrated my heart and it was then that I told the Lord, 'I am all in!'"

Camp Growth

It was exciting to think that the first official FCA Lacrosse Camp that included girls, in 2010, attracted 27 female campers and less than a decade later, more than 200 girls would join more than 300 boys and nearly 100 volunteer coaches and huddle leaders at Lebanon Valley College for camp.

It was disappointing to transition our camp's location from Gettysburg College after more than 20 years there (because the U.S. Olympic Soccer Development Committee leased the entire campus for their summer teams), but God opened a door at Lebanon Valley College and would later lead camp to Lancaster Bible College in Pennsylvania.

The most important thing is that hundreds of girls, boys and amazing volunteer coaches and huddle leaders were coming from all over the country to better learn the Creator's game and to grow in their relationship with God.

It has been amazing to see the FCA Lacrosse Camp grow from nine participants in 1988 to more than 500 boy and girl campers and nearly a hundred volunteer coaches and huddle leaders.

CHAPTER 70

Club Growth

"Still other seed fell on good soil, where it produced a crop—a hundred, sixty or thirty times what was sown."

Matthew 13:8

From the original six club teams in Maryland, the FCA Lacrosse club ministry grew rapidly.

About five years after the first club teams in 2012, Ryan Horanburg, the FCA Lacrosse director, was concerned about coordinating tryouts, practice fields, gear and tournament scheduling for up to twelve teams now competing under the FCA Lacrosse banner. That would mean more than 500 boys trying out and approximately 300 boys making one of the Maryland FCA club teams. And, that meant a lot of FCA Lacrosse Camp scholarship offers to those boys who didn't make one of the club teams.

It also meant significant growth of the annual FCA Maryland Club Lacrosse Retreat that first weekend in December at River Valley Ranch. The Retreat now had to be divided into two 24-hour blocks, with nearly 150 youth and middle school boys coming Friday night at 5 p.m. through Saturday at 4 p.m., and another nearly 150 high school boys coming Saturday night at 5 p.m. through Sunday at 4 p.m. And dads were still invited, so it was becoming quite a weekend of Influence.

One year, one of the younger campers, Fisher Putnam, whose father John was in attendance, came forward after one of the fellowship and huddle times, and asked if he could get baptized to fully express his new commitment to Christ. The challenge was that it had snowed five inches that day and the only place nearby with water was the small river that ran right through the campsite.

Our platform speaker that year, John Smith, a former college (UMBC) and FCA Lacrosse player himself, ended up baptizing him right there in the river with the snow falling and many of the campers looking on.

As Fisher's dad, John, watched his son get baptized, he stepped into the water to hug him, then asked to get baptized himself.

It was an inspiring reminder of the power of the Good News to bring new life to those who receive it.

It wouldn't be long before FCA Lacrosse girls club teams would be started, and they would need retreat time as well. We would have to start thinking about hiring FCA staff to run the club lacrosse ministry.

It was emotional to see a son and his father both ask to be baptized in the middle of a snowstorm at our annual FCA Maryland boys club lacrosse retreat.

Pruning Leads to Expansion

The Great Recession that occurred between 2007 and 2009 caused major challenges for many businesses and non-profit organizations across the country.

It turned out to be a very difficult time for Kelly Benefits, when one of our key leaders made some unwise and hidden financial decisions, exacerbating the effects of the economic downturn. In order to weather the storm, our family had to pool our personal finances and make some painful staff reductions.

Those issues brought us to our knees and challenged us to remember and apply the truth from one of the Proverbs in God's Game Plan to "Trust in the Lord with all your heart and do not lean on your own understanding. In all your ways acknowledge Him, and He will make your paths straight."[1] It was hard to understand what was happening and why, and it didn't make sense on many levels, but we did our best to surrender the situation and trust the Lord to lead us out, and He did.

Fortunately, that time of pruning and financial stress ultimately led to another period of fruitful growth. Again, God showed Himself gracious and faithful in our time of need.

That recession also led to reduced donations to many faith-based organizations, including FCA. On a national level, FCA was forced to reduce expenses and realign staff. Instead of eighteen regional vice presidents, there would be twelve, and the FCA sports-specific ministry position, held by Sean McNamara, would be merged into the various regions. Sean would end up taking a position as the FCA Northeast Region vice president. This proved to be providential, as Sean was the perfect person to help start and oversee an FCA Lacrosse ministry and club program in that region.

Sean McNamara (with his beautiful family) came to faith as a sixteen-year-old at FCA Lacrosse Camp in 1992 and has been on staff with FCA in various leadership roles and locations for more than 25 years.

In 2015, Sean hired Solomon "Sol" Bliss, who had been a multi-time All-American and National Champion defenseman at Syracuse University, to oversee the FCA Club Lacrosse program in Upstate New York (where the Creator's game originated). And of the seventeen boys and girls FCA Club Lacrosse teams in the area as of this writing, many of the players have a Native American heritage, which has helped their teammates gain more respect for the game.

In one of the huddle times, Sol asked one of the Native American players named Croix Snow of the Seneca Nation to tell everyone more about the origin of the game.

Croix was always ready and willing to give his teammates a glimpse into the history of lacrosse. Sol noticed that when the FCA players learned more about lacrosse's spiritual roots—the Creator's game—they upped their level of respect for the game and changed the way they play. They started to define success by how they treated the game, their teammates and their opponents.

Croix told his teammates, "Players who respect the game aren't going to throw their sticks. That stick represents the game, and the game was created to give you joy, medicine and healing. Players who respect their teammates welcome them into the community of athletes who love lacrosse. Teammates are not merely competitors for playing time. You never know when or

Coach Sol Bliss (back row, standing with gray shirt) and the FCA Upstate New York 2021 Box Lacrosse Championship team that had several players with a Haudenosaunee background

where your paths will cross away from the field. And players who respect their opponents don't taunt or trash-talk them because without opponents, you don't have a game."

Respect for the game and FCA Lacrosse's emphasis on the athlete's spiritual journey are reasons why players and parents tell Sol all the time that they love FCA for more than the lacrosse. "We can play lacrosse anywhere," they say, "but we can't get FCA Lacrosse anywhere else."

In 2019, Sol hired former Marywood University head women's lacrosse coach, Katie Tutak, to be director of operations and soon after, the FCA Upstate girls' lacrosse director as well. Katie hit the ground running and her heart to minister "to and through the coach" was evident from day one. Her effectiveness as a leader resulted in five new FCA girls club teams in Upstate New York, and a great deal of influence in other areas as well.

Lacrosse in the Sunshine State

Russ LeBlanc was a volunteer with FCA Lacrosse in Maryland when he felt led to move his family to Florida in 2018 to start an FCA Lacrosse ministry there. Russ recounts how God opened doors for him to use the Creator's game to share the Gospel on the Treasure Coast of Florida:

"To spread the word about FCA Lacrosse when I arrived, I ran free clinics at middle schools to help kids understand the game. I visited a different high school each day and made myself available to the lacrosse coaches. I told them, 'I'll work with a brand-new kid. I'll help with the offense. I'll clean up balls. I'll do anything you want me to do.'"

Coach Russ LeBlanc in Florida

All Russ asked in return was the chance to offer a voluntary huddle after practice for any of the guys or girls who wanted to stick around. Russ introduced FCA Lacrosse, invited them to free clinics and gave them the opportunity to play for an FCA tournament team. Russ' first tournament team was with a group of high school girls.

Three of the high school coaches Russ volunteered for were also coaching club teams. They told Russ what a headache the teams were to manage. They trusted him as a coach and pitched him an idea: they would turn the teams over to Russ to coach, organize, manage and schedule tournaments, and they would just show up and help coach.

Once Russ made sure all the coaches were okay with the vision, mission and values of FCA, as well as letting him lead the huddles, in the fall of 2019, FCA Lacrosse in Florida added a high school boys A-team, B-team and C-team to its club lacrosse lineup.

For the boys and the girls, playing for FCA Lacrosse was a different experience. Russ held a huddle after every practice to discuss what was going on in their lives and apply biblical truths to whatever they were going through. Russ created a team culture in which players learned the game and biblical truths in a safe, positive environment.

For many kids, the message of salvation, hope, joy and peace was brand new. For others, it was reinforcement. "Anything I can do with lacrosse to spread the Gospel in the state of Florida is what I'm all about," Russ said.

MORE TO THE STORY...

To and Through the Coach – Katie Tutak

I was the head women's lacrosse coach at Marywood University in Scranton, Pennsylvania, recruiting at the Capital Cup tournament, when I saw an FCA sticker on another coach's water bottle. *Hmmm. Should I be recruiting at FCA, whatever that is?*

I jotted "FCA" down in my recruiting notebook and Googled it when I got home. When I read about FCA's summer camp, which brought lacrosse and God together, I decided I had to go and see for myself. I applied to volunteer as a coach at the 2014 camp in Gettysburg.

I was totally blown away by how Jesus was central to everything at the camp. I was blown away by how the other coaches lived out their

Coach Katie Tutak with FCA Lacrosse Upstate New York

faith, and that an organization existed for sports and Jesus, the two primary loves of my life.

The atmosphere was so different than any other camp where I had coached. Those other camps were high intensity. The head clinicians were often very critical of the kids, and at times even pitted the coaches against each other—who ran the best drills? Whose players executed better?

At the FCA Lacrosse camp, the coaches made sure the campers learned the skills properly, but in an encouraging and loving environment. We worked together and encouraged one another. Huddle leaders constantly asked what they could do to serve us and help with the drills.

At FCA Lacrosse, I found fellow coaches who understood what I was going through. We clicked as a group and talked about our experiences on a much deeper level than we could with most other people.

Experiencing that kind of fellowship, watching the kids grow in their faith and ultimately become huddle leaders themselves, and having a father tell me that his daughter who struggles with anxiety "hasn't been this happy in years," kept me going back to FCA camps. I developed friendships that have lasted to this day.

I stepped away from coaching in 2018 and moved to Buffalo, New York. FCA Lacrosse in Rochester was just over an hour away, and I started coaching one of FCA's first girls club teams. The following year, Sol Bliss and FCA Lacrosse Upstate were looking for a director of operations. As I considered taking the position, Frank Kelly was the first person I called about raising support. He has always been an encourager and willing to help me however he could. We all agreed the job was a good fit for me, and I joined the staff. The FCA Girls Club Lacrosse director position opened up two months later and I added that role to my plate.

Over the years, we have looked for more and more ways to effectively encourage and positively influence women's coaches. A major focus of FCA's outreach is "to and through the coach," and from personal experience, I knew the significant challenge college coaches experience. Most people have no idea of all that coaches do and the pressures they face, especially those who are followers of Jesus.

Since 2010 we've held a breakfast meeting at the annual Intercollegiate Women's Lacrosse Coaches Association (IWLCA) convention. FCA recently became an official sponsor of the IWLCA convention, which gave us a role in planning the convention. It's our opportunity to serve the women's lacrosse community and spread the message of FCA Lacrosse face-to-face with 600 coaches and facilitate fellowship for coaches who are open to growing in their relationship with God.

From coaching our girls club teams, to being a lead clinician at FCA Lacrosse camp, to serving women lacrosse coaches at the IWLCA Convention and throughout the year, I love what I do in and through FCA.

Sports and Faith Don't Mix – Russ LeBlanc

"Sports and faith don't mix."

So said the coach of a girls club lacrosse team when I told him about FCA Lacrosse. Our program was just getting off the ground on the Treasure Coast of Florida—which stretches roughly from Vero Beach to Port Lucie—and I was still introducing myself to other coaches and players in the area.

"I think you're a really good guy, and I think FCA is a really good program, but I just don't think sports and faith should combine," he said.

Over the next year, he saw us around the fields, and his daughter was involved with other FCA groups, but he kept his wall up and never allowed me access to his team.

Then one day in December, he called me. He had tried to enter his team into a weekend tournament but couldn't get in. We had two teams playing.

"Hey, I'm in a tough spot," he said. "Could my daughter and some of our players join your team for the tournament?"

"We'd love to have them," I said.

I found out that his birthday was on the Sunday of the tournament, so on Saturday, I brought an FCA Lacrosse Christmas shirt for him.

"Can I give this to you as a birthday present?" I asked. "I'm not offended if you don't want it. I know how you feel."

"Are you kidding? I'll definitely take it!" So on Sunday, I'm looking over at a coach and a father, who once didn't want anything to do with me, wearing an FCA Lacrosse shirt and watching his kids play on my team.

After the game, all the players and families, including the coach, gathered around for prayer and praise and to recognize our seniors. My daughter, Morgan, one of my assistant coaches, prayed for the seniors and the team.

The coach is a good friend now. I love how God, our Creator, connects people to Himself and others through the Creator's game.

CHAPTER 71

Do Not Give Up
Meeting Together

"And let us consider how we may spur one another on toward love and good deeds, not giving up meeting together, as some are in the habit of doing, but encouraging one another—and all the more as you see the Day approaching."

Hebrews 10:24-25

I n 2008, when I was coaching Stephen in 11-13 football, our LTRC team was trying to defend its championship from the prior year. We were into the playoffs and our November practices were starting to get cold. We only had two full practices before our next playoff game, so when two of my assistant coaches told me they had to leave early to be part of a small group they committed to through their church, my curiosity was piqued.

"You guys attend a Catholic church, don't you?" I asked, knowing that most Catholic churches I knew did not have small-group Bible studies or cell groups.

"Yes," they said. "We attend Church of the Nativity, right near Ridgely Middle School," which is where I went to middle school.

"And what are you studying in your small group?" I asked.

They said they were studying a book called *The Purpose Driven Life.*

I said "Let me get this straight. You guys are leaving our playoff football practice early to attend your small group and discuss the all-time best-selling book in history (next to the Bible) written by a pastor named Rick Warren through your Catholic

Two of our football coaches left our playoff practice early to go to their newly established small group through The Church of the Nativity. That piqued my interest, and I was thankful we still won as well.

church, Nativity?" I knew the book well as it was one of my favorite books to give away.

"That's right, Frank," they said. "We'll see you at practice on Thursday night."

"Wow! That is great. Let me know how it goes."

I went home that night and told Gayle I wanted to check out Nativity. We had attended Grace Fellowship for more than 20 years, and had invited many people to join us, but the church had been through some leadership transitions and we weren't growing like we used to, and I didn't feel excited about bringing guests there anymore.

Music, Message and Ministry

I'll never forget going to church my first time at Nativity, when Father Michael White gave his homily based on a teaching series he was doing called "Catholic Atheists." *What a crazy series title,* I thought to myself, and wondered what he would possibly say. That day, he spoke on "prayer" and how many Catholics, at times even himself, often live like "prayer atheists." Then taught that prayer was simply communicating with God, who wanted to have a personal relationship with us through his son Jesus Christ. It was a simple, clear and biblical message. Nativity's focus on music, the message and ministry were relevant and very encouraging.

For about a year, we attended both Grace Fellowship Church and Nativity, until we sensed we could reach more people in our spheres of influence by being fully committed to Nativity. I communicated clearly with the leaders of Grace, and they supported our move. They had even invited Father Michael to give a message at Grace one weekend.

Since 2010, we have attended Nativity full time and have been very involved in leading small groups in our home and Gayle has been one of the small group teachers for the weekly video series they produce. Nativity's more than 200 small groups meet each week, watch a brief video message, and then work through discussion questions about the sermon from Sunday, the small group message and/or relevant scriptures.

It's exciting that some FCA staffers and a good number of the FCA Maryland boys and girls club lacrosse coaches, players and their families attend Nativity. In many ways, the messaging of FCA and Nativity have been aligned in reinforcing the importance of having a personal relationship with God, the Creator, and the importance of sharing His love and truth with others, including the blessing of giving.

The Joys of Generosity

One of Nativity's most impactful message series to me had to do with generosity and giving. We were reminded that God is very generous, and when we are generous with our time, talent and treasure, we are being like God.

In particular, the series challenged everyone to practice the biblical principle of "tithing," or giving away the first ten percent of your income, and what they called the "Four Ps of Giving:" making financial giving a Priority, developing a Plan, committing to giving away a Percentage of your income—even if it was just one or two percent to start—and, to consider Progressively increasing your giving over time.

This teaching reminded me of my time in Japan, when my friend Scott challenged us to memorize Luke 6:38 and Jesus' challenge to "Give, and it will be given to you..."

Gayle and I had practiced these principles since our first days of marriage, so giving for us became a habit and a lot of fun. We actually set up a separate "tithe" checking account and the first part of our income goes into that, which has given us even greater joy and freedom in giving. As we have given, God has graciously allowed our income to grow.

I have heard it said that "you can't outgive God" and that has definitely been our experience. I don't think we should "give to get," but somehow "when you give, you get."

I often laugh at my good friend, Ed Bradley, who spent more than 30 years in the financial markets before retiring to go on staff at Nativity, serving in the areas of finance, development and training. We had been in a number of small groups together over the years, and God used me to challenge him in the area of tithing and giving.

Ed jokes that our friendship cost him more money than any other, because since we met, he began to practice the principle of tithing and giving away an increasing percentage of the treasure God had entrusted to him. He has given away more than he ever imagined. I always ask him what happened to God's provision in his life after he met me and began applying God's Word and truth to his giving. He always laughs and shakes his head at God's grace and blessing.

Others who practice generous giving have helped fund and fuel FCA, realizing that almost every FCA staff person is faith-financed, so each staff person has to raise their own budget, with God's blessing of course.

Gayle and I love being on the financial support team of dozens of FCA staffers in our area, across the country and around the world. Kelly Benefits has been blessed by the opportunities to support many FCA events and activities as well.

My feeling is that if FCA staffers have the courage to be on the front lines of sports ministry, the least we can do is give and support their efforts.

A Big Brother

The benefits and joys of generosity and giving financially apply to nonprofits and faith-based groups like FCA Lacrosse as well.

One way FCA has raised money over the years is through golf tournaments. Businesses provide sponsorships in exchange for foursomes that allow relationships to be built, the FCA story to be told and financial resources to be developed.

FCA Lacrosse has not done a golf tournament, but we have helped support other ministry golf outings, including the FCA Hockey Golf Tournament, held each fall in Annapolis, Maryland. The proceeds go to help fund FCA Hockey, which was started by Rick Randazzo and his wife, Shannan, in 2008.

Rick had played hockey at West Point, where he was a top scorer before coaching at the U.S. Naval Academy. He would ultimately leave his coaching and later business career and travel with his wife and five children around the country, running FCA Hockey camps in all 50 states before deciding to move to Minnesota to officially establish the FCA Hockey headquarters and co-found the Northstar Christian Academy for Hockey.

He saw what the Creator was doing with FCA Lacrosse and sensed that God was calling him to "go" and start FCA Hockey. Inspired by a verse in Isaiah, which says, "Then I heard the voice of the Lord saying, 'Whom shall I send? And who will go for us?' And I said, 'Here am I. Send me!'",[1] the Randazzos made the move. FCA Hockey has impacted thousands of hockey players, coaches and fans at the youth, high school, college and professional levels ever since.

FCA Hockey board member Todd Steinweg and his friend Mark Tomchik agreed to start and run the FCA Hockey Golf Tournament more than a dozen years ago.

Todd notes, "Kelly Benefits and FCA Lacrosse have sponsored our FCA Hockey golf outing every year since we started. They have no reason to do that other than their love for God and to see another sport-specific ministry grow and have an eternal impact. In many ways, FCA Lacrosse has become a big brother to FCA Hockey."

With the fun connection to FCA Hockey, it was exciting to learn that Stan Fisher, whom I coached in lacrosse at Calvert Hall and who was a member of one of our first FCA Huddles in 1989, has started and is coaching a local FCA ice hockey club team. I love the ripple effect of FCA.

FCA Lacrosse was also thrilled to see FCA Wrestling get started in 2008, when Tim Johnson, FCA vice president of field ministry in the Midwest, worked with our former FCA Lacrosse director and then new FCA vice president of sport-specific ministry, Sean McNamara. Tim was a high school and college wrestling legend, a highly respected wrestling coach, and a Hall of Fame wrestling broadcaster. In 2011, Tim and the FCA Wrestling Board hired a former All-American, national champion wrestler and highly regarded wrestling coach from the University of Illinois, Carl Perry, to become full-time director of FCA Wrestling. He has been leading the ministry since.

Again, God used the growth and impact of FCA Lacrosse to influence another sport with a very specific culture, and their impact on the wrestling community at every level—locally, nationally and even globally, including the worldwide Olympic wrestling community, is truly inspirational.

Influence is about helping others fulfill their unique mission, purpose and calling in life. FCA Lacrosse has helped inspire and encourage FCA Hockey, FCA Wrestling and other sports like baseball, soccer, volleyball and surfing. In many ways, FCA Hockey and FCA Wrestling now inspire and encourage FCA Lacrosse to continue to serve the lacrosse community with excellence.

That is what brothers and sisters should do—encourage and inspire each other to maximize their potential and expand their influence.

PART XII

Do You Believe in Miracles?

CHAPTER 72

The Fields Are Ripe for Harvest

"...I tell you, open your eyes and look at the fields! They are ripe for harvest."

John 4:35

Afew years after Ryan Horanburg became our FCA Lacrosse director, he was at the Vail Lacrosse Shootout helping oversee the two FCA youth teams that were there competing. One day as he was on the sideline gazing out over the fields at four different huddle groups meeting with their leaders (each of whom were current college lacrosse players) with the majestic Gore and Swatch mountains in the background, he smiled and thought, *Look at this picture! God, You are so good. This is what it's all about.*

Ryan recalls, "After savoring that moment, I turned to walk down the sideline and—*What was that?* Something hit me in the back of the head. I glanced back at the huddles. There was nothing and no one behind me, except maybe the Holy Spirit. I turned and began walking, and there they were. Yes, we had 40 kids on our two teams in huddles, but in front of me stood 80 parents, some of them hurting and in just as much need of Jesus as the kids, and we weren't doing anything for them."

Ryan knew I had a heart and plans to influence the parents on the teams I was coaching, but nothing had been formally structured to serve the parents on the various national teams that were playing under the FCA banner.

"What would it look like to impact the parents? I thought of a flight attendant's in-

FCA Lacrosse Director Ryan Horanburg with his wife Kate and their four sons by Vail's famous Gore Creek

struction for oxygen masks: If you're traveling with small children and there is a loss of cabin pressure, parents, please put your masks on first before you put a mask on your children," noted Ryan.

FCA Lacrosse became more strategic about serving the players' parents so they would be better prepared to support their child after their FCA Lacrosse team experience. Ryan and the staff designed FCA parent huddles and a "Word of the Day" to be shared with the parents right there on the field prior to their sons' or daughters' first game of the day.

Many of these tournaments were over the weekends, so attending church was off the table and thus, we decided we would strategically bring the Good News to where the parents and children were—there on the lacrosse fields.

God blessed our efforts and a few years later, there were more than 800 FCA players, parents and family members connected to the twelve FCA Lacrosse teams that were spread across the Vail Lacrosse Shootout fields. Ryan and the team even figured out a way to get everyone together for a big country western-style meal to celebrate all that the Creator had done and was doing through FCA Lacrosse. 4 Eagle Ranch was the perfect place to gather for an amazing meal, fun outside activities and an incredible time of fellowship for hundreds of people.

Hundreds of FCA laxers and their families enjoying a western dinner at 4 Eagle Ranch

Ryan loves to remind the parents that "This tournament trip is not just for your kids, it's for you too. We believe no one is here by accident, and we pray that you and your family each take that next step in your relationship with God because of our time together."

Every Parent Sees Two Games

As our sons got older and continued playing competitive sports and I was no longer on the sidelines coaching them, I noticed that as I watched the games from the bleachers or stands, I was dealing with more and more emotions in my heart and mind. Why was I getting upset or concerned if they won or lost a JV basketball game? Or got limited playing time in a varsity football or lacrosse game? As they began playing at the Division I collegiate and then professional levels, some of those emotions continued and at times even intensified.

I realized that every parent of an athlete watches two games when they watch their child compete no matter what the level. There is the actual game being played that everyone sees with the final score, etc., and then there is the game we as parents see through the situation of our sons or daughters.

Of course, we cheer for our team, but it's hard not to notice our child's situation in the game. *Did they start? Are they on the bench? Did they get solid playing time? Did they play well? Were they on the extra-man offense or power-play unit? Did they get injured? Or make a play that helped the team win? Or a mistake that caused the team to lose?*

I have come to realize that so much of the emotion we experience as parents while watching our children compete is tied to expectations. If we can manage and properly align them with God's Word, we will have more peace and joy regardless of the outcome—easier said than done for me.

Competition is not for the faint of heart, as every time you compete, there are winners and losers. Some will play well, and others will have off days. You can learn so much about life as a coach and an athlete but, in some ways, the hardest role in sports is that of a parent.

FCA often teaches about being "three-dimensional" (or 3D) coaches and athletes—developing the mental, physical and spiritual dimensions of coaches, athletes and fans by focusing on coaching the heart. There is a Scripture that reminds us, "Above all else, guard your heart, for everything you do flows from it."[1]

Even as parents, it takes work to guard our hearts and minds—to have peace, joy and proper perspective. It was exciting that FCA Lacrosse was now focusing on serving the hearts and minds of parents, as well as the coaches and athletes on the field.

Influencing the Influencers in Lake Placid

As the Creator's game exploded in growth—statistics have shown that lacrosse is the fastest-growing team sport in the country—so have the number of tournament locations.

The Lake Placid Summit began in 1990 with a modest seven-team field. It rapidly became a popular location for collegiate and post-collegiate teams, including Masters Teams (like our FCA "Gideon's Army" Masters team in 2004), but then expanded significantly as a national youth tournament location and today has evolved into a week-long event with more than 250 teams. Talk about a bunch of full fields.

Ryan notes, "Our tournament geography has shifted some in recent years. While Vail remains an important destination in our history and national team schedule, Lake Placid has become another hub, which is fitting since this part of New York is the home of the Mohawk Nation of the Haudenosaunee or Iroquois Confederacy, where as the 'Keepers of the Eastern Door,' they also played the Creator's game."

And since Lake Placid was the site of the 1980 Winter Olympics "Miracle on Ice," where the USA men's hockey team upset the heavily favored Soviet Union team and ABC sportscaster Al Michaels famously asked in the last seconds of the game, "Do you believe in miracles?," the FCA teams always tour the Olympic Village and hockey rink where the USA won a gold medal. It's a perfect place to discuss the history of lacrosse and FCA's "Miracle in the Mountains" team—We like to talk about miracles!

We get to discuss how that historic ice hockey game played a part in breaking down the wall of communism, just as FCA Lacrosse helps break down the walls keeping us from connecting with our Creator.

The Lake Placid tournament is usually in late July or early August, so it is one of the last tournaments on the summer schedule and has been a great place to bring the FCA National boys and girls teams. Being "select" teams, getting a spot on an FCA Lake Placid team has become a greatly valued opportunity for players across the country. Like Vail, with hundreds of players and parents descending on the fields and coming together under the FCA banner, the need for Godly coaches and huddle leaders is of absolute importance.

Fathers Reunion

In August 2021, I was blessed to be in Lake Placid, standing on the sideline of a field, watching our youngest, JK, play for the FCA National High School Team, when who did I run into, but Peter Schaffer, Dave Pietramala and Ronnie Klausner. Dave and Ronnie had played for the Greene Turtle team that FCA defeated in the 1992 Miracle in the Mountains game, and Peter led the team Colorado team the FCA defeated in the semifinal of that same tournament.

Here we were, nearly 30 years later, watching our sons play against each other, as their three boys were playing for HEADstrong—a team named for the HEADstrong Foundation founded by Nick Colleluori, a player at Hofstra University known for his mental toughness. Nick died of cancer fourteen months after his freshman season. Before he died, he started the foundation to provide financial, residential and emotional support to families affected by cancer, and his mother, father and three brothers have built it into one of the most amazing organizations anywhere, serving families facing a cancer diagnosis and inpatient hospital treatment.

As the whistle blew to start the game, we noticed JK was covering Peter's son, Gavin. While we watched, Peter shared with me that only six months prior, Gavin had been diagnosed with stage-four lymphoma, and that he was now in remission and cleared to play. As JK marked Gavin, a strong left-handed attackman, Peter told me Gavin was wearing number 27 in honor of Nick Colleluori, who wore number 27 when he played at Hofstra.

Miracles continue in Lake Placid with Gavin Schaffer overcoming lymphoma to play with HEADstrong and battle JK and FCA (with their proud dads on the sidelines).

Later in the game, I looked across the field, and JK was now defending Dominic Pietramala, Dave's son, who was also wearing number 27. Dominic was rated one of the top attackmen in his class and had committed to play at North Carolina. Dave, Ronnie, Peter and I were shaking our heads and laughing about all the ways lacrosse connected us, and now our sons as well.

Many of the high school players on that field would go on to play college lacrosse at schools like Virginia, Duke, Cornell, Georgetown, Ohio State, Yale and Johns Hopkins, but for that day they were united by the Creator's game in a cause much bigger than themselves or their future teams.

"Influencing the Influencers" in the lacrosse world was one of the goals of Coaches Sol Bliss, Drew Wardlow, Ben Savick and Michael Sisselberger with the 2021 FCA National High School Team.

Next-Gen Leadership

With the growth of the FCA National Lacrosse Camp and the number of FCA Lacrosse teams playing on fields around the country, Ryan and the FCA Lacrosse Board decided to establish a summer internship or "Fellows" program to secure and develop more quality youth coaches and huddle leaders.

Interested college lacrosse players have to apply and go through a fairly extensive interview process in order to secure one of these full-time, paid intern positions, which begin each summer in early June and end in mid-August.

There is a goal to have ten (five men, five women) full-time FCA Lacrosse interns each summer, and I have a goal that two of our twelve Kelly Benefits summer interns will be joint Kelly Benefits/FCA Lacrosse interns as well. So, there are usually twelve total FCA interns (made up of current college lacrosse players) who live for free with local host families, including our family, and share times of fellowship and learning—studying and living God's Word while getting real-life ministry experience coaching and discipling kids.

For the Kelly Benefits/FCA Lacrosse interns, we pay them for the work they do at Kelly Benefits, and we give them the freedom and flexibility to take time off to volunteer and serve with FCA Lacrosse as well. This joint internship allows them to experience a top-quality summer business experience so they can check that box on their resume and we encourage them to volunteer and work at least three FCA Lacrosse summer events, so they are learning the value of flexibility, service and living an integrated life.

And although they work many hours, they tell me that they love it!

Ryan Horanburg leading our boys FCA National High School Team and their families in prayer after their tough one-goal loss in the 2018 Lake Placid Summit Championship. You can see the famous Olympic ski jump in the background.

MORE TO THE STORY...

Coach Said – Les Steckel

When I traveled the country as president of FCA, I got more questions about our FCA Lacrosse ministry. Being an NFL coach for over 25 years, I didn't know much about lacrosse, but I know a lot about the influence of coaches and competition.

How do I explain the boom in FCA Lacrosse youth teams? There's no question that more and more parents wanted their sons and daughters exposed to the quality of coaching and the role modeling they get on an FCA Lacrosse team.

Parents see how their young athletes are positively influenced—and influence has been the theme of FCA since 1954—by Christian coaches who care about their kids more than just winning on the scoreboard.

I remember getting a call from the son of a man I coached at the University of Colorado back in the seventies named Don Hasselbeck. Don had two sons who both ended up playing quarterback in the NFL, Matt and Tim. They're both on ESPN now. I've known them since they were in diapers.

Matt was calling me about his son, Henry, who played high school football and lacrosse in Massachusetts. "Can you do me a big favor?" he asked.

"Sure," I said. He wanted to find out how Henry could possibly play on the FCA National High School Lacrosse Team playing in Lake Placid that summer. I connected him with Dan Britton, who connected him with the FCA Lacrosse staff, and they selected him to play on that very talented team.

After his FCA Lacrosse Lake Placid experience, I received a beautiful thank you note from Matt about the amazing experience Henry and the entire Hasselbeck family had, both on and off the field. Matt shared how much Henry appreciated the FCA Lacrosse coaches and their influence on him and the entire team.

Over the years, I spoke at many FCA banquets and conferences, and I always quoted Billy Graham, who said that "a coach will influence more people in one year than most people will in a lifetime." And I always shared that two of the most powerful words ever spoken to an athlete are, "Coach said."

FCA Lacrosse has gained momentum because it has influenced so many coaches to provide an excellent lacrosse experience on the field, and practical and powerful teaching from God's Word off the field. Both the players and their parents want more of that kind of influence.

Never Know Who Is Watching – Matt Hasselbeck

I grew up in a football family. My dad played in the NFL, and my brother Tim and I both ended up playing quarterback at Boston College and then in the NFL. I knew very little about lacrosse until my son, Henry, and daughters, Annabelle and Mallory, started playing and loved it.

When Annabelle and Mallory, who played on Boston College's 2021 National Champion Women's Lacrosse Team, played at the Lake Placid summer tournaments, their younger brother, Henry, often roamed around the fields to watch the boys' games. One year he told me about "this really good team called FCA National."

I knew what FCA was about because I had attended an FCA Huddle at Boston College, led by the football team's strength coach, Jerry Palmieri. Jerry later followed Boston College's head coach Tom Coughlin to the Jacksonville Jaguars and New York Giants and won two Super Bowls.

The FCA team was fun to watch, and we rooted for them. Henry dreamed of playing for FCA in Lake Placid when he was old enough. When he turned fifteen in 2021, he asked, "Dad, do you know how I can try out for the FCA Lacrosse team?"

"I have no idea," I said. FCA Lacrosse had no staff or teams near us in the Boston area. "But I'll try to find out."

I poked around on their website. I then happened to get a call from FCA president and former NFL coach Les Steckel. Toward the end of the call, he said, "Matt, if there's anything I can ever do for you, let me know."

I said, "Well, there is something. I'm trying to find out how my son can try out for the FCA National High School Lacrosse Team that will be playing in Lake Placid, New York this summer. I see there are FCA Lacrosse teams in Baltimore and Upstate New York. We're willing to travel—it's that important to us."

"I don't know the answer," Les said, "but I know our FCA Vice President Dan Britton, and he will definitely have the answer."

Within five minutes I'm connected to Dan Britton who connects me by email to three FCA Lacrosse staff guys. They liked Henry's lacrosse resume—he played varsity as a freshman at a high school that won back-to-back-to-back championships in 2015-17—and invited him to play in Lake Placid.

We both loved the experience. Henry didn't know anyone on the team before he got to Lake Placid, but now he keeps in touch with several guys from Maryland and New York, and I still keep in touch with FCA staffers Kyle Savick and Sean McNamara.

In my five years playing college football and eighteen years in the NFL, my teams prayed in the locker room before and after every game, and some of us would circle up at the 50-yard line with a group from the opposing team to pray after the game. You don't get that in youth sports around where we live, so it was cool to see prayer back on the field in Lake Placid with FCA Lacrosse. And not only prayer, but huddles for the kids and "Word of the Day" Bible verses for the parents on the sidelines.

We made it to the championship game, and before the game—which can be very stressful for parents—Kyle spoke to us about sportsmanship and urged us to honor the FCA Lacrosse gear we were wearing. He also challenged us to find some way after the game, win or lose, before coaching up our kids, to tell them how much joy it gave us to watch them play.

It wasn't easy in a fast, physical game that we lost by one goal, but I can say that we were one of the best-behaved parent groups I can remember in my spectator career!

Top to bottom, from the quality lacrosse to the team dinners to the hiking and cliff jumping, the week was an incredible experience for everybody. I was impressed with Kyle's coaching and organizing, and how he did it all with a nice demeanor about him.

Here's how I can tell how much Henry likes FCA Lacrosse. He has at least ten backpacks around the house, but which one does he use for school every day and take everywhere else? His FCA Lacrosse backpack from Lake Placid.

I love their approach: Let's answer our calling; let's use the gifts God gave us; let's go out and maximize our talent, and play physical and play hard, and be the best we can be at this game. Let's try to win this thing and honor God as we play and shine a light on the lacrosse world.

FCA planted seeds in me in college that others watered for the rest of my life. I have a lot of hope for the seeds FCA Lacrosse is planting now. It's a fruitful ministry and an all-out cool experience.

FCA Lacrosse staffer Kyle Savick leading his FCA National High School team in prayer after a Lake Placid tournament game

Talking About Love – Lilly Stephens

How does a 20-year-old FCA Lacrosse intern and coach like me make a 50-something-year-old mother cry? By talking about love in an FCA Lacrosse parent's huddle at a tournament in Lake Placid.

"Growing up playing lacrosse in Baltimore," I told the parents, "It's a tough world. You always want to be the best, and you always want to be recognized, but there's always something you're doing wrong and something you can do better. But none of these girls want to hear that. The only thing they want to hear is that their parents love them and are so proud of them."

Then I told them how my dad loves me no matter how I play.

"Every time I come off the field—I could have zero goals, zero ground balls and ten turnovers—my father still gives me a hug and tells me he loves me."

One of the moms came up to me in tears after the huddle. "Now I see the impact you and the

FCA National Girls Team being led in a prayer huddle by intern Lilly Stephens with the 1980 Olympic Torch in the background

other coaches have on my daughter and all these young girls. I want that love. I want Jesus! I want Him to know my heart."

For all the tournaments I had played and coached in with FCA Lacrosse, I never realized the importance of the parent huddles until that moment. God, you're so cool. You are using me in ways I never could have imagined.

Return to My Spiritual Roots – Myles Cohen

I would not be the person I am today if it weren't for my internship with FCA Lacrosse.

I played lacrosse at Boys' Latin School in Baltimore and was blessed to receive a scholarship to play defense and long pole at Furman University.

Curious to live life on my terms, unsure of who I was, and caught up in the college experience of a high-level athlete, I drifted away from the Lord my freshman year at Furman. Everything came to a screeching halt my sophomore year after I fractured my tibia in a game against the University of North Carolina. The metal rod in my leg and the inability to do much of what I was used to doing spun me into one of the most difficult periods of my life.

After a couple of months of expressing my heart through reading and writing, I knew I had to return to my spiritual roots. I started a Bible study with my teammates because I knew many of them were struggling with similar questions about their identities. Over 20 of us met every week to talk about life and learn more about who we were on a spiritual level. That was a cool experience that helped me exponentially.

My teammate Matt came to me one day, all pumped up. "Myles, I've got to tell you about my summer internship with FCA Lacrosse. You would love this!"

I applied, was accepted and interned for the next two summers.

I'm naturally a quiet guy. Back in college, sometimes I did not like talking to people. But the internship involved interacting with different groups—working as a team with the other interns, getting to know the kids and coaching them, leading huddles, and communicating with parents. Those roles forced me out of my comfort zone, and I learned how to express myself and let people know who I really am.

Since college, I've coached multiple FCA Lacrosse teams and led huddles for various FCA National Teams. FCA's influence led me to start LRV Lacrosse (Live-Rise-Vitalize) which helps prepare high school athletes for the overall experience of a student-athlete—from balancing academics and athletics to dealing with mental health obstacles. I have also been fortunate to work at STX, one of the top lacrosse equipment manufacturers in the world.

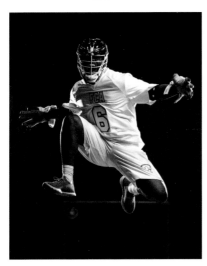

FCA Intern Myles Cohen showcasing some "hot" FCA Lacrosse gear

In all my current roles I communicate with people all the time. Using the skills I learned and developed as an FCA Lacrosse intern, I'm trying to impact the lives of many young athletes the way FCA Lacrosse has impacted me.

CHAPTER 73

Like Arrows in the Hands of a Warrior

*"Children are a heritage from the Lord, offspring a reward from him.
Like arrows in the hands of a warrior are children born in one's youth.
Blessed is the man whose quiver is full of them..."*

Psalm 127:3-5

Although my brothers, John, David, Bryan and I only played together on a lacrosse team one time—the 1992 FCA Lacrosse Miracle in the Mountains team—our children played on many teams together.

Between us, we have 21 children. John and his wife Tee have six children—three boys and three girls. David and his wife Melissa have four boys and two girls, including Eyasu and Gibby, whom they adopted from Ethiopia. And Bryan and his wife Heidi have five sons. So, when you include Gayle and our three sons and one daughter, our parents have attended literally hundreds, if not thousands of their grandchildren's youth, high school, college and even professional lacrosse games.

Each of the 21 Kelly cousins played at least a year or two of lacrosse, but not everyone loved the game. People often ask, "Who belongs to whom, and where have all the Kelly children played?" As of this writing, twelve of the fifteen boy cousins have played at Calvert Hall and most

KELLY KIDS, WHO CAME FROM ASIA AND AFRICA, COMMITTED TO LOCAL LACROSSE TRADITION

In a 2021 local newspaper article titled "Adopting the Family Game," (L to R) my brother Bryan's son Joshua, my brother David's son Eyasu, my brother John's son Micaiah, our son JK, and my brother David's daughter Gibby were all highlighted for playing high school lacrosse.

have played or committed to play college lacrosse, including my nephew David at Rutgers ('14); five cousins at North Carolina, including Frankie ('14), Patrick ('16), Stephen ('17), Timmy ('19), and Jacob ('22); Johnny at Ohio State ('17); Daniel at Maryland ('24); Micaiah at Denver ('25); JK at Cornell ('26), while Joshua has committed to Georgetown ('27) and Eyasu to Dickinson ('27). Most of the girl cousins played at least a couple of years of high school lacrosse, but none had a passion to play at the collegiate level.

Each of the boys have attended many FCA Lacrosse camps and played on numerous FCA Lacrosse teams that have influenced not only each of them, but many of their friends as well. Most of the boys ended up captains of their high school and/or college teams, so their chance to influence others both on and off the field was expanded further.

You don't have to win to have influence, but it didn't hurt when our son Stephen and my brother David's sons Patrick and Timmy won a National Championship with UNC over Maryland in 2016, while my brother John's son Johnny helped lead his Ohio State team to the National Championship Game in 2017. And then in 2022, my brother Bryan's son, Daniel, who played on one of FCA's most talented club teams growing up, was on the Maryland Terrapin team that beat Cornell in the National Championship Game. You know my parents and a bunch of us were in East Hartford, Connecticut for that game.

With Daniel Kelly and his younger brothers Eli and Caleb after Maryland won the 2022 National Championship in East Hartford, Connecticut

Pro Field Lacrosse

In 2001, Major League Lacrosse (MLL) was established as a legitimate professional field lacrosse league. Pro indoor/box lacrosse had been around since the 1980s and was continuing to grow (even without me playing—just kidding!) and had expanded to more than a dozen franchise teams in the U.S. and Canada.

To me, the reality of pro field lacrosse was particularly exciting and important for the growth of the Creator's game. It would also allow some of the Kelly cousins and a good number of other FCA laxers the chance to keep playing at a high level after college if they wanted to and could make a team.

After graduating from UNC in 2016, my nephew Patrick would play two years with the Florida Launch and Ohio Machine of the MLL, before having to let lacrosse go to focus on medical school and pursue becoming a doctor.

Frankie ended up on the MLL's Atlanta Blaze practice squad and helped coach and run the box for them on game days. Timmy was pursued aggressively by the Denver Outlaws but decided not to play after college due to multiple concussions he experienced during his Tar Heel career.

Stephen graduated from UNC in 2017, and he wanted to continue to compete at the highest level—the professional field game matched his skill set perfectly.

It was disappointing that UNC was knocked out of the NCAA playoffs in the first round Stephen's senior year, thus they were not playing in the Final Four and National Championship games, which are always Memorial Day weekend. Instead, he was hanging at the beach with a bunch of family and friends on the back patio of our Fenwick Island, Delaware beach house watching and listening to the MLL draft, when we heard his name selected in the fourth round by the Chesapeake Bayhawks.

Bayhawks and Archers

The Bayhawks played their home games in Annapolis, Maryland, so although Stephen was moving to Atlanta, Georgia for his new job at OneDigital (a large national health insurance and employee benefits broker), his professional home lacrosse games would be close to our Baltimore home.

Stephen with John Michael Knight after a Bayhawks game. JMK was a great high school faceoff athlete who wore #24 because of Stephen before he had a brain stem stroke his senior year of high school that left him paralyzed.

In Stephen's second year with the Bayhawks, he was selected to play in the 2018 MLL All-Star Game at Harvard Stadium just outside Boston, Massachusetts.

I felt like I had seen this movie before when the MLL all-stars played the U.S. Senior Men's National Team at Harvard Stadium. That brought back memories of 1994 when I played with the guys who were cut from the U.S. National team in an exhibition game, when we beat the U.S. National Team. Stephen enjoyed the same outcome in the MLL All-Star Game, a thrilling grudge match that went into overtime. Stephen won the overtime faceoff against Trevor Baptiste and

Stephen (#24) getting ready to take the faceoff in overtime of the MLL All-Stars vs. Team USA game

Will Manny scored the winning goal in the 15-14 MLL victory.

Unfortunately, Stephen hurt his knee in the last regular MLL game of the season in New York and couldn't play in the MLL play-offs. The Bayhawks lost in the semifinals—because they struggled winning faceoffs.

When Paul and Mike Rabil founded a new professional league, called the Premier Lacrosse League (PLL) in 2019, Stephen faced a tough decision: stay with the Bayhawks and the MLL, where he was that year named an All-Star, or go with the uncertainty of an upstart league where many of the best players seemed to be going. The new PLL had a contract with NBC Television that allowed them to pay salaries four or five times higher than the MLL and the players were being given equity in the new league that increased in value with each game in which they would play. It was a tough decision, but how could he say "no"?

I prayed about it. Stephen prayed about it.

"Dad, I feel I need to make the move," he told me. "I can't miss this opportunity."

The Archers Lacrosse Club selected Stephen and on opening day, June 1, 2019, at Gillette Stadium in Foxboro, Massachusetts and live on NBC Sports TV, Stephen won the first faceoff, picked up the first ground ball and, eleven seconds into the game, scored the first goal in PLL history. We had seen him do that before!

Later that season, encouraged by FCA staffer and life coach Mark Stephens, he started a team Bible study and led a movement of players gathering after games on the center of the field to kneel and give thanks to the Creator of the Creator's game and all of life.

Stephen (second from right) leading a PLL prayer circle after an Archers LC vs. Redwoods LC game

After the season, FCA Lacrosse's director of digital media, Mark Vernago, asked to capture Stephen's faith story on "The X," the digital video and media production that spotlights the testimonies of various players and coaches of the game, and is then shared on multiple social media platforms. Thousands around the world would see and hear Stephen's story, including the first goal in PLL history, on *Stephen Kelly: The X* that FCA Lacrosse posted on YouTube.

This poster was released after the first-ever PLL game. Scan to see "The X" and first goal in PLL history.

All-Stars and Cannons

In 2021, Stephen's third year in the PLL, he was selected to the PLL All-Star Game in San Jose, California, and played alongside his friend, Garrett Epple, whom he had played with on FCA youth teams and at Calvert Hall. Since then, they've battled against each other in college—Garrett played at Notre Dame—and in the PLL, but were teammates again for a game.

In the spring of 2022, Stephen was traded from Archers Lacrosse Club to Cannons Lacrosse Club. The Cannons LC was the one team that came from the MLL when the MLL folded in 2020 and decided to merge with the PLL.

He was disappointed to be leaving his good friends and Archers teammates, but this trade would put him on a team with two lacrosse legends; the Canadian superstar defenseman Brodie Merrill, and the all-time NCAA Division I points leader and two-time Tewaaraton Trophy (the Heisman Trophy of lacrosse) winner, Lyle Thompson. Many consider Lyle one of the top lacrosse players of all time.

Lyle is the youngest of four brothers, including Jeremy, Miles and Jerome, all of who achieved great success in college and professional lacrosse after growing up in

Stephen with his longtime Calvert Hall and FCA Lacrosse teammate Garrett Epple at the 2021 PLL All-Star Game in San Jose, California

the Onondaga Nation, which is really the center of the Six Nations Haudenosaunee or Iroquois Confederacy.

Lyle, his brothers, and his father, Jerome, have done more than anyone I know to share the true meaning and historical and cultural significance of the Creator's game. In the ESPN Films *Fate of a Sport,* about the formation of the PLL by Paul and Mike Rabil, Lyle said, "People say 'It's our game,' but it's not our game we brought to the people of this earth. It is a gift to us from the Creator; we're just passing this on."[1] FCA Lacrosse wants to share it and pass it on as well.

In 2022, the PLL negotiated a new television contract with ABC Sports and ESPN. On June 18th, the game between Stephen's new team, Cannons LC, and former team, Archers LC, would be broadcast live on ABC's main network. This would be the first live lacrosse game broadcast on ABC since they covered the 1977 NCAA Division I National Championship Game, when Cornell defeated Johns Hopkins 16-8. (That was the game we were watching 45 years earlier, when my brother John's friend, Dan Llewellyn, said that he could see me playing at Cornell one day, even though I had not yet played organized lacrosse.)

Despite Stephen scoring two goals in the *Stephen with Lyle Thompson*
first half and winning 70% of his faceoffs, the
Cannons LC lost, but the statistics for viewership came in, and the game turned out to be the most-watched lacrosse game in history.

After that game, I was thankful to snap a picture of Stephen and Lyle Thompson—teammates in the Creator's game.

Gen 3s in the Business

Although more and more players are able to make a decent living as full-time lacrosse professionals, others like Stephen maintain full-time jobs that allow them the flexibility to play.

At Kelly Benefits, we like to encourage family members and others to play and coach their sport of interest, as long as their work gets done. We continue to support flexibility as a value in our culture.

As a family, we also believe God currently wants us to build a "legacy business," by bringing the next generation of Kellys (we call them Gen 3s) into the business if they feel so led and it is a good fit. Working with an excellent group of faith-based family business advisors, we have encouraged any of our children, nieces or nephews who want to come into the business to spend three to five years working somewhere else after college first.

As of this writing, my nephews David Jr. and Johnny have joined the business, and my sons Frankie and Stephen will be joining after gaining incredible experience working other jobs that will bring instant value to Kelly Benefits.

Our children, nieces and nephews are definitely a blessing from the Lord, and will hopefully continue to be arrows of light, hope and truth to all the world, including the lacrosse community.

MORE TO THE STORY...

My Middle Name Could be "Lacrosse" – Janet Kelly

Over the years, I have been to so many lacrosse games and tournaments that

My mom (called "MeMom" by her 21 grandchildren) with my nephew Daniel after he and Maryland won the 2022 NCAA National Championship

I feel like my middle name could be "Lacrosse." Even though my vision is poor, and I can't see who is doing what, I like to be there to support and pray for my sons, my grandchildren, and their teammates and friends. From five-to six-year-old tyker games to college and club national championships, and even Stephen's professional games, I have tried to be there and be present when I can, especially after the game, win or lose.

One time, my grandson Daniel came up to me after his high school soccer game, and he was wearing a white uniform. By mistake, I was cheering for the yellow team, his opponents, the entire game. We laugh about that to this day.

I didn't get him, or his Maryland team, confused when they won the NCAA Lacrosse Championship in 2022, and I was happy to get a picture with him after that game.

I am grateful that almost all of my kiddos—sons, grandsons, granddaughters and daughters-in-law—have been involved with FCA Lacrosse. It has been a wonderful place for them to develop friendships, get to know God better and share the gifts they have received from Him.

Faith, Academics and Sports – Brother John Kane

I became president of Calvert Hall in 2014, and one of the first families I met was the Kellys. Big Frank and Frank Kelly III had each served on our board, Bryan was the head varsity lacrosse coach and John and David combined with their brothers to send more than a dozen of their sons to The Hall. The Kellys were everywhere!

One of the things I learned soon after I arrived at Calvert Hall was the history of a club called FCA. Frank III had started the FCA Huddle in 1987 and many of our students—and not only lacrosse players, but coaches and athletes from other sports (and even non-athletes—would show up by choice.

Calvert Hall President Brother John Kane with Big Frank after a game on Kelly Field, sporting his jacket with the numbers on his sleeves of ten different grandsons who played at The Hall. He's actually missing two, and will likely have two more coming in the future.

We want to be the best at Calvert Hall, but there is a whole level beyond winning that is important to us. We don't want to separate faith, academics and sports, because it's all integrated. To have a ministry like FCA and FCA Lacrosse aligns with our values and only strengthens us.

Confidence to Lead – Jacob Kelly

I'm 100% certain that I wouldn't be the man I am today without FCA Lacrosse.

My years playing FCA club and youth lacrosse in seventh and eighth grade and for a few years in high school were probably the most important years of my life. That's when I was discovering my identity. To have older huddle leaders I looked up to, like Kacy Kapinos and my cousin Patrick, leading the Bible studies and the conversations about who Jesus is and what He has done for me, kick-started everything.

Without their courage to put their faith in action and pour their wisdom and experience into a bunch of middle schoolers, I don't know if I would have had the confidence to get involved with FCA at Calvert Hall.

In high school, talking about your faith and outwardly displaying commitment to your faith are not necessarily the most popular things to do. My involvement with the Calvert Hall FCA Huddle, especially when I was elected president my senior year, pushed me to become more comfortable and confident in myself, and not afraid to say that I'm a child of God, and a follower of Jesus. In working through that process with my friends in the huddle, I discovered I was not alone.

Through the fellowship, the Bible studies, videos, and guest speakers that my Uncle Frank and Drew Wardlow led and organized for the Calvert Hall Huddle, I found out that the most

FCA Huddle leaders and coaches Kacy Kapinos (Left) and Drew Wardlow

impactful and powerful thing you can have in your life is a personal relationship with God built on a solid foundation. Without that huddle experience, who knows if I would have co-led our team Bible study at University of North Carolina, or have been selected as a team captain?

All the ways my huddle leaders influenced me inspired me to help younger guys in the same way. My buddies Liam Bateman (who played at Loyola University), Brendan Curry (who played at Syracuse) and I coached and led huddles for my little brother Caleb's FCA Lacrosse club team when he started as a fourth grader. The most rewarding aspect was teaching them the simple truths of who Jesus is and what He's done for us. Those seasons with Caleb and his friends are special, full-circle memories for me.

Our UNC team Bible study was similar in many ways. For me, one of the coolest things was to hear guys who were young in their faith or exploring faith for the first time ask the same kinds of simple questions the young kids ask and have the open door to tell them the story of Jesus.

As a team captain, I had additional opportunities to influence my teammates every day. I tried to keep an eye out to make sure everybody felt valued because everyone is truly valued in the eyes of God. Whether they're a freshman or a senior, whether they play a ton of minutes or not many, I wanted them to know that God wants what is best for them, and so did I.

I can't emphasize enough how thankful I am that my dad and aunts and uncles stepped out in faith to take an FCA team to Vail in 1992, and for all that has happened with the growth and influence of FCA since.

CALVERT HALL
FCA TURKEY BOWL BREAKFAST

For years, our Calvert Hall FCA Huddle has hosted an annual FCA Turkey Bowl Breakfast a couple of days before the big Thanksgiving Day rivalry football game.

When Baltimore Ravens Chaplain Johnny Shelton (next to me, standing, 2nd from left) comes each year with different Ravens players, who are passionate about their relationship with God and willing to share their personal faith stories, hundreds of students, including most of the football team, usually show up.

When our Calvert Hall FCA Huddle started in 1987, we never had to worry about running out of chairs in Room 108, where we still meet most weeks. But for this huddle meeting and others, which the Calvert Hall Kelly cousins have all attended and some have led, we need to meet in the auxiliary gym, which is always a lot of fun.

I love the influence of FCA!

NFL All Pro Baltimore Raven Marlon Humphrey (pictured with Calvert Hall FCA Huddle Coach Zach Rowe, President Brother John Kane and me) spoke at our FCA Turkey Bowl Breakfast in 2019 before the 100th consecutive Calvert Hall vs. Loyola Thanksgiving Day game.

CHAPTER 74

The Pandemic

"For God gave us a spirit not of fear but of power and love and self-control."

2 Timothy 1:7 (NKJV)

O ver the years, we have all faced situations that appear to be hopeless or overwhelming. I have also faced times when things on the outside appear to be fine, but inside I am battling a spirit of fear that tends to take me down a road of negative thinking. Often times, those emotions of anxiety and fear are not logical or based on a realistic view of the circumstances, yet the feelings are still real.

Other times, circumstances in our lives justify greater fear and concern, yet God's Word reminds us that despite the situation, His Spirit can give us power, love and a sound mind, and although the situation may appear to be dire, He can still use it for good.

None of us saw COVID-19 coming. It was March of 2020 when our world of work, school, church and group activities was literally shut down because of the coronavirus pandemic. Worldwide, the coronavirus had infected over 600 million people and killed over 1 million in less than three years.

Sports seasons and FCA Huddles, camps, club leagues and tournaments were all canceled. Businesses, including Kelly Benefits, were forced to have employees work remotely from home or wherever they felt safe.

How would we survive this?

It has been said that "necessity is the mother of innovation," and sure enough, we responded and overcame.

Zoom

I had never heard of a "Zoom" meeting before, but I would learn soon enough. It wasn't long before I was on multiple Zoom calls each day for business, family connections and FCA.

Our Baltimore City FCA metro area director, Sirena Alford, had just built her new advisory board, and everyone was excited and ready to go. The first couple of Zoom board meetings were a little bumpy, with various technology glitches and at times, audio and/or video issues. But we pushed through, and before we knew it, our monthly Zoom meetings were highly efficient and really well attended. We went from having around a dozen of our more than 20 advisory board members showing up to our in-person meetings, to more than 20 showing up for our Zoom calls. It eliminated all the travel time issues, and even allowed board members to join the meeting if they were out of town or on the road driving somewhere.

Our FCA Baltimore City board chair, John Shearin, did a great job leading the meetings and getting everyone involved. As a former Dunbar High School football player and coach, and family pastor at Mt. Pleasant Church in Baltimore City, he had the perfect skill set and disposition to lead what had become one of the most diverse FCA advisory boards in the country.

A Baltimore City FCA Advisory Board Zoom meeting

Business Challenges

During this time, we continued to support FCA and other non-profit organizations, despite being significantly challenged by the pandemic's effects. We went from having nearly 500 employees coming into one of our three corporate offices daily to about 20 who were considered "essential."

Many of our clients were hurt badly and had to lay off or furlough employees, which hurt us as well. We typically get paid a fee per head, per month for each employee covered on their group insurance plan and on their payroll, so as the number of employees for many of our clients shrunk, so did our revenue. Fortunately, our monthly expenses also shrunk with less travel and entertainment, as well as the difficult decision we faced to let about 30 of our people go.

Zoom calls and video messages sent via email became primary modes of communication, and even after the pandemic subsided, we, like many other employers, remained a hybrid workplace with about one-third of our employees coming into the office daily, one-third on a multi-day rotation, and one-third being fully remote.

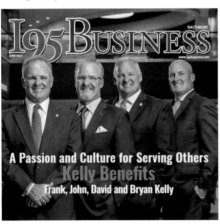

A Passion and Culture for Serving Others
Kelly Benefits
Frank, John, David and Bryan Kelly

As of this writing, many of our clients who shrunk have added back employees, and we are almost back to our pre-COVID revenues, with exciting opportunities for growth before us. In June 2021, a local business publication called *I95 Business* did a cover story on me and my brothers, and the amazing People of Kelly Benefits, as we were hoping that our history and culture would help us come out of the pandemic stronger than ever.

A Growing Family

Despite COVID-19 causing many group gatherings and functions to be canceled, in October of 2021, we were able to go forward with the wedding of our son Stephen and his beautiful fiancée Caroline.

God answered every one of Gayle's "weather prayers" in the affirmative. "Dear God, may the weather for Stephen and Caroline's wedding please be warm, but not hot, cool but not cold, breezy but not windy, and the ground kept dry. Amen!"

We knew from multiple stories in the Bible that the Creator had the power to control the weather if He wanted to. We believed God chose to bless the day in every way, and we gave Him praise and thanks not only for the amazing weather, ceremony and reception, but for the health and well-being of every Kelly family member in attendance—my mom and dad, my three brothers and their wives, the 21 Kelly cousins, as well as Frankie's wife Acacia (who was pregnant at the wedding and would give birth to our first grandson, Francis X.

"Quin" Kelly V just a couple of months later), and now Stephen's wife Caroline. And by then, my nephew Patrick was engaged to Kelly Boyd, soon to be Kelly Kelly—how's that for a name?!

It was also a huge blessing to have Gayle's 87-year-old mom, Grammy, there, with her dancing shoes on, and her brother Steve and other Schmith family members as well.

Our family was continuing to grow.

Our growing Kelly family at Stephen and Caroline's wedding in October 2021

Passing the Baton

It has been said that "the only constant in life is change," and like every family, business and organization, with growth and change come new challenges and opportunities.

When Mark Stephens passed the FCA Maryland state director baton to Shaun Smithson in 2017, he assumed a new role focused on the growth of FCA in East Asia.

Even though Mark never played lacrosse growing up, he gladly transferred his passion as a former high school and college wrestler to lacrosse when his four daughters all started playing the Creator's game. Mark and his daughters became regulars at FCA Lacrosse Camp and on several FCA National Teams, so when Dan Britton connected Mark to Reon Tay (who was on staff with FCA in Singapore and started FCA Lacrosse there), he was happy to help Reon in any way.

Mark worked with Dan and Reon to establish the Singapore Lacrosse Association, and to build teams for boys, girls and even adult men and women. Mark and Dan brought a ton of lacrosse equipment with them to be given away when they went to Singapore to help run the lacrosse clinic that Reon organized.

After the COVID-19 pandemic hit, Mark received a call from Reon with a unique request.

"Do you have somebody that could give lacrosse lessons via Zoom, while all our players are stuck inside?" Reon asked.

"I know a couple of high school guys that are going to be playing college lacrosse," Mark said, thinking of Jason and Eric Kolar. "They've lost their season and are stuck inside too. I'll ask them."

Reon Tay of FCA Singapore and Mark Stephens

Jason and Eric are brothers who played lacrosse at Urbana High School in Frederick County, Maryland, and attended an FCA Huddle that Mark held in his home, along with other athletes from different sports. They were willing but had no idea how they could possibly give lacrosse lessons from 9,600 miles and thirteen time zones away.

"Get your sticks and balls, fire up Zoom in your basement, and show them a few things," Mark suggested.

Over the next six weeks, Jason and Eric set up Zoom calls at 9 p.m. on Friday nights—10 a.m. Saturday morning Singapore time—and gave live lacrosse lessons for an hour. The kids in Singapore loved them.

Jason went on to play at the University of Delaware and Eric committed to play at the University of Maryland.

In a sense, Mark's association with FCA Lacrosse pre-dates its founding. In the fall of 1982, in his sophomore year at Salisbury University, he was finding his way back to following God after wandering on the wide road for a year or two when one of his physical fitness teachers—Hank Janczyk, who was an assistant coach for the Salisbury men's lacrosse team (before he became head coach at Gettysburg College)—said in front of a class of 150 students, "I've been telling you about your health and heart rate, but if you want to know more about the

Calvert Hall FCA Huddle meeting during the pandemic

spiritual side to you, while I can't really talk to you about it here, you can follow me to my office if you're interested."

Mark followed, and Coach Janczyk helped lead him back into a vital, life-changing relationship with God. And now, Mark was helping lead many others, including those in Singapore, to find life in the Creator.

A Relay Race

Shaun Smithson would do an amazing job as FCA Maryland state director. Under his leadership, the number of FCA staff in the state would increase from 40 to over 70. He would help strengthen the FCA Maryland club lacrosse program, working with Ryan Horanburg and FCA Northern Maryland Director Steve Medinger, to recruit and train Drew Wardlow as the FCA Maryland boys' club director (after he served in various roles with FCA Lacrosse for more than a decade). And his support of Coach Garrick Williams and the FCA Park Heights Saints program was critical during the building of the Park Heights Community Center, as well as during the period of deep grieving following the untimely death of Garrick Williams Jr., "Coach Dip."

During the pandemic, we were forced to cancel our annual FCA Maryland Victory Celebration and Fundraising Banquet for the first time in more than 25 years. When Shaun came up with the idea to do a "Virtual Banquet," former Baltimore Oriole Brian Roberts agreed to be our guest speaker, and although we had fewer people on the Virtual Banquet, we still netted the resources needed to fund the ministry. It's a lot less expensive to host a banquet on Zoom than in a banquet facility, and our FCA Banquet sponsors (including Kelly Benefits) were still pleased with their name recognition, especially since the Zoom banquet was recorded and could be shared with hundreds of people who could not attend the shortened, live Zoom presentation, in the future.

In 2022, the FCA Maryland Victory Celebration and Fundraising Banquet would again be in person at Martin's West in Baltimore, and there would be another "baton passing" ceremony. Kind of like a relay race, Shaun would announce his new role as FCA director of talent advancement for the Mid-Atlantic region, then introduce Brandon Johnson as our next FCA Maryland state director. What was so exciting about this was that Brandon was a product of FCA Lacrosse, having been connected to the Creator, and committing his life to Christ in 2004 as a rising high school senior playing on an FCA Lacrosse National High School Team. He would go on to star as an attackman at Robert Morris University before serving on staff with FCA in Carroll County, Maryland.

It is just as exciting that Brandon's FCA Maryland board chair would be

Brian Hubbard, who also came to faith through his FCA experiences more than 30 years ago with our Calvert Hall FCA Huddle, and our first FCA Lacrosse Miracle in the Mountains team.

The influence of FCA and FCA Lacrosse is truly generational, and the message, mission and movement carry on with or without a pandemic in our midst.

Shaun Smithson (Left) passing the FCA Maryland state director baton to Brandon Johnson, as FCA Maryland board chair Brian Hubbard looks on

MORE TO THE STORY...

Our Future Leaders – Brandon Johnson

Who are the seventeen-year-old athletes out there who will be the leaders of FCA and FCA Lacrosse 20 years from now?

That was me in 2004, a typical high school lacrosse player who sought popularity by going to parties, looked for my name in the sports pages and desperately wanted a college coach to want me.

Exposure to college recruiters was my only concern as a rising high school senior when I tried out for various summer teams, including what my mother called "that Christian team," FCA. I made FCA's first-ever national elite team, and my two weeks with them changed my identity, changed my purpose, changed my life.

I grew up going to church but there I was on a team that married the sport I loved with faith in God. I had played on maybe 50 teams before—each for a quick two weeks and then on to the next one. But after only fourteen days with the FCA team, I felt a relational bond with my teammates like I had never felt before. What was it about this team? There was more to it than winning lacrosse games. There was a spiritual dynamic and a lacrosse dynamic I had never experienced. God was doing something.

In our huddle devotions and discussions, we dove into the Scriptures in a way I never had before. Coaches Matt Hall, Sean McNamara, Drew Wardlow and Josh Hoffman spoke my language, and the message of who Jesus was and what

He did for me got through.

After we packed up the cars to go home following the last game of our last tournament, all the players and coaches gathered in a circle and hugged good-bye as the rain fell, and I welled up with tears. I sensed God communicating with me. The culmination of the devotions, the worship, the conversation, and the prayer over the two weeks stirred my mind and overwhelmed my heart and opened my eyes. That was the moment Christ revealed Himself to me, and I entered an eternal relationship with Him.

Oh, and did I mention coaches from Robert Morris University saw me at the tournament and recruited me to come play for them?

I didn't know anyone when I arrived on the Robert Morris campus a year and a half later, and I stood at a crossroad: would I live out my faith, or would I join in the worldly life of most lacrosse players?

Facebook was new back then—you needed a college email address to make a profile page—and on my page, I added my favorite Scripture verse: "Do you not know that those who run in a race all run, but only one receives the prize? Run in such a way that you may win".[1] I typed it in a super small font but one of my teammates noticed and invited me to a Wednesday night worship service offered by a campus ministry called Chi Alpha.

At Chi Alpha, we sang the same songs I had sung while worshiping with my FCA Lacrosse team, and the music took me back to that moment when I welled up in the parking lot. God was connecting the dots for me again. I joined a Bible study and met a group of guys who took me deeper into my faith and laid a biblical foundation for me.

During and after college I played on a couple more FCA Lacrosse teams in Ocean City, Maryland, worked at the Gettysburg and Lebanon Valley camps, and helped coach teams in Vail and Lake Placid. I was married in July of 2012 and, after a week at Amelia Island in Florida, my new bride, Ashli, and I extended our honeymoon while I coached a U15 team in Orlando.

Around that same time, God began to give me a restlessness in my heart. He confirmed to me that my sales support job was not my long-term career path, but I had no idea what my next step should be. At my church, I signed up for a mission trip to Haiti and met Jimmy Page, then the FCA regional vice president, at the trip planning meeting.

After the meeting, I shook Jimmy's hand and said, "Thanks for all you do for FCA. FCA changed my life, and I wanted to say thank you."

The first words out of Jimmy's mouth were, "What do you think about coming on staff with FCA? We have an opening in Carroll County." At that moment

I knew in my heart that God was calling me to the organization that had so strongly influenced my life. In 2012, at age 24, I joined the FCA staff as the area representative.

My vision at that time, and my vision in 2022 as I moved into the Maryland state director's position, was to provide the same opportunity that I had as a high school athlete to athletes in the community where I was raised. I see myself in a lot of those athletes—and the coaches. Their identities are wrapped up in all the wrong things, just like mine was. I feel called to introduce them to an identity that's unshakable, unbreakable and eternal, through the avenue of sports.

Frank Kelly has been a major influence on my development within FCA and the entire FCA ministry in Maryland. He is always thinking and dreaming and casting a vision for ways to propel the ministry forward. It's no wonder Frank was the first person from Maryland to enter the FCA Hall of Champions. He's the glue that ties much of the ministry together—from staff to donors to volunteers to athletes and coaches. Frank is a connector.

In 2004, I was just your average high school athlete. Two weeks with an FCA Lacrosse team changed my life and reshaped my identity and positioned me to one day oversee more than 70 FCA staff members throughout the state of Maryland. That's my story, and it moves me to ponder, who are the young men and women in FCA huddles and camps and playing on FCA teams who will be in positions like mine 20 years from now, telling a similar story?

CHAPTER 75

Defense Wins Games

*"Put on the full armor of God, so that you can take your
stand against the devil's schemes."*

Ephesians 6:11

T here is a common saying in team sports that, "defense wins games."

When our youngest, JK, turned six years old, he started playing soccer and lacrosse. He was strong, fast and aggressive, but naturally gravitated toward the defensive end of the field and would end up being the only Kelly cousin (and only Kelly other than Uncle Bryan) to play defense with a long pole.

I coached his youth lacrosse teams, including our first-ever FCA Maryland Club 9-10 B-Team in 2012, and boy, did we take it on the chin that first year when we were almost a full year younger than the other teams we played.

We would improve over time, and four years later won all of our elite-level summer tournaments, including the prestigious Vail Lacrosse Shootout—the same year that our

Micaiah, Shuey and JK Kelly on one of the early FCA Maryland Club teams

As a middle schooler at FCA Lacrosse Camp with his FCA club teammates, (L to R) JK, Daniel Owens, Jordan Wray and Luke McAuliffe

son Stephen (who had just won a National Championship at UNC), and his good friend Ben Pridemore (who played for Notre Dame) were our assistant coaches and team huddle leaders. The kids loved Stephen (Bones) and Ben, especially when Ben told the boys he would let them shave his

Our FCA 2022 Club Team won the 2016 Vail Lacrosse Tournament on famous Ford Field.

big "mullet" head of hair if we won our first tournament championship—which we did! We were all cracking up as the boys gave him a reverse mohawk, shaving a huge strip down the center of his head.

Our team ended up being ranked in the top five club lacrosse teams in the country in our age group that year, and the boys really benefited from their huddle times with Bones and Ben as they shared from God's Word and honestly about their personal faith stories and relationships with God.

Following Footsteps

JK ultimately followed the footsteps of his brothers Frankie and Stephen as well as his cousins David, Johnny, Patrick, Timmy, Jacob, Daniel and Micaiah to Calvert Hall. His freshman year he was fortunate to make the varsity team. That year, the team went undefeated, and won the 2019 MIAA Championship.

The next year, the COVID-19 pandemic completely wiped out the Calvert Hall season and much of our FCA club seasons as well. JK would start on defense as a junior and senior, both years helping lead The Hall to the MIAA semifinals played at Navy-Marine Corps Memorial Stadium in Annapolis, Maryland. As a senior captain, JK would earn *Baltimore Sun* All-Metro honors.

In 2022 as a senior captain, JK (#4) with his cousins Shuey (#9) and Eyasu (#52)

The Kelly family with Daniel (#45), Micaiah (#29), JK (#51) and Coach Bryan Kelly (back row with grey shirt and red hat) after winning the 2019 MIAA Championship

Cardinals vs. Dons

JK also played football for the Cardinals, and a real highlight was when he made the varsity football team as a sophomore and played in the 100th consecutive Calvert Hall vs. Loyola Thanksgiving Day Turkey Bowl game in 2019, which The Hall won 33-10. By chance (or Providence), he wore #41, which I had forgotten was the same number I wore in the Turkey Bowl 40 years earlier (the next year and thereafter, I wore #24) when I played on Calvert Hall's last undefeated varsity football team as a sophomore in 1979.

JK playing football reminded me of how important Calvert Hall football was in my life, and that it was a key reason I went to The Hall—which ultimately led me to playing the Creator's game. My brothers soon followed, and as of this writing, thirteen of our sons have attended The Hall as well.

I am thankful that although the Loyola Dons still lead the Turkey Bowl football series, between me, my brothers and our sons Frankie, Stephen and JK, the Kelly family and Calvert Hall have won eleven of the twelve Turkey Bowls we've played in.

And even though I rarely beat Loyola in lacrosse (my brothers and I all lost championship games to them), JK was fortunate to never lose to the Dons, whose team was also full of a number of our FCA club players whom we loved dearly.

Hey, Coach Frank!

On September 1st of JK's junior year, he and a number of our FCA club players got calls from some of the top college coaches in the country. Over the next couple of months, a number of the boys who I and others helped coach for many years made their college commitments. Jordan Wray committed to Georgetown, AJ Larkin chose Maryland, Luke McAuliffe and EJ Vasile both committed to Lehigh, Cole Myers picked Hofstra and Evan Huffman chose Salisbury University.

JK, after being recruited by Ohio State, Yale, Brown, Marquette and Notre Dame, decided on Cornell and the Big Red. Yes!

I was thrilled and loved fielding all the calls from my former Cornell teammates, other alums, and even Coach Richie Moran, all congratulating me on one of the Kellys finally heading north.

After 25 years of coaching what I've calculated to be more than 1,000 youth and high school games in a variety of sports, I sensed that with JK heading to college, this would be a good time to take a little break. I must admit though, one of my favorite things to hear around town, or even around the country, when I run into former players I've coached is, "Hey, Coach Frank!"

The influence of coaching goes both ways.

JK playing for his FCA "2022" Club Team

JK on "signing day" after he committed to attend Cornell and play for the Big Red

Back to Ithaca

It brought back many memories when Gayle and I dropped JK off at Cornell in August of 2022, exactly 40 years to the week since my parents dropped me off as a freshman. One of the many reasons I'm thankful that JK chose Cornell is that Tom Howley would be his strength and conditioning coach.

Tom played football at Tulane in the late 1980s, and through the influence of a friend in FCA there, committed his life to Christ. In 1995, as a young man strong in his faith, he was hired at Cornell as the strength and conditioning coach to oversee the design and implementation of athletic performance programs for all varsity sports.

Over his long tenure at Cornell, he wrote a book, *Complete Conditioning for Lacrosse*, and has become a living legend amongst the athletes he has trained.

In 1997 Tom helped start, and continues to lead, an FCA Huddle at Cornell, and in 2020 joined FCA staff full-time—the first FCA staff person at Cornell. He's still the part-time strength and conditioning coach with the men's lacrosse program, so I'm excited that JK has Tom as both a coach and spiritual mentor. And I have been honored to work alongside Tom as the chair of his Cornell FCA Board of Advisors, a role he asked me to take in 2021.

Our son JK is part of a Big Red story come full circle, from all the way around the world!

Dropping JK off at Cornell as a freshman and being reminded that "It's Great to Be Here!"

MORE TO THE STORY...

Let's Go Red! – JK Kelly

I know what you're thinking, but no, my father did not push me to go to Cornell. He sometimes jokingly dropped hints, but to be honest, the fact that he's an alum was more like a deterrent for me. I think my father was wise enough to know that pushing me would backfire and decrease my chances of going there.

My mindset was simply: whoever recruits me, I'll go with the flow. Cornell recruited me without my sending them letters of recommendation and highlight reels. They had seen me play in various tournaments and on their own reached out to me, so I knew they wanted me. All the Cornell players and coaches I met had the kind of values, work ethic and outlook on life that made me want to be around them. The players told me that going to school and playing at Cornell was one of the greatest experiences of their lives. I could see myself becoming close friends with them. I could see myself liking Cornell even if I got hurt in the first practice and never played a minute of lacrosse.

I look forward to getting involved with the FCA Huddle at Cornell. My huddle with my FCA Lacrosse club

JK, #41, in his first fall ball scrimmage for the Big Red vs. Maryland

team—which my father coached since I was in second grade—helped me plug more into my faith because all the guys were in the same stage of life, and we helped each other by talking through our common problems and sharing our experiences. I hope that I'll find that same kind of close fellowship and opportunities to grow in my faith at Cornell.

Now that I'm attending Cornell, I think it's pretty cool that I'll hopefully graduate from the same college as my father. Go Big Red!

CHAPTER 76

New Wineskins

"And no one pours new wine into old wineskins.
Otherwise, the wine will burst the skins, and both the wine and the wineskins
will be ruined. No, they pour new wine into new wineskins."

Mark 2:22

Les Steckel, FCA's CEO from 2005-2017, was an amazing leader. No one could out work him. He was definitely "old school" when it came to technology, but as far as personal contact was concerned, no one was better. Every board member and all 2,000 staff around the country and around the world received a personal call from him on their birthday. I still have a voicemail message he left me on my phone from more than five years ago that I listen to from time to time (don't ever discount the power of an encouraging word!).

Les traveled the country tirelessly sharing the FCA vision, mission, values and strategy. God used Les and his wife Chris to bless and encourage many coaches and athletes and inspired many others to give resources to help fuel the ministry, which grew rapidly under his leadership.

I was honored to serve as a trustee for the last three years of Les' tenure, and to serve under several amazing board chairs, including Buck McCabe, former chief financial officer of Chick-fil-A, and Darlene Johnson, the first female African American board chair in FCA history.

In 2017, the board announced the hiring of Shane Williamson to replace Les as the next president and CEO of FCA, which was so exciting because Shane is a true product of the movement, having come to a personal faith in Jesus as a high school athlete attending an FCA camp in Black Mountain, North Carolina.

Shane's passion and energy are contagious, and he is not afraid to push change. He realizes that the world of youth, high school, college and professional sports is ever-changing and that our culture is requiring new paradigms and wineskins in order to accomplish FCA's mission "to lead every coach and athlete into a growing relationship with Jesus Christ and His church" and FCA's vision "to see the world transformed by Jesus Christ, through the influence of coaches and athletes."

One Word – "Every"

Each year, FCA picks a short theme, usually one word, that is woven into all that FCA does that year, including their summer camps, which will minister to more than 100,000 coaches and athletes each summer.

The 2022 theme was "Every," which was in perfect alignment with FCA's mission to reach and serve "every coach" and "every athlete" in "every sport."

Under Shane's direction, a new wineskin has been established called FCA Sports, which recognizes that fewer and fewer people are attending church, and only a small percentage of sports are being played on high school and college campuses, so there is a real need to take the Good News more proactively to where the coaches and athletes are.

Shane considers FCA Lacrosse a "forerunner" and a "paradigm-shaper" for FCA's new strategy. FCA has identified multiple sport environments with the goal of executing its ministry strategy of engaging, equipping and empowering coaches and athletes to become disciples (or followers) of Jesus, who make disciples in their sport environment. Each sport environment represents groups of coaches and athletes with like-minded competition and culture perspectives.

Under the relatively new FCA Sports pillar, FCA will be focusing on serving club and league sports, action sports, outdoor sports, motorsports, pro and elite sports and all-ability sports, which refers to coaches and athletes who compete with physical and/or intellectual disabilities.

In FCA, "Every" means "Every"—every coach and every athlete in every sport, and that includes all those who coach, play or want to play the Creator's game.

I am so thankful FCA Lacrosse has helped shape and influence this new FCA Sports paradigm and these new wineskins. From day one, FCA Lacrosse has been committed to reaching and serving the lacrosse community locally, regionally, nationally and internation-

ally. We love the challenge and focus to serve every lacrosse coach and athlete, including those with a unique set of abilities and needs.

MORE TO THE STORY...

Paradigm Shaper – Shane Williamson

FCA Lacrosse is the forerunner, the paradigm-shaper for the opportunities that have surfaced for FCA's off-campus initiatives.

The way FCA Lacrosse evolved to stay relevant—from the first team in 1992 to multiple tournament teams to club teams—created a model for FCA to replicate in other sports. That model has helped birth FCA Sports, the brand identity for our global off-campus initiative.

FCA Lacrosse played a pivotal role in helping us get there, and Frank Kelly has been directly involved as a member of the FCA Sports committee of our board. He and Gayle have generously invested their time, talent, treasure, and decades of experience in helping develop FCA Sports.

FCA President Shane Williamson is a "football guy" who loves coaching women's volleyball and sharing the influence of FCA.

Three aspects of the FCA Lacrosse model were especially important to replicate. The first is their holistic approach—holistic not only in the spiritual, emotional and physical dimensions of the players, but also in their ministry to both players and their families. Influencing entire families establishes deep community roots.

The second aspect is the way FCA Lacrosse established their brand identity. When parents and players on the sidelines recognize the FCA Lacrosse colors, logo and gear, they start talking about the other ways that FCA Lacrosse is different, and those conversations can spark interest in their holistic approach.

Third, I admire FCA Lacrosse's willingness to help coaches establish teams and programs across the country and around the world. What started in Maryland—perhaps the epicenter of the lacrosse world—didn't stay in Maryland. Frank and the staff share what they know with anyone interested. I'm not surprised because, as a board member, Frank advocated for FCA to look beyond the U.S. borders and embrace its international opportunities.

Frank is a multi-dimensional, impactful leader. I've watched his love for the Lord, for lacrosse and for FCA play out at the global level, the regional level and in Baltimore, the city he loves. His passion and tenacity for seeing the world changed by the Gospel have influenced the FCA ministry for over 35 years.

A Great Teammate – Darlene Johnson

I met Frank Kelly when I attended my first FCA Board of Trustees meeting that was held in Baltimore, Maryland. Frank was a trustee and was hosting the meeting in his hometown. I could not help but notice this man's passion, energy, commitment, transparency and kindness. He was one of the first to introduce himself, welcome me and ask about my family. He was a true ambassador for the Board and made me feel comfortable as a recruit.

Former FCA Board of Trustees Chair Darlene Johnson

As I moved into a leadership role and ultimately became chair of the Board, Frank was a great teammate who brought enthusiasm and a real business savvy to our trustee meetings. And he was a bridge between the Board, staff and what was going on in the field, especially with his heart for Baltimore City (my heart was with urban ministry as well) and the lacrosse community around the world.

All-Abilities Camp – Ryan Horanburg

My vision for an all-abilities camp was cast in 2006 when I watched my wife Kate's niece, Lizzie, who had ALS (Lou Gehrig's Disease), play baseball in a wheelchair.

Fast forward to a recent summer, when I watched videos from an FCA all-abilities camp in Cincinnati and thought, *This is something FCA Lacrosse needs to pray about and consider.* As I prayed, I felt that God wanted FCA Lacrosse to move forward, so I sat down with the staff to ask what they thought about the idea.

When our FCA men's Ministry Coordinator Kyle Savick told us about his special-needs cousin, we all concluded: We need to do this!

We partnered with various organizations, such as the Kennedy Krieger Institute at Johns Hopkins Hospital, Parkville Adaptive Lacrosse, and several local churches that have special-needs programs. Calvert Hall High School made its gym and fields available to us.

We ran the camp on a Friday night and Saturday morning. Twelve campers participated, ranging from a two-year-old blind child to a 22-year-old with Down Syndrome. We had autistic children and children with cerebral palsy. Over 70 volunteers worked at the camp—a tremendous outpouring of community support.

For our opening ceremony, I called each camper up front and presented them with a lacrosse stick. For most of them, it was their very first stick. Now I know what it feels like to be Santa Claus! The kids beamed with joy and energy as they showed off their new sticks to the crowd around them. It's a sight I'll never forget.

Then they used their new sticks to throw, catch, shoot and scoop through various practice stations, guided by their team of huddle leaders which included a college student, two high schoolers and a middle schooler for each camper.

I firmly believe that God can reach the heart of anyone regardless of their ability or disability, so each group held huddles where they prayed together and worked through thought-provoking discussion questions. As a full camp, we acted out Bible stories—such as David and Goliath—and gave each camper a role to play in telling the story.

Parents of special-needs children face unique pressures and stresses, so we blessed them with a gift card to use for a date night during camp hours. The parents couldn't stop thanking us, and many told us they wanted to be involved in organizing future camps.

Within hours of posting our first camp pictures on social media, I received a flood of messages. "Could we do this in Texas?" "I'd love to have an all-abilities camp in Florida!" "We could start an all-abilities league!" "My son is in a wheelchair. Is there any way to include him on a club team?"

On Saturday we added outdoor activities, including a dunk tank where the campers shot a ball and dunked a huddle leader.

We concluded with a medal ceremony to celebrate all that God accomplished at the camp. The huddle leaders also honored each camper with a letter they wrote and read out loud to the entire camp, affirming the special ways that each camper blessed their huddle leaders and fellow campers.

We started the All-Abilities Camp with a vision and a blank canvas. We threw some paint on it and watched God turn it into a masterpiece before our very eyes.

I only wish Lizzie could have been there. She passed away in 2020 at the age of 23, which was sad, but also a blessing in a way because her doctors didn't think she would live past age two.

But Lizzie's mother and father, Claudine and Joe, came from Florida to observe the camp. They also had opportunities to share their experiences and encourage other parents. I'm sure they felt Lizzie's presence, and I believe Lizzie was looking down on the camp and smiling.

Something for Them – Dean Curtis

I first learned about FCA Lacrosse in 2006 when I met a fellow Ohio State alum, Scott Hodgson, as he was manning the FCA Lacrosse booth at the US Lacrosse convention.

I wanted to get involved so I brought my high school team to a One Way 2 Play tournament. That tournament was run in a different way than any other tournament I had ever played in. Yes, the teams wanted to win, but the overarching message was not all about competition. There was prayer, fellowship and speakers who talked about the things of God.

I've always sought out ways to be involved in organizations that I believe in, and since the One Way 2 Play tournament, I've kept connected to FCA Lacrosse as a player on a Master's team, a coach at Lake Placid and camps, a parent of Emelie and Sophia, who played on FCA National Teams, a board member and even as an FCA Lacrosse board chair. It has been an awesome journey with so many opportunities to have people of FCA Lacrosse pour into my family and me, and then to give back and pour into others.

FCA Lacrosse is a light in a place that has a lot of darkness. I love a lot of aspects of the lacrosse community, but FCA Lacrosse brings a different purpose to the game. We give kids an experience in the lacrosse world that's not all about how good they are, but who they are as a person. We touch kids' spiritual lives and help them see that Jesus is at the center of it.

We bring a sense of humanity to lacrosse experiences. Relationships matter, and the people you meet matter far more than the final tally on the scoreboard.

Many of the connections I've made have continued throughout the players' high school and college years. We exchange text messages and get together for lunch if they live in the area. They like keeping in touch because they're used to everyone wanting something from them, but they know that I, like all FCA Lacrosse coaches, just want something for them.

The landscape in the lacrosse community is changing. There's a lot of growth in the game, which is terrific, but with that growth has come a rise in "super elite" club teams and a widening gap of talent. FCA Lacrosse will continue to adapt in the ways we reach the full spectrum of coaches and players.

The mission field will continue to grow, and FCA Lacrosse will continue to find new ways to reach and serve coaches and athletes and shine light where there's darkness.

CHAPTER 77

Coaches, Conferences and Conventions

"In their hearts humans plan their course, but the Lord establishes their steps."

Proverbs 16:9

In order for an organization to be successful—whether it be a team, a business or a nonprofit ministry – it must have a clear mission.

In the early 1990s, I took my dad, who was then president and CEO of our business, to an overnight conference called "Business by The Book." We both had read the Bible and were believers, but neither of us realized how much God's Word had to say about business and organizational excellence. From hiring to firing, to borrowing and lending, to how you pay and treat your teammates, it was all there.

I came away from the conference challenged, yet encouraged, and with the clear sense that we needed to write and clarify our mission, which we did. To this day, Kelly Benefits is a mission-driven organization.

One of the benefits of getting away to a conference or convention, is that it usually gives you a chance to learn, to think and potentially craft a better way forward. Yet the Scriptures remind us that even though we plan or organize our days and our ways, as we surrender our lives to the Creator, He establishes our steps.

A number of years ago, FCA developed a simple way to summarize their plan to accomplish their mission by focusing on what they called the Four Cs —Camps, Campuses, Communities and Coaches. Today, the commitment to minister and serve "to and through coaches" has only increased. The focus to encourage, equip and empower coaches to fulfill their true calling and purpose is a top priority.

In order to reach coaches, you have to go where they are, and one way to do that is by having a presence at their annual coaches conventions and conferences. Almost every sport has some type of conference or convention where coaches gather to learn, grow and network.

Since the seventies, FCA has had a major presence at the American Football Coaches Association Convention and the NCAA Basketball Final Four Coaches gathering. Since the late eighties and early nineties, FCA Lacrosse has had a consistent presence at what used to be one and is now three separate lacrosse coaches conventions or conferences.

Realizing the importance of building relationships with coaches, FCA Lacrosse has always provided some type of free meal and program that is planned to attract, serve and bless every coach who chooses to attend.

For decades, we have been at every US Lacrosse (rebranded USA Lacrosse in 2021) Convention with a booth in the vendor area to interact with any coach who may walk by, and provide and promote a free outreach breakfast, lunch or dinner geared towards sharing the Good News and blessing, encouraging and challenging coaches to live out their true calling and purpose.

In this book, I have shared a number of stories from our FCA Lacrosse coaches outreaches at not only the USA Lacrosse Convention, but the Intercollegiate Men's Lacrosse Coaches Association (IMLCA) and the Intercollegiate Women's Lacrosse Coaches Association (IWLCA). The IMLCA now calls their gathering a "Summit" and the IWLCA calls their gathering a "Symposium" and both host a major high school recruiting tournament attracting hundreds of teams to their location, which is usually in a beautiful, warm place like Florida or Texas, around a long weekend in early December.

At these gatherings, coaches often have one day dedicated to their specific conference or rules meetings, and our FCA Lacrosse leadership team has followed suit. Each year during the USA Lacrosse Convention, our FCA Lacrosse director, Ryan Horanburg, calls together an FCA Lacrosse Leadership Summit and planning day that includes all FCA Lacrosse staff and board members from around the country and even around the world.

I love this picture from our January 2020 FCA Lacrosse Leadership Summit at the USA Lacrosse Convention (held in Philadelphia that year), which includes about half the group of FCA Lacrosse staff and leaders that were in attendance.

Working the Floor

It's not just during official meetings or meals that relationships with coaches and other centers of influence are built. We are always intentional after our FCA Lacrosse Leadership Summit gathering to head to the convention floor and work the FCA Lacrosse booth and more importantly, to just be present amongst the other vendors and many coaches who are just roaming around.

I also have several exhibitors I like to connect with each year, especially at the Iroquois or Haudenosaunee booth. I love when I get a few minutes to talk with Alfred Jacques, the famed Onondaga stick-maker, or to say hello to Oren Lyons, the former All-American lacrosse player from Syracuse University and the Native American Faithkeeper of the Turtle Clan who was raised in the culture and practices of the Seneca and Onondaga Nations, or to catch up with the legendary Bucknell University coach, Sid Jamieson of the Cayuga Nation, who actually recruited me to play football and lacrosse during my senior year at Calvert Hall. Coach Sid is the only Native-American head coach in the history of NCAA Division I Lacrosse and was also the first head coach of what was to become the Iroquois or Haudenosaunee National Team, which is now one of the top teams in the World Lacrosse Championship every four years.

I was thrilled to buy this antique 1890s lacrosse stick from Alfred Jacques (center of left picture), the famed Onondaga stick-maker, and to connect with Native American Coach Sid Jamieson at the 2023 USA Lacrosse Convention. I also ran into Rufus Ntiamoah (right picture), who started lacrosse in Ghana and is now the president of the Africa Association for Lacrosse on behalf of World Lacrosse. He attended our free friends of FCA Lacrosse dinner at Sabatino's in Baltimore.

Realtime

I also love how FCA pulls all of their staff, board members and key volunteer leaders from across the country and around the world together every couple of years at their Realtime conference. It is an amazing time of fellowship, worship, teaching and fun!

Like the various lacrosse conventions and conferences, Realtime has breakout sessions. I was blown away by our FCA La-crosse breakout session in 2022, especially with how many FCA staffers and leaders from around the world showed up, because they are using lacrosse or want to start

FCA Lacrosse leaders breakout session at Realtime in 2022

lacrosse or an FCA Lacrosse outreach in their area or country.

We have come a long way from when we had eight coaches at our first FCA Lacrosse Coaches Breakfast at the US Lacrosse Convention.

Being at the USA Lacrosse Convention and FCA Realtime gathering, both with so many coaches in attendance, always reminds me of the coaches who have influenced my life and the many young athletes that I, and FCA Lacrosse, have been able to coach and influence. I thank God for the picture below of my former Calvert Hall high school football coach Augie Miceli, with his son and my dear friend Augie Jr., and his grandson Augie III wearing an FCA Lacrosse sweatshirt.

Three generations of Augie Micelis

God used Coach Miceli to re-cruit me to Calvert Hall. Calvert Hall Lacrosse Coach Mike Thomas convinced me to play the Creator's game, lacrosse. I ended up at Cornell playing lacrosse and there, committed my life to the Lord. After graduation, and a summer mission to Japan, I returned to Baltimore and started FCA at Calvert Hall, out of which developed FCA Lacrosse. And more than 40 years later, Coach Miceli's grandson was a part of an FCA Lacrosse club team, which hopefully had, and will continue to have, a positive eternal influence on the rest of his life.

God's Word is always true. In our hearts and minds, we can plan our course, but God establishes our steps, and His purpose prevails, whether at a conference, convention or anywhere in life.

That is cool! That is God! That is FCA!

CHAPTER 78

The Four

"I pray that the eyes of your heart may be enlightened in order that you may know the hope to which he has called you, the riches of his glorious inheritance in his holy people, and his incomparably great power for us who believe..."

Ephesians 1:18-19

I n the summer of 2022, Gayle and I would fly to Istanbul for our 35th wedding anniversary getaway to follow the missionary journeys of the Apostle Paul through Turkey and Greece. The day we toured Ephesus, I received a brief, but powerful God-story video clip from one of the Kelly Benefits/FCA Lacrosse interns, Caleb Newman, showing another intern, named RJ Mellor, sharing his personal faith story at the FCA Lacrosse camp.

In front of the ruins of the library and nearby synagogue in Ephesus, Turkey, that date back to the time of the Apostle Paul with our dear friends, the Bradleys (Left) and Knudsens (Right)

It's a God story because, only weeks before, Gayle and I had hosted our annual FCA intern "get to know you" dinner with "Baltimore's Best" ribs from the Corner Stable and crab cakes from Pappas Restaurant for all five interns who would be living in our basement for the summer.

Our son JK and daughter Jackie joined us as we went around our kitchen table, and I asked each guy to tell us a little about themselves and why they decided to dedicate their summer to serving as an FCA Lacrosse intern. Each guy enthusiastically talked about their unique faith and college lacrosse stories, until we got to the last intern, RJ, who happened to be sitting next to me. He got very quiet and kind of nervous.

"To be honest Mr. Kelly, I'm here because one of my coaches thought it would be a good idea for me to do this. His name is Brett Bernardo, and he was an FCA Lacrosse intern who lived in your basement a few years ago."

"I remember Brett," I said. Every summer for the last ten years, we have had anywhere from two to five FCA interns live in our two finished basement bedrooms.

RJ went on, "It's a long story, but I played high school lacrosse in western Maryland, which is not known as a 'hotbed' of lacrosse talent, and I didn't get heavily recruited to play in college. I ended up getting some interest from Messiah College in Mechanicsburg, Pennsylvania. They were a solid Division III program, so I thought this was my best chance to play lacrosse at the next level.

"I grew up in a family that had no faith background, so the fact that Messiah College was a Christian school meant nothing to me. I guess with a name like 'Messiah,' I should've realized, but I was just focused on lacrosse."

RJ continued, "I barely survived my freshman year and decided to not return as a sophomore. I missed the fall semester, and then received a call from a new assistant coach named Brett Bernardo. I had been thinking about giving Messiah another try, but his call put me over the top.

"Throughout the lacrosse season, Coach Bernardo encouraged and challenged me. I could tell he really cared about me. And then as our season was coming to an end in May, Coach Bernardo encouraged me to apply for this FCA Lacrosse Fellows Internship program. I really had nothing else to do this summer, and because of my respect for Coach Bernardo, I decided to give it a shot! So here I am."

"Wow! Thank you for sharing your story, and being so honest about how you got here," I said.

I then asked the group if they had been through the FCA Lacrosse intern training on "The Four," and if they had been given an FCA "Four" bracelet yet. They said they had heard a little about it but had no formal training or bracelet yet.

I usually wear an FCA "Four" bracelet or two, realizing it might become a conversation piece and lead to an opportunity to share. At the table, I took off my bracelet and asked RJ if he had seen and knew the meaning yet. He did not.

I explained the four symbols on the bracelet: a heart, which represents

God's amazing love for us; a division sign, which represents our sin that divides and separates us from God; a cross, which represents Jesus' sacrifice on the cross for us; and a question mark, which represents our decision— what will we do with Jesus—accept Him, reject Him or neglect Him?

I asked RJ if he had ever opened his heart and mind to accept Jesus or invited and received Him into his life.

Again, being honest, he said "No, not yet."

"Would you like to receive Jesus, put your trust in Him and follow Him?" I asked.

You could have heard a pin drop, as all of us around the table awaited his response.

"Yes!" he said. "I think I would like to do that."

And right there, I led RJ in a simple prayer that he repeated after me:

"Lord, I acknowledge that you are perfect, holy and loving. I acknowledge that I am imperfect, broken and a sinner, and that my sin has divided and separated me from You. I acknowledge that You, Jesus, lived, died and rose again, and that through Your shed blood on the cross, my sins can be forgiven so I can be rightly connected to You, Lord, my Creator. Today, June 2, 2022, I ask you to forgive me of my sins and I accept, invite and receive You into my life. Please come and make me the person you created me to be. Thank you Lord! Amen."

We all looked on in awe as RJ lifted his head, and with tears in his eyes and a big smile on his face, said "That felt great!"

I affirmed RJ and his decision of faith to put a stake in the ground that he could remember. I then gave him my "Four" bracelet and he put it right on his wrist. "I will definitely keep and wear this," he said.

You can only imagine how thrilled I was to see the video clip Caleb Newman sent me from FCA Lacrosse Camp four weeks later, where RJ was sharing his story with hundreds of campers and explaining "The Four" to them. That's influence!

Camp Stories

With more than 500 boys, girls, and volunteer huddle leaders and coaches attending FCA Lacrosse Camp at Lancaster Bible College, many stories of life change continued to stream in throughout the weeks after camp concluded.

Rain caused the 2021 FCA Lacrosse Camp picture to be taken inside.

One of the things I love about FCA camps is that often, the people influenced the most are the coaches and huddle leaders who come to camp to serve. They think they are there to lead and show the young campers the way, but many times, their lives end up being the most challenged, impacted and transformed by the nightly fellowship and huddle times.

One story that really touched me was about Tommy Meehan, a star defenseman at High Point University, who helped coach one of the FCA Maryland club teams during the month of June and was a last-minute addition to the FCA Lacrosse Camp coaching staff. His girlfriend, Logan Tingley, who was playing on the women's team at High Point, was one of the female interns for the summer and was also at camp as a coach and huddle leader.

As Tommy left camp and was driving home, he was overcome with emotion and tears as he reflected on his experience that week sharing God's love with hundreds of campers through the Creator's game. Yet he knew he wasn't fully right or connected with the Creator himself.

Logan, who knew that Tommy (in his own words), had "one foot in and one foot out" of a relationship with God, sensed that he was ready to go "all in" and fully surrender his life to Jesus, and called him 20 minutes after he left and encouraged him.

"For some reason, I feel strongly that you need to turn around and come back," Logan said to him.

As she and a bunch of other coaches and huddle leaders were still at camp, discussing all the amazing things they had experienced together, Tommy had been thinking the same thing.

When he returned, he told the group he wanted to go "all in" and how God had led him to turn around and come back. Logan and the other huddle leaders and coaches who were still there hugged him, prayed with and over him and cried tears of joy with him as the eyes of his heart were opened and he humbly invited and received Jesus into his life to be both his Savior and Lord. That was powerful!

Women's Team Serve

The summer of 2022 also provided a unique opportunity to serve the women's world lacrosse community and to share The Four, when appropriate, through our first-ever FCA Lacrosse Women's "Team Serve."

The Women's World Lacrosse Championships were coming to Towson University and more than 30 countries would be participating. It was right in our backyard, but it would still be a lot of work to pull together a group of women FCA laxers who would be willing to volunteer and serve the Women's World Lacrosse community, USA Lacrosse (who was hosting the games) and the teams who were coming to Maryland for this incredible competition.

Thankfully, FCA Lacrosse staffers Robyn McCormick and Katie Tutak (from Upstate New York), and Russ LeBlanc (from Florida), agreed to coach FCA Team Serve, and Mark Stephens agreed to be the general manager and coordinate all the lodging, meals and scheduling logistics for the team.

It was so exciting to see Dan Britton's daughter, Abby, and our former FCA Lacrosse Advisory Board chair, Dave Britton's daughter, Ashley, help lead the team on the field. Also on the team were Russ LeBlanc's daughters, Heidi and Kate, and Mark Stephens' daughter, Lilly (Frostburg), my friend Glen Miles' daughter, Jordan (High Point), Baltimore Ravens Head Coach John Harbaugh's daughter, Alison (Notre Dame), and Ron Leubecker's daughter, Hannah (Maryland) all playing together and serving. FCA Lacrosse interns Rachel Delate, Ellie Pruitt, Logan Tingley, Abby Zeigenfuse and Kati Paavola played or helped coach as well.

The Team Serve players all grew in their relationships with God, and in their hearts for the other nations, as they practiced with, scrimmaged and served national teams from Israel, Switzerland, Latvia, Italy, Austria and China. In several cases, they got to share "The Four" with them,

FCA Women's Team Serve after scrimmaging Team China

as they gave each player from the other team an FCA Four bracelet as a token of appreciation for the "friendly" match.

Team China at first declined to play FCA because of our faith-based background. "We want to play lacrosse and help your team get better prepared," Team Serve's general manager Mark Stephens assured them, and then instructed his players not to broach the topic of faith unless someone asked. China agreed to play and, afterwards, presented Team Serve with souvenir towels from China. That opened the door for Team Serve to reciprocate by offering The Four bracelets to Team China's players.

"Then we invited Team China to an all-American cookout at Nick and Tina Wasielewski's house, whose daughters Ella and Maci played for us," Mark said. "Over dinner, we had the opportunity to get to know them personally and demonstrate the love of God. Many of the girls connected on social media so the conversations will continue."

Team Serve's mission was to serve the other teams at the tournament, but the fellowship impacted many on our team as well. Ellie Pruitt recruited two of her college teammates to the team, both of whom arrived struggling with anxiety over situations at home and school. "Meeting other girls who go through the same struggles helped them start to dig out of the holes they were

Huddle time with Team Switzerland after a practice game

in and see that there's more to life when you live for God," Ellie said.

The Four was used to share a message of hope, healing and transformation for the women of Team Serve and each of the teams they were able to play.

MORE TO THE STORY...

Bigger Than Lacrosse Games – Alison Harbaugh

Team Serve was my first FCA event ever. I heard about it when my dad forwarded me a text from Mark Stephens. It sounded like an amazing opportunity that I couldn't pass up, and I came back early from our family vacation to play.

My thought going into it was that scrimmaging against some of the best players in the world would be a great way to prepare for my college season the next spring. But right away, on the first day, I realized that Team Serve was much bigger than lacrosse games.

I was nervous when I arrived because I didn't know any of my teammates, but they welcomed me with open arms and made me feel like a part of the team. That made me realize that the Holy Spirit puts us in special places at special times in our lives. In only six days, I got to know all the girls and our spirits connected on a deep level.

Alison Harbaugh with her dad, John, the Baltimore Ravens Super Bowl Champion Coach

As a college student, it's easy to get caught up in material things, parties, social media and to talk about shallow and surface-level issues. But in our Team Serve Bible studies, our faith brought us together and we talked about God's presence in our lives and our personal thoughts and experiences.

My faith grew stronger hanging out with amazing young women my age who played lacrosse and were also inspired to live their lives the way God created them, and the way God wanted them to—with Him in the forefront. *Wow, I can do that too!*

I think God brought me to Team Serve to send me the message to devote everything to Him and live my life through His words. And, oh yeah, the lacrosse was fantastic! The games brought me together with young women from different countries and different cultures that I didn't even realize played lacrosse.

We all love the sport but live such different lives and I was blown away by the opportunity to meet and talk to players from across the ocean. I played attack, and when the ball was on the other side of the field, I would ask my defenders about their countries and lives. I learned so much and my eyes were really opened.

Two of the teams we played were extra special for me. Team Switzerland was like a barrel full of monkeys—so lively, sweet and fun. The defender who guarded me had played on the Swiss hockey team in the Olympics.

Team China didn't want to play us at first because of our Christian beliefs, but they eventually agreed, and we invited them to a barbecue afterward. At dinner, many of them asked questions about FCA and Christianity, which opened the door for conversations about Jesus. I'm still in touch with a couple of the girls on Instagram.

I would love to be a part of Team Serve again in four years. I came for lacrosse but received so much more than I expected—a stronger faith and friendships for the future I would otherwise never have had the opportunity to forge.

Ambassadors for the Creator and the Creator's Game – Ryan Horanburg

We united 27 girls from different schools and different states across the country to put together the first-ever FCA Lacrosse Women's Team Serve, right in our backyard at Towson University in Maryland. For six days before the opening ceremonies of the Women's World Championships, we served, scrimmaged and broke bread in American homes with nine different teams from around the world.

One highlight came as a complete surprise. USA Lacrosse called me and said they needed volunteers for the opening ceremony. I said, "Sure, we have 27 players and five more volunteers that would love to help out in any way, shape or form."

"Great, we'll take all of you," USA Lacrosse said. That showed me what a strong relationship FCA Lacrosse has built with USA Lacrosse and World Lacrosse. Our whole emphasis was that Team Serve was there to do anything they needed us for, and they included us in maybe the most visible element of the entire event.

FCA Team Serve members were happy to carry the flags and signs for each country during the Opening Ceremony.

Five hours before the opening ceremonies, we picked up our credentials and looked to see what our jobs would be. "Ambassadors," the sheet read. *Okay, sounds good, whatever it means.*

What it meant was that an FCA Lacrosse player or volunteer was assigned to each of the 30 teams to help them get organized and in line for the opening ceremony and walk them into the stadium. Then, USA Lacrosse added another request: for our players and volunteers to carry the flag or the country name sign for their teams!

So, there was FCA Lacrosse, center stage in front of thousands of fans in the stands and millions more around the world watching on ESPN. A once-in-a-lifetime experience for all of us.

What an honor to be an ambassador to the world for the Creator and the Creator's game.

Supernatural Living – Caleb Newman

When I arrived at Cornell as a freshman lacrosse player in 2020, I was ready to party.

My father was a pastor, so I grew up in the church and was involved with FCA in high school, but I felt religion was forced on me. I was running from God, but I made one concession to my parents—I would go to an FCA Huddle at Cornell.

The huddle leader, Tom Howley, who is also the strength and conditioning coach at Cornell, was excited about having us read a book that a Cornell lacrosse alum had donated: *The Holy Spirit: The Key to Supernatural Living,* by Bill Bright.

With my church background, I could explain God the Father and Jesus, but I was not at all familiar with the Holy Spirit. By the end of that first semester, my heart began to open up and soften toward the Holy Spirit.

On a break, I visited my brother who worked on a missionary base in the Hawaiian Islands. There, I encountered the power of the Holy Spirit for the first time in a real way and it rocked my life. I became a believer.

I told Coach Howley about my newfound faith when I returned to Cornell. "This book on the Holy Spirit has changed my life," I said. "I'd like to contact the guy who donated them and thank him."

Coach gave me the email address of a man named Frank Kelly.

I emailed Mr. Kelly to tell him my story and thank him for the book. I found out immediately how Mr. Kelly operates: the moment you send him an email, you get a phone call right back.

We talked on the phone for about an hour and a half because our stories have so much in common. We both came to Cornell living the lacrosse life, the party life, far from God. His life was transformed in a Bible study with Athletes in Action, a ministry my four grandparents help to start. He attended AIA's Ultimate Training Camp, which my grandpa, Wendell Deyo, helped create.

Mr. Kelly then reinvested the spiritual legacy he received through my grandparents into Cornell by serving Coach Howley as chair of the FCA Cornell Board of Advisors and donating the book that helped transform my life.

Meeting Mr. Kelly was a divine appointment. Our relationship blossomed during that first phone call, and he became a mentor. I called him whenever I struggled to live out my faith because I knew he had been through the same struggles.

On one call, Mr. Kelly happened to mention his company, Kelly Benefits. I remembered that's where two of my teammates, Luca Tria and Danny Boccafola, worked as interns the previous spring when our season was shut down because of the COVID-19 pandemic. Both Luca and Danny shared with me the amazing spiritual impact they experienced while living with the Kellys and working at Kelly Benefits. I didn't say anything to Mr. Kelly then, but I began praying, *God, if I could have the opportunity to go to Kelly Benefits and be around Frank Kelly, I would jump on it—whatever kind of business it is that he runs.*

The next time I talked to Mr. Kelly, I mentioned the differences that I saw in the way my teammates lived their faith after their internship with Kelly Benefits. "Well," he said, "if you would want to do something like that next summer, we could set up the same thing."

"Yes!" I said.

Mr. Kelly talked to me about the value of flexibility and living an integrated life—which doesn't mean work hard/play hard but work hard/serve hard. His visionary internship required me to work at Kelly Benefits and also volunteer for at least three FCA Lacrosse events. I wouldn't be paid for the lacrosse service, but the company would give me the time off and schedule flexibility I needed.

Caleb Newman (Left), pictured with Ben Savick, worked the joint Kelly Benefits/FCA Lacrosse internship, which led him to FCA coaching and playing opportunities around the country, including Vail, Colorado and beautiful Piney River Ranch.

For my first FCA Lacrosse service experience, I went to Colorado to help coach one of the FCA youth teams playing in the Vail Shootout. As a coach and huddle leader, I loved working with the kids and sharing God's love and truth with them. After that, I was asked to stay and play in the Open Division of the Vail Lacrosse Shootout with the 30th Anniversary FCA Lacrosse Team that Frankie and Timmy Kelly were leading. I was honored to play on that team and be a part of FCA Lacrosse history, while building some amazing relationships with my new teammates.

It was great to have the youngest of 21 Kelly cousins, Eli (Center) and Caleb at FCA Lacrosse Camp, where dozens of volunteer lacrosse players, like Caleb Newman, coached and led huddles.

I returned from Vail, worked a week at Kelly Benefits, then left for Lancaster,

Pennsylvania to serve 500 kids for a week at the FCA Lacrosse Camp. I finished my lacrosse service by coaching and then playing with FCA national teams in Lake Placid, New York.

The Kellys let me live at their house for the summer, and Mr. Kelly modeled to me how to live an integrated life, which he does better than anyone I know. Everything he touches points to God and gives Him glory—FCA Lacrosse, his business, his family, his friends, even his basement! The walls are covered with pictures and stories of God's grace and glory over Mr. Kelly's life. That's how I desire to live my life.

My whole summer was a total God thing, so divine that He brought Frank Kelly into my life. The joint Kelly Benefits/FCA Lacrosse internship gave me the business experience I wanted and the flexibility for the lacrosse ministry I desired.

And it was great to meet people like Lilly Stephens, who played lacrosse at Frostburg State University, and also worked the joint Kelly Benefits/FCA Lacrosse internship. Lilly's main FCA Lacrosse focus was the Women's World Lacrosse Championships (which were being played only a few miles from our Kelly Benefits office), and the first-ever Women's Team Serve. She would get to the office early to get a head start on her work, leave for a few hours to go scrimmage or practice with a team like Austria or Italy, then hustle back to the office to finish her Kelly Benefits projects.

To see it all work together in an integrated fashion was life changing.

CHAPTER 79

I Lift Up My Eyes

"...I lift up my eyes to the mountains—where does my help come from?
My help comes from the Lord, the Maker of heaven and earth."

Psalm 121:1-2

I t was déjà vu all over again, to borrow the words of the Yankees sage, Yogi Berra.

The day before our flight to the 2022 Vail Shootout—which marked the 30th anniversary of FCA's Miracle in the Mountains victory and the 50th anniversary of the tournament itself—one of our players tested positive for COVID-19. That put the team not one player short like we were in 1992, but five down, to only fifteen players.

Between the pandemic, which was subsiding but still making many people sick and squeamish about traveling, an inflation spike that nearly doubled the cost of flights and lodging, the typical family commitments of a holiday week-end, and work schedules, it was tough for the team leaders—my son, Frankie, and nephews, Timmy and David—to recruit players for the FCA Lacrosse Elite Division "Anniversary" team.

"When we started recruiting players in February, our idea was to put to-gether a reunion tour of guys who had recently played on the FCA U19 teams, played high-level college lacrosse, and were 25 or younger," Frankie said. "Then we'd add a few of us 30-ish veterans, like David and me, who could hold their own on the field but would mostly be there as a leadership presence off the field. We thought we would easily get 25 players, but that wasn't what the Lord had in mind."

"We let everyone know up front that while we would compete hard to win games, the real mission was a five-day retreat in the mountains," Timmy said. "That cost us a couple of guys who were more interested in the Vail nightlife or coming home with a championship trophy, but we didn't want to overpromise."

Timmy had the most to lose if the FCA team didn't come together. He played for the 2021 Vail Shootout champion Mohawk Tile, but this year chose to play for FCA rather than help his former team defend its title.

Timmy was all in. "It was an honor for me to work with my cousin Frankie," he said. "It was a lot of work and frustrating at times, but the least I could do to say 'Thanks' to my Uncle Frank and everyone who has worked with him for so many years to build the FCA Lacrosse ministry."

When we heard about the positive COVID test the day before the team was to arrive in Colorado, Gayle and I dropped to our knees and asked God to please raise up players, and quickly—guys who loved lacrosse and were open to growing in their relationship with God. I called Caleb Britton, Dan Britton's nephew, who is one of Liberty University's all-time leading scorers.

Frankie had offered Caleb a spot on the team earlier in the year, but he said he couldn't make it because of his summer job commitment. I felt led to make a last-minute appeal and let him know that several players from the original team had offered to offset a major portion of the flight costs—a sacrifice bigger than when Gayle and I fronted the money for 20 flights in 1992 because we got paid back. With a last-minute request, Caleb's boss graciously let him take the time off and he agreed to play.

All summer, four FCA Lacrosse interns, all college players, lived in our basement. I had asked them several times to come to Vail but they had reasons why they couldn't. Gayle made one final, last-ditch plea. She explained the need to fill the roster and the lower cost, and within an hour, three of them, Griffen Agawa, RJ Mellor and Addison Bennett agreed to go, and they recruited their multiple-time Division III All-American friend, Brett Gladstone, to also join the team. Gayle booked them all on a 6 a.m. flight the next morning.

God was gracious and faithful, and the team was set with 20 players, the same number as in 1992. "Proverbs 16:9 played out before our very eyes," Frankie said. *The mind of man plans his way, but the Lord directs his steps.*[1]

As the players made final preparations to leave, we prayed for something they didn't have to worry about much in 1992—our flight schedules. Frankie noted, "We were traveling during 'airline armageddon' week. The airline industry was still digging out of the pandemic shutdown, and there were national shortages of pilots, flight attendants and baggage handlers. Thousands of flights were delayed or canceled every day across the country, and thousands of passengers were stranded in airports for hours or days. We had twelve different flights descending into Denver on Thursday. If only one or two didn't make it, our team was in trouble for our two games on Friday."

Transforming the Generations

God answered our prayers, and everyone arrived on time for the team practice at 6 p.m. on Thursday. Standing on the sideline—I was not going to pick up a stick—I realized they were practicing on the same field where the 1992 team played its first game. So many memories washed into my mind and heart. All four Kelly brothers scored in that victory. Would multiple Kelly cousins find the back of the net in a game 30 years later?

Frankie and Josh Hoffman extended to me the honor of closing the practice in prayer. I thought of Big Frank—my dad and Frankie's grandfather—running out on the field after the miracle victory to pray with his sons.

FCA split the two games on Friday, and the Kelly cousins lit up the scoreboard. David Jr. played defense, but his minutes were limited by his vision challenges. Frankie and Timmy combined for eight goals in the first game (seven by Timmy) and five in the second game. Frankie even shot one of his two goals between his legs off of a faceoff—"The coolest goal of my life," he said.

After the second game, we got a number of family and team pictures which sparked more flashbacks, for which we were grateful.

Three generations of Kellys (L to R), Gayle, me, Quin, Frankie and Acacia on Ford Field

How About Them Unis

And how about those uniforms! Thirty years ago, the numbers that were taped onto our practice pinnies were falling off by the end of the tournament. Now the kids on the FCA club and national teams think FCA Lacrosse Under Armour gear is so cool that some have worn it for their official player profile pictures and to tryouts for showcase or All-Star teams.

I looked at the four FCA Lacrosse interns with us—including Caleb Newman, who had recently completed his sophomore year at Cornell and was interning at Kelly Benefits—posing in the photo. In 1992, I couldn't dream that

FCA Lacrosse would hire ten to twelve college interns every summer.

Most of the other FCA Lacrosse interns and staff were 3,000 miles away making final preparations for the FCA Lacrosse Camp at Lancaster Bible College, where more than 500 campers, coaches, huddle leaders and staff had signed up. What an increase from the nine kids at our first FCA Lacrosse Camp in 1988, and the 80 or so that attended the camp at Gettysburg College that Dan Britton and I helped run after we returned from Vail 30 years prior.

Timmy Kelly going to the goal in the 50th Vail Lacrosse Shootout

And at the same time, back in Baltimore, several of the women FCA Lacrosse interns and staff were scheduling scrimmages and fellowship dinners for our first-ever FCA Women's Team Serve outreach later that week at the 2022 Women's World Lacrosse Championships.

I glanced over at Jakub Lipczik, who traveled 5,300 miles from Poland to play with FCA after his Polish national team dropped out of the tournament due to the travel costs. Jakub had taught the game to Vova Demediuk, our FCA Lacrosse staff member in Ukraine, and now he was here with our anniversary team in Colorado—his first-ever FCA Lacrosse experience.

Jakub shared with us that 50 kids signed up for a lacrosse camp in Ukraine, which was under attack—again—by Russia, and 60 were coming to a camp in neighboring Poland, where 5 million Ukrainian refugees (including Vova and his family) had fled to safety.

I thought about the team picture being taken on another field for the FCA U19 girls' team who also played in the tournament and the recent years that FCA entered up to a dozen teams in the youth divisions. It was growth unimaginable considering the minor miracle it took for our first team to get into the tournament off the waitlist, something that "never happens" according to the original Vail Shootout organizers.

Where Does Your Help Come From?

On Saturday, FCA jumped out to a 4-1 lead, but the score tightened by halftime. With under two minutes left in the game, FCA led by two with possession of the ball, but in a gut-wrenching reversal gave up three unanswered goals and lost 10-9. So many of FCA's shots hit the pipes and two shots that were clearly goals were not counted. Someone slashed Frankie's knee—it swelled up like a grapefruit and he hobbled around on crutches after the game.

It appeared that God had put a lid on that game and FCA was not meant to win. Why? Only God knew, but I had a hunch. Because of the loss, FCA didn't play again until Sunday afternoon, which freed up Sunday morning for a mountaintop chapel service. Gayle and I joined the team on the gondola ride to the top of the Vail Mountain to worship at its simple but beautiful amphitheater, 14,000 feet above sea level, overlooking the still snow-covered Rocky Mountains and the Mountain of the Holy Cross.

Frankie led a devotion from Psalm 121:1-2: "I lift up my eyes to the mountains—where does my help come from? My help comes from the Lord, the Maker of heaven and earth." Then he challenged us to find a quiet spot and ask ourselves where we look for help, self-worth and contentment. Do we look to God, our Creator, or someone or something else?

Sunday morning fellowship time on top of Vail Mountain. Now that is one beautiful chapel!

"The Greatest Lacrosse Tournament in the World"

In Sunday afternoon's game, FCA fell behind by a bunch of goals, then during halftime, thunder and lightning rolled in. The officials called off the game 30 minutes later.

It was tough losing like that, but the early ending gave us time for a bumpy, hour-long drive to Piney River Ranch for a hike and a campfire—except it rained the entire way there. *Well, this is a bust.*

Then ten minutes after we arrived, the rain stopped, and the clouds broke up to show us one of the most beautiful sunsets I've ever seen (like the one on the dustjacket of this book—which is an actual picture from Piney River Ranch).

Piney River Ranch is a special place for things like our grandson Quin's first "shoulder ride" with his Poppy, or a huddle led by Sol Bliss around the campfire.

Sol Bliss, our FCA Lacrosse Upstate New York director and former Syracuse lacrosse All-American, who at 43 was our oldest player, shared his faith story around the campfire with the lake and mountain range in the background.

Sunday afternoon's loss also set up the final game on Monday on Ford Field against Mohawk Tile. I believe God ordained or destined that matchup, not only because of Timmy's connection to Mohawk Tile, but also because their general manager, Jim Soran, was a founding father of the Vail Lacrosse Shootout 50 years earlier.

Without Timmy, and also missing their star defenseman Mike Nathan (who also played with FCA), Mohawk Tile had won only one game, but FCA wasn't at full strength either. Frankie's knee limited his minutes, and former Calvert Hall and Johns Hopkins star Phil Castronova was nursing a separated shoulder with ice and Advil. It wasn't exactly "God Squad Upsets Turtles" as in 1992, but beating the defending champs 10-5 was an encouraging and upbeat finish to the tournament.

After the game, both teams gathered at midfield and I thanked Jim for founding and hosting "The Greatest Lacrosse Tournament in the World," where everyone has the opportunity to connect with the Creator through the Creator's game in the beautiful Valley of Vail.

FCA and Mohawk Tile celebrating the Creator's game and their general manager, Jim Soran (standing next to me, fifth person in from the right), for starting the Vail Lacrosse Shootout 50 years earlier

A Mountaintop Experience

Moved by our worship, fellowship, testimonies, prayer and fun in the majestic Rocky Mountains, many connected more closely with the Creator that weekend.

Caleb Newman and Ben Savick, our goalie who had starred at Robert Morris University, spoke at length with Jakub from Poland about what it means to have a relationship with God and encouraged him to get involved with Vova and FCA Lacrosse back home.

Timmy said that Mike Nathan, his former teammate and close friend from UNC, opened the Bible for the first time.

JD, who had just finished his freshman year at the University of Georgia, opened up to Frankie about how he had never taken his faith seriously and that this week was the first time he had met older men of faith that he could respect.

David Jr. shared that Phil had some deep conversations with Caleb, and expressed interest in reading the Bible more, and a refreshed desire to grow in his relationship with God and His Word.

Timmy's roommate in Denver, Patrick, played for Mohawk Tile but joined us at the Sunday morning chapel and Piney River Ranch Sunday night. He thanked Frankie for an uplifting experience and said he'd be interested in playing on the next FCA team.

Frankie, Timmy and David might have had the most stirring mountaintop experience of any of us. Their big takeaway was trust, they said. They learned to trust in each other through a frustrating planning process. "We became each other's psychologists," Frankie said. They called each other to celebrate when a player committed to coming and reminded each other that the Lord would get the guys to Vail that He wanted.

"Trust in God was the umbrella component over everything," Timmy said, and not only for the roster and the travel logistics, but even for the weather. It was supposed to rain the whole day we planned a team golf outing, but the rain stopped long enough to get in all eighteen holes and allow us to really enjoy God's creation.

The forecast called for rain on Sunday morning as well, but it held off until the afternoon to give us a beautiful morning for our chapel service on top of the mountain, a storm-shortened game, and plenty of time at Piney River Ranch. Rain or shine, we would give thanks, but we were especially grateful for the way we sensed God, our Creator, allowed the weather to unfold over our long weekend together.

Mostly, Frankie, Timmy and David trusted God that the weekend would impact the lives of the guys and rejoiced about the stories of influence that they heard.

The team finished seventh out of 14 teams, which wasn't the goal, yet the total FCA experience more than compensated for the numbers on the scoreboard.

"I have been blessed to play on championship teams at Calvert Hall and North Carolina and with the U.S. U19 team and FCA," Timmy said. "Winning is still important to me because I am an intense competitor, but what I have continued to learn is that what matters most are the relationships, community, friendships and fun that come from playing the Creator's game. And no one I know balances it better than FCA."

Through the work of the Creator of heaven and earth, we all left Vail more thankful for the Creator's game, the powerful ministry of FCA and their collective influence in our lives and the lives of many others.

The hope and dream are for the legacy of influence to continue for generations to come.

In 1992, Gayle and I brought eight-month-old Frankie with us and his "Uncle" Steve Paletta held him up in the back row of the team photo. In 2022, Frankie and his wife Acacia brought their six-month-old, Francis X. "Quin" Kelly V and Quin's Uncle David held him up in the back row. I see more than my grandson in that photo; I see a picture of God's faithfulness, grace and blessing, and His desire to influence and transform the generations through FCA, the Creator's game and all of life.

The 1992 Miracle in the Mountains FCA Lacrosse Team

The 2022 30th Anniversary FCA Lacrosse Team

CONCLUSION

"The one who calls you is faithful, and he will do it..."

1 Thessalonians 5:24

If there is one word I think of when I think of God, the Creator, it would be "faithful."

He is faithful and true to His character of love, grace, mercy, righteousness, holiness and perfection. He has been so gracious, patient, loving, kind and faithful to me, my family, our business and the ministry of FCA in schools and throughout the lacrosse community.

As part of His faithfulness, God says in His Game Plan, the Bible, that "...Those who honor me, I will honor..."[1] That certainly does not mean everything is easy and goes perfectly well for those who are trying to please and honor God. At times, it may feel that life is even harder for those who choose to follow, obey and serve Him.

Yet, as I look back on the ups and downs, wins and losses, and even challenges and disappointments over the years, I see God's faithfulness, blessing and all that He has done along the way.

When He spoke to me through His words recorded in Acts 1:8, during my time in Japan, after my senior year at Cornell, I had no idea what God had in store for me if, as imperfect as I am, I chose to obey and honor Him and His call—one step, one day, one year at a time.

The impressions were clear that I was supposed to go back home and start in my Jerusalem—Baltimore—and in some way focus on business, school(s), lacrosse and my friends. I thought it was a one-year assignment and I often joke that I feel like I have been on an annual renewable contract for more than 35 years. I still take time each August to pray and discern if God still wants those to be areas of focus for me.

This book recounts just some of the ways God worked in my life and the lives of many others after he used the Creator's game, to ultimately humble and connect me to Him, and then connect many others to Him as well.

It certainly wasn't a part of my plan or any "deal" I made with God, that He would choose to honor or allow me to be honored in each of those areas, but that's what He did.

It was June of 2012 when the Maryland Association of Health Underwriters (MAHU), our insurance and benefits industry association, inducted me into the MAHU Hall of Fame for my role as a leader in our industry and for my many years of involvement as a board member, and then president of both the Baltimore and Maryland Association of Health Underwriter associations.

When I first joined our family business, I felt that in some ways I was wasting my life, when God's Word reminded me that "whatever you do, do it with all your heart as if for the Lord..."[2] So I decided if I was going to be in this business, I needed to be a good "witness" and give my best effort to serve not only Kelly Benefits, but our industry and community at large.

It was really special that a year later, in June of 2013, Ernst & Young honored our family and business at their annual Entrepreneur of the Year Awards celebration with their Family Business Award of Excellence. I love the picture they took of us—my mom and dad, with me and my brothers, as well as our dear family friend and Baltimore Oriole Hall of Famer, Cal Ripken Jr., who was the "surprise presenter" for this prestigious award.

In 2013, I also learned that both my high school, Calvert Hall, and FCA wanted to honor me. What?!

When God impressed "schools" on my heart, my mind went right to Calvert Hall, which is where we started (or restarted) FCA in Maryland. Little did I know I would help lead the Calvert Hall FCA Huddle for the next 35 years, and that new FCA huddles would get started in over 300 other schools in Maryland.

Because of some of the success I had, and the fact that I helped coach lacrosse for many years, served on the Board of Trustees and served as co-chair for a large fundraising campaign, Calvert Hall decided to induct me into their Alumni Hall of Fame. At the ceremony, in front of hundreds of people, I was able to give honor to God and thank Coach Miceli for recruiting me to play football at The Hall, Coach Thomas for convincing me to play lacrosse and for Coach Tom Keigler for believing in me as my first official lacrosse coach on the JV team.

What are the chances that later that year, FCA would announce that I was being inducted into the national FCA Hall of Champions, the first person from the state of Maryland ever recognized with this honor.

FCA chose to do the presentation at a big dinner in December at Calvert Hall, which was perfect since not only did FCA Maryland get restarted there, but in many ways, the FCA Lacrosse ministry really started there as well. It was special that a number of former Calvert Hall Huddle members and current FCA Lacrosse players that I had coached gave testimony to the impact that FCA and FCA Lacrosse had and was having on their lives.

Five years later, in 2018, I was blown away when I found out I had been selected into the US Lacrosse Greater Baltimore Chapter's Hall of Fame. Even though I didn't really start playing lacrosse until high school, and my career and connection with the game almost ended my sophomore

FCA's Mark and Rhonda Stephens presented me and Gayle with my FCA National Hall of Champions induction plaque at a celebration dinner at Calvert Hall in December 2013.

year in college, here I was being recognized and inducted with other lacrosse legends like Henry Ciccarone Jr. (the star midfielder at Johns Hopkins), whom I looked up to when I first started playing.

At the ceremony, which was held on a cold Saturday night in January, who appeared out of nowhere but Coach Moran! He had driven down from Ithaca, New York to remind me with his presence that "It's Great to Be Here!" as he was a big part of me being there that night.

I asked my brother Bryan to introduce me. As I went up to give my speech and looked out over the audience, a flood of emotion enveloped me when I saw all my family—Gayle and our children, my mom and dad, my brothers and other family members, a number of former high school and college teammates (like Augie Miceli Jr. and Steve Paletta) and other friends from the lacrosse community and FCA.

I remembered how God used the Creator's game to draw me into a personal relationship with Him, and then allowed me to be a small part of helping to grow the game around the world and to see the game, with dozens of FCA Lacrosse staff and volunteers, now across the country and around the globe, being used to help draw others to the Creator as well.

I shared some funny stories about myself, our family and lacrosse and was able to publicly thank God for the game, and for all the coaches and teammates who influenced me along the way.

That night further inspired me to keep going—we wanted to see lacrosse become an Olympic sport again, and the influence of FCA Lacrosse to continue to grow and expand around the world. This wasn't an end, but a chance to reflect on the joys and successes of the past and move forward with a refreshed vision for the Creator's game in the future.

It was a special night in January 2018 being inducted into the US Lacrosse Greater Baltimore Chapter Hall of Fame with my family by my side. And it was an honor to be inducted alongside Henry Ciccarone Jr. and to have Coach Moran there as a surprise guest.

An Integrated Life

If there is one word I would want to define my life, it would be "faithful." I want to live a life full of faith and be reliable, dependable and faithful to the work and ministry of influence to which God has called me and to hopefully, at the end of my days, hear the words, "...Well done, good and faithful servant!..."[3]

I never did any of the activities in business, with FCA in schools, playing and coaching lacrosse, or with my friends to receive any type of recognition or honors. As imperfect and broken as I am, my desire has been to share God's love, grace and truth in a way that others in my spheres of influence could understand, comprehend and receive. My heart is for everyone to experience God's best in their lives, and I believe God wants that as well.

My dad was right when he told me if I joined the family business, even if just for a year (as I originally planned), that I would have to work really hard, but could enjoy the quality of life that only flexibility in my schedule could provide (including the flexibility to be on the job 24/7/365). I would not have to punch a clock, and I could, with freedom, pursue all four areas of the calling God gave me. In essence, I could live what I have come to call "an integrated life."

An integrated life wouldn't allow me to separate my life into "sacred" and "secular" activities, but would challenge me to keep the Creator, Jesus, at the center of everything I did—the center of my marriage and family, the center of our business, the center of playing and coaching sports, the center of sharing the influence of FCA in schools and the lacrosse community, as well as the center of my friendships and other relationships and activities.

I remind people often that FCA—the Fellowship of Christian Athletes—is not the Fellowship of "Perfect" Athletes, Coaches or Fans, but the Fellowship of "Imperfect, Broken, Forgiven and Restored" Athletes, Coaches and Fans. The true influence of FCA is sharing that love, grace and truth in an integrated way through all of life and all sports, including the Creator's game.

God Bless You and Your Story!

I hope you have enjoyed the many stories (and pictures!) of family, faith and lacrosse that were shared in this book. I am humbled and grateful that you would take the time to read and learn about my story, and more importantly, about the stories of so many amazing people I have been blessed to interact with along the way. And I hope you have been encouraged learning more about the "Influence" of FCA and "the Creator's game."

Most importantly, I hope you have come to learn and appreciate more about God's story and the supernatural stories He has written and desires to write in and through your life as well.

Thank you for hanging in and working through what has turned out to be a much longer book than I ever expected. To be honest, I feel a little like the Apostle John, who wrote in his Gospel of the same name, "Now there are also many other things that Jesus did. Were every one of them to be written, I suppose that the world itself could not contain the books that would be written."[4]

Nothing can compare to the life, work and stories of Jesus, yet I know many more powerful stories God has done through my family, friends, FCA and the Creator's game that if I were to record them all, the volumes would be too numerous to count. And I am excited about the stories of hope, healing and transformation that He continues to orchestrate today, and those that will be lived out and written through us in the future. By faith, I believe the best stories are yet to come!

My good friend Jon Gordon, who graciously wrote the Foreword to this book, encouraged me to keep the book "brief" and "easily digestible." It is certainly not brief, but I hope these stories have been digestible, enjoyable and inspiring, and that in some way this book has blessed, encouraged and influenced you to take the next step in your personal faith story and relationship with God.

Finally, my heart's sincere hope is that this book of stories has honored the Creator, the Creator's game and all the incredible servants of FCA.

Special Tributes

The Power of a Kind Word

"Anxiety weighs down the heart but a kind word cheers it up."

Proverbs 12:25

My first semester as a freshman at Calvert Hall was a very challenging time.

The transition from a co-ed public middle school to a large all-boys Catholic high school was not easy for me. I was struggling on the football field and in the classroom and I thought, I'm not going to make it, and considered transferring to Dulaney High School to be with my middle school friends.

Never underestimate the powerful influence of a kind word on another person. Kind words from a teacher and two friends kept me at The Hall when I was 80% out the door.

Brother Gregory "The Rock" Cavalier's timely and kind words during my freshman year kept me at Calvert Hall.

I thank God for Brother Gregory Cavalier, a.k.a. "The Rock." He claimed he was the toughest teacher there was. He taught my honors French class and fortunately, took me under his wing and believed in me when I didn't believe in myself.

"Hey Kel, you're no ordinary ham and egger," he told me.

Brother Gregory loved sports and I was a freshman football player in his class with mostly sophomores. "How about the little freshman here?" he announced to everyone in class one day. "Four touchdowns and 250 yards rushing the other day all in the first half. Way to go, Kel!"

I was seriously doubting whether I could make it athletically or academically at Calvert Hall, and I was very concerned about this honors French class. I was in way over my head, and felt like I was drowning, when one day, Brother Gregory walked by me while I was taking a 20-question true/false quiz. He looked over my shoulder, and said, "Kel, if I were you, I would look again at numbers four, eleven and fifteen." He threw me a bone! That act of grace and encouragement, for some reason, relieved a huge burden from my shoulders.

A couple of the sophomores in the class, Rick Roesner and Andrew Kimmel, probably don't even know it, but their light-hearted words of encouragement and affirmation more than 40 years ago were also significant in my decision to stay at The Hall.

The timely affirmations from Brother Gregory, Rick and Andrew helped me stick it out that first semester and had a huge ripple effect. Without their words of encouragement and influence, which impacted my decision to stay at Calvert Hall, who knows if I would have even played lacrosse, or if my younger brothers, three sons, and many nephews would have attended The Hall; if my brother Bryan would have become the head lacrosse coach there in 1996 and go on to win more than 300 games and five MIAA lacrosse championships; or if there would be a Kelly Field that our family helped to get built? More importantly, would FCA Lacrosse ever have taken off? In many ways, the foundation of FCA Maryland and FCA Lacrosse were laid at Calvert Hall.

A few words of encouragement can really go a long way!

Brother Gregory transitioned to eternity on October 5, 2021, at the age of 92, but his words of encouragement live on in my life and the lives of many others.

Greater Love

"Greater love has no one than this, than to
lay down one's life for his friends."
John 15:13 (NKJV)

Peter Kohn was a special friend to the FCA Lacrosse ministry. For nearly 20 years, he served as the equipment manager at numerous FCA Lacrosse camps and for many of our national teams in Vail.

Peter's selfless love and service attracted many young athletes to the Creator, including a high school camper named Sean McNamara. Years later, when Sean came on staff to lead FCA Lacrosse in 1998, we felt led to create an FCA Lacrosse Service Award in Peter's honor. We would present it annually at our FCA Lacrosse Coaches Breakfast or Lunch at the US Lacrosse Coaches Convention (and later at the IMLCA Convention), to a person who laid down his or her life in acts of service to benefit the lacrosse community and others in need.

Sean McNamara and Peter Kohn

The FCA Peter Kohn Service Award would be presented annually to a member of the lacrosse community who embodied the Scripture, "Greater love has no one than this, than to lay down one's life for his friends" and exemplified the FCA values of integrity, excellence, teamwork and serving, both on and off the lacrosse field.

Peter was born into a wealthy Jewish family in Baltimore—the co-founders of the Hochschild Kohn department store chain that was a Baltimore mainstay from 1897 to 1984. Most believe Peter was on the autism spectrum, with noticeable traits of Asperger syndrome.

I first met Peter the summer after my freshman year at Cornell in 1983, while working at Coach Richie Moran's Quick Stick Lacrosse Camp.

"Hey, Frank Kelly," Coach Moran called to me. "There's a guy named Peter Kohn coming, an equipment manager, a great guy. I want him to stay in your apartment and keep an eye on him. I gave him your address so he will be coming in sometime tonight."

"Sure, Coach."

My other roommates and I came home late that night and were so startled when we opened our apartment door that we jerked back a step before walking in. We thought someone robbed us and ransacked our apartment. Wet clothes were hanging from every lamp and table and chair. Then, in one of the bedrooms, we found this guy laying down on top of newspapers, buck naked except for a jockstrap. He had shaved his entire face and blood was everywhere.

"Are you Peter?"

"Hello, alright. I'm Peter," in his unique voice.

My roommates and I shook our heads and laughed at Peter for a day or two. By the middle of the camp, we were laughing *with* him. By the end, we had fallen in love with him.

Peter graduated from the Park School in Baltimore, and he loved to sing his school alma mater over and over. The kids and coaches loved it. I got to know the Park School alma mater better than I knew Cornell's and Calvert Hall's. For decades, Park School's alma mater was the most famous school song throughout the high school and college lacrosse community.

Peter was not athletic enough to play high school sports, but he was always around the games as the team manager. One day he was working the scoreboard at a basketball game against St. Paul's School. When the game ended, the St. Paul's scorekeeper had them winning by a point, but the Park School scorekeeper showed Park winning by a point. They looked at Peter's scorebook to decide the official result. Park wins!

One of the players on St. Paul's was Jerry Schmidt, who became a three-time All-American lacrosse player at Johns Hopkins, and to this day is the only lacrosse player ever to appear on the cover of *Sports Illustrated* (April 23, 1962). Jerry was playing for the Carling Lacrosse Club after graduating from Hopkins when he ran into Peter.

"You're the guy who cost us that basketball game back in high school!" Jerry said.

Peter was so gracious that Jerry asked him to help manage their club team, and Peter stepped into the world of lacrosse. I reconnected with him at the first FCA Lacrosse Camp at Gettysburg College in 1988 when Hank Janczyk brought him along to help at his lacrosse camp, which was held the same week, and Hank brought him over to help with our small group of players as well.

At camp, Peter and I had several conversations about "God and Jesus," and Peter told me that, through reading the Bible and the influence of various people that God brought into his life, he had come to believe that Jesus, the Jewish carpenter from Nazareth, was the Messiah.

Between managing for Carling Lacrosse Club, and later for Coach Moran, Coach Janczyk, FCA, Middlebury College, and four U.S. National teams, Peter traveled across the country and around the world serving lacrosse coaches and players.

Peter Kohn singing his famous "Park School" fight song at one of our early FCA Lacrosse camps on the fields of Gettysburg College

Everywhere he served, Peter was the first person on the field and the last to leave. He served with the same joyful spirit, no matter the task. I still remember Cornell Lacrosse camp when he was holding up the bottom half of a cut-off T-shirt and walked around the entire field asking, "Did anybody lose this?"

"Pete, I think that's trash."

"I need to find who it belongs to. Someone might be looking for it and I want to find them."

At a typical practice, a team will start with 50 balls and if they finish with 45, they're happy. Not Peter. He would crawl on his stomach in the bushes and under the stands until he found every last ball.

He filled water bottles, laid wet towels on players' necks to cool them off, picked up trash and did whatever it took to reconnect a lost mouthpiece to its rightful owner. Everyone loved watching Peter and anyone who saw him for the first time had the same reaction: *Who is that guy?*

Peter never, ever had a bad word to say about anyone. We used to tempt him by telling him about problems between players, such as a fight that broke out. "Who do you think was right?" we would ask.

"I think they are both beautiful men. I love them both dearly."

"But one of them had to be right and one of them had to be wrong," we would insist.

"I would rather not say. I believe they both have points of view that should be considered."

Peter saw the good in everything. In a scene in the 2005 documentary about him called *Keeper of the Kohn* (from his days as the equipment manager for the Middlebury College lacrosse team), directed by David Gaynes, Peter is hiking in the mountains in Vail and picks a dandelion. "Some people think dandelions are weeds," he says. "I

Scan to watch Keeper of the Kohn.

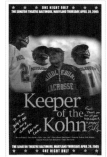

think they are beautiful because God created them."

A Hall of Fame Contributor to the Game

We worked hard to get Peter inducted into the National Lacrosse Hall of Fame, and he entered as a contributor to the game in 2004.

"The most important thing that happened to me," he said in his acceptance speech, "was to be loved and cared for, for what I am...And I thank God so many people put up with me when many times they could have fired me."

One of the extraordinary blessings of my life was speaking at Peter's funeral in 2009, along with Richie Moran, Jim Grube, the head coach at Middlebury College, and Bob Scott, the former legendary head coach at Johns Hopkins.

In my eulogy, I recounted the stories that epitomized Peter's life. I added that every day, Peter modeled one of our aspirations in FCA—to live an "I am third" life, where God is first, others are second, and I am third. We all know that Peter loved the Lord and loved and cared for everyone else more than himself.

With Peter Kohn at an early FCA Lacrosse Camp at Gettysburg College

By the world's standards, Peter Kohn didn't have much to give. But God doesn't care how much you have. He cares about how much you do and give from what you have. Peter took the gifts God gave him and fully gave of himself to bless and serve his Lord, thousands of players and coaches, and his friends.

Rarely have I ever seen a greater love.

Farewell "Darky"

After filming *The Middie* video for US Lacrosse in 1988, I drove home with Jimmy "Darky" Darcangelo, a three-time All-American midfielder at Towson University, a three-time U.S. National Team member and National Lacrosse Hall of Famer, who also appeared in the video.

"Frankie, I want to fly an idea by you," he said. "I'm thinking of opening a lacrosse-only store. Check out my logo." He showed me a picture of a player with his hands raised after scoring a goal—it was Darky from one of his Team USA games.

"I want to call it Lax World," he said.

"I think it's a fantastic idea," I said. Six months later he opened his first store and grew Lax World into a national chain of sixteen stores with locations in five states and the District of Columbia.

I played with Darky for several seasons at the Maryland Lacrosse Club. Despite his age, he still had the magic in his game and a positive outlook that raised the spirits of everyone around him.

Jimmy died in 2020, but because of the COVID-19 pandemic, USA Lacrosse waited until June 2022 to honor his life, and I attended with my brother David.

Several family members and friends eulogized Darky, including Terry Corcoran, who played high school lacrosse with Darky in Upstate New York on teams coached by Terry's father. Terry had a distinguished coaching career himself and he coached my brother John at Washington College.

Terry told a story about staying out late with Darky at the 2001 US Lacrosse Coaches Convention. One beer turned into two beers, three beers, four beers, and the next thing they knew, it was after one in the morning. Darky turned to Terry and said, "Cork, I need you to do me a big favor."

"Sure, what is it?"

"I've been invited to the FCA breakfast at 7 a.m. I'm afraid I'm not going to know anybody there. Would you go with me—number one, to make sure I'm there, and number two, so I have someone to sit with?"

I squirmed in my seat. *Uh oh, he's going to say something negative or a joke about FCA and our FCA Lacrosse Coaches Breakfast,* I thought.

But Terry recounted how Darky knew everybody there, "and FCA Lacrosse presented Darky with one of his favorites among all the awards he ever received, the FCA Peter Kohn Service Award."

Then, Terry quoted John 15:13. "The award is based on the scripture: 'Greater love has no one than this, than to lay down one's life for his friends.' Like Peter, Darky laid down his life for his friends. That verse captures his life, and I'm honored to have known him."

Amazing! Right there at the USA Lacrosse Headquarters and National Teams training facility and field in front of hundreds of people, Terry honored God's Word, Jesus' example, FCA, Peter Kohn and Darky.

I turned to David sitting next to me. We looked at each other and I thought, *That was a God-wink!*

FCA LACROSSE
PETER KOHN SERVICE AWARD WINNERS

"Greater love has no one this, than to lay down one's life for his friends."
(John 15:13)

1998: Peter Kohn
1999: Hank Janczyk
2000: Buddy Beardmore
2001: Jim Darcangelo
2002: Susan Powell
2003: Bob Scott
2004: Jerry Schmidt
2005: Richie Moran
2006: Jim Grube
2007: Ed Britton
2008: Dave Urick
2009: Richie Meade
2010: Brad Corrigan

2011: Dr. Frederick Douglass Opie
2012: The Colleluori Family
2013: The Kelly Family
2014: Steve Stenersen
2015: Aimee Dixon
2016: Sgt. James J. Regan
2017: Mike Jolly
2018: Tom Hayes
2019: Brendan Looney
2020: Mary Schwartz
2021: Greg Bice
2022: Janine Tucker
2023: Steve Koudelka

The Logistics Queen and Mary

"And God has appointed in the church...
gifts of healing, helping, administrating..."

1 Corinthians 12:28 (ESV)

In the early days, it wasn't just Dan Britton and me running around organizing all the teams, coaches conventions and camps. During the first ten years, from 1988 to 1998, before Sean McNamara came on staff with FCA Lacrosse, and as Barry Spofford was helping grow and solidify FCA in the state of Maryland, my wife Gayle was intimately involved in so many organizational and administrative tasks. All along, Gayle gave me the freedom to use my gifts to help grow our family business and pursue my passion of sharing God's love and truth through sports, while she served in her areas of gifting.

In the FCA Lacrosse world, Gayle earned the name "The Logistics Queen" because she arranged all the flights, all the lodging, all the meals, and all the activities off the field, so that the players, coaches, and families could enjoy the lacrosse and the fellowship on and around the field. Over the years, whether our FCA teams traveled to Vail, Colorado, Tampa, Florida, Lake Placid, New York, Australia, Africa, Israel, or wherever God opened

One of Gayle's favorite "early days" pictures at Piney River Ranch in Vail, Colorado after one of many FCA Lacrosse trips she helped to organize

doors—Gayle dotted all the "i's" and crossed all the "t's."

And the growth and impact of our business and FCA would also not have happened without the incredible administrative gifting and work ethic of my long-time assistant at Kelly Benefits, Mary Iampieri.

In my role as a vice president of sales, then president, and ultimately CEO of

Kelly Benefits, I could not have asked for a more dedicated, loyal and hard-working assistant.

A single mom raising five children, Mary was my right hand for 23 years until she retired at 72, and soon after was diagnosed with cancer and went home to be with the Lord. Mary supported the administration of everything FCA in Maryland and FCA Lacrosse, from the huddle communications at Calvert Hall, to the banquet planning and logistics, to the numerous lacrosse camps, trips and coaches conventions. Baltimore City FCA wouldn't be anything near its current level of influence without Mary's support and dedication over her years of work with me.

When Mary passed away in 2013, the FCA Park Heights Saints Football and Cheerleading teams added an image of an angel with the name "Mary" on the back of hundreds of Saints shirts worn by the players, cheerleaders and coaches. And they continue to honor and recognize Mary to this day.

In many ways, Gayle and Mary laid the administrative foundation of FCA Maryland and FCA Lacrosse and handed over a well-oiled machine with ten-plus years of folders, files and prototypes once we got full-time FCA staff in place.

Although Gayle and Mary never sought and rarely received any public recognition for the behind-the-scenes administrative work they did that led to the growth of FCA in our region and in the lacrosse community, Gayle did get her fifteen seconds of lacrosse fame in an unexpected way.

Gayle was an accomplished high school and college athlete, but very modest about it. In 2016, when our son Stephen's University of North Carolina team was on its playoff run toward winning the NCAA championship, one game after Stephen scored a big goal off of a fastbreak faceoff, the ESPN game announcer, Paul Carcaterra, on national television, talked about what a great year Stephen was having and mentioned "His mother played three sports (cross country, field hockey and lacrosse) at Mary Washington University."

Gayle's phone lit up, with text messages from her college friends. "Hey three-sport athlete, way to go!" Gayle just smiled and shook her head.

Little did they know what an amazing wife, mother, grandmother, woman of faith and Logistics Queen she is as well.

Honor Your Father and Mother

"'Honor your father and mother'—
which is the first commandment with a promise—"

Ephesians 6:2

My story, and many of the stories in this book, would not have been possible without the love, support and encouragement of my mother and father. My parents were always there and always present and through them, I have learned that a person's presence is one of the greatest signs of love.

My Mom

My mom, Janet DeMaine Kelly, anchored our home—breakfast, lunch, dinner—every meal, every load of wash, every homework assignment that needed her assistance.

On top of all that, she ran the operations of our family business for ten years after she and my father started it in 1976 in the basement of our family home.

She never played sports growing up and didn't really care about them. Since her four sons ended up loving football, and especially lacrosse, and because success on the athletic fields mattered to us, it mattered to her.

My mom is smart, focused, disciplined and likes things done well—we actually got our competitive spirit from her.

Later in life, my mom has battled vision issues. Like my brother John, and my nephews David and Johnny, she has a degenerative eye condition called Best disease. She can no longer drive a car and needs a huge screen to magnify words so she can still read a bit. Yet that has never stopped her from attending many dozens of her sons' games, and literally hundreds of her 21 grandchildren's games.

She can't see, but she can pray, and her presence at games and other activities has brought a certain peace, joy and perspective.

My mom is gifted in many ways, but one of her greatest gifts is wisdom. The Creator, through the Holy Spirit, has allowed my mom to bestow tremendous wisdom on her children, grandchildren and all who interact with her.

I often joke with my mom that I would never have graduated elementary school if she had not been there to help me figure out various homework assignments and projects. I would often get stuck, really frozen with fear about how to move forward, and she always had a way to help me see what I needed to do. Her presence and wisdom have given me the confidence to do what God has created me to do, including this book.

Another significant gift and lesson my mom bestowed on our family and me is empathy. She had a special-needs sister—Aunt Joan. My mother ingrained in me and my brothers to always reach out, include and care for the person furthest out, or down and out.

The wisdom and empathy my mom bestowed on me, and our family have influenced the way we see life, treat others, coach and help lead FCA and FCA Lacrosse. Her presence and influence has been life-changing for our entire family and many others.

My Dad

My dad, whom most call "Big Frank" or "BF," is a true people person, and more present than anyone I know. He is with who he is with, which makes people feel good when they are in his presence or even talking with him on the phone.

When he and my mom started our family's business, he helped bring in the clients, while my mom made everything work. And amazingly, after choosing to double mortgage their home to start the business with five children under the age of fourteen, he was recruited two years later to run for State Senate over a crazy property tax issue that he and others opposed. He won that election and served three four-year terms from 1979 to 1991.

With all that going on, he was still very present. Sometimes, the Maryland General Assembly, or Senate Session in Annapolis, which ran from mid-January to mid-April each year, caused scheduling conflicts during lacrosse season. But even that didn't often stop him. One year, my brother Bryan had a big lacrosse game for Calvert Hall and my dad missed a vote on the Senate floor to be at the game. Some people took shots at him for that, but he was straightforward about it. "My son had a really big game and I thought that's where I should be," he said. "I need to keep my priorities in order."

He drove the ten-hour round trip to Ithaca many times for my Cornell games and always wore his bright green Irish cap so I could find him in the stands. After college, he came to my Maryland Lacrosse Club games enough times for my teammates to get to know and love him.

In 1992, he was there in Vail, Colorado to watch his four sons play together for the first, and what would be the last time. After we beat the Greene Turtle team in the Miracle in the Mountains game, he ran out on the field to join the celebration and knelt with us in our prayer of thanksgiving. He is front and center in what is arguably our most famous FCA Lacrosse picture, known as "The Power of Prayer." He was there on his knees in the huddle with the rest of us, wearing his signature Kelly green shirt.

Big Frank praying with his grandsons Jacob and Daniel before a big Calvert Hall game, with their little brother Caleb joining the huddle

He has attended hundreds, if not thousands, of his grandchildren's games, and too many Calvert Hall games to count. Before most games he would find time, either in person or over the phone, to pray with and over any of his grandchildren that were playing prior to their game.

He has been a faithful supporter of FCA and FCA Lacrosse. He and my mom have been the largest donor to FCA Baltimore City for more than 20 years. He pitched in and was there with our FCA Team Serve at the World Lacrosse Championships in Denver in 2014, and again in Israel in 2018. My dad has been so generous with his time (presence), and treasure, and his gift of exhortation and encouragement has inspired me and many others to take risks and pursue God's best.

In 2022, FCA inducted him and my mom into their Ring of Honor, which recognizes "major donors who are living a legacy of impact for generations to come."

When I think of Influence and the Creator's game, very few have had a bigger behind-the-scenes impact than my mother and father. Their presence says it all!

ACKNOWLEDGMENTS

I have always loved team sports like lacrosse and have come to realize that writing a book is a true team effort. I want to thank and acknowledge all of my teammates who helped make the dream of this book become a reality, including:

Bill Tamulonis, for interviewing more than 75 people, and helping write and re-write many of the enclosed chapters.

My wife Gayle, who listened to all my crazy ideas and read and listened to more drafts than you can imagine.

My assistant Kira Voit DiStefano, who kept me from pulling my hair out, or at least not pulling all of my hair out, with her steady and positive disposition and amazing typing, editing and organizational skills.

Jen Jardell and Michele Reber, who read, re-read and suggested edits and corrections to many of the spelling, grammar and sentence structure challenges I inadvertently hid throughout the text.

All of the People of Kelly Benefits, who edited content and gave valuable feedback, including Heather Kness, who helped design the cover, and Amanda Merrey, who helped inform our usage of Scripture.

Jen Kozak, who designed and did the layout and refined the cover with her creative skill and brilliance, and the Schmitz Press team for their commitment to excellence.

My teammates who serve through the ministry of FCA, especially Danielle Ripley-Burgess, whose copy and line edit skills truly challenged my thinking and greatly enhanced the stories that are told as well as Shaun Smithson and Ryan Horanburg, whose review and feedback were invaluable.

Many friends along the way who read various drafts and gave valuable input, including Jay McCumber, Bruce Barbour, Ted Squires, Sue Dilli, Jack Gilden, Jeff Caliguire and Frankie Kelly.

The dozens of people who have encouraged, prayed for and cheered me on in this process. You know who you are and I appreciate you.

My Creator and heavenly Father, His son Jesus Christ, and the Holy Spirit for loving me, saving me and empowering me to be a small part of these stories of healing, hope and transformation.

Thank you, team! I am grateful for the many ways you have blessed and served me and this book, and I am honored to call you teammates.

ENDNOTES

Dedication

    (1) Billy Graham

Introduction

    (1) *The Creator's Game: Lacrosse, Identity, and Indigenous Nationhood* by Allan Downey, p. 11

    (2) Kayla Emerson – 11/27/12 – "The Creator's" – *Reporter Magazine*

Chapter 2 – God Squad Upsets Turtles

    (1) Colossians 3:23 – The Bible

Chapter 11 – Peace

    (1) John 3:3 – The Bible (NASB)

Chapter 18 – The Calling

    (1) Romans 10:17 – The Bible (NKJV)

    (2) 2 Timothy 4:2 – The Bible (NIV)

Chapter 24 – My Grace Is Sufficient for You

    (1) James 5:16 – The Bible (NIV)

Chapter 37 – Loaves and Fishes

    (1) *Lacrosse Magazine*, August 2009

    (2) *Lacrosse Magazine*, August 2009

Chapter 40 – Gideon's Army

    (1) Judges 7:12 – The Bible (NASB)

Chapter 47 – Thumbs Up

    (1) *FCA Magazine* – 2017, Volume 89, Issue 2

    (2) *FCA Magazine* – 2017, Volume 89, Issue 2

Chapter 53 – Team Serve

    (1) *Lacrosse Magazine*, September 2014

    (2) *Lacrosse Magazine*, September 2014

Chapter 55 – "The Cross" in Kenya

    (1) ILWT reporter Anna Taylor, August 6, 2019

Chapter 56 – YouTube and Ukraine

    (1) *FCA Magazine*, March 2018

Chapter 61 – The Dead Sea to The Mount of Olives

(1) Acts 1:8 – The Bible (NIV)

Chapter 64 – The Saints Go Marching In

(1) *Baltimore* magazine, February 2020

Chapter 65 – A City on a Hill

(1) Ephesians 6:12 – The Bible (NIV)

Chapter 66 – Watch God Do It

(1) *Baltimore* magazine, February 2020

Chapter 70 – Club Growth

(1) Proverbs 3:5-6 – The Bible (NASB)

Chapter 71 – Do Not Give Up Meeting Together

(1) Isaiah 6:8 – The Bible (NIV)

Chapter 72 – The Fields Are Ripe for Harvest

(1) Proverbs 4:23 – The Bible (NIV)

Chapter 73 – Like Arrows in the Hands of Warriors

(1) ESPN Films – *Fate of a Sport*

Chapter 74 – The Pandemic

(1) 1 Corinthians 9:24 – The Bible (NASB)

Chapter 79 – I Lift Up My Eyes

(1) Proverbs 16:9 – The Bible (NASB)

Conclusion

(1) 1 Samuel 2:30 – The Bible (NIV)
(2) Colossians 3:23 – The Bible (NIV)
(3) Matthew 25:23 – The Bible (NIV)
(4) John 21:25 – The Bible (ESV)

Fields of Faith...

I hope you enjoyed reading about the various "Fields of Faith" where my life and the lives of so many others were influenced.

From the very small field in our family's suburban Baltimore backyard to the synthetic turf field of Cornell's famed Crescent stadium, to the grass fields of the beautiful Vail Valley and the outback fields of Australia, to the Olympic fields of Lake Placid and the red dirt fields of Africa, to the fields nestled in the historic hills of Israel, and back to the fields of inner city Baltimore, the Creator, God, has visited His favor and blessing upon us in so many ways.

Four of my favorite family lacrosse pictures from famous fields in the U.S. were painted for me by Tommy Johnson, a gifted artist, whom I had the pleasure of coaching at Calvert Hall. He went on to play at Loyola University and currently lives (and paints) in California. If you have a favorite picture that you want to have painted, you can reach out to Tommy at artisttommyjohnson.com or tommy@laxartist.com.

Me winning a fast-break faceoff on Cornell's Schoellkopf Field in 1986

FCA Power of Prayer after the 1992 Miracle in the Mountains on Ford Field in Vail, Colorado

Frankie Kelly winning a fast-break faceoff on North Carolina's Fetzer Field in 2014

Stephen Kelly winning a fast-break faceoff on Johns Hopkins' Homewood Field in 2016

ABOUT THE AUTHOR

Frank Kelly III is CEO of Kelly Benefits, a family business he leads with his three brothers.

A 1986 graduate of Cornell University, Frank was recognized as a Red Key Scholar-Athlete, played football, and captained the lacrosse team, where he was a first-team All-Ivy selection. His interest in lacrosse continued after college, playing several seasons of professional indoor lacrosse, many years of high-level field lacrosse, and coaching youth and high school lacrosse for decades.

Frank has served on boards and in leadership roles for many nonprofit organizations and has been inducted into the Halls of Fame of his high school (Calvert Hall), business/industry (Maryland Association of Health Underwriters) and lacrosse community (US Lacrosse Greater Baltimore Chapter) as well as the Fellowship of Christian Athletes Hall of Champions. Frank is also the author of *Look & See* and a highly regarded national platform speaker.

Frank and his wife, Gayle, are the grateful parents of four children, two beautiful daughters-in-law, and a precious grandson. They live in Lutherville, Maryland.

Look & See is a picture book
about better appreciating
and experiencing the blessings
and provision of God.

www.FrankKellyIII.com